SHEMARYAHU TALMON

LITERARY STUDIES IN THE HEBREW BIBLE
FORM AND CONTENT

לזכר אבי מורי יום-טוב ליפמן זלמנוביץ
ולזכר אמי מורתי חנה לבית אֵל
ולזכר אחיותי לאה ורבקה   הי״ד

LITERARY STUDIES IN THE HEBREW BIBLE

FORM AND CONTENT

Collected Studies

SHEMARYAHU TALMON

JERUSALEM — LEIDEN

THE MAGNES PRESS, THE HEBREW UNIVERSITY

E. J. BRILL

Published with the generous help of the
Aryeh (Leo) Lubin Foundation
in memory of his parents Lilian and Moshe Lubin

© The Magnes Press, The Hebrew University, Jerusalem 1993
Printed in Israel
Typesetting: Beverly Butrin Fields

Distributed in Israel by The Magnes Press, The Hebrew University,
Jerusalem
Distributed in the other territories of the world by E. J. Brill, Leiden

Library of Congress Cataloging-in-Publication Data

Talmon, Shemaryahu, 1920-
    Literary studies in the Hebrew Bible: form and content:
    collected studies / Shemaryahu Talmon
          p. cm.
    Includes bibliographical references and index
    ISBN 9004098755
    1. Bible. O.T.—Criticism, interpretation, etc. 2. Bible. O.T.—
Criticism. Form. I. Title
BS1192.T34 1993
221.6'6—dc20   93-4248
                                                       CIP

CONTENTS

PREFACE

The studies in this volume focus on some major issues in biblical research to which I have given attention over several decades:

The applicability of the "comparative method" toward the elucidation of biblical modes of thought, literary problems, and textual cruces, over and against an interpretation based on insights derived intertextually from the biblical writings.

The identification of specific biblical literary techniques in this endeavor to gauge pivotal aspects of the ancient Israelites' conceptual universe.

In the introductory chapter, the methodological problems that inhere in the comparative approach are set out. They are then illustrated by several examples pertaining to sociopolitical institutions and theological concepts, as well as to philological and literary aspects of the biblical writings. The ensuing in-depth analyses of selected issues—the pertinence of the biblical רְפָאִים to the Ugaritic *rpu/i(m)*, the mythic concept of the "navel of the earth," the ancient Israelites' understanding of "revelation," the conjectured existence of a biblical national epic, and the prophets' presumed propagation of a "desert ideal"—culminate in findings that differ substantially from the views on these matters that prevail in contemporary biblical scholarship.

These studies underpin the proposition that by probing specific literary patterns and modes to which various biblical authors and editors repeatedly had recourse, one can elicit facets of speculative thought which the ancient Israelites entertained, but which do not find expression in the Hebrew writings in systematic and comprehensive accounts. This approach is illustrated by an examination of the pivotal concept of "eschatology" in relation to the biblical understanding of "history." It is here that the interplay of form and content comes into full view.

In this context, I highlight some prominent techniques that biblical writers applied in the structuralization of larger literary units. The "resumptive repetition" enabled a writer to preserve, in his necessarily one-dimensional

7

narration, the synchroneity of discrete but nevertheless interrelated events that occurred simultaneously in diverse locations. By splitting the line of discourse and interspacing the parallel-running threads of the complex narrative, carefully marking the cutoff and resumption by the reiteration of key phrases, an author succeeded in impressing on his readers the concurrence of the events he was reporting. Their coincidence would have been lost in a one-line presentation, which would have created the impression of a sequential occurrence. A "redactor" would have used the very same technique for secondarily inserting initially independent units into an already "closed" corpus of literature. The "resumptive repetition" is thus seen as a technical mode, whose impact can be traced in the biblical texts on various levels of their transmission.

The widespread employment of the "resumptive repetition" and other such compositional techniques proves that they cannot be considered idiosyncracies of one or another author, nor characteristics of one or another literary stratum or source. Rather, they must be adjudged tools of the trade of the biblical literati generally, throughout the entire period of ancient Hebrew creativity. This phenomenon should be taken into account when the historico-critical method is brought to bear on the elucidation of the composition of biblical literary entities and their interpretation. This desideratum is exemplified in the analysis of a composite pericope of historiography—2 Kgs 17:24–41.

In the concluding essay, I present in detail my understanding of the book of Esther as a historicized "wisdom-tale," identifying in it themes and collocations that reveal in the tale of Esther and Mordecai the presence of the "type-plot" of the low exile who rises to prominence at a foreign king's court.

I wish to thank the editors and publishers of the periodicals and co-authored books in which these studies originally appeared for granting permission to republish them in this collection. While the scholarly discussion of the issues investigated was not brought up to date, practically all the essays have been reworked and expanded, several to a significant degree.

My thanks are due to Daniel Cochavy and Samuel Cardillo, who proofread the initial manuscript and the final pages, respectively. Special thanks go to Mrs. Beverly Fields, who prepared the indexes, edited and typeset the entire manuscript with indefatigable care and exemplary patience.

I wish to thank both the Committee of the Federmann Fund of the Hebrew University of Jerusalem for granting a subsidy towards the publication of this book and the Academic Committee and the Director of Magnes Press for their resolve to include this volume in their publication program as a follow-up to the two previous volumes, *King, Cult and Calendar* (1986) and *The World of Qumran from Within* (1989).

I dedicate this book to the memory of my father, Yom-Tov Lipmann, my mother, Hanna, and my sisters, Gerda and Regina Zelmanowicz, who perished in the Shoah.

THE COMPARATIVE METHOD IN BIBLICAL INTERPRETATION: PRINCIPLES AND PROBLEMS

I. General Observations

Modern studies of the Hebrew Bible, from the inception of the historico-literary or *literarhistorische* approach, constitute an illuminating example of interdisciplinary contacts and of the transfer of methods applied in one field of research to another. Thus the principles underlying the analysis to which the ancient Hebrew literature has been subjected, especially since the beginning of the nineteenth century—the days of de Wette, Ewald, Kuenen, Graf, and Wellhausen, to mention only a few outstanding names—in essence had been formulated by students of Classical Greek literature. They were adopted and adapted by biblical scholars to meet the requirements posed by the particular character of the writings of the Old, and for that matter, the New Testament.[1] Another illustration of the fructification of biblical studies by other disciplines can be observed in the overall complex of "oral tradition" and the "traditio-historical" method, which has freely emulated analytical and interpretative techniques and procedures developed by students of ancient Scandinavian lore and of the epic literature of Eastern European peoples.[2] Similarly *Werkinterpretation* or "close reading" and similar schools, which crystallized in general literary criticism, influenced and

---

1.   For the history and survey of the literature, see, int. al., H. F. Hahn, *Old Testament in Modern Research* (Philadelphia: Muhlenburg, 1956); H. J. Kraus, *Geschichte der Historisch-Kritischen Erforschung des Alten Testaments* (Neukirchen: Neukirchener Verlag, 1969); and R. Smend, *Wilhelm Martin Leberecht de Wettes Arbeit am Alten und Neuen Testament* (Basel: Helbing & Lichtenhahn, 1958).

2.   The following are only a sample of the relevant studies: E. Nielsen, *Oral Tradition* (London: SCM, 1954); I. Engnell, "Methodological Aspects of Old Testament Study" ([VTSup 7; Leiden: E. J. Brill, 1959] 13–30); idem, "The Traditio-Historical Method in Old Testament Research," *Critical Essays in the Old Testament* ([trans., J. T. Willis; London: SPCK, 1970] 3–11).

still influence heavily the contemporary study of biblical literature *qua* literature with concomitant repercussions on other areas of biblical research.[3]

The restating of these well-known facts may be likened to "carrying coals to Newcastle," since the dependence of biblical scholarship on other humanistic disciplines with respect to fundamental outlooks as well as tools of the trade is generally admitted and recognized. The perusal of any "History of Modern Biblical Studies" or "Introduction to Biblical Literature" will prove the point. However two considerations induce me to preface my paper with these cursory remarks of a general nature: the lack of a fully detailed, up-to-date analysis of this interdependence which still remains a desideratum; and the fact that the "comparative method," on which I aim to focus attention, did not emerge independently within the frame of our discipline but rather was devised and developed in other areas of historical and phenomenological research from which comparative biblical studies derived their impetus. Again, this dependence will be readily acknowledged and likewise the legitimacy of applying to biblical literature techniques worked out in quite disparate fields of scholarly endeavor.

Unfortunately there seems to be a decisive difference between these other disciplines and our own. Sociologists, anthropologists, ethnographers, and historians bestow constant attention to the evaluation and reexamination of the conceptual modes by which they guide their comparative investigations. It would appear, however, that comparative investigations concerning the ancient Hebrew society, its literature and world of ideas, deal preponderantly with particular cases of parallels which are found or are assumed to be present in other cultural complexes. Scholars seem to be less given to scrutinizing their methods in the light of the experience gathered from their "field work" and seldom ponder basic questions such as whether the comparative method intrinsically operates under the "assumption of uniformity," as one school opines, or whether the aim should be "a comparison of contrasts rather than a comparison of similarities," as another school would have it.[4]

---

3. M. Weiss ("Die Methode der 'Total-Interpretation,'" [VTSup 22; Leiden: E. J. Brill, 1971] 88–112) provides a survey of the state of the art and bibliography; idem, *The Bible From Within: The Method of Total Interpretation* (Jerusalem: Magnes, 1984) 1–46.

4. Cp. K. E. Bock, "The Comparative Method of Anthropology," *Comparative Studies in Society and History* 8 (1965–66) 269–80; and E. R. Leach, "The Comparative Method in Anthropology," *International Encyclopedia of the Social Sciences* 1. 339–45.

The even more fundamental dichotomy between comparativists and noncomparativists which is very much in the foreground of contemporary anthropology has barely found an echo in biblical scholarship.[5] Specifically it may be said that so far as biblical studies were affected at all by the vigorous forays of the structuralists against the comparativists, the impact came from social scientists like Mary Douglas and E. R. Leach (following C. Lévi-Strauss) who applied to biblical literature the structuralist concepts fashioned in the science of anthropology.[6]

Analogous to what was and to a degree still is the practice in other areas of comparative research (history, sociology, ethnography, anthropology, folklore, etc.), so too in biblical studies two main approaches can be discerned. On the one hand we encounter what Marc Bloch defines as "the comparative method on the grand scale . . . the basic postulate of this method, as well as the conclusion to which it constantly returns, is the fundamental unity of the human spirit or, if you wish, the monotony and astonishing poverty of human intellectual resources during the course of history."[7] An even more critical note is sounded by Bouquet: comparison of religions always runs the risk of sinking "to the level of collecting dead insects or pressed flowers, which in the process lose all their colour and reality."[8] This generalizing trend, which catalogues rather than explains the phenomena under review, entails a "loss of uniqueness and variegation" and suggests a

5. A thorough discussion of the problem is presented by A. J. F. Köbben ("Comparativists and Non-Comparativists in Anthropology," *A Handbook of Method in Cultural Anthropology* [ed. R. Naroll and R. Cohen; New York: Columbia University Press, 1970] 581–96). Köbben notes (p. 583) that the two trends, one following the principle of "specificity" and "specification" and the other that of "homogeneity," had already been differentiated by Kant in his Critique of Pure Reason: "This distinction shows itself in the different manner of thought among students of nature [and of culture], some . . . [are] almost averse to heterogeneousness, and always intent on the unity of genera; while others . . . are constantly driving to divide nature [or society] into so much variety that one might lose almost all hope of being able to distribute its phenomena according to general principles."

6. A notable exception is J. W. Rogerson (*Myth in Old Testament Interpretation* [BZAW 134; Berlin: de Gruyter, 1974]), especially his analysis of "The Structural Study of Myth" (pp. 101–27). A critical survey and full bibliography of Mary Douglas' research is provided by S. R. Isenberg and D. E. Owen ("Bodies, Natural and Contrived: The Work of Mary Douglas," *Religious Studies Review* 3 [1977] 1–17). For Edmund Leach and his critics, see below, n. 48.

7. M. Bloch, "Two Strategies of Comparison," *Comparative Perspectives: Theories and Methods* (ed. A. Etzioni and F. L. Dubow; Boston: Little, Brown, & Co., 1970) 41. See further: R. Bendix, "Concepts and Generalizations in Comparative Sociological Studies," *ASR* 28 (1963) 532–39.

8. S. C. Bouquet, *Comparative Religion* (London: Penguin, 1962) 21.

uniformity which does not really exist in social behavior.[9] By fastening attention on what is or appears to be identical or similar in historically and geographically diverse, even widely removed, societies, this trend lumps these features together, thus providing proof for the axiomatic basic likeness of men and their societies which serves as a philosophical launching pad for the comparative method on the grand scale. At the same time, and in full awareness, it completely loses sight of what makes cultures, societies, and men ready objects for comparison, namely the peculiar and sometimes particularistic traits which one developed independently of and in distinction from others. Says Kröber, "Our concern is with differences and likenesses."[10]

In the framework of Old Testament studies, this approach is represented by J. G. Frazer's classical multivolume work *Folklore in the Old Testament*,[11] an offspring of his even more comprehensive opus *The Golden Bough*.[12] These works constituted the summation of scholarly endeavors in the second half of the nineteenth century and concomitantly provided the momentum for numerous less-ambitious studies which issued forth from the school of social scientists inaugurated by that eminent British scholar. In the study of the Hebrew Bible, the comparative approach "on the grand scale" is still practised by researchers who like to find resemblances between biblical stories and narrative motifs in other cultures. In doing so they lean heavily on Frazer's work, which shows that their approach received its major impetus from the outside. It echoes the emphasis laid on the method in a wide range of general disciplines, primarily but not exclusively in the social sciences, including the study of religion and literature. It tallies with the evolutionist theory which up to the first half of this century had a pronounced impact on the sciences generally and, nearer home, also on modern critical research on the Hebrew Bible. Scholars of various disciplines who adopt this approach in their comparative endeavors meet on shared philosophical premises in spite of the diversity of their pursuits.

The comparative method on the grand scale will concede that the fundamental equality in thought processes, social organization and societal progress is more decidedly an outstanding characteristic of the "primitive"

---

9.   Köbben, "Comparativists," 582 (see above, n. 5).
10. After Köbben, "Comparativists," 590.
11. J. G. Frazer, *Folklore in the Old Testament* (London: Macmillan, 1918).
12. J. G. Frazer, *The Golden Bough* (London: Macmillan, 1890), subsequently republished in constantly expanding editions.

or "preliterate" stages of human development than of the structures and the philosophical horizons of "higher" societies. However it presumes that the intrinsic unity of mankind manifests itself in relics from those early phases which can be identified and then compared in societal and conceptual molds of more developed historical peoples, even up to modernity. Comparisons can be drawn, therefore, between any two (or more) cultures and social organisms which exhibit some similar features, although they are far removed from one another in time and space. Given this underlying persuasion of the intrinsic equality of men and their societal structures, any extensive investigation of diverse cultures will bring to light parallels in social customs, ritual, and lore in as distinct and disparate settings as those of the South American Indians and the kings of France, the Teutons and ancient Egypt, Tiv law and British law, biblical Israel and Arab Nomads. Accords and agreements of this kind are the more readily detected the more atomistic the approach, viz., the more pronounced the discussion of the compared phenomena in isolation from their overall cultural and civilizational context. For example, if we should consider modern bylaws against spitting on the floor in vehicles of public transport or other public places without reference to the pertinent context of contemporary mores and attitudes toward hygiene, they could be compared with the prohibition of spitting in the solemn assemblies of the Judean Covenanters (1QS vii 14), for which a parallel can be found in Josephus' account of Essene customary law. But to construe the "similarities" which comparitivists evince as evidence of "similar concepts" in such diverse cultures produces staggering and indeed nonsensical results. Bronislaw Malinowski's classic stricture, that "in the science of culture to tear out a custom which belongs to a certain context leads nowhere,"[13] can be widened to include clusters of customs or groups of phenomena which may turn up in different cultures.

The criticism which in the main is aimed at the Frazer school is well taken. Random comparison without reference to the general structure and profile of the overall scale of values and beliefs of the societies involved can only mar and distort, as will yet be explicated. Seemingly identical phenomena which may occur in different cultures are often quite differently weighted in the one and in the other. When dealing comparatively with separate features of social and religious life or with single concepts, motifs,

---

13.   As quoted by Köbben, "Comparitivists," 584.

and idioms, it is imperative to view them in relation to the total phenomena of the groups involved. As Emile Durkheim observed, "Social facts [in the widest sense of the term] are functions of the social system of which they are a part; therefore, they cannot be understood when they are detached. For this reason two facts which come from two different societies cannot be fruitfully compared merely because they seem to resemble one another."[14]

Of a different scope and character is another type of comparative procedure that has become prominent in biblical research since the thirties of the present century in the wake of momentous developments in Ancient Near Eastern archaeology. The discoveries significantly broadened the outlook of scholars with regard to social and religious phenomena, modes of thought, literary achievements, and linguistic habits which distinguish biblical culture. This more recent comparative approach has carved for itself a secure niche in contemporary Old Testament studies. Again we observe a parallelism between developments in comparative study generally and in the domain of the Hebrew Bible. Marc Bloch defines this method as one "in which the units of comparison are societies that are geographical neighbors and historical contemporaries, constantly influenced by one another. During the historical development of such societies, they are subject to the same overall causes, just because they are so close together in time and space. Moreover they have, in part at least, a common origin."[15] While the comparative method on the grand scale may be likened to general linguistics which deals with all human languages, the historically and geographically circumscribed method is closer to comparative philology which is concerned with "language groups within which signs of a common historical origin can be detected,"[16] for instance the Indo-Germanic or the Semitic language families.

It would be difficult to grade the importance of geographic proximity, historical propinquity, and other factors for the application of comparative analysis. However we would tend to accept as a basic rule, *mutatis mutandis*, the scale proffered by James Barr with reference to comparative philology: sources closer to the Hebrew Bible in time take pride of place over considerations of geographic proximity; however, because of that proximity even

14. After Köbben, 590.
15. Bloch, "Two Strategies," loc. cit. (see above, n. 7).
16. J. Barr, *Comparative Philology and the Text of the Old Testament* (Oxford: Clarendon, 1968) 77.

features observed in relatively late sources may retain traces of earlier common cultural conditions. Thus *date* appears to be more important than *place*. Within this framework a general closer *affinity* should decide on the actual investigative procedure, viz., the decision as to which two of an available selection of compared features culled from different cultural settings are most likely to represent a common basic phenomenon. It appears that in dealing not only with linguistic issues but with a wider array of cultural traits which are to be compared, the maxim to be followed is M. J. Herskovits' characterization of the comparative method as pertaining to "the analysis of cultures *lying within a given historic stream,*" since it takes adequately into consideration the aspects of historical and geographical proximity as well as those of cultural affinity.[17]

The historically and geographically defined method of comparison successfully removed biblical Israel from the cultural and conceptual seclusion imposed upon it by the isolationist ideology which characterizes generally the biblical, and in particular, the prophetic outlook. Careful observation, classification, and interpretation of the new information which excavators made available to the historian and the sociologist, to the student of literature and of religion, discloses an elaborate network of channels which linked the ancient Hebrews with the nations (and the cults and cultures of those nations), in whose proximity, indeed in whose midst, they lived: from Egypt in the south, throughout the Canaanite expanse on both sides of the Jordan, and on to Mesopotamia in the northeast. A synoptic view of the everincreasing information brought to light from the archives of Ugarit, Nuzi, Mari, and the Hittite lands made it exceedingly clear that in the two millennia before the common era the peoples of the Ancient Near East indeed lived within a "historic stream" created and fed by the geographic-historical continuity which made possible a steady transfer and mutual emulation of civilizational and cultural achievements. The availability of a lingua franca, in addition to the basic linguistic affinities between the languages spoken in the region, and the existence of propitious physical means (such as a well-developed network of roads which opened up the area and furthered communication in times of war and peace) made that part of the Ancient Near East a veritable marketplace for the exchange of ideas in the realm of cult, culture, and their literary concretizations.

17.   After S. L. Thrupp, "Editorial," *Comparative Studies in Society and History* 1 (1958–59) 3.

Propelled by these internal developments, even more than by the momentum provided from outside the discipline, students of the Hebrew Bible proceeded to assemble a veritable host of facts which witnessed to the interweaving of Israel in that fabric of concepts, customs, and social structures in which other peoples of the area were enmeshed. The rapidly growing efforts along the lines of the historical-geographical comparative method brought on a wave of publications which demonstrated parallels between Israelite culture and the cultures of her neighbors in various fields: language, literary conventions, articles of belief and of ritual, social, and political organization. The sheer bulk and compass of these materials wrenched biblical Israel from the position of "a people dwelling alone and not reckoning itself among the [other] nations" (Num 23:9), which biblical ideology had assigned to her.

With specific regard to the cult, this vigorous scholarly endeavor reached its peak in the "myth and ritual" school. While the question of the origin and identity of the sources of this approach in biblical studies is still under discussion, J. W. Rogerson is most probably correct in presuming that three factors played a decisive role in its evolution: "the emergence of the ritual theory of myth, the publication of certain Babylonian and Assyrian texts about the New Year Festival, and the diffusionist anthropology which apparently dominated England in the 1920s."[18] S. H. Hooke (who initiated the myth and ritual position) and his followers construed it to prove the existence of a common Canaanite and Mesopotamian cultic pattern, also containing Babylonian elements, to which biblical Israel was a partner. In fact they did not stop short at the discernment of a general cultic pattern. Instead they widened the scope of the comparative inquiry so as to give it a more comprehensive range and to include within its frame of reference conceptual and societal phenomena which cannot be accommodated under the rubric "cult" in the restricted sense of the term. On the basis of comparison, it is presumed that the specific configurations of the myth-and-ritual pattern were affected by general societal phenomena and developments: the originally *agricultural* Canaanite version of the shared basic cult supposedly turns up in Israel in a typically *urban* variant, possibly influenced by the Babylonian pattern which also was urban in character.

18.   Rogerson, *Myth*, 67 (see above, n. 6).

Again, there is no need to go into the intricacies of the issue under discussion, as they have been adequately dealt with in recent publications, most extensively and profoundly by Rogerson. What is of concern is the emergence of a "pattern of culture" school that operated under the premises worked out by the myth-and-ritual position. The method adopted by that school for the analysis of myth, whose legitimacy was defended recently by H. Ringgren (namely "to break it down into small units and to find out where these units occur and what combinations they build up"), was in fact not only applied to the science of mythology from which it originated, but also became the path taken by scholars who analyzed phenomena of a completely different nature.[19] For this reason, and not simply because of the application of such analysis to myths, the school came under heavy criticism from quarters that insisted on the existence of individual patterns of culture among the diverse peoples of the Ancient Near East. It is somewhat difficult to concur with Ringgren in the argument that "both parties are right," because they employed the term *pattern* in different ways. While it is true that a synoptic view of the discussion discloses a discrepancy in the use of the term *pattern,* the division between these schools of thought remains much more fundamental: it derives from the unbridgeable dichotomy between an "atomistic" and a "holistic" approach.[20]

The myth-and-ritual as well as the pattern-of-culture schools, which received their initial impetus from the "historical-geographical stream" method of comparison, proceeded to disclose their Frazerian philosophical underpinnings. The fundamentally nonfunctionalist position represents in fact a cloaked and scientifically more acceptable return to the comparative approach "on the grand scale." While the pattern school in the Hooke tradition is indeed not satisfied with comparing elements alone, it views more comprehensive configurations *sub specie* "combinations," i.e., not as original self-contained units, but rather as secondary cultural constructs. In contrast the holistic method first tries to understand a cultural configuration in its entirety. To quote E. Leach, "An element has significance only because of its position in the overall structure in relation to other elements of the set."[21]

---

19. H. Ringgren, "Israel's Place among the Religions of the Ancient Near East" (VTSup 23; Leiden: E. J. Brill, 1972) 6.

20. See D. C. Phillips, *Holistic Thought in Social Science* (Stanford, CA: Stanford University Press, 1977).

21. E. Leach, "The Legitimacy of Solomon," *European Journal of Sociology* 7 (1966) 63.

Without disregarding resemblances between constitutive elements in two different civilizations within the same "historic stream," it emphasizes the individuality and dissimilarity conferred upon these identified components by their very existence within specific organic cultural totalities. Scholars like T. Jacobsen and H. Frankfort are much more interested in what B. Landsberger defined as the *Eigenbegrifflichkeit* of the diverse cultures (predominantly based on a religiopolitical circumscription) than in their presumed similarity or similarities. This insistence on the particularity of the Hebrew culture and its dissimilarity from neighboring cultures, coming from scholars whose expertise is the study of the archaeology, history, sociology, linguistics, and phenomenology of the Ancient Near Eastern civilizations, should serve students of the Old Testament as a guideline in their comparative studies.

The diversity and the comprehensiveness of biblical phenomena that invite a comparison with their likenesses in other Ancient Near Eastern cultures will not allow for a full presentation of the problems involved. Nor will it be possible to cover all the different aspects of the materials which can be and indeed are submitted to comparative study and which in practice constitute separate subdisciplines in Old Testament research. One could argue in favor of a synoptic view which conceives of these diverse aspects as a continuum and thus would submit complex rather than simple structures to comparative analysis. In the present context, however, it appears advisable to approach the matter in accord with the stratified treatment it is given in contemporary research. Again, selection is imperative. Therefore we shall illustrate some shortcomings of the procedures often followed by comparativists and what appear to be necessary rectifications by examples drawn essentially from two aspects of the study of the Hebrew Bible: (1) sociopolitical institutions, with some reference to matters pertaining to cult and myth; and (2) issues of a philological or literary nature such as emendations based on external parallels, literary imagery which signifies concepts and modes of thought, and literary forms or *Gattungen*.[22] The order of presentation aims at placing increasingly in relief the prevalent atomistic or isolationist approach in comparative research in contrast to the required investigation of total phenomena, i.e., of single features in relation to their cultural context and

---

22.   The ensuing presentation aims at viewing concisely and in a more comprehensive framework several issues which are discussed elsewhere in this volume in greater detail.

their function in more comprehensive organic structures or, with Rowton, of "organic processes."[23]

II. Sociopolitical Institutions[24]

(1) *Nomadic Survivals*. The discussion of procedures which I tend to view as an unqualified application of the comparative method to socio-historical aspects of biblical Israel will necessarily be sketchy. In introducing it I propose to dwell shortly on the presumed presence of a "nomadic ideal" in the ancient Hebrew world of ideas. The issue hinges on the basic assumption of the comparative approach grounded in the evolutionist tradition that early stages in human and especially in societal development will reveal themselves in vestigial form in higher and later phases of the societies under review. Adopting this line of thought, K. Budde, P. Humbert, and their followers discerned in the social web of Israel in the settlement period, and even in the phase of advanced urbanization under the monarchy, residues of nomadic mores which decisively affected Hebrew society throughout biblical times. Furthermore primitive nomadic life with its simplicity and direct trust in God, unencumbered by cultic paraphernalia, showed to advantage against the background of the corrupted city society which progressively crystallized in Israel after the establishment of the monarchy. The ideal to which the spiritual leaders of Israel (*lege* the prophets) aspired was not urban comfort and civilization, not even the agriculturist's life, polluted as it was by the unavoidable attachment to pagan fertility cults. Rather it was the ascetic lifestyle to which the Rechabites adhered, who shunned all forms of settlements and whom Jeremiah assumedly extolled and held up as a socioeconomic and religious paradigm for all Israel to emulate (Jeremiah 35). One view represents the Rechabites as the best-known group to organize a return to the desert and to the nomadic ideal. This ideal supposedly transcends the confines of the Hebrew Bible. It still appears, we are told, in the ideology of some constituent groups of post-

---

23. The structural approach is well employed by M. B. Rowton in an important series of articles (in process) in which he discusses "the role of dimorphic structure and topology in the history of Western Asia." For a full listing see OrAnt 15 (1976) 17, n. 4.
24. A concise presentation of the issue in general is offered by S. N. Eisenstadt ("Social Institutions: Comparative Study," *International Encyclopedia of the Social Sciences*, 14.421–29).

biblical Judaism, such as the Qumran Covenanters, whom most students of the Qumran finds tend to identify with the Essenes. In fact some scholars perceive the Qumran community as a late offshoot of the possibly pre-monarchic clan of the Rechabites, again on the basis of an apparent "similarity" but without any evidence to prove the presumed historic continuity.[25]

It must be put on record that some scholars did sound a warning note. In his discussion of the "nomadic ideal," R. de Vaux exhorts us to beware of hasty comparisons "which may overlook essential differences." But having said that much, he nevertheless concurs with the opinion that when the ancient Israelites came to settle as a nation after having first lived as nomads or semi-nomads, they still retained some characteristics of that earlier way of life.[26] When investigated in detail this statement does not stand up to scrutiny. It appears to refer simplistically to a presumed internal development of the Israelite society, somewhat along the lines which determine the development of most societies in the Ancient Near East and assumedly also in other parts of the world and in other historical settings. At this juncture the comparative approach on the grand scale comes into play, and the issue at hand assumes much wider proportions. De Vaux reasons that Arabs of pre-Islamic times and even of today are either full-fledged nomads or at least exhibit nomadic habits and traits and that "what we know of pre-Islamic, modern and contemporary Arab life can help us to understand more clearly the primitive organization of Israel."[27]

This comparability of the ancient Israelite and the appreciably later Arab societies according to some scholars applies not only to social organization but also to the constitutive characteristics of the Yahwistic faith. S. Nyström[28] summarized and systematized features and parallels which some of his predecessors (e.g., J. Wellhausen, A. Causse, and M. Buber)

---

25. Cp. S. Talmon, "The Desert Motif in the Bible and in Qumran Literature," in this volume, pp. 216–64; "*Har* and *Midbar:* An Antithetical Pair of Biblical Motifs," *Figurative Language in the Ancient Near East* (ed. M. Mindlin, M. I. Geller, and I. E. Wansbrough; London: SOAS, 1987) 117–42; מדבר *midbār,* ערבה *ʿaṛābāh,*" *TWAT* 4.660–95; "Wilderness," *The Interpreter's Dictionary of the Bible, Supplementary Volume* (Nashville: Abingdon, 1976) 946–49.

26. R. de Vaux, *Ancient Israel: Its Life and Institutions* (trans. J. McHugh; London: Darton, Longmans, Todd, 1961) 12ff. = *Les Institutions de l'Ancien Testament* (Paris: Cerf, 1958) 1.28ff.

27. Ibid., p. 3; French original, p. 15.

28. S. Nyström, *Beduinentum und Jahwismus* (Lund: Gleerup, 1946).

already had pointed out. But the precariousness of the comparison of ancient Israelite with Arab culture and the slim foundation on which it rests are revealed by I. Engnell's contrasting statement in reference to issues of a literary character: "comparing Israelite material with relatively far-distant lands and cultures—India and Iran, for instance—actually can be more fruitful than comparing it with closer regions, such as Arabia. As a matter of fact, the latter can even be characterized as distinctly dangerous."[29] One wonders on what evidence the one view bases itself and on what opposing evidence the other is founded. Is it not perhaps that both derive from intuitive insights and personal predilections rather than from inquiries and investigations carried out according to appreciably objective criteria?

The issue is further complicated if one takes into account the opinion first expressed by W. F. Albright and C. H. Gordon that the patriarchal society exhibits characteristics of *tamkaru* life and that the forefathers of Israel could be more readily likened to "merchant princes" than to bedouin sheikhs. One realizes that even in the traditions about the historically hazy "Desert Period," Israel is not actually depicted as a typical desert people. Also the bedouin characteristics discovered in the traditions pertaining to her settled life as a nation are questionable. In short, the exceeding tenuity of the "nomadic theory" and of the comparison with pre-Islamic or Islamic Arabic society is set in full relief.

Even more disturbing than the overeager search for "similarities" to nomadic societies (with which biblical Israel is assumed to lie in the same historic stream) is the disregard for internal analysis as a means to elicit from the biblical literature itself the ancient Hebrews' concept of the ideal life. Even a cursory survey of the biblical sources shows that nomads and desert-dwellers are abhorred and that the wilderness is conceived of as the abode of ghoulish spirits, wild beasts of prey and roaming marauders. The vast expanses of parched earth are shunned as the embodiment of all that is dangerous and evil. In contrast to this haunted world, Israel's societal ideal is portrayed in the visions of "the latter days," which are modelled in a restorative fashion on the idealized *Urzeit,* the days of the kingdom of David and Solomon when "Judah and Israel dwelt in safety, from Dan even to Beersheba, every man under his vine and under his fig tree" (1 Kgs 5:5).[30] A comparison of the essential features of the hoped-for *Endzeit,* even of the

---

29. Engnell, "Traditio-Historical Method," 8 (see above, n. 2).
30. See S. Talmon, "Types of Messianic Expectation at the Turn of the Era," *KCC,* 202–24.

vocabulary and imagery employed in its portrayal, with the above summary of Solomon's reign makes manifest the distortion which inheres in the attribution of a "nomadic desert ideal" to ancient Israel and to the biblical prophets. Thus Micah conceives of that blissful age: then all the nations "shall beat their swords into mattocks and their spears into pruning-knives; nation shall not lift sword against nation nor ever again be trained for war [cp. Isa 2:2], and each man shall dwell under his vine, under his fig tree, and no one shall frighten [them]" (Mic 4:3–4; cp. 1 Kgs 5:5). The internal analysis of the Israelite conception of the ideal life produces results which are indeed different from those which ensue from the comparison with desert cultures and societies, whether on the "grand scale" or geared to the "historic stream" approach.

(2) *Democratic Institutions*. Scholarly endeavors to interpret the term עם הארץ and to arrive by way of exegesis of the extant references at a satisfactory characterization of the social group or groups so designated are severely hampered by the apparent inconsistency in the employment of the term in biblical literature. The problem is compounded by the absence of any innerbiblical attempt to define the conceptual framework within which the term should be understood beyond the mere recording of some events in history in which the עם הארץ had been actively involved. This silence on principles and the lack of systematization is the rule rather than the exception and possibly reflects some basic attitudes and ancient Hebrew modes of thought, which seem to have been more empirical (fastening on concrete facts) than analytical and tending towards abstract syntheses.[31] It is for these reasons that the suggestions offered in explanation of the term עם הארץ and its content differ widely.

We would go too far afield if we tried to survey the discussion of the issue in detail. Such a review is easily accessible in recent publications, of which I shall mention three, since they seem to represent views which differ on principles of analysis and method. E. W. Nicholson, who bases himself almost exclusively on the biblical material, concludes his study of the עם הארץ with the statement that "the term has no fixed and rigid meaning but rather is used in a purely general and fluid manner and varies in meaning

---

31.　See S. Talmon, "Literary Motifs and Speculative Thought in the Hebrew Bible," *HSLA* 16 (1988) 150–68.

from context to context."[32] This appears to be a counsel of despair which helps in elucidating neither the etymological meaning of the term nor, what is more important, its societal content. In contrast, H. Tadmor and the present writer have proposed specific interpretations of the entire range of usages of the term in the Bible, assuming, though, synchronic differences and diachronic developments in its employment. However, despite accord with regard to the circumscribed meanings inherent in the term עם הארץ and their diachronic variance, Tadmor and I arrive at different characterizations of the group or groups thus designated within the framework of the biblical polity. This difference arises from the diverse paths taken in the attempt to offer a solution. Tadmor addresses the issue within the wider context of the relation between "'The People' and the Kingship in Ancient Israel," comparing what he considers to be parallel phenomena in Ephraim and Judah.[33] He further broadens the scope of his investigation and compares the Hebrew term and its signification with parallel expressions in other historical and societal contexts, such as עם הארץ in Byblos and *niše māti* in Assyria. Adopting a much more restricted approach, I dealt with the Judean עם הארץ exclusively in historical perspective, setting aside comparative considerations for the time being.[34]

The differing procedures result in quite disparate conclusions. Tadmor subtitles his essay "The Role of Political Institutions in the Biblical Period," thus revealing his intent to present the עם הארץ and similar phenomena as constitutionally representing the populace vis-à-vis the king, viz., as institutions whose intervention in matters of the body politic was apparently regulated by mutually acknowledged rules. The references to institutions which acted on behalf of "the people," both in Ephraim and in Judah, indeed with different degrees of frequency, recur in the summarizing paragraph of Tadmor's essay. It culminates in the statement: "when powerful social groups, such as army commanders, decided upon questions of state, they derived their authority from 'the people,' and drew their power from the people's traditional institutions."[35]

---

32. E. W. Nicholson, "The Meaning of the Expression *ʿam haʾareṣ* in the Old Testament," *JSS* 10 (1965) 59–66.
33. H. Tadmor, *Journal of World History* 11 (1968/69) 46–68.
34. "The Judaean *ʿam haʾareṣ* in Historical Perspective," *KCC*, 68–78.
35. Tadmor, "The People," 66.

The choice of terms, such as "decided upon questions of state," "derived their authority from the people," and "the people's traditional institutions," implies the existence of a situation in which the ascription of roles and the division of power between the monarchy and "the people" in ancient Israel were formally and legally regulated by what amounts to a constitution. Contrast with this view my conclusion that "contrary to the institutionalizing tendencies which haunt biblical research, the עם הארץ of Judah cannot be viewed as a democratic or otherwise constitutionally circumscribed institution. Rather it is a body of Judeans in Jerusalem that rose to some importance, whose tactical power was ultimately derived from their loyalty to the Davidic dynasty. The עם הארץ constitutes a sociological phenomenon that illustrates a power structure which appears to be typical of hereditary kingship without clearly defined constitutional foundations. The support readily given to the monarchy by groups like the עם הארץ helps in maintaining the political equilibrium by counteracting the potentially erosive impact of an ascending class of courtiers and ministers. Unwavering loyalty arising from kin ties balances a pragmatic allegiance rooted in vested interests."[36] Again, while both authors draw attention to the sporadic nature of the intervention of the עם הארץ (and other such groups, according to Tadmor), the manner of its going into action is differently conceived. According to Tadmor, "the people's institutions convened and acted only sporadically—when the dynastic continuity was disturbed," etc.[37] Against this, I maintain that "The עם הארץ never was formally convened or called upon by the king or some other agent," because "this body was not an institution at all, but a fairly loosely constituted power group," et sim.[38]

In the present context we are especially concerned with the divergence on principles: on the one hand one discerns a tendency to identify "institutions," of a more or less "democratic" character, which played an important role in the Israelite body politic.[39] At the other end of the spec-

36. Talmon, "The Judaean ʿam haʾareṣ," 78 (see above, n. 34).
37. Tadmor, "The People," 68.
38. Talmon, "The Judaean ʿam haʾareṣ," 75.
39. In the case of the עם הארץ this was done most succinctly at the beginning of the century by M. Sulzberger (*The Am Ha-aretz: The Ancient Hebrew Parliament* [Philadelphia: J. H. Greenstone, 1910]) and was repeated some decades later by E. Auerbach, who defined it as the "great national council," the democratic representation of the nation vis-à-vis the king ("עם הארץ," *Proceedings of the First World Congress of Jewish Studies* [Jerusalem: Magnes, 1952] 362–66).

trum is the "non-institutional" explanation of the term with its application to ever-widening circles in the population: *Landadel,* landed gentry or "lords of the land" (M. Weber, R. Kittel, A. G. Barrois, R. Gordis, S. Daiches, et al.) or even *Die Gesamtheit der Judäischen Vollbürger—l'ensemble des nationaux* (M. Noth and R. de Vaux).[40]

The presentation of this controversy in some detail is not intended to prove (what does not require proof) that the same biblical evidence can be interpreted quite differently by different scholars and thus leads to disparate conclusions. The crux of the matter lies in the method applied. The institutionalist who buttresses his arguments by having recourse to assumedly comparable materials from extrabiblical sources and non-Israelite political organisms never asks the fundamental question whether or not ancient Israel was at all inclined to solidify political institutions within the framework of the monarchy or before its inception. Phrased differently, does what we know from the sources at our disposal concerning the intrinsic structure of biblical society and biblical social thought recommend the suggestion that public opinion ever expressed itself in "institutionalized" forms and bodies, even if only of the variety found in "primitive democracies"? To answer this question adequately, a deep and comprehensive analysis of biblical society is required, which cannot be attempted here. However I would venture the suggestion that such an analysis will produce a negative answer. It will prove that with the exception of the institutions of kingship and priesthood the social components of the ancient Israelite society expressed preferences on political issues by means of a power-play acted out by groups that consolidated pragmatically and sometimes constituted themselves ad hoc.

When one looks at the wider sociological context, one discerns a correspondence between diverse types of political structures and the forms in which divergent or dissenting opinions asserted themselves against the established leadership. In every instance this or the other particular element will have to be judged and defined, not in isolation, but with a view to its functional relation to the totality of the social phenomena and especially against the background of the "deep" principles of the societal structure. Scholars of the Hebrew Bible will be well advised to pay heed to the criticism which E. Leach levelled against ethnographers and anthropologists who approached their own materials similarly in a "atomistic" fashion: "The

---

40.　For bibliographical details, see Talmon, "The Judaean *ʿam haʾareṣ*" (70-71 [above, n. 34]).

classical comparative method, the diffusionist reconstructions of the cultural historians, and the various styles in a cross-cultural statistical analysis all rested on the proposition that 'a culture' ('a society,' etc.) is to be conceived of as an assemblage of traits which can be separately compared. Functionalist social anthropology rejects this view. Societies are systems which can be compared only as wholes."[41]

The same considerations apply to another issue of the institution-versus-noninstitution controversy. In discussing the internal historical events which occurred in Israel after the death of Solomon, A. Malamat attempted to show that when Rehoboam, Solomon's son and successor to the throne, was challenged by the people to reduce the burden of taxes that Solomon had imposed upon them, he put the matter to a council that represented the people vis-à-vis the king. Rehoboam, in fact, took counsel with two bodies.[42] One, constituted of the "elders," זקנים, is often referred to in biblical literature and is therefore well known. The other, that of the "young men," ילדים, is never mentioned apart from the events described in 1 Kgs 12:1–17. Discarding other possibilities with regard to the composition and nature of this group, Malamat arrives at the conclusion "that the assemblies of elders and 'young men' of Rehoboam are not mere spontaneous gatherings of the populace; but they constitute rather formal bodies of official standing in the kingdom."[43] He then goes on to compare this official "bicameral" Israelite assembly with a parallel institution which is reflected in the Sumerian "Gilgamesh and Agga" epic, equating the Hebrew זקנים with the Sumerian *abba uru*, "elders of the city," and the ילדים with their assumed Sumerian counterpart *guruš,* "council of men." Both bicameral bodies are taken to evidence a "political system which Thorkild Jacobsen aptly named 'primitive democracy.'[44] This form of government rested on *representative institutions* [my italics] which functioned alongside of the central powers."[45] Without overlooking "the different circumstances in Sumer and Israel and the individual character of each of the sources," Malamat nevertheless in-

41. Leach, "The Comparative Method," 343 (see above, n. 4)
42. A. Malamat, "Kingship and Council in Israel and Sumer: A Parallel," *JNES* 22 (1963) 247–53.
43. Ibid., 250.
44. Ibid.
45. T. Jacobsen, "Primitive Democracy in Mesopotamia," *JNES* 2 (1943) 159–72 = *Toward the Image of Tammuz and other Essays on Mesopotamian History and Culture,* (HSS 21; Cambridge, MA: Harvard University Press, 1970) 157–72.

sists that "both of the examples are similar from a typological point of view," and therefore it is of minor importance whether the Sumerian assembly of *guruš* and the Israelite council of ילדים "differed in their very essence and subsequently in their respective functions."[46]

In his criticism of Malamat's thesis, D. G. Evans draws attention to "the difficulties which confront us in discussing political bodies (and indeed others) in the Ancient Near East. Not only does the slenderness of the evidence oblige us to make the most of it to a dangerous extent, but it increases the risk, which is always present in studies of the remote past, of importing into our sources modern constitutional ideas and practices which have no place in them."[47] Evans then analyzes the biblical tradition in detail, as Malamat had done. However his reading of the sources leads to the statement that "to conclude that the $z^eqēn\bar{i}m$ and $y^elād\bar{i}m$ at Shechem were political bodies of official standing in the kingdom seems to me more than the evidence will support," since neither of the councils at Shechem, if indeed there were two and not one, enjoyed sovereignty but at most acted in an advisory fashion. Decisions were taken and put into practice by the people's assembly or the king. Although in the biblical tradition the term זקנים often indicates a group of men that has a specific standing in the body politic, in the instance under review it would appear that the word is not to be understood in this technical sense. The opposition to ילדים, which is never employed elsewhere as a sociopolitical term, instead suggests a contrast which is only relevant to this one tradition. The reasons for Rehoboam's preference of one group over the other should be sought in the "generation gap" between men who belonged to the father's generation, on the one hand, and to his own, on the other.

It appears that also in this latter instance the comparison of two literary units which pertain to two quite different cultural settings, one to the Mesopotamian society and the other to the Israelite society, cannot be discussed in isolation from the intrinsic structures of the two societies involved. Such a discussion in isolation would result in an unfounded identification of informal political groups in Israel of the monarchic period with constitutional political bodies in Mesopotamia. The present writer would certainly opt for a noninstitutional explanation of the Israelite phenomena under review.

---

46. Malamat, *JNES* 22 (1963) 252.
47. D. G. Evans, "Rehoboam's Advisers at Shechem, and Political Institutions in Israel and Sumer," *JNES* 25 (1966) 273–79.

(3) *Divine Kingship*. The final example pertaining to the sociopolitical dimension concerns the position of the king in the Israelite body politic. There is a widespread tendency among students of the Old Testament and the Ancient Near East to discern in the biblical literature a concept of monarchy which invests the king with the status of divinity or at least accords him aspects of sanctity which elevate him above mere human beings. This idea seems to derive from an oversimplified literary interpretation of idioms and expressions which extol the greatness of kings in terms culled from the realm of the divine. The comparison of such terminology with parallels found in Ancient Near Eastern literatures, and also the conceptual modes to which these idioms assumedly give expression lead scholars to perceive an identical notion of divine kingship in the biblical world of ideas. The impact of the pattern school comes into full relief in the "divine kingship" theory precisely because the phenomenon combines fundamental features of myth and ritual with wider aspects of a pattern of culture. The "divine kingship" theory demonstrates a fusion between two quite diverse aspects of Israelite culture: the world of myth and cult as an expression of Ancient Near Eastern religiosity coalesces with the political and social dimension in which tangible history expresses itself. Most likely as a result of this facet of comparative biblical studies, structural analysis (initially applied exclusively to nonhistorical phenomena) was applied to the interpretation of biblical historical events and situations. In dealing with biblical phenomena, the anthropologist Edmund Leach took his departure from the Genesis traditions considered as myth.[48] Professional Bible scholars regarded this attempt with tolerance, equanimity, or a mild lack of interest. Subsequently, however, Leach transferred his attention to the historical books of Samuel and Kings in the endeavor to lay bare "Some Structural Aspects of Old Testament History" in the traditions about Solomon's succession to the throne of David.[49] He claims to discern in these historical traditions structural patterns of a general character which usually are applicable to mythical lore. While acknowledging the challenge for a reconsideration of the traditional work on biblical materials which issues forth from Leach's

48. E. Leach, *Genesis as Myth and Other Essays* (London: Cape, 1969) 7–23; "Lévi-Strauss in the Garden of Eden: An Examination of Some Recent Developments in the Analysis of Myth," *Reader in Comparative Religion* (2d. ed.; ed. W. A. Lessa and E. Z. Vogt; New York: Harper and Row, 1965) 574–81.
49. Leach, *Genesis*, 25–83.

studies, professional Bible scholars have been reluctant to endorse the indiscriminate application of myth-oriented structural analysis to reports of actual historical events.[50]

Let me turn now to a critical review of the established divine-kingship theory and its inherent patternism, through an examination of the meaning which adheres to the act of "anointing" the king.[51] The practice of anointing the ruler was well established in Ancient Near Eastern societies but in Israel obviously was an innovation of the monarchic regime. It is never mentioned in the preceding period of the Judges or "Saviors," nor in the days of Joshua, Moses, or the Patriarchs. Anointing, however, was known to the Hebrews in the context of the cult. Not only were cultic implements anointed, thus to confer upon them a degree of sacredness (Gen 31:13; Exod 30:26; 40:9–11; Num 7:1, 10, 84, 88), but also the special standing of certain cultic functionaries and other persons of renown was symbolized by the pouring of oil on their heads. There is one biblical report about anointing a prophet. Elisha is thus appointed by Elijah to become his successor (1 Kgs 19:16). It is of interest to observe that this act is juxtaposed with Elijah's being commanded concurrently to anoint Jehu ben Nimshi king over Israel. The very conjunction of prophet and king with reference to anointing can also be found in Ps 105:15, אל תגעו במשיחי ולנביאי אל תרעו, and in 1 Chr 29:22 with reference to Solomon and Zadok the priest.

Anointing was practised particularly in connection with the High Priest (Exod 28:41; 29:7, 36; 40:13–15; Lev 8:10, 12; Num 3:3; 30:25; et al.), who therefore could be designated הכהן המשיח (Lev 4:3, 5, 16; 6:15).

Explicit references to the anointing of kings are found in the Bible only in some instances: David (1 Sam 2:4; 5:3; Ps 89:21), Solomon (1 Kgs 1:39), Jehu (2 Kgs 9:1ff.), and Joash (2 Kgs 9:12). Accordingly opinions are divided as to whether anointing was an indispensable feature of the rites of enthronement or was applied only when special circumstances, such as an interruption of dynastic succession, required a renewed affirmation of the ʹ king's assumedly sacral status. Without attempting to arrive at a definite

---

50. See especially the aforementioned discussion by Rogerson (above, n. 6); critical studies by A. Malamat, M. Pamment, and R. C. Culley are reviewed in J. A. Emerton's treatment of the issue ("An Examination of a Recent Structuralist Interpretation of Genesis XXXVIII," *VT* 26 [1976] 79–98).

51. See S. Talmon, "Kingship and the Ideology of the State" (*KCC*, 9–38). For a comprehensive survey of the issue, cp. E. Kutsch, *Salbung als Rechtsakt* (BZAW 87; Berlin: de Gruyter, 1963).

conclusion, it may nevertheless be said that the familiar term משח למלך, in the meaning of "to enthrone" (Judg 9:8, 15; 2 Sam 2:4; 1 Kgs 19:15; et al.), and the recurring designation of kings as משיח ה׳ (1 Sam 24:6, 16; 26:9, 11, 16, 23; et al.) seem to suggest that every king (in Judah and in Ephraim) was anointed, even though our sources are silent about the fact. The dimension of sacredness which adheres to the act of anointing with holy oil (שמן הקדש), which was kept at first in the Tabernacle (Exod 25:6; 22:29; Lev 8:2) and subsequently in the Temple (1 Kgs 1:39), makes it natural that the rite was performed by a priest (1 Kgs 1:39) or by a prophet (1 Sam 10:1ff., cp. 9:16; 16:12–13; 2 Kgs 9:6ff., cp. 1 Kgs 19:15–16) at divine command. What calls for some explanation, however, is the fact that the rite of anointing the king is sometimes reported to have been executed by the "people" or possibly by the people's representative(s). According to 1 Chr 29:20–22 "they [i.e., the assembly of all Israel] . . . appointed Solomon, David's son[52] . . . and *anointed him* as the Lord's prince, and Zadok as priest."

In a similar instance concerning the coronation of Joash the son of Ahaziah, king of Judah, 2 Kings reports that "they [either the people or the temple guards] made him king and *anointed him* [וימליכו אתו],[53] and they [LXX^L + the people] clapped their hands and shouted, 'Long live the king'" (2 Kgs 11:12), whereas the parallel version in 2 Chr 23:11 reads, "Jehoiada [the priest] and his sons anointed him." Again we are told in 2 Kgs 23:30 that "the עם הארץ took Jehoahaz the son of Josiah, and they anointed him and made him king in his father's stead." Lastly, in 2 Sam 19:11 the people propose to rally around David after Absalom's death had brought an end to his rebellion, since "Absalom whom *we anointed over us*, אשר משחנו עלינו, died in war."[54] These references seem to imply that while "anointing" was indeed considered a sacral-ritual act, which by definition must be carried out by a prophet or a priest, it more decisively bore sociopolitical significance.

---

52. The MT reading וימליכו שנית ("a second time") is missing in the LXX. שנית was possibly introduced in order to remove a contradiction between the Chronicles version (1 Chr 29:22) and the parallel in 1 Kgs 1:38–40, where the High Priest Zadok is credited with the performance of the ritual. Another similar case of the introduction of שנית into the MT may be found in Josh 5:2. There too the main LXX tradition does not render the presumably redundant vocable. See S. Talmon ("חתן דמים," *EI* 3 [1954] 94).

53. The LXX render the pertinent verbs in the singular, obviously referring them to Jehoiada the priest, as is the case with the MT reading in 2 Chr 23:11.

54. The phrase is tantamount to המלכנו עלינו, as can be shown by comparison with מלך אבשלום בחברון (2 Sam 15:10).

Even though conceptually the act of anointing conferred the immunity of sanctification upon the king, in actuality the rite gave concrete expression to the king's dependence on the people (and/or the priest and the prophet as the representatives of the divine sphere). In historical reality the ritual of anointing was a ceremonial manifestation of the checks and balances which inhered in the Israelite monarchy. Through the granting or withholding of anointing, either one of the above-mentioned agents (people or prophet/ priest) could effect an important measure of control over the ruler.

When Israelite kingship is viewed in the context of biblical social institutions and against the background of preceding forms of government, instead of being defined predominantly by means of assumed similarities which comparative research discovers in other Ancient Near Eastern societies, the basic singularity of the biblical concept of the monarchy is accentuated. Contrary to widespread scholarly opinion, the presumedly sacral-ritual act of anointing did not enhance the Israelite king's status and power but rather circumscribed it. He was in fact more vulnerable than the earlier nonmonarchical rulers. Before the establishment of the monarchy, a leader of the people (like the judge, who was divinely inspired but not anointed) was never deposed once he had been established in office, even if he was found to be failing. Neither the mission of Samson, who angered his parents by marrying a Philistine woman (Judg 14:3; cp. Gen 26:34–35; 27:46), nor that of Gideon, who by erecting the Ephod in Ophra sinned and caused others to transgress (Judg 8:27), was terminated before it had run its course. However the first king, Saul, is also the first appointed leader of Israel to be dethroned by the prophet who had anointed him (1 Sam 8:13–14; 15:26–28). Because Solomon sinned by marrying foreign wives (like Samson) and set up objectionable cultic places (like Gideon), the rule over ten tribes was divested from his dynasty (1 Kgs 11:1–13) and assigned to Jeroboam ben Nebat (1 Kgs 11:29–39). Ahab's transgressions caused his son to be deprived of the throne, and Jehu ben Nimshi was made king over Ephraim (2 Kings 9). The very possibility that the rule of a king could be terminated *de jure,* and not only *de facto* in the wake of rebellions, strongly suggests that kingship was not considered sacrosanct and that the king himself was not believed to have acquired such status. The very possibility that a king's mission could be revoked—whether by God's emissary, by a prophet (as in the case of Saul, Solomon, and Ahab), or by the people (as in the case of

Rehoboam)—evidences a concept according to which kingship was firmly confined within the human sphere.

A functional analysis of biblical traditions about the monarchic period, undertaken in cognizance of the traditions which portray the premonarchic times, proves that biblical idioms, imagery, and motifs which appear to disclose an underlying conception of the Israelite king as being imbued with "divinity" are mere figures of speech, a *façon à parler,* adopted into the Hebrew vocabulary after having lost their original mythocultic significance. The apparent similarity with Ancient Near Eastern royal terminology is external and should not be construed to indicate the existence of a shared cultural pattern of cultic divine kingship. In his discussion of the supposed divinity of the Israelite kings, H. Frankfort succinctly makes the point: "Much is made nowadays of Canaanite and other Near Eastern elements in Hebrew culture, and a phenomenon like Solomon's kingship conforms indeed to the type of glorified native chieftainship which we have characterized. . . . But it should be plain that the borrowed features in Hebrew culture, and those which have foreign analogies, are least significant. In the case of kingship they are externalities, the less important since they did not affect the *basic oddness* of the Hebrew institution" [my italics].[55]

In concluding this part of the discussion, I wish to stress again that my present interest does not lie in the assessment of the accuracy of this or another specific theory, but rather in illustrating the assertion that in dealing with fundamental issues concerning the social and religious history of biblical Israel, scholars often revert to a comparison with external "parallels" without the prerequisite definition of a methodology of procedure and before examining the phenomena under consideration in their innerbiblical context.

One cannot but concur with the strictures Ringgren has voiced concerning this approach: "Comparative research in the Biblical field has often become a kind of 'parallel hunting.' Once it has been established that a certain Biblical expression or custom has a parallel outside the Bible, the whole problem is regarded as solved. It is not asked whether or not the extra-Biblical element has the same place in life, the same function in the context of its own culture. The first question that should be asked in comparative research is that of the *Sitz im Leben* and the meaning of the

---

55.   H. Frankfort, *Kingship and the Gods* (Chicago: The University of Chicago Press, 1948) 339.

extra-Biblical parallel adduced. It is not until this has been established that the parallel can be utilized to elucidate a Biblical fact."[56]

III. Philological and Literary Aspects[57]

(1) *Comparative Philology and Textual Emendation.* Probably the most spectacular development in comparative biblical studies can be observed in the domain of "language" in the widest sense of the term. One takes note that in linguistics the endeavor to define exact rules for scholarly investigation has borne more fruit than in other areas. According to J. Barr comparative linguistics concern "the comparative study of language groups within which signs of a common historical origin can be detected" and which can be fitted into "an historical common scheme."[58] In the explanation of linguistic facts, the historical analysis is supplemented by a synchronic or structural examination of the material at hand from a "holistic" point of view, rather than in the "atomistic" fashion.[59] While in actual practice these guidelines are not always followed, it nevertheless can be said that linguistic scholarship has been placed on firmer theoretical ground than other fields of biblical research. The closer the affinity of one language to another, in structure and other basic features which point to a common historic origin, the wider the scope for the comparison of their respective vocabularies. Comparative philology can help in the explanation of *hapax legomena* or rare words and idioms in one language which in a sister language are more widely used and better understood. Comparativists can point to impressive achievements in the interpretation of some difficult biblical texts predominantly, though not exclusively, through the utilization of Ugaritic materials. However along with the salutary effect it has exercised, the Ugaritic-biblical comparative research increasingly has laid itself open to incisive criticism.

The more scholars engage in the search for parallels, the more "atomistic" the approach; personal inspiration often takes the place of systematic investigation, and impressionistic déjà vu insights substitute for the

---

56. Ringgren, "Israel's Place," 1 (see above, n. 19).
57. See R. Wellek, "The Crisis of Comparative Literature," *Comparative Literature* (ed. W. P. Friedrich; Chapel Hill, NC: University of North Carolina Press, 1959) 149–59.
58. Barr, *Comparative Philology,* 77 (see above, n. 16).
59. See M. H. Goshen-Gottstein, "Linguistic Structure and Tradition in the Qumran Documents," *Aspects of the Dead Sea Scrolls* (ScrHier 4; Jerusalem: Magnes, 1958) 101–37.

required procedural principles. The results are a mixed blessing. Together with many "good figs," to use Jeremiah's simile, students of the Hebrew Bible are fed from an ever-growing bag of not-so-good fruits of research. Handled with care and the necessary restraint, the collecting of Ras Shamra Parallels[60] can be and indeed often is illuminating. But when imagination is given free reign, the resulting "parallelomania"[61] gives Old Testament studies a bad name and puts in question the reliability of biblical lexicography and comparative research generally. To be sure it would be futile and counterproductive to advocate a radical purism which, because of some doubtful hypotheses and questionable textual emendations, would abstain altogether from the application of the comparative method to biblical literature. What is to be demanded is that attention be paid to a given set of rules, the definition of which requires the cooperation of scholars engaged in the clarification of cruces in diverse fields of biblical research. One of these rules will be mentioned at this juncture: the solution of a crux in the biblical text should be attempted first and foremost by reverting to the immediate context and to synonymous expressions in similar contexts. Direct and "distant parallelism" hold out special promise for the elucidation of opaque or obscure expressions. Comparison with extrabiblical material should be brought into play only when a properly executed innerbiblical analysis does not produce satisfactory results. Even then it would be wise to pay heed to the warning sounded by Y. Muffs, namely that "only after new meanings emerge naturally from the context of one language should comparative material be brought into the picture."[62]

The comparison of biblical literature with Ugaritic writings presents a particular problem. The similarity of the two languages and the obvious contacts Hebrew cultures had with Ugaritic/Canaanite culture, both lying within the same "historic stream," have caused scholars to consider the two literatures to be of one cloth. H. L. Ginsberg opined that "from the philological point of view . . . the Hebrew Bible and the Ugarit texts are to be regarded as one literature, and consequently a reading in either may be emended with the aid of a parallel passage in the other."[63] However one wonders whether

---

60. *Ras Shamra Parallels* (AnOr 49–51; Rome: Pontificium Institutum Biblicum, 1972–1981).
61. S. Sandmel, "Parallelomania," *JBL* 81 (1962) 1–13.
62. Y. Muffs, "Two Comparative Lexical Studies," *JANES* 5 (1973) 296.
63. H. L. Ginsberg, "The Ugaritic Texts and Textual Criticism," *JBL* 62 (1943) 109–15

this sweeping statement can pass unchallenged.[64] Methodological considerations and some comparative techniques which resulted from this dictum cause one to judge the situation less sanguinely. Two literatures such as the biblical and the Ugaritic, which emanated from different cultures, akin as they may be, can never be identified so unreservedly lest we consider the Semitic cultures to exhibit "the monotony and astonishing poverty of human intellectual resources" which the old-style comparative method on the grand scale took as a fundamental postulate. Paraphrasing a statement by A. L. Kröber[65] I would say that in comparative studies generally our concern is and should be with differences as much as with likenesses.[66] The particularity of Hebrew literature on the one hand, and of Ugaritic writings on the other, must not be blurred so as to facilitate and legitimize their being judged as one cultural whole.

In his aforementioned essay, Y. Muffs quotes as an instance which emerges naturally from within the biblical literature H. L. Ginsberg's novel interpretation of the common word עז, "anger," in Qoh 8:1, which he achieved by working out the meaning innerbiblically and relating it subsequently to Akkadian ezzu, "anger, wrath." Here Ginsberg followed the recommended procedure. However in other cases, predominantly where assumed Ugaritic parallels are involved, one sometimes observes a significant departure from this rule because of the posited "identity" of Hebrew and Ugaritic literature. Occasionally Ginsberg will emend a difficult biblical text on the ground of a Ugaritic parallel without attempting first to solve the problem innerbiblically.[67] A case in point is Ginsberg's famous and widely acclaimed emendation of the puzzling ending of one line in David's lament over Saul and Jonathan: הרי בגלבע אל טל ואל מטר עליכם ושדי תרומת (2 Sam 1:21). Numerous proposals were put forward for the restoration of the assumed original reading underlying the awkward expression ושדי תרומת, which does not make sense in the context, some utilizing the ancient versions, others resorting to conjectures. None was convincing enough to gain general

---

64. With regard to aspects of linguistics, see the critical remarks by A. S. Rainey ("כלים האוגריתית לחקר חדשים," *Lešonenu* 32 [1966] 250–53); J. Greenfield, in a review of M. Dahood (*Ugaritic-Hebrew Philology* [BibOr 17; Rome: Pontifical Biblical Institute, 1965]) in *JAOS* 89 (1969) 174–78.

65. After Köbben, "Comparativists," 590 (see above, n. 5).

66. I apply this maxim also in the study of the Qumran literature. See "Between the Bible and the Mishnah" (*WQW*, esp. 19–47).

67. See S. Talmon, "Emendation of Biblical Texts on the Basis of Ugaritic Parallels," *Studies in Bible* (ScrHier 31; Jerusalem: Magnes, 1986) 279–300.

support. By contrast, there was an almost immediate acceptance of Ginsberg's suggestion to read *šr͑ thmt*, "waters of the abyss," derived from a line in the Dan'el epic, which appears to be the exact equivalent of the above Hebrew phrase, being set in a functionally identical context: *bl ṭl bl rbb bl šr͑ thmtm* (CTA 19 = 1 Aqht 1.44).

However the rare attestation of *šr͑* in the Ugaritic vocabulary where it may well be a *hapax legomenon*, which moreover has no counterpart in the Hebrew Bible, detracts from the appeal of the proposed emendation. There also arose doubts concerning the correct reading of the passage in the Dan'el epic. But this emendation of a biblical crux by means of a Ugaritic parallel is still recognized as a classic,[68] despite reservations entertained by critics.

The "waters of the abyss" hardly constitute a proper parallel to "dew" and "rain." In biblical, as in Ugaritic imagery, the "abysmal floods" always carry a negative, not a positive connotation, such as is required in the context under review. It seems preferable to conceive of שדי תרומת as a parallel to הרי בגלבע, both referring to "heights" or mountains on which men are killed in battle. This *Leitmotif* in David's elegy is often employed in other biblical descriptions of wars. A similar idiom is present in the Song of Deborah, which exhibits striking affinities with David's lament with respect to genre, function, and setting. There the tribes of Zebulun and Naftali are extolled by the singer for having "risked their very lives . . . on the heights of the battlefield" (Judg 5:18). The crucial Hebrew expression is על מרומי שדה. On the strength of this phrase in Deborah's song, it seems plausible to suggest that ושדי תרומת in 2 Sam 1:21 is a synonymous idiom in which the sequence of components has been inverted. It should be understood as (ו)תרומת שדה, with תרומה/תרומת being derived from רום/רמה as a by-form of מרום/מרומים, denoting "height" here, not "offering" or "contribution" which is its prevalent connotation in Biblical Hebrew. שדה, probably identical with Akkadian *šadu*, is equivalent here (as in many other biblical passages) to הר, "mountain."

Another variant of מרום/תרומה in combination with שדה/הר turns up in Lam 4:9 in a literary and situational context which is almost identical with that in which David's lament is set. There we encounter the expression מתנובת שדי in relation to Jerusalemites or Judahites slain in battle. Translations of the crucial passage שהם יזובו מדקרים מתנובת שדי, such as "for

---

68. T. L. Fenton, "Comparative Evidence in Textual Study: M. Dahood on 2 Sam i 21 and CTA 19 (1 Aqht), I.44–45," *VT* 29 (1979) 162–70.

these pine away, stricken through, for want of the fruits of the field" (RSV) or "these wasted away, deprived of the produce of the field" (NEB), make no sense in the context. The meaning of the stich must be determined by the parallel in the first half of the verse which has been correctly rendered "They that be slain with the sword are better than they that be slain with hunger" (RSV) or "Those who died by the sword were more fortunate than those who died of hunger" (NEB). It appears obvious to translate the second line accordingly, "for they shed their [blood], speared on the height of the mountains." I suggest that מתנובת resulted from a misreading of מתרומת still extant in 2 Sam 1:21. Therefore the latter verse should not be translated "Ye mountains of Gilboa, let there be no dew or rain upon you, neither fields of offering" (RSV); nor, following Ginsberg's emendation, "Hills of Gilboa, let no dew or rain fall on you, no showers on the uplands" (NEB); but rather, assuming an elliptic-chiastic parallelism, "Hills of Gilboa, no dew and no rain upon you, mountain heights."[69]

I wish again to emphasize that the analysis presented here is not intended merely to prove or disprove the validity of an emendation suggested on the ground of a presumed external parallel. Rather, it is meant to illustrate the need for a definition of the proper procedure to be followed in the comparative philological study of biblical texts and to adduce proof for the maxim that the innerbiblical analysis always should precede the comparison with extrabiblical texts.

(2) *Literary Imagery.* As already stated biblical thinking seldom if ever expresses itself in a conceptual system. The Hebrews' ideas and concepts can be gauged, rather, from events narrated and from the narrators' attitudes which can be elicited, to a degree, from an analysis of the text. Recurring idioms, phrases, imagery, and motifs are of considerable help in the discernment of matters and reflections with which the writers' minds were preoccupied; they constitute a form of capsule descriptions which substitute for the detailed presentation of intricate thought processes. On the cognitive level literary images can be employed as concretizations of abstract notions and thus facilitate the transmission of ideas, e.g., in the realm of myth and religious thought.[70] Therefore it can cause no surprise that literary imagery is

---

69. J. P. Fokkelman arrived independently at a similar explanation of the passage ("שדי תרומת in II Sam 1:21ᵃ: A Non-Existent Crux," *ZAW* 91 [1979] 290–92).

70. In the studies mentioned above (nn. 25 and 31), I endeavor to illustrate the utilization of such literary patterns towards the elucidation of ancient Israelite speculative thought.

a ready object for comparative research (both on the grand scale and in the "historic stream" manner), often in detachment from the immediate literary or cultural context. In some instances such research abuts on comparative linguistics or philology. The method has special appeal in the explanation of texts or expressions whose connotation cannot be established with the help of the biblical lexicon or on the basis of etymology.

A case in point is the speculation about cosmogony and the conception of the world which hinges on the mythic-existential notion of a center of the world, as captured in the idea and the image of the *omphalos*.[71] Essentially the term and the imagery point to a representation of the world in the form of a human body. Its center is marked by a tall mountain representing the navel from which issues forth an imaginary umbilical cord, the *vinculum*. Just as the embryo is bound to its mother's body by the navel cord, it links our world with the higher spheres, the world of the gods. W. Roscher, the innovator of modern *omphalos* research, proved the widespread existence of this idea in the classical world. He showed that the principal sanctuaries of ancient Greece—Delos, Epidaurus, Paphos, Branchides, Miletus, and Delphi—were each considered by their respective adherents to be at the center of the earth, i.e., to constitute its navel. Roscher further demonstrated that the image of an imposing mountain as the center of the earth was already current among the nations of the Ancient Near East. His hypothesis was developed by Wensinck who assembled impressive evidence that the *omphalos* idea persisted in postclassical Greek thought and Jewish-Hellenistic and rabbinic sources as well.

The term *omphalos* appears twice in the Septuagint as the translation of the Hebrew term טבור הארץ. One of these places is the Abimelech story of Judg 9:37 and is connected there, one way or another, with the area of Shechem. The other occurrence is in Ezekiel's vision of the onslaught of Gog on the people of Israel who have been gathered into their land (Ezek 33:10–12). טבור thus far has evaded precise etymological determination, nor can its biblical connotation be definitively established. It is beyond doubt that ὄμφαλος of the LXX and *umbilicus terrae* of the Vulgate reflect an understanding of טבור as "navel," in perfect accord with its meaning in Mishnaic Hebrew. However it remains open to discussion whether the existence of the pre- or extra-biblical mythic concept "navel of the earth" in the

---

71. See S. Talmon, "The 'Navel of the Earth' and the Comparative Method," in this vol., pp. 50–75.

Ancient Near East as well as the postbiblical notion of a "center of the world," designated טַבּוּר/טְבוּר or ὄμφαλος, are indeed decisive proof for the presence of that very same concept in the biblical world view. The paucity of the evidence for the assumed existence of a biblical ὄμφαλος concept, two solitary usages of the unexplained term טבור הארץ, appears to neutralize its import when compared with the prevalence of the concept in other, both earlier and later, cultures. Furthermore the absence in the above-mentioned biblical passages of any reference to a sanctuary, a feature integral to the classical Greek as well as the most significant Ancient Near Eastern examples of the "navel of the earth" myth, surely constitutes negative evidence. This deficiency is "remedied" by postulating that since the events related in the Judges passage take place in the vicinity of Shechem and reference is made to "the tops of the mountains" (Judg 9:36), the term טבור הארץ surely must pertain to holy Mount Gerizim on the top of which the Samaritan temple stood during later periods. Likewise the recurrent mention of הרי ישראל in Ezekiel's Gog of Magog vision (Ezekiel 38–39) is construed as being synonymous with Jerusalem. Thus טבור הארץ in that context is understood as an attribute of the holy city and her sanctuary.

Despite the frailty of this argumentation, Hebrew Bible scholars have endorsed the identification of biblical טבור הארץ as "navel of the earth" on the basis of the above extrabiblical parallels. In this they were joined by phenomenologists who could now add ancient Israelite culture to the group of cultures in which the *omphalos* myth was present, thus buttressing the proposition that the idea of a cosmic center was a universal component of the human conception of the world. Furthermore some patternists attempted to elicit from the biblical sources evidence for the former existence of an Israelite *omphalos* myth. By infusing an abundancy of imagination into the comparative procedures, the *omphalos* myth was placed at the very center of Israelite religion, in fact was made the "navel" of her conceptual world.[72] This development illustrates the snowballing effect of the search for similarities by which distinct civilizations can be forced into one pattern of cult and culture.

The contemplation of the טבור הארץ issue first and foremost in the context of and in relation to the bases of ancient Hebrew religion, instead of or even concomitant with its review in the comparative manner, should have

---

72. S. Terrien, "The Omphalos Myth and Hebrew Religion," *VT* 20 (1970) 315–38.

convinced scholars of the improbability that the Mesopotamian, Jebusite, or Canaanite mythic idea of the *omphalos* could have served as a pillar of ancient Israel's spiritual world. While vestiges of pagan beliefs certainly filtered into the popular cult and religion, it is far-fetched to assume that they were emulated by authoritative biblical authors, such as the prophet Ezekiel. Terrien's insistence that "in all probability, the myth of the navel of the earth, far from being an incidental aspect of worship at the temple of Jerusalem, constitutes in effect the determining factor which links together a number of its cultic practices and beliefs that otherwise appear to be unrelated"[73] remains without proof if one bears in mind the fragility and questionability of the evidence on which this claim rests. Indeed the treatment of the issue by comparativists fully bears out the critical description and evaluation of their procedures which E. Leach offers: "The practitioners displayed a prodigious range of erudition in that they were familiar with an extraordinary variety of ethnographic facts. . . . The ethnographic evidence was always used to exemplify general propositions with the implication that such propositions are validated by an accumulation of positive evidence. Neutral or negative evidence was never considered."[74]

From this discussion emerges a very simple but fundamental rule which should be observed in the study of biblical texts and their conceptual import: when linguistic aspects provide but unclear and difficult hints in the explanation of textual cruces, one should not depend on the forced testimony of assumed external parallels ferreted out by the comparative method. Rather, the elucidation of difficult terms and ideas must be achieved from the biblical books themselves. They are the only reliable firsthand evidence which mirrors, albeit fragmentarily, the conceptual horizon of ancient Israel and the linguistic and literary modes in which it found its expression. Internal parallels are of greater help than external ones; their identification can be achieved in a more systematic fashion than the pinpointing of similarities in extrabiblical sources. It appears to be quite appropriate at this juncture to cite the exegetical principle formulated by E. J. Kissane, which has lost nothing of its force but unfortunately is often lost sight of by exegetes of the Hebrew Bible: "The context is the guide to interpretation, and disregard of the context leads to chaos."[75]

---

73. Ibid., 317.
74. E. Leach, "The Comparative Method in Anthropology," 342 (see above, n. 4).
75. After Engnell, "Traditio-Historical Method," 5 (see above, n. 2).

In the case under review, the significance of the rare expression טבור
הארץ, the application of this procedure produces results which are quite
different from the thesis put forward by the comparativists. A contextual
analysis of the Ezekiel passage, and to a lesser degree of the relevant
passage in the book of Judges, makes it evident that in both occurrences the
term טבור הארץ has no mythic implications whatsoever but rather describes
an open place of settlement, ארץ פרזות, where people live peacefully, assured
of their safety without the need of fortifications and ramparts. This idea is
clearly the tenor of Ezekiel's oracle about Gog. It sounds a warning to the
enemy of his imminent fall and gives assurance to the people of Israel who
have returned to their homeland to live there in tranquility. The *Leitmotif* of
the oracle is "life in security," which echoes a recurring divine promise that
pervades biblical literature (Lev 25:18–19; 26:5; Deut 12:10; 33:28). It
applies to Israel's existence in history (see, e.g., 1 Sam 12:11; 2 Sam 7:10;
and esp. 1 Kgs 5:5) as well as to the future restoration of her fortunes (Isa
32:17–18; Jer 32:37; Ezek 28:26; 34:27–28; Hos 2:20; Mic 4:4; Zech 14:11;
et al.).[76] In Ezekiel the motif is reiterated in a series of expressions, one of
which is "dwell on the טבור הארץ." The equation of טבור הארץ with "secure
place" as the most tangible historicogeographical meaning which can be
elicited from a close reading of the Ezekiel passage is applicable also to the
reference in the Abimelech tradition. It can be buttressed by a comparison of
the situation described in the Gog oracle with similar descriptions of
inimical onslaughts on a peaceful population. The most noteworthy example
is found in Judg 18:7–10, 27–28, which depicts the attack of the Danites on
the people of Laish. There phrases are employed which are synonymous with
those used in the Gog oracle: "They dwell in security, יושב(ת) לבטח, . . . quiet
and safe, שקט ובטח, . . . and quarrel with no one, ודבר אין להם עם אדם, . . .
[living] in a wide-open land, והארץ רחבת ידים, . . . in the valley next to [the
city of] Bet Rehob, בעמק אשר לבית רחוב (cp. further 1 Chr 4:40; Jer 39:31–32;
et al.).

In summary, the elucidation of the twice-used term טבור הארץ by means
of a contextual analysis and an innerbiblical comparison with synonymous
expressions in functionally similar settings suggests that no mythic element
whatsoever adheres to the term. There is no need or justification for saddling

---

76. See my remarks on the matter in a review of W. D. Davies, *The Gospel and the Land: Early
Christianity and Jewish Territorial Doctrine* ([Berkeley: The University of California Press,
1973] in *Christian News from Israel* 25 [Jerusalem, 1975] 134–36).

it with a mystic import by means of eisegesis based on the comparative method in the pattern-of-cult tradition.

(3) *Literary Gattungen*. I turn now to the problem of the comparability of biblical literary forms or *Gattungen*. Once more our interest will focus on Ugaritic literature because of the proven similarity of its structures, imagery, and phraseology with those found in biblical writings. Before presenting a specific example, it may be useful to make a preliminary remark. *Per definitionem*, a literary *Gattung* has a specific *Sitz im Leben*, i.e., a well-circumscribed anchorage in the cultic and cultural structure of the society which produced it. It is the formalized literary expression of ideas, social concepts, and cultic values which that society fostered. Therefore the identification of a *Gattung* evidenced in the literature of one society also in the creative writings of another requires the additional proof that in both it had the same *Sitz im Leben*. This means that a comparative study of *Gattungen* must take into account the social context in which specific literary types and forms arise. What must be shown is that this *Gattung* and what it expresses do actually find their place in the cultic and conceptual framework of both societies. A *Gattung* cannot be contemplated in isolation from the overall sociocultural web of a society.

Our present concern will be with the application of these thoughts to the question of whether there ever existed an Israelite national epic. There can be no doubt that we have no evidence of an epos in biblical literature.[77] U. Cassuto, to whose discussion of the question we shall return, states quite unequivocally that neither the epic nor the epic song proper is found in the biblical books. This statement would achieve common consent unless one were to maintain that the Hebrew Bible in its entirety constitutes the national epic of the ancient Hebrews. There remains, however, the consideration of the *Vorgeschichte* of the present canon of biblical writings. It is correctly assumed that in the stages before its crystallization in the form of books, Hebrew literature was current as only loosely connected, preponderantly oral traditions. It is within these earlier stages of this literature which are no longer extant that the search for lost epic cycles has been conducted. Scholars concentrated their attention on the supposedly tangible remnants of and references to epic songs submerged in the present prose texts, especially the obscure ספר מלחמת ה׳ (Num 21:14, with a barely intelligible quotation

---

77. See S. Talmon, "Did There Exist a Biblical National Epic?" in this volume, pp. 91–111.

from that work), and the twice-mentioned ספר הישר (Josh 10:13; 2 Sam 1:18;
again with quotations).[78] With the exception of Tur-Sinai, who took ספר to
mean "oral transmission" or "recitation" of God's mighty deeds,[79] it is
unanimously held that the sources do refer to epics which were still known
at the time of the historiographers who quote from them.

With S. Mowinckel the hypothesis achieved its fullest form.[80] According
to him, the surmised *Israelitische Nationalepos* had successfully fused heroic
epic tales, portraying the historical exploits of the Israelites and their God in
the post-Davidic period, with an epic of cosmogony which rightfully belongs
in the category of myth. Central to our present concern is the closing section
of Mowinckel's essay which widens the scope of the inquiry (until then
based altogether on biblical material *sensu strictu*) as the author turns to
Ancient Near Eastern epic literature in order to support the postulated existence of a Hebrew national-religious epic.

The employment of the comparative method in search of the lost biblical epic reached a new height in the writings of Cassuto, at whose disposal
lay the newly discovered Ugaritic literature.[81] Cassuto collected a good
number of isolated expressions and word combinations scattered in biblical
prose texts which bear the stamp of poetry or even are reminiscent of specific literary turns in Ugaritic epics. The evidence which he assembled certainly strengthens the case for the generally accepted notion that biblical Israel had been imbued with vestiges of Ugaritic/Canaanite culture, including
elements borrowed from epics of which the Hebrew authors must have
known sizeable portions. Yet to jump from the collation of such obviously
borrowed materials to the supposition that they help to prove the existence
at one time of an originally Hebrew epic (or epics) is a far cry indeed. It is
interesting to observe that Cassuto was almost compelled to make this assumption by his correct insight that biblical Israel hardly would have taken
over lock-stock-and-barrel the polytheistic literature of the Canaanites. The
antagonistic attitude toward the pagan cult and ritual with which the

78. The proposed retroversion of ἐν βιβλίῳ τῆς ᾠδῆς mentioned in a Greek addition to
     1 Kgs 8:53 (3 Kgdms 8:53a [8:13]) and also found in one witness of the Vetus Latina into
     ספר השיר and the latter's identification with ספר הישר (by inversion) is rather questionable
     in view of the apparent dissimilar content of these two compilations.
79. N. H. Tur-Sinai, "Was There an Ancient 'Book of the Wars of the Lord'?" *BIES* 24 (1960)
     146–48 (Heb.).
80. S. Mowinckel, "Hat es ein israelitisches Nationalepos gegeben?" *ZAW* 53 (1935) 130–52.
81. U. Cassuto, "The Israelite Epic," *Biblical and Oriental Studies* (trans. I. Abrahams;
     Jerusalem: Magnes, 1975) 2.69–109.

Ugaritic epics are intimately connected simply ruled out such a transfer. Therefore he maintains that as far as remnants of epic literature are recognizable in the biblical writings, they perforce must derive from original Hebrew epic songs.

It is at this state of our survey that we encounter once more the issue of method. The combined evidence marshalled by scholars from their survey of biblical literature cannot provide a sound basis for positing the existence of full-fledged Hebrew epics in the biblical period. The evidence as a whole is circumstantial. It is based on inference from observations about the assumed developmental process of national literatures generally, and Ancient Near Eastern and foremost Ugaritic literature especially. In addition the presumed ancient Hebrew epic is discussed in complete isolation from other forms or *Gattungen* extant in the biblical writings. There can be no doubt that in the historiographies, the narratives, Psalms, and even in the prophetic books we do encounter features which are characteristic of the epic genre: poetic rhythm, parallelistic structure, and formulaic language. However these features are found also in literature to which the designation "epic" cannot be applied. We still have to ask ourselves the fundamental questions of what makes an epic an epic and in what way can an epic be clearly distinguished from other forms of narrative "epic-type" literature. Not one of the scholars who engaged in the study of the issue attempted to provide a clear definition of the "epic" as a special *Gattung*, nor was a satisfactory definition offered by students of the history of general literature and of literary criticism.

Of even greater import is the following fact. The outstanding predominance in the Bible of straightforward prose narration fulfills the functions for which other literatures revert to the epic genre: heroic tales, historiography, even myth and cosmogony. The phenomenon is too striking to be coincidental. It appears that the ancient Hebrew writers purposefully nurtured and developed prose narration to take the place of the epic genre which by its content was intimately bound up with the world of paganism and appears to have had a special standing in the polytheistic cults. The recitation of epics was tantamount to a reenactment of cosmic events in the manner of sympathetic magic. In the process of total rejection of the polytheistic religions and their ritual expressions in the cult, epic songs and also the epic genre were purged from the literary repertoire of the Hebrew authors. Together with the content its foremost literary concretization fell into disrepute and was banished from the Israelite culture. The epic elements which did survive—

preponderantly in the literature of the monarchic period, viz., from a time when the prophets were active—were permitted to infiltrate other forms of biblical literature as building blocks because they had lost their pagan import and had been neutralized. These survivals constitute examples of figurative language whose original connotations had been so diluted that they no longer evoked objection. However the initial rejection of the epics and the epic genre seems to have been so thorough that they could never be reintegrated into the technical apparatus of the Hebrew literati. It can be surmised that the closure of biblical literature against the epic was helped along by the progressive falling into desuetude of this genre in the Semitic world from about the second quarter of the first millennium BCE. The following observation may be added: in the framework of the cult, the Hebrew writers developed the historiographical psalm as a substitute for the epic. The great acts of God in the creation of the world and in history thus were related and possibly recited in a specifically and originally Israelite genre.

In summing up this discussion it can be said that the epic is not simply a *Gattung* which can be identified by a given number of literary techniques such as were specified for example by W. Whallon.[82] It is, rather, the expression of a specific societal *Gestalt*. Its presence can be empirically established in those societies which did produce epics and in which it has a special *Sitz im Leben*.[83] It cannot be reconstructed where it does not exist. With reference to the epic as a specific literary genre, Israel presents a deep societal structure which differs from those of her neighbors. The cosmological epic requires a rich background of myth for its development; Israel was lacking that background, having rejected myth from the outset. The historical epic has been shown by D. F. Rauber to have flourished in societies in the heroic stages of their development.[84] It is therefore striking that biblical literature did not record even Israel's heroic age (the days of the judges and the early kings) in the form of epics.

Comparativists generally, and in the field of biblical studies especially, would do well to pay heed to differences between cultures and not only to likenesses. Adequate attention must be given to the interpretation of the

82. W. Whallon, *Formula, Character, and Context: Studies in Homeric, Old English, and Old Testament Poetry* (Cambridge, MA: Harvard University Press, 1969).

83. Cp. the interesting observations on the position of the epic poet in Homeric Society in S. C. Humphreys, "'Transcendence' and Intellectual Roles: The Ancient Greek Case" (*Daedalus* 104 [1975] 91–118).

84. D. F. Rauber, "Observations on Biblical Epic," *Genre* 3 (1970) 318–38.

dissimilarities from other cultures of the Ancient Near East which made biblical civilization the peculiar and particular phenomenon it was. These considerations lead us to answer in the negative the question posed by Mowinckel and echoed by Cassuto: "Hat es ein israelitisches Nationalepos gegeben?" Biblical Israel did not produce epics nor did it foster the epic genre.

IV. Conclusion

In closing this presentation I wish to return to the issue of procedure to which reference was made in the introductory part and to stress once more the need for the definition of a set of rules which should serve biblical scholars as a guideline in their pursuit of comparative studies. It must be emphasized that the formulation of a methodology of comparative research in matters pertaining to ancient Israelite culture and biblical literature is a task which transcends the framework of this paper and which cannot be carried out single-handedly because of the comprehensiveness and the variety of issues to which this research applies itself. It demands an interdisciplinary and synoptic grasp, thus requiring the cooperation of experts in diverse areas: philology, literature, folklore, theology, sociology, history, and the history of ideas. All that could be attempted here was the delineation of some basic, not necessarily new principles which should be followed in the intercultural comparative study of biblical phenomena.

These can be summarized as follows. The interpretation of biblical features—whether of a sociopolitical, cultic, general-cultural, or literary nature—with the help of innerbiblical parallels should always precede the comparison with extrabiblical materials. In the evaluation of a societal phenomenon, attention should be paid to its function in the developing structure of the Israelite body politic before one engages in the comparison with parallel phenomena in other societies. Such comparisons can be applied to societies which lie in the same "historic stream" as biblical Israel. Comparisons on the "grand scale" are better avoided. In this respect, the methodological concerns expressed by Walter Goldschmidt are most pertinent: "Because each culture defines its own institutions there is always an element of falsification when we engage in institutional comparisons among distinct cultures."[85]

---

85. W. Goldschmidt, *Comparative Functionalism* (Berkeley: University of California Press, 1966) 131.

In any such study the full range of the available evidence must be taken into consideration: the "holistic" approach should be given preference over the "atomistic." The abstraction of a concept, an aspect of society, cult, or literature from its wider framework and its contemplation in isolation more often than not will result in distortion; its intrinsic meaning ultimately is decided by the context and therefore may vary from one setting to another.

The required application of these principles is illustrated in detail in the analysis of specific ideational and literary phenomena as presented in several studies included in the present volume. They address themselves to a variety of pertinent issues, foremost in: "The 'Navel of the Earth' and the Comparative Method," "Biblical רְפָאִים and Ugaritic *RPU/I(M)*," "The Desert Motif in the Bible and in Qumran Literature," and "Eschatology and History in Biblical Thought."[86]

---

86. See further, int. al., "Kingship and the Ideology of the State," *KCC*, 9–38.

THE "NAVEL OF THE EARTH" AND THE COMPARATIVE METHOD

I

The comparative method has carved itself a secure niche in modern biblical research. It significantly broadened the field of discussion of the social phenomena and principles of thought that distinguished the culture of Israel. This method of study removed biblical Israel from the isolationist ideology which characterizes in general the biblical and in particular the prophetic outlook. Careful observation disclosed an elaborate network of channels linking Israel with the nations in whose midst she resided: from Egypt in the south, through the Canaanite expanse on both sides of the Jordan, and on to Mesopotamia in the northeast. In the two millennia before the common era, this geographical-territorial proximity made possible a close and constant "give and take" on the social and intellectual plane, despite the limited means of communication.

A multitude of facets points toward the interweaving of Israel within the net of interaction among the peoples of the area. The sheer abundance of parallels drawn from various aspects of life, language, literary forms and conventions, articles of belief and of ritual, methods of social and political organization brought to light by "comparativists" wrenched biblical Israel from the ideological position of "a people dwelling alone and not reckoning itself among the nations" (Num 23:9).[1]

Comparative research did not limit its compass to contemporaneous cultural systems, viz., to the discernment of similarities between linguistic, literary, and intellectual values of biblical Israel and those of other nations of the Ancient Near East. Instead the comparative method widened the scope of inquiry to include also cultures that were chronologically and geographically far removed from ancient Israel: the Arab society of the

1.   See "The Comparative Method in Biblical Interpretation," in this vol., p. 18.

pre-Islamic period,[2] the culture of classical Greece and its later Hellenistic expressions.

The comparison with such extrabiblical materials, whether culled from contemporaneous literatures of the Ancient Near East or from postbiblical writings, recommends itself when one comes to examine a term or concept that occurs rarely in the Bible or is altogether a *hap. leg* that cannot be satisfactorily explained either through etymological derivation or from the context. An extrabiblical source in which the subject matter is sufficiently clear sometimes offers an analogy by which a biblical crux can be satisfactorily solved.

There can be no quarrel with the comparative method as long as it is employed within the bounds of reason and does not divorce the issue under discussion from its proper context in the culture compared.[3] However, sometimes researchers seem to let their penchant for resemblances and parallels run wild, relentlessly searching the great expanse of Ancient Near Eastern literature for every possible similarity or likeness with presumed biblical counterparts, often closing an eye to factors which differentiate one cultural system from another.

Despite the wide and varied ramifications of comparative research, the time may not yet be ripe for drawing general conclusions from unconnected facts which have been assembled piecemeal. The formulation of a methodology of comparative research demands a synoptic, interdisciplinary comprehension and requires the participation of experts from distinct fields of research: language, literature, sociology, and intellectual history. Such a concerted effort is still a desideratum. But the comparison of any biblical facet with a presumed counterpart in other cultures should in any case be guided by this principle: before positing a resemblance of a biblical phenomenon with a contemporaneous, a prebiblical, or a postbiblical counterpart, it is imperative to examine biblical literature itself for possible parallels, foremost the immediate context under discussion. This rule is especially important when one deals with literary motifs or with bases of biblical thought which embody incipient religious concepts destined to come to full flower in postbiblical Jewish thought and literature.

---

2.   J. Wellhausen, *Reste arabischen Heidentums* (Berlin: G. Reimer, 1885) remains the fundamental work in this area. Cp. M. Buber, *Königtum Gottes* (Berlin: Schocken, 1932).

3.   Exceptions are phenomenological aspects and theoretical models that apply to many cultural systems and are not particular to the one or the other.

II

We shall exemplify the approach outlined by examining the connotation of the term טבור הארץ, found only twice in the Bible, in Judg 9:36–37, "And when Gaal saw the men, he said to Zebul, 'Look, men are coming down from the mountain tops' . . . and he said, 'Look, men are coming down מעם טבור הארץ"; and in Ezek 38:11–12, "I will go up against the land of the unwalled villages; I will fall upon the quiet people who dwell securely . . . who dwell על טבור הארץ."

The meaning of טבור has not been ascertained etymologically.[4] J. Boehmer sought to link the term with Aramaic, Syriac, and Arabic *tur;* and טבור, equally תבור, with Akkadian *duppuru* and Ethiopic *dābār,* all of which are nouns sharing the common meaning "mountain."[5] Albright connected טבור with Ugaritic *tbrrt,* meaning "brightness," "splendor," or "purity."[6] D. Winton Thomas suggested the derivation of טבור from נבר and conjectured that it approximates Ethiopic *henbert* and Amharic *enbert,* whose meaning is identical with rabbinic טַבּוּר/טַבּוּר and biblical שׂר ("navel").[7] This suggestion is undoubtedly intended to support the hypothesis that in the two above-mentioned biblical occurrences of טַבּוּר, the term is equivalent to טִבּוּר in Mishnaic Hebrew. Indeed, it was so understood by the LXX, which rendered it ὀμφαλός in both instances, and by the Vg., where it is rendered *umbilicus.* As a result of the identification of טַבּוּר (isolated from its biblical context) with טַבּוּר/טִבּוּר of rabbinic usage and with ὀμφαλός of the LXX, the mythical idea of the "navel of the earth," which is marked by a major sanctuary, was introduced into biblical thought. It is claimed that in

---

4. No etymological derivation of טבור is given in W. Gesenius and F. Buhl, *Hebräisches und Aramäisches Handwörterbuch über das Alte Testament* (17th ed.; Berlin: Springer, 1949); L. Köhler and W. Baumgartner, *Lexicon in Veteris Testamenti Libros* (Leiden: E. J. Brill, 1953–58); or E. Ben Yehuda, "טַבּוּר/טִבּוּר," *Thesaurus Totius Hebraitatis et Veteris et Recentioris* (4.1836). A. Kohut seeks to derive the noun "from the Samaritan word *tᵉbar = Hochpunkt,* i.e., an elevated point on the human body" (*Aruch Completum* [New York: Pardes, 1955], 4.13).

5. J. Boehmer, "Der Gottesberg Tabor" (*BZ* 23 [1935] 33–41); idem, "Der Name Tabor" (*ZS* 7 [1929] 161–69). Biblical tradition does not give Mt. Tabor a special status of holiness. Tabor is viewed, rather, as one mountain among others (Josh 19:22; Judg 4:6, 12, 14; 8:18), comparable with Mt. Carmel (Jer 46:18) and Mt. Hermon (Ps 89:13).

6. W. F. Albright, "The Role of the Canaanites in the History of Civilization," *The Bible and the Ancient Near East* (ed. G. E. Wright; Garden City, NY: Doubleday, 1961) 252, n. 7.

7. D. Winton Thomas, "Mount Tabor, the Meaning of the Name," *VT* 1 (1951) 229–30.

Ezekiel, Jerusalem and her Temple are regarded as the focus of the world, whereas in Judges, Mt. Gerizim is conceived as the "navel of the earth,"[8] reflecting the central role which that site was to play in the faith of the Samaritans, who refer to it by טברא בריכא and sometimes by טורא בריכא, as a competitor with Mt. Zion and Jerusalem. The representation of the world in the form of a human body, a disc, or a square,[9] whose center is marked by a tall mountain which represents its navel, is prevalent in the mythical traditions of many cultures. Just as the embryo is bound at the navel to the mother's body, so the world of man as well as of the underworld is linked with the higher spheres, the world of the gods, by the central mountain, the likeness of the umbilical cord (*vinculum*). From this image sprang the identification of a sanctuary atop an imposing mountain, or the "tallest mountain" (though this need not be the geographic reality), with the "navel of the earth."[10]

The currency of the conception of the sanctuary as the center or navel of the earth in Greek mythology was proven by Roscher, who may be considered the innovator of modern ὄμφαλος research.[11] In the *Odyssey* (1.50) Homer describes the geographical center of the sea as its navel: "the sea-washed island, the navel of the sea," νήσῳ ἐν ἀμφιρύτῃ ὅθι τ' ὀμφαλός ἐστι θαλάσσης. Roscher speculated that the image had its place even in the most ancient representations of the world as a whole, though the first explicit occurrence is with Epimenides (Plutarch, *Moralia*, 409E), who appears to refute that image: "nor was the center of the earth a navel."

---

8. See G. Lanczkowski: "In Palästina galt der Garizim als N[abel] der Erde (ṭabbûr haaraeṣ: Ri 9, 37)" ("Nabel," *RGG* 4.1286); cp. H. W. Hertzberg, "Garizim" (*RGG* 2.1202); "The Mythology of Pre-Israelite Shechem" is investigated in detail by G. R. H. Wright, who provides further bibliographical information on the issue (*VT* 20 [1970] 75–82); B. Mazar, "מקום שכם-תחום מקודש לבני ישראל" (*Canaᶜan and Israel: Historical Essays* [Jerusalem: Bialik, 1974] 144–51, esp. 148).

9. W. Roscher, *Omphalos* ([ASGW 29; Leipzig: Teubner, 1913] part 9, p. 20).

10. Historians of religion discovered this "Symbolism of the Center" in practically all cultures. A concise presentation of the matter may be found in M. Eliade, *Cosmos and History: The Myth of the Eternal Return* ([New York: Harper, 1959] 12–17).

11. See Roscher, *Omphalos*; *Neue Omphalosstudien* (ASGW 31; Leipzig: Teubner, 1915) part 1; *Der Omphalosgedanke bei verschiedenen Völkern, besonders den semitischen* (SSAW 70; Leipzig: Teubner, 1918) part 2. Cp. N. V. Herrmann, *Omphalos* (OrAnt 13; Münster: Aschendorff, 1959); E. A. S. Butterworth, *The Tree at the Navel of the Earth* (Berlin: de Gruyter, 1970); S. Thompson, *Motif Index in Folk Literature* (Copenhagen: Rosenkilde & Bagger, 1955–1958) A 875.1, 151.1; L. I. J. Stadelmann, S.J., *The Hebrew Conception of the World: A Philological and Literary Study* (AnBib 39; Rome: Pontificium Institutum Biblicum, 1970) 147–53.

Roscher demonstrated that the principal sanctuaries of Greece, Delos, Epidaurus, Paphos, Branchidae, Miletus, and especially Delphi, were viewed by their respective adherents as the center of the earth, viz., its navel. He further argued that the image of a mountain as the center of the earth was already current among the nations of the Ancient Near East. On a Babylonian map of the heavens and the earth, for example, the city Babylon is presented as the center of the world. More than once a temple standing on the height of a mountain is spoken of as the "link between the heavens and the earth"; the heavens have their foundation in the mountains which serve them as supporting pillars. However, in these instances this center of the world is not designated *abbunatu*, which is the Akkadian equivalent of "navel"— ὄμφαλος; Rab. Heb. טַבּוּר/טִבּוּר.

Roscher's hypothesis underwent a further development at the hands of Wensinck, who determined that the idea of the "navel" in the ancient world (and in Jewish thought as well) was expressed in five sub-images: (1) the center of the earth; (2) the highest elevation in the surrounding area; (3) the meeting-point of the upper and the lower world; (4) the matrix of the created world; and (5) the source of nourishment for the world and its inhabitants.[12] Such concepts are indeed present in Jewish-Hellenistic literature; there they represent the city of Jerusalem and the Temple which is regarded as the heart of the city. The images are also reflected in ancient maps of the land of Israel, obviously as a concept more than as a reflection of geographic reality (see illustrations on p. 55).

The idea emerges in the Letter of Aristeas (line 83), where Jerusalem is portrayed as it is viewed by a diaspora Jew who made a pilgrimage to the Holy City: "When we arrived (in the land of the Jews) we saw the city situated in the middle (or in the center) of the whole of Judaea on the top of a mountain of considerable altitude" (*APOT* 2.103).[13] A similar description is offered in the book of *1 Enoch* (26:1–6) in the course of the description of Enoch's journey through the universe: "And I went from there to the middle of the earth, and I saw a blessed place in which there were trees with branches [of a dismembered tree] abiding and blooming. And I saw a holy mountain, and underneath the mountain to the east there was a stream, and

---

12. A. J. Wensinck, *The Ideas of the Western Semites Concerning the Navel of the Earth* (Amsterdam: Johannes Müller, 1916) xi.
13. R. H. Charles, ed., *The Apocrypha and Pseudepigrapha of the Old Testament* (Oxford: Clarendon, 1913).

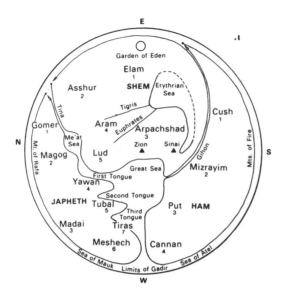

The World according to the *Book of Jubilees,* by Francis Schmidt
Courtesy Yad Izhak Ben-Zvi, Jerusalem

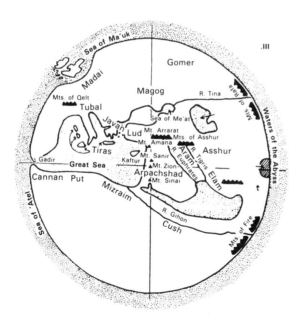

Jubilees Map, Reconstructed by P. S. Alexander
Courtesy Yad Izhak Ben-Zvi, Jerusalem

it flowed to the south. And I saw towards the east another mountain higher than this and between them a deep and narrow ravine: in it also ran a stream underneath the mountain," (*APOT* 2.205). The author resorts to similar language in his description of the site of Gehinnom (*1 Enoch* 90:26): "a like abyss was opened in the midst of the earth, full of fire" (*APOT* 2.259). Likewise, Philo of Alexandria pictures Jerusalem as being in the center of the world (*Legatio ad Gaium* 37.294). The identical conception, though focused on the Temple rather than on the city, is employed by Hecataeus of Abdera (ca. 300 BCE), as cited by Josephus Flavius (*Ag. Ap.* 1.197ff.). In his description of the Jews and their land, Hecataeus notes that in addition to many fortresses and villages in different parts of the country, there is one fortified city called Jerusalem, and "nearly in the centre of the city," κατὰ μέσον μάλιστα τῆς πόλεος,[14] stands the Temple (LCL 1.243).

The term ὄμφαλος is present in Josephus' description of Judea on the eve of the rebellion against the Romans (*J.W.* 3.3.5 §51–52): "In breadth it stretches from the river Jordan to Joppa. The city of Jerusalem lies at its very centre, for which reason the town has sometimes, not inaptly, been called the ὄμφαλος of the country" (LCL 2.590–91). It is impossible to determine with precision whether the word "country" (χώρα) here signifies Judea or the world as a whole. It appears that Josephus fused two ancient concepts. One of these is apparent in the book of *Jubilees* (8:19) in an early midrash on Gen 10:25: "for in his days the earth was divided." In the division of the world among the sons of Noah, the central expanse falls to the lot of Shem, who "knew that the Garden of Eden is the holy of holies, and the dwelling of the Lord, and Mt. Sinai the centre of the desert, and Mt. Zion the centre of the navel of the earth: these three were created as holy places facing one another" (*APOT* 1.26).

The identification of the central portion of the world as its "navel" is often found in rabbinic literature, occasionally with an abstraction of its primary meaning. In a midrash on the various appellations of Tiberias, the name of the city is connected with the term טבור: "Why is she called Tiberias? Because she is situated in the very centre [טבור] of the land of Israel" (*b. Meg.* 6a). In *b. Sanh.* 37a the verse "Your navel is a rounded bowl . . ."

---

14. Josephus employs a similar phrase to position the earth "in the midmost place," (of the universe), καὶ γὰρ αὕτη τὸν μεσαίτατον τόπον ἔχει, as the ἐσσῆν, חשן is set in the midst of the priest's garment (*Ant.* 3.185; [LCL 4; London: Heinemann, 1930; reprinted Cambridge, MA: Harvard University Press, 1957] 404).

(Cant 7:3) is expounded as follows: "'Your navel'—that is the Sanhedrin. Why was it called 'navel'? Because it sat at the navel [טַבּוּר] of the world." Rabbi Shelomo Yitzhaki (Rashi) ad loc. adds the explanation: "The Temple is in the center of the world." Jellinek maintains that the Hellenistic basis of the image of the navel is evident in a late midrash which reads: "'In wisdom God founded the earth' [Prov 3:19]. The Holy One, Blessed be He, created the world like the infant of a woman. In the beginning a newborn develops from the navel and extends from there. What is the navel of earth? This is Jerusalem. And its central point is the altar. And why was it called the foundation stone? Because from it the entire world was established."[15] This midrash is certainly tied to a similar one found in *Midr. Tanḥuma* on Lev 16:1 (קדושים, § 10): "Just as the navel is in the center of the human [body], so the land of Israel is the navel of the world; as it is written, '[They] who dwell at טבור הארץ' (Ezek 38:12). The land of Israel is at the midpoint of the world, and Jerusalem is in the middle of the land of Israel and the Temple in the middle of Jerusalem and the Holy Place, היכל, in the middle of the Temple and the Ark in the middle of the Holy Place, and before the Sanctuary is the Foundation Stone, אבן שתיה, from which the world was established."[16] This midrash implies that already in the days of its author טבור הארץ in Ezek 38:12 was understood as a designation of Jerusalem, the center of the land of Israel.

Wensinck's claim that the idea of the "navel of the earth" is as widespread in Jewish tradition as in the traditions of other peoples is based largely upon rare evidence of this sort.[17] In any case, since he bases his assumption solely on postbiblical sources, no direct support can be derived from them for the interpretation of the term טבור in biblical literature. Seeligmann was undoubtedly correct in observing "that the concept of the 'navel

---

15. A. Jellinek, ed., בית המדרש (Jerusalem: Bamberger & Wahrmann, 1938) vol. 2, part V, p. 63.

16. S. Buber, ed., *Leviticus-Deuteronomy* in *Midrash Tanḥuma* (Lemberg, 1883; repr., New York: Sefer, 1946) 2.78, § 10. H. Z. Hirschberg, "The Temple Mount in the Arabic Period (638–1099)," *Jerusalem Through the Ages* (ed. J. Aviram; Jerusalem: IES, 1968) 109–11 (Heb.). See also M. Gruenbaum: "Der Tempel bildet den Mittel—punkt des Talmud wie Palästina als Umbilicus terrae galt" ("Beiträge zur vergleichenden Mythologie aus der Haggada," *ZDMG* 31 [1877] 199).

17. Wensinck, *Navel of the Earth,* chap. 1 (see above, n. 12). It should be pointed out, however, that the great majority of usages of טַבּוּר/טבור in rabbinic literature carry the physical notion of the human navel and that the metaphorical use of the term is rare. See E. Ben Yehuda ("טבור/טַבּוּר," *Thesaurus* 4.1836).

of the earth' in later Judaism originated in Greek mythography which characterizes the center of the world by the term ὄμφαλος. Jewish-Hellenistic diaspora literature, conferred upon the mythographic motif a rationalistic
dimension so as to present Jerusalem as the center of the world, at a time
when the city served as a pilgrimage center for Jews from all over the
world."[18]

The foregoing discussion implies that the biblical term טבור cannot be
explained either by having recourse to conjectured mythic parallels from
cultures of the Ancient Near East, which themselves are not above doubt,[19]
or through reference to rabbinic טַבּוּר/טַבּוּר or its rendition in the LXX by
ὄμφαλος, which derives from a classical, mythopoeic notion. In order to establish the actual meaning of the biblical term, we must turn to motifs and
vocabulary in biblical literature which resemble those found in the relevant
passages from the books of Judges and Ezekiel.[20]

III

It is helpful to open the comparative innerbiblical discussion with the
passage from Ezek 38:10–13, reasoning *a maiori ad minus*. For even scholars
who hesitate to propose a mythological interpretation of טבור הארץ in the
Abimelech episode (Judg 9:37) cast little doubt upon its applicability to the
futuristic assault of Gog on Israel and Jerusalem in Ezekiel. The passage
reads as follows:

10. כה אמר אדני ה' והיה ביום ההוא יעלו דברים על לבבך וחשבת מחשבת רעה

11. ואמרת אעלה על ארץ פרזות אבוא השקטים ישבי לבטח כלם ישבים באין חומה ובריח
ודלתים אין להם

12. לשלל שלל ולבז בז להשיב ידך על חרבות נושבת ואל עם מאסף מגוים עשה מקנה וקנין
ישבי על טבור הארץ.

10. Thus says the Lord God, "On that day thoughts will come into your mind, and you
will devise an evil scheme

18. I. L. Seeligmann, "Jerusalem in Jewish-Hellenistic Thought," *Judaea and Jerusalem*
(Jerusalem: IES, 1957) 192–208, esp. 200ff. (Heb.).
19. See R. J. Clifford, *The Cosmic Mountain in Canaan and the Old Testament* (HSM 4; Cambridge, MA: Harvard University Press, 1972) 135, 183.
20. See S. Talmon, "הר *har*," *TWAT* 4.471–83 = *TDOT* 3.427–47.

11. and say, 'I will go up against the land of unwalled villages, and I will fall upon the quiet people who dwell securely, all of them dwelling without walls and having no bars or gates,

12. to seize spoil and carry off plunder, to assail the waste places now inhabited and the people who were gathered from the nations, who have gotten cattle and goods, who dwell at [or "on"] טבור הארץ.'"

The *Targum of the Prophets* translation, תוקפא דארעא, and the Peshitta's שופרא דארעא, the "strong point" or the "best" of the country, seem close to the meaning at hand. The LXX on the other hand translate the term ὄμφαλος τῆς γῆς and the Vulgate *umbilicus terrae*, thus giving the Hebrew term a mythic thrust. Medieval commentators explain the phrase similarly, without doubt in the wake of its use in the rabbinic tradition. Thus, e.g., Kimchi "The land of Israel is called טבור הארץ, for it is in the middle of the world, just as the navel is in the middle of the body." Rashi combined this interpretation with that of the targum: "on the height and strength of the land that slopes down on all sides, as the navel is in the middle of the man."

The LXX (and the Vulgate) are responsible for the tendency of most modern commentators to perceive in the text an expression of the mythic belief that Mt. Zion and the city of Jerusalem stand in the center of the land of Israel and of the world as a whole. Some modern commentators adopt a cautious stance on the matter. Thus W. Zimmerli observes that in the book of Ezekiel, in particular in the vision of the Temple (Ezekiel 40–48) and indeed throughout the Bible, Jerusalem is not presented as the heart of either Israel or the world. He nevertheless subscribes to the opinion that the above passage does not speak of a war like any other war but of a cosmic war to be waged "am Ort der Mitte der Welt."[21] But this explanation cannot be substantiated by the Hebrew text, as the ensuing inquiry will demonstrate.

Since neither etymological nor comparative research helps in explicating satisfactorily the Hebrew collocation טבור הארץ, let us now turn to an examination of the problem by taking our departure from the vocabulary, the context, and the structure of the passage. Zimmerli defines Ezek 38:10–13 as an expansion of the basic speech concerning Gog (38:1–9) and sees in the remaining part of the chapter three interpretative additions which were

---

21. W. Zimmerli (*Ezechiel* [BKAT 2; Neukirchen-Vluyn: Neukirchener Verlag, 1969] 955–57) obviously depends upon the opinions of Roscher and Wensinck (see above) and of H. Schmidt (*Der heilige Fels in Jerusalem* [Tübingen: Mohr, 1933]) and W. Caspari ("Tabur-Nabel," *ZDMG* 11 [1933] 49ff.).

appended to the basic text in the course of time (vv. 14–16, v. 17, vv. 18–23). The core prophecy is continued in 39:1–5. Ezek 38:10–13 is therefore perceived as an independent unit. I accept this argument with two reservations: (1) vv. 14–16 are not an independent unit but must be discussed in connection with vv. 8–9, which are related to them by content and language; (2) the prophet's basic address to Gog ends with v. 7 and not with v. 9 (against the masoretic division). These suggestions are strengthened by a structural examination of the passage, which reveals sundry literary-technical means which the editor or 'arranger' of the text employed in the structuring of the Gog episode: summary line, inversion, conflated phrases in which each of the constituent components is derived from a different subunit, and the *inclusio* pattern.[22]

Summary Line. This method of signifying the close of a subunit in a series of passages which were combined to form a comprehensive complex is applied here in the pericope as a whole as well as in its constituent components. The Vision of the Dry Bones (Ezekiel 37) which directly precedes the cluster of prophecies concerning Gog ends with the closing formula: "Then the nations will know that I the Lord sanctify, מקדש, Israel, when my sanctuary, מקדשי, is in the midst of them for evermore" (Ezek 37:28). This very closing formula further serves within the complex to distinguish secondary units whose definition will be discussed below: "that the nations may know me, when through you, O Gog, I vindicate my holiness, בהקדשי, before their eyes" (Ezek 38:16); "So I will show my greatness and my holiness, והתקדשתי, and make myself known in the eyes of many nations" (38:23); "and the nations shall know that I am the Lord, the Holy One, קדוש, in Israel" (39:7).

Inclusio. The essence of this pattern lies in the author's (or editor's) taking up in similar terms at the end of a passage what had been stated at its beginning, so much so that the two elements enclose the passage as if within brackets. Thus the opening and closing formulae delineate the extent of a literary unit as it was conceived by the author or of a self-contained passage which an editor inserted secondarily into a given literary complex. By the discernment of this pattern in the text under review, 38:10–14

---

22. These methods of *literary composition* require separate treatment. For the present, see S. Talmon and M. Fishbane, "The Structuring of Biblical Books: Studies in the Book of Ezekiel" (*ASTI* 10 [1976] 129–53); S. Talmon, "The Presentation of Synchroneity and Simultaneity" (in this vol., pp. 112–33).

Opening Formula 38:8–9

1	מימים רבים תפקד	After many days you will be mustered:
2	באחרית השנים תבוא אל ארץ	in the latter years you will go against the land
3	משובבת מחרב מקבצת מעמים רבים	restored from war, where people were gathered from many nations
4	על הרי ישראל אשר היו לחרבה תמיד	upon the mountains of Israel, which had been a continual waste;
5	והיא מעמים הוצאה וישבו לבטח כלם	its people were brought out from the nations and now all dwell securely.
6	ועלית כשאה תבוא כענן לכסות הארץ תהיה	You will advance like a storm; you will come like a cloud covering the land,
7	אתה וכל אגפיך ועמים רבים אותך	you and all your hordes and many people with you.

Closing Formula 38:15–16

1	ובאת ממקומך מירכתי צפון אתה	You come from your place out of the farthest north,
4	אתה ועמים רבים אתך	you and many peoples with you,
5	רכבי סוסים כלם קהל גדול וחיל רב	all riding on horses, a great host, a mighty army;
6	ועלית על עמי ישראל כענן לכסות הארץ	you will come up against my people Israel, like a cloud covering the land.
7	באחרית הימים תהיה והביאותיך על ארצי	In the latter days I will bring you against my land.

CHART A — EZEKIEL 38

emerges as an originally independent unit whose extent is marked by the closing formula in vv. 15–16 which employs nearly identical terms with those found in the opening formula, vv. 8–9 (see Chart A). The first and the last element of the closing formula are presented in a precisely chiastic order in relation to their parallels in the opening formula, thereby illustrating the technique of *inversion*.[23]

This parallelism of the opening and closing formulae, with slight lexical alterations, is bound to play a major role in the mutual clarification of exegetically difficult expressions. In the present instance the parallelism shows that the phrase "in the latter years" (v. 8) is synonymous with "in the latter days" (v. 16) and that both connote "after many days" (v. 8). Likewise "my land" (v. 16) illumines the phrase "the land that is restored from war" (v. 8). This important interpretative principle will figure prominently in our discussion of the meaning of the term טבור.

Inclusio patterning is also present within the unit bracketed by Ezek 38:8–9 and 38:15–16. This structural technique allows us to recognize 38:12–13 as a secondary unit whose unique vocabulary sets it apart from the immediate context:

12.	to seize spoil	13.	[Have you come] to seize spoil
	and carry off plunder		to carry off plunder
	who have gotten cattle and goods		to take away cattle and goods

Chart B reveals four distinct elements of which the unit 38:10–14 is constituted: (1) Introduction—v. 10; (2) Strophe A, Gog's speech—v. 11; (3) Strophes B[1,2], which encompass a dual interpretation of Gog's evil intentions: once in the words of the Lord or his prophet—v. 12; and once in the words of Sheba and Dedan—v. 13; (4) Conclusion, which completes the introduction—v. 14. The pericope as a whole is bracketed by the opening (vv. 8–9) and the closing (vv. 15–16) formulae.

The author-editor emphasizes the contextual continuity of the distinct elements by means of composite phrases which serve as connecting links between the different constituent subunits: we have already pointed out the

---

23.   The second part of v. 8, from מקבצת מעמים רבים to the end of the verse, is not part of the structural scheme and will be discussed below.

Opening Formula

8. After many days you will be mustered;
   in the latter years you will go against the land restored from war,
   where people were gathered from many nations
   upon the mountains of Israel, which had been a continual waste;
   its people were brought out from the nations and now all dwell securely.
9. You will advance like a storm; you will come like a cloud covering the land,
   you and all your hordes and many people with you.

מימים רבים תפקד 8.
באחרית השנים תבוא אל ארץ משובבת מחרב
מקבצת מעמים רבים
על הרי ישראל אשר היו לחרבה תמיד
והיא מעמים הוצאה וישבו לבטח כלם
ועלית כשאה תבוא כענן לכסות הארץ תהיה 9.
אתה וכל אגפיך ועמים רבים אותך

Introduction

10. Thus says the Lord God,
    "On that day thoughts will come into your mind,
    and you will devise an evil scheme

כה אמר אדני י׳ 10.
והיה ביום ההוא יעלו דברים על לבבך
וחשבת מחשבת רעה

Strophe A

11. and say, 'I will go up against the land of unwalled villages;
    I will come upon the quiet people who dwell securely,
    all of them dwelling without walls, having no bars or gates;'

ואמרת אעלה על ארץ פרזות 11.
אבוא השקטים ישבי לבטח
כלם ישבים באין חומה ובריח ודלתים אין להם

Strophe B¹

12. to seize spoil and carry off plunder;
    to assail the waste places which are now inhabited
    and the people who were gathered from the nations,
    who have gotten cattle and goods,
    who dwell at טבור הארץ

לשלל שלל ולבז בז 12.
להשיב ידך על חרבות נושבת
ואל עם מאסף מגוים
עשה מקנה וקנין
ישבי על טבור הארץ

Strophe B²

13. Sheba and Dedan and the merchants of Tarshish
    and all its mighty men will say to you,
    'Have you come to seize spoil?
    Have you assembled your hosts to carry off plunder,
    to carry away silver and gold,
    to take away cattle and goods, to seize great spoil?'"

שבא ודדן וסחרי תרשיש 13.
וכל כפריה יאמרו לך
הלשלל שלל אתה בא
הלבז בז הקהלת קהלך
לשאת כסף וזהב
לקחת מקנה וקנין לשלל שלל גדול

Conclusion

14. Therefore, son of man, prophesy, and say to Gog,
    "Thus says the Lord God:
    'On that day when my people Israel are dwelling securely,
    you will know;

לכן הנבא בן אדם ואמרת לגוג 14.
כה אמר אדני ה׳
הלוא ביום ההוא בשבת עמי ישראל לבטח
תדע

Closing Formula

15. you will come from your place from the farthest north,
    you and many peoples with you,
    all riding on horses, a great host, a mighty army;
16. you will go up against my people Israel, like a cloud covering the land.
    In the latter days I will bring you against my land,
    that the nations may know me,
    when through you I vindicate my holiness before their eyes, O Gog.'"

ובאת ממקומך מירכתי צפון 15.
אתה ועמים רבים אתך
רכבי סוסים כלם קהל גדול וחיל רב
ועלית על עמי ישראל כענן לכסות הארץ 16.
באחרית הימים תהיה והבאותיך על ארצי
למען דעת הגוים אתי
בהקדשי בך לעיניהם גוג

CHART B —EZEKIEL 38

63

parallels between the Opening and Closing Formulae as well as the resemblances between the beginning and end of Strophe B (vv. 12 and 13). The Introduction and the Conclusion are, moreover, linked through the formula "Thus says the Lord God, 'On that day . . .'" (vv. 10 and 14); whereas תדע (v. 14) stands in opposition to and at the same time completes the words addressed to Gog, "Thoughts will come into your mind, and you will devise an evil scheme" (v. 10). Common to Strophe A and to the Closing Formula are the phrases עלית על עמי ישראל (v. 11) and אעלה על ארץ פרזות (v. 16), as well as אבוא (v. 11), ובאת (v. 15), and והבאותיך על ארצי (v. 16). The connection between Strophe A and the Conclusion will be discussed below.

It is noteworthy that Strophes B[1,2] share no linguistic resemblance with either the Introduction or the Conclusion; nor for that matter with Strophe A. Thus they signify the distinctiveness of Ezek 38:12–13 (B[1,2]) within the complex 38:10–14. On the other hand the phrase "the waste places which are now inhabited, and the people who were gathered from the nations," which sets off v. 12 from v. 13, indicates the connection of Strophe B[1] with the Opening Formula: "the land where the people were gathered from many nations upon the mountains of Israel, which had been a continual waste; its people were brought out from the nations" (v. 8). At the same time, the phrase קהלת הקהלת, "you assembled your hosts," which sets off v. 13 from v. 12, echoes the expressions קהל רב (v. 4) and וכל קהליך הנקהלים (v. 7) of the basic speech concerning Gog, as well as קהל גדול of the Closing Formula (v. 15). It follows that the opening stich of v. 13, "Sheba and Dedan and the merchants of Tarshish and all its villages," which has no parallel in v. 12, must be seen as an allusion to the similar expression in the basic speech: "Persia, Cush, and Put are with them . . . Gomer and all his hordes" (vv. 5–6).

IV

Of special import for our concern, viz., for the clarification of the term טבור הארץ, are phrases which give expression to a central and recurring theme in the prophecies concerning Gog, namely the security of the people of Israel who returned to their land. This idea is given added emphasis in the appendices (38:10–13) to the basic speech (38:1–9). It may be said that the clause "the people of Israel dwelt securely in their land," with linguistic variations yet to be discussed, is the *Leitmotif* that characterizes most units

64

constituting the comprehensive complex Ezek 38:8–16: Opening Formula, "[its people were brought out from the nations] and now all dwell securely" (v. 8); Strophe A, "[I will come upon] the quiet people who dwell securely" and the accompanying phrase "all of them dwelling without walls, having no bars or gates" (v. 11); "[on that day] when my people Israel are dwelling securely, בטח (v. 14).

An echo of this motif is heard as well in the close of the Prophecy of Return (39:25–29) which concludes the complex of oracles concerning Gog: "when they dwell securely in their land with none to make them afraid" (v. 26).[24] This expression is retained once more, by principle of opposition, at the end of the basic speech: "I will send fire on Magog and on those who dwell securely in the coastlands" (39:6).

Ezek 38:1–16 presents a description of a tranquil settlement which does not depend upon fortifications to ensure its security because God protects it. This settlement is situated "upon the mountains of Israel" (38:8, cp. 21; 39:2, 4, 17) or "on the land of Israel" (38:8, 9, 16, 18, 19; 39:26, 28), which is the land sanctified by the God of Israel and not to be polluted (38:12–16). It is worthy of note that in all these occurrences we have found not one allusion to the idea that this land is the center of the world or that Jerusalem is the heart of the land.

Due to the wide currency of the theme of "Israel dwelling in security" in the diverse components of the complex of prophecies concerning Gog, it is surprising that this motif does not find an explicit expression in Strophes B[1,2]. Although, as said, these strophes are distinguished from the other components of the pericope, the editor nevertheless sought to integrate them in the literary continuum by means of expressions, similar to those which turn up in other components. This prompts an examination of the phrase ישבי על טבור הארץ, the core of the problem under review. The other collocations connected with the verb ישב, discussed above, are all concerned with the secure dwelling of the people of Israel in their land or on the mountains of Israel. It may therefore be conjectured that the unexplained noun טבור also has a similar connotation, whether expressing altogether the very notion of security, בטח, or whether signifying an area which is regarded as being militarily more

24. In these collocations there reverberates a core motif of the biblical "Promise of the Land" divinely bestowed upon Israel, which Ezekiel shares with other biblical sources (Ezek 28:26; 34:27–28; cp. Lev 25:18–19; 26:5; Deut 12:10; 33:28; 1 Sam 12:11; 2 Sam 7:10; 1 Kgs 5:5; Jer 32:37; Hos 2:20; Mic 4:4; Zech 14:11, et al.).

secure than others. The term טבור is clarified through the adjacent reference to the people that dwell there as having "cattle and goods," מקנה וקנין,[25] just as the expression "all of them dwelling without walls, having no bars or gates" (v. 11) explicates the collocations "the land of unwalled villages" and "the quiet people who dwell securely."

This description reflects a similar image couched in almost identical language in Ezek 28:25–26:

כה אמר אדני ה' בקבצי את בית ישראל מן העמים אשר נפצו בם ונקדשתי בם לעיני הגוים
וישבו על אדמתם. . . . וישבו עליה לבטח ובנו בתים ונטעו כרמים וישבו לבטח.

Thus says the Lord YHWH, "When I gather the house of Israel from the peoples among whom they are scattered and manifest my holiness in them in the sight of the nations, then they shall dwell in their own land. . . . And they shall dwell securely in it; they shall build houses and plant vineyards and dwell securely."

These collocations are obviously biblical formulaic expressions (not in the book of Ezekiel alone) in which is captured the notion of an open and secure settlement in a spacious location whose inhabitants live at peace with their neighbors and do not fear for their future, until in some instances, destruction suddenly descends upon them. In Jeremiah's oracles against the nations, the campaign of Nebuchadnezzar king of Babylon against Kedar and the king-dom of Hazor is described in similar images: "'Rise up, advance against a nation at ease, that dwells securely, יושב לבטח,' says the Lord, 'that [whose cities] has no gates or bars, that dwells alone. Their camels shall become booty, their herds of cattle, מקניהם, a spoil'" (Jer 49:31–32). We may also compare the ancient genealogical tradition concerning the town of מבוא גדור, conquered by the Simeonites who were in search of pasture for their flocks: "There they found rich, good pasture, and the land was wide open, quiet, and peaceful," והארץ רחבת ידים ושקטת ושלוה (1 Chr 4:40). The text then pro-ceeds to explain that "the former inhabitants there belonged to Ham," im-plying that they were not part of the autochthonous population and were not allied with their neighbors. The equally ancient tradition concerning the Danites' conquest of Laish likewise exhibits both contextual and linguistic similarities, to the point of employing idioms found in Ezekiel and in other

25.   קנין may in fact be synonymous with מקנה, as in Gen 34:23; Josh 14:4; and Jer 49:32: גמלים ‖ מקניהם. It is of interest to note that Ps 105:21, שמו אדון לביתו ומשל בכל קנינו probably has an echo in the extracanonical Psalm 151A from Qumran (11QPs^a xxviii 1–2) as: וישימני רועה לצונו ומושל בגדיותי.

parallel passages mentioned above: "[They] saw the people who were there, how they dwelt in security . . . quiet and secure . . . and how they were far from the Sidonians and had no dealings with anyone,"[26] ויבאו לישה ויראו את העם אשר בקרבה יושבת לבטח . . . שקט ובטח . . . ורחקים המה מצדנים ודבר אין להם עם אדם (Judg 18:7, 27–28); and again: "When you go, you will come to a secure people. The land is broad . . . a place where there is no lack of anything on earth," כבאכם תבאו אל עם בטח והארץ רחבת ידים . . . אשר אין שם מחסור כל דבר אשר בארץ (Judg 18:10).[27]

It becomes apparent that the term טבור הארץ in Ezek 38:12 is simply one other expression which defines the propitious situation of the people who returned to their land, to "the [former] waste places which are now [securely] inhabited," and occupy themselves with raising livestock on sites which do not need fortifications or other defense installations. Nothing in this vision reflects the idea of a "center of the earth" or "of the land of Israel." It is even doubtful whether the text suggests that this settlement stands on a high mountain. *Au contraire*, for that settlement "on the mountains of Israel," mentioned recurrently in the Gog passage, certainly is not situated on the peaks of the mountains but in an area on the terraces or hollows between them. This interpretation of the pertinent phrases is buttressed by the parallelism of טבור הארץ and ארץ פרזות, "the land of unwalled villages" (v. 11). In the latest biblical usages of the term פרזות, those characteristics and traits are as prominent as in Ezekiel. The sense is that of a comfortable expanse for the raising of cattle: "Jerusalem will be inhabited as villages without walls because of [to accommodate] the multitude of men and cattle in it" (Zech 2:8). Again, "the Jews of unwalled villages, who live in settlements" refers to communities that differ from those who live in fortified towns like Susa the capital (Esth 9:18–19). We should possibly see in this light also the

26. It is widely held that instead of אדם we should read ארם here, which is in agreement with several ancient versions and would be in keeping with the context.
27. It would appear that the imagery and the phraseology of Ezekiel's Gog-vision possibly reverberates in the description of "the dwelling of Shem" which Noah allocated to his son, as reported in *Jub* 8:17–21: "He knew that the Garden of Eden is the holy of holies . . . and Mt. Sinai the center of the desert and Mt. Zion the center of the navel of the earth" (8:19). I tend to presume that "center" is the original translation of טבור הארץ in the Hebrew *Vorlage* to which subsequently a second rendition, ὄμφαλος, was added, resulting in the doublet "the center of the navel of the earth." It should not go unnoticed that in that context (describing Shem's territory) *Jubilees* combines Ezekiel's טבור הארץ image with phraseology employed by the Danites' envoys in their praise of the territory in which Laish is situated. "A blessed and spacious land, and all that is in it is very good" (*Jub* 8:21) can be retroverted to [כי ראינו את] הארץ והנה טובה מאד . . . והארץ רחבת ידים :read (Judg 18:9–10).

67

term פרזון in the Song of Deborah (Judg 5:7). Although the etymological derivation of פרז has not been sufficiently clarified, the most likely sugges-tion is that its meaning corresponds to Arabic *farez* which denotes a hollow between mountains,[28] viz., a sheltered valley, well suited for the raising of livestock, whose location may indeed evoke a comparison with the position of the navel in the human body.[29]

In summary, the phrase טבור הארץ in Ezek 38:12 is not to be explained by having recourse to extrabiblical parallels which refer to an elevated site, a mountain peak that is the center of the surrounding expanse, whether the land of Israel or the entire earth; nor is it to be burdened with mythic ideas concerning the centrality of Jerusalem and the Temple in the universe. Simi-lar expressions in the immediate context or in parallel biblical texts not only serve to blunt the purported mythological point of the term; they actually bring us to a realistic topographic-ecological interpretation of it.

V

The meaning of the term טבור הארץ which emerges from the analysis of Ezek 38:12 applies also to the other occurrence of the phrase in Judg 9:36–37:

וירא געל את העם ויאמר אל זבל הנה עם יורד מראשי ההרים ויאמר אליו זבל את צל ההרים אתה ראה כאנשים. ויסף עוד געל לדבר ויאמר הנה עם יורדים מעם טבור הארץ וראש אחד בא מדרך אלון מעוננים.

And when Gaal saw the men, he said to Zebul, "Look, men are coming down from the mountain tops!" And Zebul said to him, "You see the shadow of the mountains as if they were men." Gaal spoke again and said, "Look, men are coming down from טבור הארץ, and one company is coming from the direction of אלון מעוננים."[30]

This text describes the descent of Abimelech's troops from the mountain tops, or from "the highest mountain of all" (Rashi), and upon their reaching

---

28. Cp. the dictionaries of Brown, Driver, Briggs, and Köhler-Baumgartner, s.v. פרז.
29. Cp. Maimonides, *Mishneh Torah, Book of Knowledge,* Fundamental Principles of the Torah 4,2: "The nature of fire and air is to ascend *from below;* that is, from טבור הארץ upward towards the sky." The term here obviously designates a depression and not an elevated site.
30. J. A. Soggin (*Judges* [OTL; London: SCM, 1981] 189) explicitly rejects my interpretation of this passage and reasserts the omphalos interpretation of טבור הארץ, however without ad-ducing any new evidence in its defense.

some level area, the division of that army into three companies in order to attack the city below.[31] Thus explained Rabbi Isaiah of Trani, "a place evenly between the towns from which one could head to this city and one to that, like a fork in the road."[32] N. H. Tur-Sinai[33] justifiably proposes that we understand טבור הארץ here in the sense of plateau, viz., the level land at the midway point of a mountain.[34]

The interpretation of טבור הארץ in the Abimelech episode as a geographical rather than a ritual-mythical term, at which I arrived on the strength of a linguistic and literary analysis, can be buttressed by having recourse to topographical factors and considerations of military tactics. Citing the medieval commentators Rashi, Kimchi, and R. Isaiah of Trani (see above), C. F. Burney stresses that "in Ezek. 38[12], the only other occurrence of the term in O. T., it is also used *topographically* [my italics], the inhabitants of Judah being described as 'those dwelling upon the navel of the earth,'" but adds "i.e. (from the Israelite point of view) the most prominent and central part of the Universe (cf. Ezek. 5[5])." Then, in reference to Judg 9:37: "In the present passage the expression is obviously a closer definition of 'the tops of the mountains,' v. [30], and probably describes some neighbouring *height* (or even *heights;* for v. [37b] seems to indicate that the bands are coming from different directions) which was regarded as the central part of the mountain range of Cana‘an."[35]

Burney was actually preceded by G. F. Moore, who cautiously states, "The meaning of the noun (טבור) is hardly to be questioned (Mishna, Talm.); the sense in which it is applied here is uncertain. . . . We should have in any case to suppose that it had become a proper name," adding in a footnote, "*Navel of the Land,* appellatively, for highest point (Ges.) is hardly possible

---

31. Similarly Kimchi, ad loc.: "Like the navel, טבור is the middle of the human body, the midpoint of the land, הארץ, and the highest point in it will be called טבור." Cp. *Midr. Tanḥ.* (see above, n. 16).

32. A. J. Wertheimer, ed., *Commentary on the Prophets and Hagiographa of Rabbi Isaiah of Trani, the Elder* (Jerusalem: Ktab waSepher, 1959) 16.

33. N. H. Tur-Sinai, "טבור ובמה," הלשון והספר (Jerusalem: Bialik Institute, 1955) 233ff. Y. Kaufmann subscribes in principle to the navel theory but states that the tradition in Judg 9:36–37 does not pertain to Mt. Gerizim (ספר שופטים [Jerusalem: Kiryat-Sefer, 1962] 209).

34. J. M. Wilkie suggests the Syriac reading *tuwnh* and translates the phrase "the inner chamber of the land" ("The Peshitta Translation of Ṭabbûr Hāʾāreṣ in Judges IX 37," *VT* 1 [1951] 144).

35. C. F. Burney, *The Book of Judges* (London: Rivingtons, 1918) 283.

Jerusalem in the Center of the World

Map of the year 1580

The World Portrayed as a Cloverleaf with Jerusalem in Its Center
Heinrich Bünting Map, Courtesy Eran Laor Cartographic Collection
The Jewish National and University Library

in the plain prose of this story."[36] M. Naor is more specific than both Moore
and Burney. He identifies טבור הארץ with a rounded hillock on the south-
western slope of the Kabir range which lies to the northeast of ancient
Shechem and Mt. Gerizim.[37] This identification was recently further underpinned by C. Eshel and Z. Ehrlich in an analysis of Abimelech's assault on
Shechem which leads them to an altogether separate טבור הארץ on Ras Kabir
from אלון מעוננים, which is situated on Mt. Gerizim. This separation engenders the conclusion that the term טבור הארץ cannot be invested with a cultic

36.   G. F. Moore, *Judges* (ICC; Edinburgh: Clark, 1895) 262.
37.   M. Naor, המקרא והארץ (Tel Aviv: Otzar Hamoreh, 1954) 134; see also T. Ilan, "מקום
         טבור הארץ," *Beth Miqra* 89/90 (1982) 122–26.

meaning, nor can it be connected with the mythic navel of the earth idea. טבור הארץ is a topographical term.[38] Nothing in the Abimelech tradition bears out Wensinck's claim that "Gerizim was of old the subject of navel-theories (Jud. 9:37)."[39]

The trend to discover in the Bible vestiges of the ὄμφαλος myth in connection with Jerusalem is not limited to occurrences of the term טבור. Thus M. Weinfeld opines "that Bethel, too, a royal sanctuary in the north (Amos 7), was thought in Israel's monarchy to be the center of the universe."[40] Since nowhere in the Hebrew Bible is Bethel referred to by טבור or by a term which resembles it or at least recalls the notion of "navel," Weinfeld has recourse to a rather convoluted argument: "This [Bethel] is the place where the ladder stood whose head was in the heavens and on which the angels of God ascend and descend (Gen 28:12). Indeed, Jacob labels it 'the gate of heaven.'" How the designation "gate of heaven" can be seen to present Bethel as the ὄμφαλος, the "navel of the universe," escapes me. In Akkadian parlance both these collocations can indeed be applied to a royal city, especially to Babylon and Nippur. But they clearly are different facets of Ancient Near Eastern imagery and cannot be transferred in tandem to the biblical scene where the one together with the other are never applied to one city.

Texts which speak of Jerusalem as standing בתוך/בקרב the nations or the land also have been invested with the mythic connotation of טבור הארץ, first and foremost in Ezek 5:5: "This is Jerusalem; I have set her in the center, בתוך, of the nations, with countries round about her." Zimmerli, like many other scholars, discerns in the verse once again the theme of the ὄμφαλος. He asserts that the two parallel stichs of the verse are meant to emphasize the distinction of Jerusalem as the center of the world and the nations.

---

38. C. Eshel and Z. Ehrlich, "The First Battle in Abimelech's War against the Shechemites and the Problem of טבור הארץ" (*Tarbiz* 58 [1989] 111–16, with a rich selection of pertinent literature). My thanks are due to Mr. Eshel for having brought these publications to my attention.

39. Wensinck, *The Ideas* (see above, n. 12). In an issue of *BA* dedicated to the excavation of Shechem, G. E. Wright superscribes his editorial comment, "Shechem, the 'Navel of the Land,'" and B. W. Anderson elaborates on the mythic qualities of that city in "The Place of Shechem in the Bible," stressing especially the notion of the city's being at the navel of the earth (*BA* 20 [1957] 2, 10–19).

40. M. Weinfeld, "Zion and Jerusalem as Religious and Political Capital: Ideology and Utopia," *The Poet and the Historian: Essays in Literary and Historical Criticism* (HSS 26; Chico, CA: Scholars Press, 1983) 107.

Zimmerli is then drawn into exaggerated conjectures, all dependent upon that same text: just as in the Roman Empire all roads came together in the forum of the capital city, and as the kingdom of China perceived itself as the "Middle Kingdom," so did Ezekiel envisage Jerusalem as the focus of the world. This status did not come to the city in any natural manner but was willed by God: "I have set her in the center of the nations."[41] This argument can easily be refuted. It suffices to point out passages in Ezekiel and other biblical books in which the term בתוך/תוך is employed without connoting "center" in any way, but instead equalling the preposition ב-, which parallels בתוך,[42] with which it interchanges: "They also shall go down to Sheol with it, to those who are slain by the sword; yea, those who dwelt under its shadow among [בתוך] the nations" (Ezek 31:17); and its parallel: "You shall be brought down with the trees of Eden to the nether world; you shall lie among [בתוך] the uncircumcised, with those who are slain by the sword" (31:18; cp. further 5:2, 5, 8, 10, 12 with 5:9, 14, 15; 20:5 with 20:8; Isa 19:19 with 19:20, et sim.).[43]

M. Weinfeld recently attempted to underpin Roscher's notion of an ancient Babylonian conception of a central temple as the navel of the earth or the universe. But the one instance of the idiom *abbunat māt nakrim* = "navel of the country" (Yos. X.33.iii)[44] which he adduces in defense of his claim has no cosmic-mythic connotation. Instead it is used in a military context which tells of the invasion of an army to the "navel of the enemy's land," exactly as Judg 9:35ff. speaks of the penetration of Abimelech's troops into the Shechemites' territory, and Ezek 38:10ff. of Gog's forces penetrating the heartland of Judah. I fully concur with D. Sperling's careful and correct observation: "In Ezek. 38:11, an invader has assembled his host in order to 'go up against the land of unwalled villages', and 'fall upon the quiet people who dwell securely'. In vs. 12 these same intended victims are described as living on the navel of the land (RSV, 'who dwell at the center of the earth'). The alternation of phrases indicates that emphasis is not upon privileged

---

41. Zimmerli, *Ezechiel,* 1.133 (see above, n. 21). Cp. Wensinck, *The Idea,* 22 (see above, n. 12).
42. See, e.g., Isa 5:2, וייבן מגדל בתוכו וגם יקב חצב בו, et al.
43. The same pertains to בקרב, which also interchanges with בתוך, as, e.g., in Isa 24:13: כי כה יהיה בקרב הארץ בתוך העמים, et al.
44. See A. Goetze, *Old Babylonian Omen Texts* (New Haven: Yale University Press, 1947).

position in the cosmos but rather upon vulnerability. The intended victims are as unprotected as the human navel in the center of the body."[45]

I would add that the understanding of the collocation טבור הארץ as an image of vulnerability rather than connoting the mythic ὄμφαλος notion brings to mind a comparable image which also derives from the poetic personification of the earth in biblical literature.[46] Like the human body, a country is especially vulnerable in its genitals. Spies are sent out to identify such soft spots in a country's defenses. Thus Joseph accuses his brothers: לראות את ערות הארץ באתם, "You have come to spy out the vulnerable points [in the defense system] of the country" (Gen 42:9, 12; cp. Isa 20:4). This collocation parallels a similar accusation which the Ammonite nobles level against the envoys with whom David sent condolences to King Hanun upon the death of his father. In actual fact they say, "[David sent these men] to spy out the city and to find out [the weaknesses in its defenses so as] to overthrow it" (2 Sam 10:3).[47] In contrast, the high officials in the province of Yahud profess their loyalty to the Persian King Artaxerxes by averring that being in his employ they certainly would not want to see the king (and his empire) becoming vulnerable: ערות מלכא לא אריך למחזא (Ezra 4:14). Therefore they warn him lest the rebuilt city of Jerusalem should become a hotbed of sedition and rebellion (4:15).

In sum, the biblical phrase ערות הארץ is a much more befitting parallel of טבור הארץ (which helps to ascertain its topographical-military connotation) than the myth-ridden concept ὄμφαλος τῆς γῆς, vinculum.

---

45.   D. Sperling, "Navel of the Earth" (IDBSup; Nashville, TN: Abingdon, 1976) 622. This entry came to my knowledge after the original version of my paper had already gone to press.

46.   In Biblical Hebrew and other Semitic languages the earth can have an eye (Exod 10:15), a face (Gen 11:9), or loins (Jer 6:22; 25:32, et al.), just as mountains can have heads, as in Judg 9:7, 25, 36 and Ezek 43:12 (Exod 19:20; Num 14:40, 44, et al.) or shoulders (Josh 15:10), loins (Judg 19:1, 18; 2 Kgs 19:23, et al.) or ribs (2 Sam 16:13). See E. Dhorme, L'emploi métaphorique des noms de parties du corps en Hébreu et en Akkadien (Paris: Lecoffre, 1923); S. Talmon, "הר har" (TWAT 4.465–66).

47.   Cp. Josh 2:1–3; Judg 18:2, 9 for the same idea but without involvement of the metaphorical imagery.

Despite the weakness of the evidence adduced in support of the conjectured identification of טבור הארץ with ὄμφαλος and the resulting mythic implications, this supposition has become a tenet of modern biblical study. It is especially prominent in commentaries to the books of Judges, Ezekiel, and often also to the book of Psalms.[48] With the proliferation of comparative studies in biblical research, this emphasis has grown even more pronounced. Motifs assuredly drawn from the Canaanite (or Jebusite) conceptual universe were traced in the biblical description of Jerusalem. B. Childs states that the Israelites perceived in Mt. Zion the foundation stone of the world; the umbilical cord connecting the heavens, the earth, and the underworld; the center of the earth, which is likened to a disk; the cosmic tree, as well as the new Garden of Eden.[49] S. Terrien went one step further, claiming that "in all probability, the myth of the navel of the earth, far from being an incidental aspect of worship at the temple of Jerusalem, constitutes in effect the determining factor which links together a number of its cultic practices and beliefs that otherwise appear to be unrelated."[50] He envisions the myth of the navel (טבור) as the vital common denominator of biblical thought and ritual. In its light all becomes explicable: the cult of the serpent and of the Underworld in the Temple in Jerusalem; sun-worship; androgynous cultic practices; and the institution of male prostitutes, for which parallels are widespread, encompassing, int. al., the temple in Delphi.[51] In Terrien's opinion the influence which this mythic belief exercised on the faith of Israel in the biblical period and thereafter cannot be overstated. He will concede that

48. See, e.g., M. Dahood (*Psalms I* [AB 16; Garden City, NY: Doubleday, 1970] 142) *ad* Ps 22:28, וישבו אל ה׳: "There may be an allusion here to the theme which made Jerusalem the navel of the earth. . . . The mention of 'all the ends of the earth', כל אפסי ארץ, suggests that this motif may be present in Ps lix 14. . . . God's governance of the world radiated from Israel, the navel of the earth." And again *ad* Ps 48:3, הר ציון ירכתי צפון, "In terming Zion 'the heart of Zaphon', the poet may be alluding to the theme of the navel of the earth" (16.290). See also W. D. Davies, *The Gospel and the Land* ([Berkeley: University of California, 1973] 6ff.) and my review of the book (in *Christian News from Israel* 25 [1975] 132–36); T. H. Gaster (*Thespis* [Garden City, NY: Doubleday, 1961] 183). Cp. Moore, Burney, Soggin (see above, nn. 30, 35, 36), et al.

49. B. S. Childs, *Myth and Reality in the Old Testament* (SBT 27; London: SCM Press, 1960) 83–93.

50. S. Terrien, "The Omphalos Myth and Hebrew Religion," *VT* 20 (1970) 317–38.

51. Cp. further G. R. H. Wright, "Joseph's Grave under the Tree by the Omphalos at Shechem," *VT* 22 (1972) 476–86, with additional bibliography.

the idea of ὄμφαλος certainly underwent novel interpretation within Israel's intellectual universe but avers that through this reinterpretation a mythical view of space was absorbed into a dynamic theology of time, and the resultant combination became a mainstay of the ideological principles attached to Mt. Zion and the Temple.[52]

Terrien admits that "these beliefs do not receive an explicit formulation in the early traditions concerning the building of the temple." He nevertheless surmises that "the allusions found in the pre-exilic psalms and prophets, Ezekiel, and his post-exilic successors clearly indicate that the acceptance of the ὄμφαλος myth, in a modified form, antedates by centuries the testimony of the Chronicler, the post-canonical Jewish literature, the New Testament, and Christian folklore."[53]

Childs, Terrien, Weinfeld, and others have defined motifs, phraseology, and ideational complexes in abundance as proof of the existence of the idea of a "world mountain" (Weltberg) identical with the "navel of the world" in biblical thought. However, a close examination of the assumed parallels which they adduce in order to bolster this conjecture reveals a castle built on sand. Unexplained terms such as טבור and general idioms like תוך or קרב become the objects of tendentious interpretation based wholly upon the assumption that Israel weaved into the very warp and woof of her conceptual universe the mythic ideas of other cultures of the Ancient Near East. While it is certainly true that biblical authors occasionally historicized mythic elements known from Ancient Near Eastern cultures, it is imperative to note that the vestiges of Mesopotamian and Canaanite (or Jebusite) mythic principles which were absorbed into the popular beliefs of various groups and factions within Israel, cannot be construed to have served as the basis of Israel's spiritual world or the belief in the holiness of Jerusalem and Mt. Zion. It is totally unacceptable to hypothesize such cultural transfers except when they can be proven by evident literary parallels. Apparent linguistic similarities in external sources cannot serve as safe bases for the explanation of a biblical text for which more secure and dependable solutions can be achieved by drawing upon illuminations that emerge from a comparison with other biblical texts pertinent to the issue.

52.   Terrien, VT 20 (1970) 338.
53.   Ibid., 319–20.

BIBLICAL רְפָאִים AND
UGARITIC *RPU/I(M)*

I

The etymological derivation of the term רְפָאִים-*rpu/i(m)* and the clarification of its connotation or connotations remain vexing problems that continue to exercise the minds of linguists, exegetes, and comparativists.[1] As is well known, the term is also found in Phoenician and other semitic languages.[2] However, those sporadic references have affected the scholarly discussion of the issue only to a minimal degree. The evidence adduced in the quest for a solution to the problem is drawn predominantly from Ugaritic literature, backed up by biblical references to רְפָאִים, which are deemed to be affiliated with Ugaritic *rpu/i(m)*.

The issue has been dealt with both extensively and intensively over the last decades[3] and no additional material is available which would shed new light on the etymology and meaning of the term in either setting. If the matter is being picked up here once more, it is solely for one reason, that is, to bring to bear on the discussion some special features of the biblical employment of the term not previously (or not sufficiently) noted. Our

---

1. A survey of the state of the art may be found in C. E. L'Heureux, *Rank Among the Canaanite Gods: El, Ba'al, and the Repha'im* ([HSM 21; Missoula: Scholars Press, 1979] 111ff.). To the publications listed there, one should add: M. Dietrich, O. Loretz, and J. Samartín, "Die magischen Totengeister *rpu(m)* und die biblischen Rephaim" (*UF* 8 [1976] 45-52); S. E. Loewenstamm, *"Repha'im"* (*EncMiq* 7, col. 404–7); M. H. Pope, "Notes on the Rephaim Texts from Ugarit" (*Essays on the Ancient Near East in Memory of J. J. Finkelstein* [Memoirs of the Connecticut Academy of Arts and Sciences 19; Hamden, CT: Archon, 1977] 163-82); and the most recent paper by I. F. Healey, "The Last of the Rephaim" (*Back to the Sources: Biblical and Near Eastern Studies in Honor of Dermot Ryan* [ed. K. I. Cathcart and I. F. Healey; Dublin: Glendale, 1989] 33–44).
2. The evidence is presented by L'Heureux (*Rank*, 112); see H. Donner and W. Röllig (*Kanaanäische und aramäische Inschriften* [Wiesbaden: Harrassowitz, 1964], 13.7-8; 14.8, S. 3).
3. See the literature listed by L'Heureux (*Rank*) and the additional publications mentioned below and in n. 1 above.

present concern is primarily with the biblical evidence concerning רְפָאִים and with its *literary* relation to or its dependence upon the Ugaritic use of *rpu/i(m)*, leaving aside any *etymological* considerations.

The Ugaritic references to *rpu/i(m)* allow for a fairly wide spectrum of interpretations and, in fact, have been interpreted quite diversely by scholars in the field. In contradistinction, the biblical mentions can be neatly arranged under two distinct headings, as was shown already before the discovery of the Ugaritic literature.[4]

(1) In one cluster of texts רְפָאִים serves as a designation of a group of human beings who inhabited specific areas in pre-Israelite Canaan, and were distinguished by bodily features which put them into a category quite by themselves. Their depiction brings to mind the portrayal of the heroes in the Classical Greek tradition, as has been recurrently pointed out.

(2) In other biblical metaphors and tropes, the term רְפָאִים unmistakably carries mythopoeic overtones that bring to the fore its relation to the conceptual framework of the netherworld.

Notwithstanding the apparent multifacetedness of the Ugaritic usage and the evident bifurcation of the biblical employment, prevailing scholarly opinion tends to derive all mentions of Ugaritic *rpu/i(m)* and biblical רְפָאִים from one common stem. Its exact meaning, however, is still disputed. The various and varying usages of the term in both literatures is taken to have arisen from diachronous semantic developments and/or is seen to reflect diverse synchronous modes of its application.[5]

Virolleaud's sweeping dismissal of any connection between רְפָאִים and *rpu/i(m)* and his flat denial of the applicability of the biblical evidence to the clarification of the Ugaritic term or vice versa[6] has not found acceptance

---

4. See P. Karge, *Rephaim: Die vorgeschichtliche Kultur Palästinas und Phöniziens.* (Archäologische und Religionsgeschichtliche Studien: Collectanea Hierosolymitana 1; 2d ed.; Paderborn: Schönig, 1917); cp. A. Caquot, "Les Rephaim Ougaritiques," *Syria* 37 (1960) 75–93; J. Gray, "The Rephaim," *PEQ* 81 (1949) 128; A. Jirku, "*Rapaʾu,* der Fürst der *Rapaʾuma*" *ZAW* 77 (1965) 82–83; et al.

5. See L'Heureux, *Rank,* 111-27; idem, "The Ugaritic and Biblical Rephaim," *HTR* 67 (1974) 265–74; and Dietrich, Loretz, and Samartín, *UF* 8 (1976) 45–52 (above, n. 1).

6. C. Virolleaud, "Les Rephaim" (*RES* 7 [1940] 77–83). Also Virolleaud, "Les Rephaim dans les poèmes de Ras Shamra" (*Comptes rendues de l'Académie des inscriptions et belles-lettres* [Paris: Imprimerie Impériale, 1939] 638-40): ". . . il résulte que les Rephaim de RS ne sont pas les âmes des morts, et qu'ils ne sont pas, non plus, un ancien peuple."

with scholars.[7] However, even if one does not subscribe to Virolleaud's extreme view, his argument cannot be dismissed out of hand. A close reading of the relevant biblical passages discloses telling differences between the two types of רְפָאִים usages[8] respective to their presumed interconnection with Ugaritic *rpu/i(m)*.[9] The comparative rarity of mythopoeic elements in the biblical use of הרפא/ה-רפָאִים as an ethnic-geographical or geopolitical designation does not display an obvious relation with the *rpu/i(m)* of the Ugaritic myth and may have to be explained independently of that term. In contradistinction, the ample additional terminology pertaining to the mythopoeic רְפָאִים and the unvarying employment of the word in the plural does indeed give reason to connect biblical usage with Ugaritic (epic) literature.

II

The bifurcation of the biblical occurrences of רְפָאִים has indeed been noted and stressed in the scholarly debate. But to my knowledge, no weight was given to the fact that the two connotations (at best only marginally connected) turn up in separate sections, as well as in diverse literary types or *Gattungen* of biblical literature. The word רְפָאִים, when used as a designation of an ethnic entity (or entities) settled in specific locations in the land of Canaan, is found exclusively in the historiographies Joshua, Samuel, Chronicles, and in historiographical passages in the pentateuchal books Genesis and Deuteronomy. There the רְפָאִים and their territories are at times juxtaposed to others of the indigenous population who are of a comparable ethnic-geopolitical character, such as the Perizzites, Amorites, Canaanites (Gen 15:20–21), Geshurites, and Maacathites (Josh 13:13). A recurrent tradition places them in Transjordanian Bashan, an area which is expressly named "the land of (the) Rephaim" (Deut 3:13). It included territories which at the time of the Israelite conquest were settled by the

7. See M. Astour, "A North-Mesopotamian Locale of the Keret Epic?" (*UF* 5 [1973] 35): "We must proceed from the premise that the *rpum* of the Ugaritic literature are the same as the *rp'm* of Phoenician texts and the רְפָאִים of the Bible, namely the shadows of the dead."
8. This very obvious fact did not escape the attention of scholars but was not sufficiently appreciated in the analysis of the רְפָאִים-*rpu/i(m)* issue.
9. Such a differentiated approach to *rpu/i(m)* is proposed by L'Heureux (*Rank*, 202ff. [see above, n. 1]) and to רְפָאִים by Loewenstamm ("*Repha'im*," 7.404–7 [see above, n. 1]).

Ammonites (Deut 2:20). Og,[10] the Amorite King of Bashan (Deut 4:47; Josh 2:10; 9:10), was considered to be מִיתֶר הָרְפָאִים, i.e., a "remnant," "survivor," or possibly "kinsman" (Deut 3:11; Josh 12:4; 13:12; cp. 11:22)[11] of the Rephaim.[12] His fabulously large bedstead reportedly could still be seen in Rabbat Ammon (Deut 3:11) at the time of writing. But he is presented as having resided, הַיוֹשֵׁב, i.e., "ruled," in the cities of Ashtaroth and Edrei (Josh 12:4–5). Tradition relates that in hoary antiquity the great Kedarlaomer, King of Elam, had defeated the Rephaim there (Gen 14:5).[13] The רְפָאִים—named זוּזִים, זַמְזֻמִּים by the Ammonites (Gen 14:5; Deut 2:20) and אֵמִים by the Moabites (Deut 2:10–11)[14]—were reckoned among the עֲנָקִים. They are described as a race of men of exceedingly tall stature (Num 13:33; Deut 2:11, 21; Josh 14:15), compared with whom the Israelites felt like "small worms" (חֲגָבִים, literally "locusts," Num 13:33), so much so that conquering the land that the giants inhabited seemed to be just impossible (Num 13:28; Deut 1:28; 9:2). But with divine assistance, Israel nevertheless vanquished them (Deut 2:21; Amos 2:9).

In all these instances, the term רְפָאִים has an obviously ethnic content. The pertinent texts do not present them as mythical creatures, notwithstanding their gigantic size. While their exceeding tallness may be defined as a "formulaic" (possibly "epic") element, it is too thin a basis for terming

10. C. Rabin explains this proper noun to mean "(great) man" ("Og," *E. L. Sukenik Volume* [EI 8; Jerusalem: IES, 1967] 251-54).

11. In some instances, like the one under consideration, biblical יֶתֶר seems to indicate an ethnic connection rather than the notion "remnant." The ethnic or familial connotation makes better sense in apocopated theophoric personal names, such as יֶתֶר (Exod 4:18; Judg 8:20; 1 Kgs 2:5, 32; 1 Chr 2:32; 4:17; 7:38); יִתְרָא (2 Sam 17:25); יִתְרִי (2 Sam 23:38; 1 Chr 2:53; 11:40). Cp. further יִתְרְעָם (2 Sam 3:5; 1 Chr 3:3); יִתְרָן (Gen 36:26; 1 Chr 1:41; 7:37). A similar dual connotation inheres in the noun שְׁאֵרִית (e.g., Amos 9:12; cp. Isa 15:9; Ps 76:11), in which שְׁאָר, "remnant," and שְׁאֵר, "consanguinity," (Lev 25:49) may have been fused (by way of double entendre).

12. On Og and his affiliation with the רְפָאִים, see J. C. de Moor, "*Rapiʾuma Rephaim*" (*ZAW* 88 [1976] 338ff.), with a survey of earlier publications on the issue.

13. The defeat predates Abraham's victorious battle against those allied kings after they had spoiled the cities of Sodom and Gomorrah and had captured Lot, Abraham's nephew. For our present concern it is of no consequence whether that tradition is based on historical facts or whether it is but a legend.

14. If רְפָאִים, זוּזִים (זַמְזֻמִּים), and אֵמִים are indeed but alternative designations of one ethnic entity, the stringing of these terms in the report about their defeat at the hands of the allied Mesopotamian kings (Gen 14:5) should be considered a case of textual conflation of synonymous readings (see S. Talmon, SROT, 335–83). But the אֵמִים and זַמְזֻמִּים (זוּזִים) also could have been subdivisions of the רְפָאִים who had occupied territories that the Ammonites and Moabites won from them in the course of history (see L'Heureux, *Rank* [see above, n. 1] 112; de Moor, *ZAW* 88 [1976] 323–45 [see above, n. 12]; et al.).

these traditions "mythopoeic." Some passages compare or even link the רְפָאִים with the primeval נפילים who are first mentioned in a patently mythical context (Gen 6:1–4). The textually somewhat difficult reference to the נפילים in Num 13:33[15] which links them with the בני ענק may well be a case of the historization of the earlier myth. However, this linkage should not be construed as proof for the relation of the two groups.[16] Rather, these passages contain a purely literary aggrandizement of those *gigantes* whom the Israelites encountered in Transjordan.

Reports which are set in the later period of David's wars tell of four giant warriors, presented as ילידי, i.e., "descendants" of הרפא/ה,[17] who were affiliated with the Philistines and engaged David's men in face-to-face combat (2 Sam 21:15–22; 1 Chr 20:4–8). The summary of that combat roster notes "these four": Ishbi-benob (2 Sam 21:16);[18] Saph (2 Sam 21:18; 1 Chr 20:4); Goliath from Gath (2 Sam 21:19), who in 1 Chr 20:5 is given a brother named Lahmi; and an unnamed warrior of "great stature"(?), איש מדין/ון (2 Sam 21:20) or מִדָּה (1 Chr 20:6). All of these men were born (נולדו) to הרפא/ה in Gath and were felled by David's fighters (2 Sam 21:22; 1 Chr 20:8). הָרָפָא/ה could be understood as a gentilic *plurale tantum*.

It should be noted that the Bible does not define the descendants of הָרָפָ/ה as Philistines. Rather they are reported to have fought in the Philistine army, possibly as mercenaries or allies. The best-known among them, Goliath the duelist, איש הַבֵּנַיִם (1 Sam 17:4, 23)[19] whom David himself

---

15. The second part of the phrase ושם ראינו את הנפילים בני ענק מן הנפלים is missing in the LXX. The MT most probably exhibits a case of conflated readings. See Talmon, "The Textual Study of the Bible: A New Outlook" (*QHBT*, 349).

16. As proposed by L'Heureux (*Rank*); de Moor (*ZAW* 88 [1976] 323–45); et al.

17. The interchange of הרפא/הרפה most probably is but another case of the well-documented variation between א and ה in (parallel) biblical texts. There is hardly room for listing רפא and רפה as "Hebrew roots of contrasted meanings," nor for the surmise that "רפאים" may be derived from the meaning . . . 'make strong, heal,' or it may be a cacophony 'weak ones' due to a desire to avoid describing them as 'strong,'" as R. Gordis suggested ("Studies in Hebrew Roots of Contrasted Meanings," *JQR* 27 [1936] 55–56).

18. The MT exhibits a hybrid reading of the qere וישבי בנב with the kethib וישבו בנב. But there is no compelling reason for emending it to וַיֵּשְׁבוּ בנב and transferring it after ודוד ועבדיו עמו in 2 Sam 21:15 (BH). It may be conjectured that originally the text read נב, which reading would not materially affect the meaning of the passage.

19. In a kind of insert in 1 Sam 17:23–25, he is again referred to by the epithet איש הבנים or by the apocopated form איש. At the end of v. 51 the equivalent expression גבור is used.

vanquished (v. 26ff.),[20] was the Philistines' protagonist and issued forth from their camp clad in heavy armor and carrying awe-inspiring weaponry (vv. 4–7). But interestingly enough, initially he is not introduced as a Philistine. Only when he addresses the ranks of the Israelites does he present himself as a פלשתי (v. 8). From then on the author uses this designation throughout his account of the duel (*passim*). At one point his Philistine origin is further highlighted by David's referring to him disparagingly as ערל, "this uncircumcised one" (v. 26), a specific characteristic which biblical writers employ as a stereotype in reference to the Philistines.

It should further be pointed out that with the exception of these war tales that are all set in David's days, no other biblical tradition presents the Philistines or a Philistine as being of gigantic stature, as the ילידי ענק (Num 13:22; Josh 14:15) and the רפאים are said to have been. Therefore, it could be surmised that the ילידי הרפא/ה by origin were not Philistines but survivors of a component of the autochthonous population of Canaan who had been conquered by the invading Philistines (cp. Josh 11:22) and either were pressed into military service or had joined their army as mercenaries,[21] not unlike the Judean David. The phenomenon as such is well known from the history of Ancient Near Eastern societies and obtained in other civilizations as well. Suffice it to draw attention to biblical texts that detail at some length the "population-mix," of which armies mustered by several nations were constituted—Egypt (Jer 46:9, et al.), Assyria (Isa 36:8, et al.), Babylon (Jer 50:37, et al.), the Phoenicians, viz., Tyre (Ezek 27:10–11). Last but not least, mention should be made of the variety of mercenaries who became part of the Israelite royal army in the days of David and Solomon. Among them the כרתי ופלתי stand out, most probably contingents of conquered Philistines (Sea People). Initially they served as the king's bodyguard and subsequently became the nucleus of a professional army which was loyal to the royal house and freed the king to an increasing degree from his dependence upon the people's *Heerbann* (2 Sam 8:18; 20:23; 1 Chr 18:17; 2 Sam 15:18; 20:7; 1 Kgs 1:38, 44).

---

20. There is no need to deal here with the vexing problem of whether the Goliath whom David vanquished should be identified with the Goliath who was killed by Elhanan the son of Jaare (Oregim), one of David's men (2 Sam 21:19).

21. If this indeed was the case, one would have to conclude that those mercenaries had adopted the combat techniques and weaponry which the Philistines had introduced into Canaan from the Aegean, as illustrated by Goliath's outfit and tactics. See Y. Yadin, "Goliath's Javelin and the 'Menor Oregim'" (*Y. Ben-Zvi Volume* [EI 4; Jerusalem: IES, 1956] 68–73 [Heb.]).

By way of an interim summary of the argument presented so far, it may be said that:

(a) The overwhelming evidence in biblical historiographical literature shows the term רָפָא/ה-רְפָאִים to designate a stratum of the pre-Israelite population of Canaan (Gen 14:5; 15:20; Deut 3:11; Josh 13:12).

(b) Their excessive height, in comparison with the Israelites and possibly other autochthonous entities, may well be an "epic" aggrandizement (Deut 2:11; 3:11, et al.) of basic actual facts. Under this heading comes also their association with the mythical נפילים (Num 13:33).

(c) The association of the ילידי הרפא/ה with the Philistines, mentioned only in reference to David's days, may be of secondary nature, resulting from the conquest of their territories by those invaders (2 Sam 21:16, 18, 20, 22; 1 Chr 20:4, 6, 8).

(d) The surmise may be entertained that the proper noun רָפָא/ה of one Judean (1 Chr 4:12) and two Benjaminites (one of them a Saulite—8:2, 37) was emulated by the Israelites from the local population that came under their sway after David defeated the Philistines and integrated into his kingdom the territories which they previously had won from the Canaanites.

(e) The majority of these references to רפא/ה-רפאים contain no unequivocal mythical allusions (their outsize stature having been explained as an "epic-formulaic" element), especially no reference whatsoever to their connection with the "netherworld." The one possible exception is the term ארץ רפאים, since in Ugaritic myth and also in biblical mythopoeic language, the term אֶרֶץ/*ʾarṣ* does indicate the realm of the dead. This aspect still needs to be considered. However, in the compass of the biblical references which have come under scrutiny so far, ארץ רפאים manifestly has an ethnic geopolitical connotation (Deut 2:20; 3:13; Josh 17:15).[22]

III

Of an altogether different nature is a cluster of eight biblical phrases in which the term רְפָאִים is employed—*nota bene*—without exception in the plural. In all these instances, the accompanying terminology, whether by syntactical association or in *parallelismus membrorum* leaves no room for doubt-

---

22. Cp. B. Margulis, "A Ugaritic Psalm," *JBL* 89 (1970) 300-302.

ing the mythopoeic character of the term and its specific appositeness to the realm of death, the netherworld. In all these instances the immediate context contains synonymous or "explanatory" vocables, such as שאול, אֶרֶץ, אבדון, שוכני עפר, יורדי בור/דומה, מתים, and several verbs and adjectives that serve to underline the "downward" movements of the human creatures who are the subject matter of these passages.

In contradistinction to the references considered in section II, all biblical citations to be discussed in this section turn up in prophetic literature (Isa 14:9; 26:14, 19), Psalms (88:11), and wisdom writings (Job 26:5; Prov 2:18; 9:18; 21:16). Not one is found in historiographical literature in which the ethnic, geopolitical references to רָפָא/ה-רפאים are concentrated.

Moreover, most if not all the pertinent passages show marked "mythological" traits. This again sets them apart from the texts adduced in section II. The fact springs to the eye in the "Oracle against the King of Babylon" (Isa 14:9), in proverbs concerning the "foreign female" seducer (Prov 2:18), "Dame Folly" (Prov 9:18; cp. 21:16), and in the "Creation" setting of Job 26:5ff. The remaining two references to רפאים in Isa 26:14 and 19 are textually similar and constitute a conspicuous element in the opening and closing lines of a unit that is distinguished from the surrounding text by the literary technique of "ring composition." While the supposition cannot be proved, it would appear that the passage (Isa 26:14–19) was probably inserted *in toto*, as a unit, into the present context and may have had a literary "prehistory"of its own.

In the ensuing deliberations the thesis will be explored that the cluster of רפאים references in nonhistoriographical biblical writings do in fact evince an impact of Ugaritic epic tradition on ancient Hebrew literature. What is more, it will be suggested that the borrowing engendered the generalization of a specific Ugaritic technical term which was assimilated into the Hebrew vocabulary as purely a "manner of speech." The transformation was furthered by a "misunderstanding" or possibly a conscious "reinterpretation" of the Ugaritic term in question and by the additional impact of the well-known technique of the "Break-up Pattern," present in Ugaritic as well as in biblical literature.[23]

23. Scholarly literature on the break-up pattern is rapidly increasing. The following listing of pertinent items in no way aims at presenting a complete roster: E. Z. Melamed, "Break-up of Stereotype Phrases as an Artistic Device in Biblical Poetry" ([ScrHier 8; Jerusalem: Magnes, 1961] 115-44); Talmon, SROT (335–83); and G. Braulik, "Aufbrechen von

The point of departure for the following analysis is the recurring epithet of Danʾil in Aqht texts (19:X): *mt rpi*.[24] Our hypothesis is that the component *mt*, which in reference to Danʾil undoubtedly carries the meaning "man of . . . ," in the process of its transfer to Biblical Hebrew and literature was identified erroneously with the Hebrew root מָוֶת ("dead" or "death"), which connotation the homonym of *mt* also has in Ugaritic. Such a misinterpretation most probably caused some confusion in the vocalization of the plural form, מְתִים, in Job 24:12, which was vocalized in MS di Rossi 193 as מֵתִים. This pointing may have been implied also in the *Vorlage* of the Syriac translation. But the prevailing masoretic tradition vocalizes it with a *shewa*: מֵעִיר מְתִים יִנְאָקוּ וְנֶפֶשׁ־חֲלָלִים תְּשַׁוֵּעַ (Job 24:12). Because of חללים ("slain") in the second stich,[25] commentators argue that a better reading and translation of the crucial passage would be achieved "with MT מְתִים, 'men,' repointed to מֵתִים, 'the dead': 'From the city the dead groan, and the throats of the slain cry out.'"[26] However, the argument hardly stands up to scrutiny. חללים ("slain") indeed can still "cry out," since the pertinent Hebrew term also connotes the "mortally wounded" (see, e.g., Isa 53:5), especially so in connection with the verb אנק. In Jer 51:52 and Ezek 26:15; 30:24, it turns up in contexts which recurrently refer to the "groans" of men caught in the "throes of death": קוֹל מִפַּלְתָּךְ (Jer 51:54–55), שְׁאוֹן קוֹלָם, קוֹל גָּדוֹל, קוֹל זְעָקָה (Ezek 26:15). Over against this, מֵתִים always indicates that final state in which any vestige of human life has been extinguished. *Per definitionem*, מֵתִים are totally silenced; they are utterly voiceless (Isa 38:18; Ps 115:17, et al.; contrast Isa 26:19). Therefore, the vocalization מְתִים should be retained in Job 24:12. The combination (מֵ)עִיר מְתִים employed there as a designation of the "citizenry" of a township is possibly a (borrowed?) *term. tech.*, which turns up twice more in Deut 2:34 and 3:6.

The possible confusion of מֵתִים with מְתִים may also be observed in the interpretation of a Ugaritic text that is of paramount importance for our pre-

geprägten Wortverbindungen und Zusammenfassen von stereotypen Ausdrücken in der alttestamentlichen Kunstprosa" (*Semitics* 1 [1970] 7–11). See also Y. Avishur, *The Construct State of Synonyms in Biblical Rhetoric* (Jerusalem: Kiryat-Sefer, 1977 [Heb.]).

24. R. Whitaker, *A Concordance of the Ugaritic Literature* (Cambridge: Harvard University Press, 1972) *s.v. rpi*.

25. The same order מֵתִים ‖ חללים is found in Ps 88:6; the inverted pattern חללים ‖ מֵתִים in Isa 22:2. Cp. also Isa 34:3, where (וּ)פִגְרֵיהֶם takes the place of מֵתִים as the B-word after וְחַלְלֵיהֶם.

26. M. Dahood, "Ugaritic-Hebrew Parallel Pairs," *RSPI* (AnOr 49; Rome: Pontificium Institutum Biblicum, 1972) 272, 374α, h.

sent concern and to which we shall now turn our attention. Also there *mtm* is used in parallelism with *rpi* (CTA IV:6:44–48):

> *špš rpim thtk / špš thtk ilnym*
> *ʿdk ilm hn mtm ʿdk / kṯrm ḥbrk whss dʿtk*

M. Pope's translation of *mtm*, "Your comrades the gods, the dead your comrades,"[27] is followed by most commentators. However, the phrase *mtm ʿdk* appears to be but an inverted synonymous parallel of *ʿdk ilm*, both referring to the "fellowship" or "community" of the gods. The trope does not necessarily involve any aspect of death, contrary to Pope's claim about the descent to the "netherworld" of Baal, the addressee of the couplet. The underlying concept of a "divine assembly" is further emphasized by the terms *ḥbrk* and *ʿdk*, which could be a miswritten *ʿdtk* (a fem. alternative of *ʿdk?*). And just as *mtm* parallels *ilm*, in the preceding line *rpim* parallels *ilnym*, again without any explicit or implied reference to "death" or the "netherworld."

Rpim and *ilnym* in the first two stichoi should, or at least could, be seen as apocopated parallels (or even synonymous terms) of *ʿdk ilm* and *mtm ʿdk* in the ensuing line, all referring to a divine "assembly," with the following *ḥbrk* and *dʿtk* expressing a similar notion.[28] All these tropes bring to mind the Hebrew term קהל רפאים found in Prov 21:16, also without an explicit mention of the "netherworld." There is implied, however, a fairly obvious threat to the one who "strays from the way of prudence" that he will ultimately "lie" (ינוח) with the רפאים, i.e., will be gathered unto them. One is inclined to propose that in the above Ugaritic text *rpim . . . mtm* should be seen as an inverted employment of the vocables which make up Danʾilʾs epithet: *mt rpu/i*. If this argument can be sustained, the presumed break-up pattern *cum inversio* will demand our attention in the ensuing interpretation of the biblical evidence.

---

27. Pope, "Notes" (see above, n.1), 176, n. 1; see also 172.
28. In this context we should recall H. L. Ginsberg's contention that "*rpʾe* is a common noun, 'community,' from a root *rpʾ*, with the primary sense 'to join,' as in Arabic. This meaning is demanded by the parallelism, *rpʾe* corresponding to *qbṣ*, 'a gathering'" (*The Legend of King Keret* [BASORSS 2–3; New Haven: Yale University Press, 1946] 41). The relevant texts are CTA 15:3:2 and 14:14; RS 34, 126. See also Pope, "Notes" (177).

IV

The starting point for the investigation will be those biblical passages in which the pertinent words מְתִים/מֵתִים and רפאים turn up in A/B order[29] in two cola of a *parallelismus membrorum*:

(1) Isa 26:14:   מֵתִים בל־יחיו רפאים בל־יקמו
לכן פקדת ותשמידם ותאבד כל־זכר למו

In neither of the possible vocalizations, מְתִים or מֵתִים (MT), does this word ever turn up in parallelism with רפאים in any of the biblical passages referred to above in section II, in which רפאים serves as an ethnic-geopolitical term. In contrast, in the present case מֵתִים clearly identifies that latter term un-equivocally as pertaining to the realm of the dead, the "netherworld." The absolute and final cessation of the life of "men," מְתִים, or "the dead," מֵתִים, like that of the רפאים to whom an afterlife or "resurrection" is categorically denied, is further highlighted by the statement that they will not be remem-bered (cp. Ps 88:6 et al.): "God has annihilated them and wiped out their memory" (cp. Isa 26:8, 13). The metaphor undoubtedly refers to the denial to those מְתִים-מֵתִים and רפאים of offspring, in whom a man's life finds a con-tinuation even after his own death.[30] This idea comes most forcefully to the fore in the LXX rendition, καὶ ἦρας πᾶν ἄρσεν αὐτῶν, which either may reflect an explanatory translation of the MT's זֵכֶר, "remembrance," or else mirrors the variant reading (vocalization) זָכָר, "male" (offspring). The latter proposition derives support from the (probably formulaic) combination of רפאים with "cessation of the family line," found in a Phoenician *Fluch-formel*:

Tabnit 1:7–8 (KAI 13):   אל יכן לם זרע תחת שמש
ומשכב את רפאם

---

29. The use of this pattern in biblical literature was conveniently surveyed by P. B. Yoder ("A-B Pairs and Oral Composition in Hebrew Poetry," *VT* 21 [1971] 471–89) and W. G. E. Watson ("Fixed Pairs in Ugaritic and Isaiah," *VT* 22 [1972] 461–67), with copious refer-ences to earlier discussions of this phenomenon.

30. See S. Talmon, "Yād Wāšēm: An Idiomatic Phrase in Biblical Literature and Its Varia-tions," *Hebrew Studies* 25 (1984) 8–17.

Biblical רְפָאִים and Ugaritic *Rpu/i(m)*

ʾEšmunʿazar 1:8–9 (KAI 14):

אל יכן לם משכב את רפאם ואל יקבר בקבר

ואל יכן לם בן וזרע

A similar apposition of מֵתִים and רפאים occurs in the closing line of the ring-composition for which Isa 26:14 serves as an opening:

(2) Isa 26:19:

יחיו מתיך נבלתי יקומון הקיצו ורננו שכני עפר

כי טל אורת טלך וארץ רפאים תפיל

Although the verse is fraught with textual difficulties, they do not obfuscate its relevancy for our present concern, viz., the employment of מֵתִים and רפאים in parallelism in the A/B sequence. The "netherworld" connotation of those two terms is underlined by the added tropes [נבלתי|ך]31 and שכני עפר and possibly also אֶרֶץ (רפאים), a word which can designate the "netherworld" both in Ugaritic and in Biblical Hebrew.

(3) Ps 88:11:

הלמתים תעשה־פלא אם־רפאים יקומו יודוך

Ps 88:11 provides one more illustration of the employment of מֵתִים-רפאים as synonymous terms in the A/B order, possibly resulting from the presumed "break-up" of *mt rpu/i(m)*. The use of יקומו(ה), by way of a rhetorical question which implies a negative reply, gives expression to the same notion of the finality of death that permeates Isa 26:14 (cp. Ps 88:5–6). Again, by way of a rhetorical question, יודוך(ה), the psalmist reiterates the observation already mentioned, that מֵתִים and רפאים represent the netherworld where utter silence reigns (cp. Isa 38:18; Ps 88:12–13; 115:17; Job 26:5–6, et al.).

A variant of the above A/B pattern in which מתים is substituted by the general noun מָוֶת is found in

(4) Prov 2:18:

כי שחה אל־מות ביתה ואל־רפאים מעגלתיה

31. The emendation of נבלתי to נבלתיך is widely accepted. The final ך after the י may have dropped out due to a *lapsus calami*, a haplography with יק at the beginning of the next word.

The inherent idea of perdition which a (foreign) adulteress will bring upon men is underpinned in the following verse, which states that whoever is ensnared by her will lose "the path to [or 'of'] life" (cp. Prov 2:22; 21:16). This "path of life" is apportioned to the righteous who are guided by Wisdom (2:1ff., esp. 7–9, 13–15, 20) and therefore "will dwell on earth" (2:21).

The latter example indicates that once the parallelism מֵתִים ‖ רפאים, derived from the presumed break-up of Ugaritic *mt rpu/i(m)*, had been absorbed into biblical imagery, it could be subjected to stylistic and syntactical variation, as will be shown. By the very nature of things, the explicit connotation of מֵתִים makes for the employment of this vocable as the A-word that defines the meaning of the less transparent B-vocable רפאים. While we cannot establish a definite developmental process, it would appear that in the course of time a semantic identity evolved which caused the two terms to become completely interchangeable, so much so that their order in *parallelismus membrorum* could be reversed. No definite proof for this hypothesis can be adduced from biblical literature. There is not one instance of the B/A pattern on record with רפאים preceding מֵתִים. However, the text already mentioned, CTA VI:6:44–48, shows that at least one such inversion is extant in Ugaritic: *rpim ... ilnym ... ilm ... mtm.*

The inverted B/A pattern is possibly still reflected in biblical literature, as well, albeit with the additional substitution of a synonym for the original A-word מֵתִים. The most obvious substitutes would be vocables that have the very same mythopoeic content of מָוֶת-מֵתִים, especially when these terms are employed in conjunction with רפאים. First and foremost שאול should be mentioned:

(5) Prov 9:18:　　　　　　　ולא־ידע כי־רפאים שם בעמקי שאול קראיה

(6) Job 26:5:　　　　　　　הרפאים יחוללו מתחת מים ושכניהם
　　26:6:　　　　　　　ערום שאול נגדו ואין כסות לאבדון

מתחת מים is a rather awkward opening phrase of the second stich in the masoretic sentence division of Job 26:5 and does not connect well with the ensuing ושכניהם. It seems preferable to link מתחת with the beginning of the verse, הרפאים יחוללו. Thus a more pronounced parallelism with the first stich

of the following verse would be achieved and concomitantly a connection
with שאול, which is reminiscent of Isa 14:9, לקראת בואך שאול מתחת רגזה לך. In
addition, the noun ושכניהם brings to mind several passages in which שכן is
employed in apposition to other netherworld terms, such as:

Job 4:19:	אף שכני בתי חמר אשר בעפר יסודם
Ps 7:6:	ירדף אויב נפשי וישג וירמס לארץ חיי וכבודי לעפר ישכן
Ps 16:9:	לכן שמח לבי ויגל כבודי אף־בשרי ישכן לבטח
16:10:	כי לא תעזב נפשי לשאול לא־תתן חסידך לראות שחת
Isa 26:19:	יחיו מתיך נבלתי[ך] יקומון הקיצו ורננו שכני עפר

(cp. further Prov 21:16). Not once do we find in these texts the word מים, not
even in the negative connotation of "water of the abyss." Rather, they are
replete with imagery which pertains to the dead who are buried or lie in the
earth: ארץ (Isa 26:19; Ps 7:6); עפר (Job 4:19); שחת and שאול (Ps 16:10).
Viewed against this backdrop, the plural possessive pronoun in ושכניהם (Job
26:5) must be taken to refer to שאול and אבדון in the following verse, and the
conjecture may be entertained that the present MT reading מים resulted from
an original מתים due to the elision of the ת (by haplography with מ?). If the
proposed restoration of מֵתים can be sustained, Job 26:5 would exhibit the
one and only biblical instance of the (inverted) B/A pattern מֵתים ‖ רפאים.

The coupling of שאול and אבדון[32] with רפאים as substitutes for מֵתים in the
A/B, or rather in the B/A, pattern in MT Prov 9:18 and Job 26:5–6 evokes
the expectation that other synonyms or variants of מֵתים may turn up conjoined with רפאים in biblical passages which similarly display the concepts
of death and the netherworld, as, e.g., in:

(7) Isa 14:9:	שאול מתחת רגזה לך לקראת בואך
	עורר לך רפאים כל־עתודי ארץ הקים מכסאותם כל מלכי גוים

The idiom עתודי אָרֶץ is employed here by way of double entendre:[33] on
the one hand it harks back to the preceding mythopoeic term רפאים; on the

---

32. Cp. Prov 15:11: שְׁאוֹל וַאֲבַדּוֹן נגד ה' אף כי־לבות בני־אדם; 1QH iii 19–20: כי פדיתה נפשי
מִשַּׁחַת וּמִשְּׁאוֹל וַאֲבַדּוֹן העליחני; and see Avishur, *The Construct State* (113 [above, n. 23]).

33. Ugaritic *rpu(m)* exhibits a comparable duality of meaning. Next to its "divine" dimension, as
in *rpᵓ mlk ᵓilm* (*UT* 5:2), it has a purely human connotation, as in Dnᵓil's epithet *mt rpm*.

other hand it refers proleptically to the "earthly kings," מַלְכֵי אָרֶץ, who are depicted as already having been transferred to the netherworld.

A further stage in the process of literary development in the suggested biblical break-up pattern מֵתִים ‖ רפאים of the Ugaritic construct *mt rpu/i(m)*, may be discerned in a verse that contains but an allusion to the component מֵתִים:

(8) Prov 21:16: אדם תועה מדרך השכל בקהל רפאים ינוח

In contradistinction to the prevalent positive connotation of נוח in Biblical Hebrew, in the passage under consideration the verb ינוח is given a negative sense. By being conjoined with רפאים (קהל), exactly as in the passages quoted above, the prevailing favorable or beneficial notion that goes with נוח in biblical phraseology was turned round completely. By binding it up syntactically with netherworld terminology, it was invested with a sense of detriment and adversity.

To summarize the results of our investigation, the analysis of the eight occurrences of the plural form רפאים in nonhistoriographical biblical texts, to the exclusion of the singular רפא/ה which is found in historiographical literature, its presumed original apposition to מֵתִים—and in ensuing stages of literary development to synonymous expressions of that term—supports the hypothesis presented at the outset of our investigation that this special employment of רפאים, in specific texts only, may disclose an impact of the mythopoeic Ugaritic terms *mt(m)* and *rpu/i(m)* on biblical literature and phraseology. As in Ugaritic, also in Biblical Hebrew the mythical overtones of these terms are further accentuated by their apposition to vocables which pertain to the realm of the dead, the netherworld, such as בור, עפר, ארץ, שאול, אבדון, and שחת.

As against this, such mythopoeic vocabulary is conspicuously absent from the historiographical biblical texts in which רפא/ה-רפאים in the singular and in the plural has a pointed and practically exclusive ethnic-geopolitical connotation. This employment should therefore be discussed separately.

DID THERE EXIST A BIBLICAL
NATIONAL EPIC?

I

The question of whether the literary genre "epic" or "epos" ever developed in ancient Israel has exercised the minds of scholars for some time, especially since the beginning of the twentieth century. The attention given to the issue and the theories advanced most probably did not arise from within the field of biblical studies or from specifically biblical interests. Actually the pursuit was probably sparked by developments in other areas of humanistic research, preponderantly in literary criticism and the history of literature. This dependence cannot occasion any surprise. Biblical scholarship on the whole has molded itself upon borrowed methods and has availed itself of tools and techniques which had been fashioned in other disciplines. It would be tantamount to carrying balm to Gilead were we to enlarge on this well-known and generally accepted feature of modern biblical studies. It suffices to refer to the impact of critical classical scholarship on the inception and crystallization of the *literarhistorische* approach in the study of the Bible,[1] or to the enrichment of the study of biblical literature *qua* literature through the adoption and adaptation of new modes of inquiry in the study of literature generally, such as *Werkinterpretation* or "close reading."[2] In short the application to particular biblical issues of methods and procedures worked out in other domains of scholarly endeavor *per se* must be recognized as eminently legitimate. What remains open to discussion and rightly evokes criticism is the unqualified transfer of scholarly instruments from the

---

1. For the history and a survey of pertinent literature, see, int. al., F. Hahn, *The Old Testament in Modern Research* (Philadelphia: Muhlenberg Press, 1956); H. J. Krauss, *Geschichte der historisch-kritischen Erforschung des Alten Testaments* (Neukirchen: Neukirchener Verlag, 1969); R. Smend, *Wilhelm Martin Leberecht de Wettes Arbeit am Alten und Neuen Testament* (Basel: Helbings Lichtenhahn, 1958).
2. M. Weiss ("Die Methode der 'Total-Interpretation'" [VTSup 22; Leiden: E. J. Brill, 1971] 88–112) provides a survey of the method of this school and relevant bibliography.

discipline to which they are germane to another without paying heed to inherent disparities. Borrowing requires selection and discriminative refinement of the imported goods.[3] These reflections have some definite bearing on the matter to be discussed here.

There cannot be any doubt that we have no palpable evidence for the existence of an epos proper in biblical literature.[4] Umberto Cassuto, to whose discussion of the question we shall return, states quite unequivocally that neither the epic nor the fully worked-out epic song is present in the biblical books. This assertion would find unanimous approval unless one were to maintain that the Hebrew Bible in its entirety (or at least the historiographies contained in it) constitutes the national epic of the ancient Hebrews, as among others F. M. Cross appears to maintain.[5] The scholar who probably came nearest to propagating this claim is Arvid Bruno. In a series of studies he attempted to reconstruct the original form of the early biblical historiographical books, thus recovering "Das hebräische Epos," which presumably underlies the prosaized configuration in which, e.g., Samuel and Kings were handed down.[6] Neither Bruno's theory nor the historical epic which he restored attracted much attention and certainly did not make a lasting impression on biblical studies.

The assertion that the epic as a specific *Gattung* is absent from ancient Hebrew literature as represented in the biblical canon does not yet close the discussion. It can be postulated, as indeed it was, that the epic may have existed at some time in the precanonical past. The canon of biblical writings

3. For a more articulate discussion of this question, see S. Talmon,"The Comparative Method in Biblical Interpretation" (in this vol., pp. 11–49).

4. See also L. M. Pakodzy, "Zur Frage des Altisraelitischen Nationalepos," *Acta Antiqua Academiae Scientiarum Hungaricae* 23, Fasc. 1–2 (1975) 77–92.

5. F. M. Cross, *Canaanite Myth and Hebrew Epic: Essays in the History of the Religion of Israel* (Cambridge, MA: Harvard University Press, 1973). From the many relevant references, I would mention his statement: "In the case of the epic materials . . . we are inclined to reconstruct a long and rich poetic epic of the era of the league, underlying JE, and to take the prose epic variants (with their surviving poetic fragments) preserved in the P work (i.e., the Tetrateuch. JEP) as truncated and secondary derivatives [p. 124, n. 38; cp. also pp. 293–96, 303ff.]. In any case we possess long, poetic epics from Old Canaan, from ancient Mesopotamia, and Homeric Greece, and to find the same phenomenon in Israel would not be surprising." On p. 143 Cross refers to "Israel's epic of Exodus and Conquest" (cp. p. 293), which he dates in "the tenth and ninth centuries" (p. 183) and which in his view is preserved only in fragments (pp. 271–72).

6. See Arvid Bruno, *Rhytmische Untersuchungen von Gen, Ex, Jos, Ri, I. II Sam, I. II Kön, Jes, Jer, Ez, 12 Proph, Ps, Mi, Spr, Ruth, Hhld, Pred, Klgl, Esth, Dan* (Uppsala: Almavista Wiksells, 1953–59) and *Das Hebräische Epos* (Uppsala: Almqvist & Wiksell, 1935).

grew over a period of a thousand years, and each of the books incorporated in it had a *Vorgeschichte*. It is quite correctly assumed that in the stages before "inlibration," which preceded crystallization in book form, Hebrew literature had been current in other forms, preponderantly as oral traditions. One cannot dismiss out of hand the possibility that in those early stages materials had been handed down in *Formen* or *Gattungen* which were lost in the process of transmission when they were transformed into the literary structures in which they were ultimately preserved in the Hebrew Bible.

The search for such presumably lost materials and literary configurations at first concentrated on references in the Bible to works no longer extant, foremost in the books of Kings and Chronicles. These references seem to pertain to compilations of a historical-narrative nature such as "the annals of the kings of Judah" (1 Kgs 14:29; 15:7, 23; 22:46) or "of the kings of Israel-Ephraim" (1 Kgs. 14:19; 15:31; 16:5, 14; et al.) and "the annals of the kings of Judah and Israel" (2 Chr 16:11; 25:26; 27:7; 28:26; et al.) To these compilations of a comprehensive character we can add the more limited historiographies mentioned mainly by the Chronicler, which related the deeds of individual kings such as "the records of David" (1 Chr 29:29), "the book of Solomon's acts" (1 Kgs 11:41; 2 Chr 9:29), "the records of Rehoboam's exploits which had been written by Shemaiah the prophet and Iddo the seer" (2 Chr 12:15) possibly referred to also as "the midrash of Iddo the prophet" (2 Chr 13:22), and the work of Jehu ben Hanani which commemorated Jehoshaphat's history and had been incorporated in "the book of the kings of Israel" (2 Chr 20:34).[7] Without fully articulating the apparent similarity, students of the Bible recalled that "lost epic cycles," of which only vague reminiscences have remained, are also suspected in classical literature.[8] However these two sets of materials cannot be compared, since the biblical references to those lost works do not imply that they had been composed in epic form.

These attempts at tracing tangible remains of ancient Hebrew epics which presumably are submerged in the present prose texts were triggered by

---

7.   J. Liver, "The Annals of Solomon," *Studies in Bible and Judean Desert Scrolls* (Jerusalem: Bialik, 1971) 83–108 (Heb.); J. A. Montgomery, *Kings* (ICC; Edinburgh: Clark, 1959) 24–38.

8.   See, int. al., G. Murray, *The Rise of the Greek Epic* (4th ed.; Oxford University Press, 1961), esp. p. 175; G. S. Kirk, *The Songs of Homer* (Cambridge: Cambridge University Press, 1962), esp. part III; A. B. Lord, *The Singer of Tales* (New York: Atheneum, 1970); K. Ziegler, *Das hellenistische Epos, ein vergessenes Kapitel griechischer Dichtung* (Leipzig: Teubner, 1934).

the broad assumption that biblical, like all prose literature, had been preceded by heroic tales in the form of epics. One considered as the most likely representatives of the epic *Gattung* in the Hebrew Bible the obscure ספר מלחמות ה' mentioned once in the roster of the Israelites' travel stations in the desert, together with a barely intelligible quotation from that work (Num 21:14); and the similarly undefined ספר הישר, referred to, again with quotations, in Josh 10:13 and 2 Sam 1:18. Both these references are set in a context of war reports. This latter circumstance strongly suggests that the ספר הישר should not be identified with the βίβλιον τῆς ᾠδῆς, which is mentioned in an addition to the LXX and also in one witness of the Vetus Latina after 1 Kgs 8:53 but is not referred to in the MT and the other ancient versions at the appropriate juncture (1 Kgs 8:13).

Although the proposed retroversion of βίβλιον τῆς ᾠδῆς into ספר השיר appears to be plausible, the identification of ספר הישר with ספר השיר by assuming a simple metathesis, שיר-ישר,[9] is more than doubtful. The apparent dissimilarity of these compilations suggested by the quite dissimilar contexts in which they are referred to, one in war settings and the other in a cultic framework, militates against this assumption. However this point is of minor importance for the present discussion since it does not affect the basic issue under consideration.

It should be noted that with the exception of Tur-Sinai,[10] who concurs with S. D. Luzatto in the opinion that ספר מלחמות ה' was not at all a book in the accepted sense of the word but rather a loose collection of orally transmitted praises of God's mighty deeds, it is *communis opinio* that the Bible indeed refers to a book which was still known to the historiographers who quote from it. The same holds true for ספר הישר. We shall not go into a detailed presentation of the views of earlier scholars—Gray,[11] Cornill,[12] Gressmann,[13] Caspari,[14] et al.—but rather shall concentrate on the more re-

9. See, int. al.: Montgomery, *Kings*, 189–92 (see above, n. 7); H. St. J. Thackeray, "New Light on the Book of Jashar," *JTS* 11 (1909–10) 518–32; P. K. McCarter, *II Samuel* (AB 8; Garden City, NY: Doubleday, 1984) 74.

10. N. H. Tur-Sinai, "Was There an Ancient 'Book of the Wars of the Lord'?" *BIES* 24 (1960) 146–48 (Heb.).

11. G. B. Gray, *Numbers: A Critical and Exegetical Commentary* (ICC; Edinburgh: Clark, 1903) 284–85.

12. C. H. Cornill, *Einleitung in die Kanonischen Bücher des Alte Testaments* (Tübingen: Mohr, 1905) 74.

13. H. Gressmann, *Mose und seine Zeit* (Göttingen: Vandenhoeck & Ruprecht, 1913) 304ff.

14. W. Caspari, "Was stand im Buch der Kriege Jahwäs?" *ZWT* 54 (1912) 110ff.

cent discussion of the matter. Y. Kaufmann speaks of these works as representing early Hebrew literature which preceded the "Torah" (not necessarily to be identified with the Pentateuch in its present form). The incipient crystallization of that ancient literature may be found in the ספר מלחמות ה׳ and ספר הישר, and in the (שירת) המשלים, in which "an *epic element* is present" (my italics).[15] The inclusion of the (שירת) המשלים from which the Heshbon song is cited (Num 21:27–30) in the roster of lost books of an "epic character" points to the direction which research has taken: an intensified search for witnesses to the one-time existence of an ancient Hebrew epic which is no longer extant.

II

A watershed in the discussion was reached in 1935 with the publication of Sigmund Mowinckel's study "Hat es ein israelitisches Nationalepos gegeben?"[16] After summarizing earlier scholarly contributions to the clarification of the issue, Mowinckel replied in the affirmative to the question posed in the title of his paper, adding further insight and details of information gleaned from biblical literature toward the reconstruction of the lost Israelite national epic. In doing so he sought to correct a prevalent supposition that the assumed diversity of the materials which had been included in the above-mentioned three works proves them to have been anthologies "von selbständigen, aus verschiedenen Zeiten stammenden lyrischen Liedern."[17] Cornill had already defined ספר מלחמות ה׳ as "eine Sammlung von volkstümlichen Kriegs—und Siegesliedern,"[18] and Gressmann had typified the quotation from it in Num 21:14–15 as a geographical "Beschreibungslied."[19] But David's Lament, which the author of 2 Samuel presumably had taken from the ספר הישר[20] actually is a קינה and can hardly be defined as a *Siegeslied*.

---

15. Y. Kaufmann, *The History of Israelite Religion* (Tel-Aviv: Dvir, 1942) 2/1.144ff. (Heb.).
16. S. Mowinckel, "Hat es ein israelitisches Nationalepos gegeben?" *ZAW* 53 (1935) 130–53.
17. Ibid., 130.
18. Cornill, *Einleitung,* loc. cit. (see above, n. 12).
19. Gressmann, *Mose,* loc. cit. (see above, n. 13).
20. This assumption is questionable. The superscription of David's Lament "as written in the ספר הישר" (2 Sam 1:18b) probably refers not to the "Lament," but rather to the song "to teach the Judahites bow [shooting]" mentioned in the preceeding stich (1:18a), which presumably served as a musical prototype on which was modelled the presentation of the "Lament." One is reminded of the use of traditional tunes by the medieval *troubadours* and

Judging from Joshua's song (Josh 10:12–13), that same compilation would also have contained a *Beschwörungsspruch*," which represents a different *Gattung* altogether. The Heshbon song (Num 21:27–30) was labelled by Gressmann a political *Spottlied*[21] of extra- and probably pre-Israelite origin.[22]

If one adds the above-mentioned LXX reference to a ספר השיר which Mowinckel and others identify with the ספר הישר, that ancient Hebrew epic work would also have contained a *Tempelweihspruch*, a special *Gattung*, which, however, is evidently not listed in the classifications suggested by students of biblical literature. Despite the undeniable disparity, Mowinckel would still bring all these literary creations under one heading. He suggests that ספר מלחמות ה' and ספר הישר, including ספר השיר, are designations of one and the same book, of which המשלים (שירת) had also formed a part. He buttresses his assumption by the correct observation that in biblical and post-biblical Israel books often circulated under more than one title.[23] On the one hand we encounter the custom, well known in the Ancient Near East, of designating a book by its *incipit* (its first line or even only the opening words or word), as is the masoretic custom in the Pentateuch: ויקרא, אלה שמות, בראשית, ואלה הדברים, במדבר. On the other hand titles are used which provide in catchword fashion a short characterization of the content of the work in question or of some of its major aspects. This type of superscription is more in keeping with the Classical Greek and Roman usage. Thus *Leviticus* is sometimes referred to in rabbinic sources as תורת כהנים, the "priestly Torah"; *Numeri* as ספר פקודים, the "book of commandments"; and *Deuteronomium* as משנה תורה.

As far as the identification of ספר מלחמות ה' with ספר הישר is concerned, the position taken by Mowinckel can indeed be defended. Reading a שׂ for the שׁ in הישר, I have proposed understanding that term as a contraction of the abbreviated tetragrammaton by ה with the verb יָשַׂר or יׂשׂר, meaning "God has made / will make war (for Israel)." No textual corroboration can be adduced for this conjecture. However it derives some support from pertinent parallel phrases such as שרית עם אלהים (Gen 32:29), וישר אל מלאך—שׂרה את אלהים (Hos

---

Meistersinger in reciting their own literary creations. The omission of קשת, "bow," in the Greek translation shows that the translator, like most exegetes, understood the superscription to mean that the "Lament" itself had been incorporated into the ספר הישר. This interpretation is put in relief in the expanded rendition of the NEB: "It was written down [+ "and can be found"] in the book of Jashar."

21. Gressmann, *Mose*, 307 (see above, n. 13).
22. See commentaries ad. loc.
23. Mowinckel, *ZAW* 53 (1935) 130 (see above, n. 16).

12:4–5), and the very name ישראל, all derived from the basic tradition about
Jacob's wrestling with "a man" at the Jabbok crossing (Gen 32:23–33), with
the abbreviated tetragrammaton replacing the original אל or אלהים (32:29,
31).[24] However when Mowinckel tries to explain the topical and formal differences between the compilations involved, he has recourse to extremely
weak and hardly admissible arguments in order to provide a basis for the insufficiently supported hypothesis of the one-time existence of a biblical
national epic. Apparently aware of the tenuous nature of this variegated evidence, he remarks that "Ein Epos braucht keine straff durchgeführte Kompo-
sition eines Verfassers sein."[25] This statement could be applied to any narrative literature and therefore is of no consequence for the question under
review.

It seems superfluous to list here all the other scattered pieces of supposedly epic remains which Mowinckel collected from the Pentateuch, exclusively from the Elohist source.[26] In the end he confidently concludes that the
Israelite national epic was composed after the consolidation of the Jahwistic
source which exhibits no epic materials at all, while the earlier Elohist
made extensive use of it. Thus he arrives at a date for the composition of
that epic in Judah between 750 and the destruction of the Southern Kingdom
in 587/586 BCE.[27] For the identification of vestiges of this epos in the Elohist, Mowinckel resorts to literary, in fact, to metric criteria. With the help
of "die metrischpoetische Form," which he considers to be "das einzige
einigermassen sichere Kriterium" (but regarding which he rejects Sievers'
definition), he brings to light epic morsels, int. al., in Exod 15:25b, taking
the line שם שם לו חק ומשפט ושם נסהו to be "ein wörtliches Zitat." Following
Caspari, he analyzes the curse put on Amalek (Exod 17:16) in a similar
way, as well as sundry verses or half-verses in the Pentateuch.

Having restored to his satisfaction the "Israelite national epic" in which
the mighty military deeds of God and his people were extolled, Mowinckel
also detects in that comprehensive epic work a religious dimension. He assumes that the creation story had also been told first in epic form. In order to
discover epic vestiges in the creation tradition, a difficulty has to be removed, namely the premise that Genesis 1–11 is part of the Jahwistic

24.   See S. Talmon, "מלחמות ה'י," EncMiq 4.1064.
25.   Mowinckel, ZAW 53 (1935) 141–50 (see above, n. 16).
26.   Ibid., 141.
27.   Ibid., 149.

source, which assumedly does not exhibit any epic traits whatsoever. Likewise, in view of the foregoing discussion, it would be unacceptable to uphold the claim that the Elohist source contained no *Urgeschichte* at all. The situation is remedied by identifying the second "Jahwistische Faden," isolated by Budde, Smend, Gunkel, and Eissfeldt in the Genesis 1–11 complex as actually representing the Elohist account.

With the help of Begrich's proposal one can do even better in the Garden of Eden tradition, since there Begrich ascribes the *Hauptfaden* to E. Epic traces are then discerned in Gen 2:5 and 23, and possibly also in 2:24 (as well as in 9:12ff.), which seem to testify to the "Benutzung einer metrisch-poetischen Vorlage."[28] This necessitates the wrenching of these verses from the framework of J or P in order to ascribe them to E, the only preserver of epic materials. Mowinckel must have sensed the fallibility of this procedure, since he summarizes his argument by stating somewhat hesitatingly: "Ist dies alles einigermassen richtig, so hat das Epos auch eine Urgeschichte enthalten. Das stimmt gut zu dem religiösen Grundton desselben."[29] Thus we arrive at the even more hazardous hypothesis that the surmised ancient *Israelitische Nationalepos* had successfully fused heroic tales, portraying the exploits of Israel and Israel's God in the post-Davidic (actually post-J) period, with an epic cosmogony which by right belongs in the category of myth. One hesitates to concur with Mowinckel's appreciation of this concatenation of hypotheses as being of great importance "für das Verständnis von dem Verhältnis zwischen J und E."[30]

While this latter statement has little bearing on the question under discussion here, Mowinckel's appeal in the final section of the paper to other Ancient Near Eastern epic literatures, so as to buttress the theory propounded in respect to biblical literature by means of the comparative method, is indeed relevant to the issue. Mowinckel apparently harbored some doubts that the epic genre did in fact originate among the Israelites. He therefore turned to neighboring Semitic cultures in search of possible sources of influence: "als literarisches Vorbild für eine epische Behandlung der Urzeit und der Heroenzeit in religiöser Beleuchtung würden sich für die israelitischen Dichter babylonisch-assyrische Epen darbieten."[31] Such a

28. Ibid., 146.
29. Ibid., 147.
30. Ibid., 150.
31. Ibid., 147.

comparison lies at hand. It requires little imagination to figure out in which Mesopotamian epics the author discovered suitable *Vorbilder* for the assumed epic strain in the biblical creation story. Since in 1935 Ugaritic studies were still in their infancy, Mowinckel drew attention to possible Ugaritic influences on the Israelite writers only as an afterthought: "Neben diesem babylonisch-assyrischen Einfluss ist auch ein Kanaanäischer denkbar. Die Ras-Šhamra Funde haben gezeigt, dass die Phöniker (Amoriter) eine epische Dichtung gehabt haben, die ihren Stoff wohl nicht nur aus der Sagen und Heroenzeit genommen hat; so ist von einem sagenhaften Keret, König der Sidonier, von Nägäb und Zebulun die Rede."[32]

Even though Mowinckel cannot be considered an adherent of the "myth and ritual" school, the direct references in his study[33] prove that he was influenced by the principles underlying this method. He does not explicitly employ the term "pattern" which in the "myth and ritual" school signifies the idea of Israel's sharing in the cultural substance common to the Canaanites and the Mesopotamian peoples. But this idea does find expression in references to the "Thronbesteigungsfest" and its connections with the New Year Festival. Mowinckel also brings the *enuma eliš* into the discussion and adduces with approval Gunkel's attempt in *Schöpfung und Chaos* to trace in the biblical writings impressions of the primeval battle of the creator god against the deities that opposed him.

III

At this juncture some remarks concerning the development of the comparative method in biblical studies may be in order. Analogous to what was and to a degree still is the practice in other areas—history, sociology, anthropology, and ethnography—two main approaches can be distinguished in biblical research. On the one hand we encounter what Marc Bloch describes as "the comparative method on the grand scale."[34] In biblical studies it is still practiced by scholars who find resemblances between biblical traditions

---

32. Ibid., 149.
33. Ibid., 147ff.
34. M. Bloch, "Two Strategies in Comparison," *Comparative Perspectives: Theories and Methods* (ed. A. Etzioni and F. L. Dubow; Boston: Little, Brown & Co., 1970) 41.

and narrative motifs in other cultures[35] historically and geographically widely removed, leaning heavily, whether explicitly or implicitly, on the work of Sir James Frazer.[36] The following statement by A. B. Lord exemplifies this approach: "The foregoing examples of the structuring of non-narrative themes in Serbo-Croatian oral epic song may, I hope, suggest that the phenomenon of parallel pairs in the Old Testament is closely akin to them. If so, then the analogy to Southern Slavic oral traditional narrative poetry will not have been in vain."[37] Of a different scope and character is another type of comparative procedure which became prominent in biblical research in the wake of the momentous developments in Ancient Near Eastern archeology in the last century. Bloch defines this method as one "in which the units of comparison are societies that are geographic neighbors and historical contemporaries, constantly influenced by one another. During the historical development of such societies, they are subject to the same overall causes, just because they are so close together in time and space. Moreover, they have, in part at least, a common origin." This approach, characterized by M. J. Herskovitz as "the analysis of cultures lying within a given *historic stream*,"[38] seems the more promising since it adequately takes into account the aspects of historical and geographical proximity as well as general cultural affinity.[39]

In biblical studies this method gained ascendancy as a result of the rapid development of Ugaritic studies since the late thirties, which brought on a wave of comparative inquiries into the nature of biblical literature. The Ugaritic writings threw welcome light on the culture and the world of ideas of the Canaanites or at least of part of the autochthonous population of the area in which biblical Israel had settled. Thus this literature admirably answered the requirements of a comparative approach which deals with cultural parallels and the process of acculturation between societies that live in historical and geographical proximity. The linguistic affinity between Ugaritic and Biblical Hebrew appeared so significant as to cause H. L. Gins-

---

35. See S. Talmon, "The Comparative Method in Biblical Interpretation" (in this vol., pp. 11–49). In this context it should be pointed out that the ancient Egyptians did not produce an epic or epics.

36. J. Frazer, *The Golden Bough* (London: Macmillan, 1890); *Folklore in the Old Testament* (London: Macmillan, 1918).

37. A. B. Lord, "Formula and Non-Narrative Theme in South Slavic Oral Epic and the Old Testament," *Semeia* 5 (1976) 93–105.

38. After S. C. Thrupp, "Editorial," *Comparative Studies in Society and History* 1 (1958-59) 3.

39. See "The Comparative Method in Biblical Interpretation," in this vol., pp. 13–17.

berg to view the two as being made of one cloth.[40] The similarities of literary aspects, the palpable sediments of Ugaritic idioms, imagery, and cultic terminology in biblical writings made the new finds an ideal instrument for probing into antecedents of biblical literature in its present form and the early stages of their development, since Ugaritic literature had admittedly crystallized and been committed to writing centuries before Hebrew literature had taken shape.

Among the first to give a systematic direction to the collating of similarities of biblical with Ugaritic literature was Umberto Cassuto. Having assembled a veritable array of Hebrew parallels to counterparts in Ugaritic epic literature, he finally asked the same question Mowinckel had asked: "Did the ancient Israelites compose epic poems?"[41] It is of interest to note that in attempting to answer the query, Cassuto did not begin with an analysis of the biblical material itself as his predecessors, including Mowinckel, had done but rather opened his discussion with the remark: "Epic poetry which tells of the deeds of the gods and of the renowned heroes, appears among many peoples in the epoch of their youth."[42] Having started out along the lines of the comparative method on the "grand scale," Cassuto then reverts to the "historic stream" approach by observing that epic literature had also flourished among the immediate neighbors of ancient Israel, the outstanding examples stemming from Ugarit.

Notwithstanding the fact that Ugarit already lay in ruins when Israel arrived on the Canaanite scene, the propinquity of these two cultures is accounted for by the proximity between Ugarit and ancient Israel and is demonstrated by the numerous parallels which modern scholarship has brought to light.[43] Cassuto perceives that the explanation of a puzzling phenomenon, viz., the excellence of biblical literature from the very outset, may be found in the antecedence of Ugarit over Israel. Contrary to expectation biblical literature does not seem to have gone through a process of development. It appears to be totally devoid of ancillary stages of literary creativity. The biblical authors apparently never experiment with rudimentary techniques. They do not fumble in their employment. Instead they

40. H. L. Ginsberg, "The Ugaritic Texts and Textual Criticism," *JBL* 62 (1943) 109ff.
41. U. Cassuto, "The Israelite Epic," *Biblical and Oriental Studies* (trans. I. Abrahams; Jerusalem: Magnes, 1975) 2.69–109.
42. Ibid., 69.
43. See *Ras Shamra Parallels* (AnOr 49-51; Rome: Pontificium Institutum Biblicum, 1972–1981).

handle them from the beginning with the aplomb of craftsmen and masters of their art. Ugarit helps us understand this surprising circumstance: Israel, says Cassuto, had taken over from the Canaanites the achievements of their literati and thus was spared the customary growing pains. If that had been the case, we would indeed have reason to assume that the Israelites not only borrowed phraseology and imagery from their Canaanite precursors but also emulated their literary *Gattungen,* the most prominent of which was the "epic."

However, here a problem emerges. As was already mentioned, Cassuto is forced to admit that "in Biblical literature, epic poetry is not represented at all."[44] Furthermore he expressly rejects Arvid Bruno's aforementioned attempt to construe the books of Samuel and Kings as epics as well as the endeavor of Mowinckel and his predecessors to fathom the content and literary character of the ספר מלחמות ה' and the ספר הישר, and to reconstruct from them the national epic of ancient Israel. In spite of the apparent negative evidence, Cassuto nevertheless abides by his conviction, born of the comparative approach, that Israel did possess Hebrew epic songs, even though none such can be found in the present collection of canonical books, nor are they ever referred to directly.

His supposition is based on isolated bits of poetry and poetic phraseology interspersed throughout the biblical prose literature. In the account of the plagues (Exod 8:20 and 9:31–32), for example, Cassuto finds epic traces in expressions and imagery reminiscent of Canaanite epic language and archaic grammatical forms (e.g., Exod 8:20; cp. Ps 73:9); in mythological elements such as God's staff in the hand of Moses (Exod 4:2–17); and in the employment of formulaic language which is considered to typify epic literature.[45] Having assembled a good number of such isolated expressions, Cassuto presents them as evidence for the one-time existence of biblical epic songs. He further concludes that these songs had been handed down in writing, basing his claim on Exod 17:14, where Moses is bidden to write down in a book the curse against Amaleq, which to him, as to Caspari and Mowinckel, bears the imprint of "epic."[46]

---

44. Ibid., loc. cit.
45. Ibid., 74–80.
46. U. Cassuto, "The Beginning of Historiography among the Israelites," *Biblical and Oriental Studies* (trans. I. Abrahams; Jerusalem: Magnes, 1973) 1.7–16.

The evidence adduced certainly strengthens the case for the widely accepted idea that biblical Israel was imbued with elements of Ugaritic culture, most of which were borrowed from epic literature. It stands to reason that the Israelite authors knew Ugaritic-Canaanite epics in their entirety or at least sizeable portions of them. But it remains to be questioned whether from the collation of such clearly borrowed materials we may jump to the conclusion that they indicate the one-time existence of two original Hebrew epics, one of a cosmological and one of a historical nature as Cassuto opines.[47] The truth is that he was practically forced into making this assumption, propelled by his correct observation that biblical Israel could hardly be expected to have taken over the polytheistic literature of the Canaanites lock, stock and barrel. The antagonistic attitude of the biblical writers towards the pagan cult and ritual with which the Ugaritic epics are shot through simply rules out such a transfer. Therefore Cassuto reasons that remnants of epic literature which he recognizes in the biblical writings must perforce stem from original Hebrew epic poetry.

IV

At this stage of our survey, we once again confront the issue of methodology. Even the combined evidence marshalled by scholars from a scrutiny of biblical literature cannot really provide a sound basis for positing the existence of full-fledged Hebrew epic songs in the biblical period. All the evidence is circumstantial; it is based predominantly on inference from unproven observations about the assumed developmental process which national literatures generally underwent, especially the literatures of the Ancient Near East, including that of Ugarit.

The underlying or explicitly stated assumption that all literatures have produced epics in their early stages derives from generalizations which require further study and verification. They cannot be applied indiscriminately to specific cases such as Hebrew literature. Furthermore we have to ask ourselves the fundamental questions: "What makes an epic an epic?" and "What distinguishes the epic from other forms of narrative literature which

47. Proceeding along similar lines N. M. Sarna concludes that: "The present narrative framework [of Job] is directly derived from an ancient epic of Job" ("Epic Substratum in the Book of Job," *JBL* 76 [1957] 13–25).

appear to exhibit 'epic-type' features?" and "On the strength of what criteria can the classical and the late Serbian epic, the medieval and the ancient Mesopotamian all be subsumed under one and the same *Gattung?*"[48] We still lack a clear circumscription and definition of the "epic" as a specific *Gattung,* both in the realm of literature generally and with respect to biblical literature specifically. The various proposals that have been put forward constitute steps in the right direction[49] but have not as yet accurately defined a battery of criteria by which to decide methodically whether to ascribe a given piece of writing to the epic *Gattung,* so much so that P. Merchant concludes despairingly that "the word 'epic' will perhaps never quite be defined."[50] There can be no doubt that in sundry strands of biblical literature (narrative portions, historiographies, Psalms, and even prophetic writings), one encounters qualities which often are taken to be characteristic of the epic genre: rhythm, parallelistic structure, and formulaic language. However these can also be found in literary genres to which the designation "epic" cannot be applied. The epic is not a clear-cut literary form which can be identified sufficiently by a given number of techniques, as suggested by Whallon.[51] It is, says M. Abrams correctly, "a family with variable physionomic similarities rather than a strictly definable genre."[52]

Returning to the immediate issue on hand, it should be stated that the quest for a biblical epic cannot be conducted in isolation from the various other *Gattungen* in which ancient Hebrew literary creativity expressed itself. Since, as the foregoing survey has shown, epics or even parts of epics cannot be identified in the biblical books without having recourse to rather strenuous exercises in exegesis and conjectural reconstruction, the question must be raised whether the ancient Israelites did not in fact develop alternative literary forms to fulfill the functions which the epic fulfills in other na-

---

48. For an attempt to define the specific social milieu in which epics arise and which ancient Israel assumedly shared, see D. F. Rauber, "Observations on Biblical Epic" (*Genre* 3 [1970] 318–39).

49. For recent attempts to arrive at some definitions, see, e.g., the publications of H. Jason ("The Genre in Oral Literature: An Attempt at Interpretation," *Temenos* 9 [1973] 156–60; "A Multidimensional Approach to Oral Literature," *Current Anthropology* 19 [1969] 413–26; *Ethnopoetry: Form, Content, Function* [Bonn: Linguistica Biblica, 1976]; "The Story about David and Goliath: Is it a Folk-Epic?" הספרות 23 [October 1976] 24–41 [Heb. with Eng. summary]).

50. P. Merchant, *The Epic* (London: Methuen, 1971) 93.

51. W. Whallon, *Formula, Character, and Context: Studies in Homeric, Old English, and Old Testament Poetry* (Cambridge, MA: Harvard University Press, 1969).

52. M. Abrams, *A Glossary of Literary Terms* (3d ed.; New York: Rinehart & Winston 1971) 51.

tional literatures. In this context attention should be drawn to the prominence of straightforward prose narration in the biblical books. The biblical prose narratives have no rival among the literatures of the Ancient Near East, either in quantity or in artistic quality. The phenomenon is too striking to be considered incidental. The narratives, historical tales, and historiography proper—even residues of myth and cosmogony—found in the Bible in a wide array of books from various periods display a surprisingly high level of literary craftsmanship. This seems to indicate that the ancient Hebrew writers purposefully nurtured prose narration to take the place of the epic genre.[53] The reason for this substitution of one literary form for the other may be found in the intimate connection of the epic with the world of paganism in which it appears to have had a special standing in polytheistic cults.

In some pagan cults creation epics were periodically recited. This verbal and sometimes also dramatic reenactment of cosmic events was considered to have the effect of renewing the work of creation by way of sympathetic magic.[54] Likewise the epic account of heroic feats in the past was accorded the force of a charm by which the listener in the present could be imbued with the courage which had been the distinction of the ancient heroes. As the religion of Israel totally rejected polytheism with its rites and cultic paraphernalia, the practice of sorcery and witchcraft, so the Hebrew authors purged the epic song and the epic genre from their repertoire. These literary forms had become identified with paganism. The epic, the foremost literary concretization of the objectionable polytheistic worldview, fell into disrepute and never gained a foothold in Israelite letters.[55] Indeed some pre- and extra-Israelite epic elements did survive in biblical literature. These were correctly identified on the whole by scholars who turned their attention to the matter, not in the least by Mowinckel and Cassuto. It would seem that these features were permitted to infiltrate into non-epic genres of biblical literature, as in the course of time they had lost their tangible pagan import and had become neutralized. This appears to be the most logical explanation for the otherwise astonishing fact that the surviving remnants of epic terminology and epic songs are found preponderantly in biblical writings which

53. R. Alter (*The Art of Biblical Narrative* [London: Allen & Unwin, 1981] 25ff.) concurs with this statement and offers an "illustration of how the modalities of prose fiction operate in biblical narrative."
54. M. Eliade, *Patterns in Comparative Religion* (New York: Harper & Row, 1958) chap. 2.
55. See Alter, ibid.

stem from the divided monarchies when the prophets, the fanatic proponents of Yahwistic monotheism, were active.

The residues of epic literature and phraseology present, or assumedly present, in the Pentateuch and the book of Psalms should be similarly judged. The normative character of the Pentateuch (including its historical accounts) as the preeminent expression of the Yahwistic faith, and the profound association of the Psalm with the Yahwistic cult, foremost in the Temple of Jerusalem, suggest that these works could absorb such epic elements only after their original pagan edges had been blunted to the point that they became acceptable to the Israelite authors and their audiences alike. They constitute examples of phraseology whose original pagan-epic connotation had been blurred until it became indistinct or imperceptible and no longer evoked objection. Thus they were given a lease on life in Hebrew literature as mere figures of speech.[56] However, such random survivals should not be construed as proof of the one-time existence of a Hebrew epic proper, nor of a full-fledged acceptance of pagan epics by the ancient Israelites. Indeed the initial rejection of those epics seems to have been so thorough that the epic genre could never be reintegrated into the professional-technical apparatus of the Hebrew literati. It can be surmised that the closure of biblical literature against the epic was helped along by the progressive desuetude of this genre in the Semitic world from about the second quarter of the first millennium BCE[57] would coincide with the gradual abatement of Hebrew literary creativity of the First Temple Period, i.e., the monarchic age, which could have provided a fertile breeding ground for the epic genre. The postexilic literature of Israel developed under sociohistorical circumstances which were not conducive to the emergence or the adoption of either the heroic or the cosmic epic, not even in the form of a historic literary survival of bygone ages.

56. This issue requires a much fuller discussion which, however, cannot be given here. For the present see S. Talmon, "The Biblical Understanding of Creation" (*ExAuditu* 3 [1987] 101–5).

57. In opposition to this F. M. Cross maintains that "The religious currents of the sixth century were incredibly rich. The old Epic traditions of the Tetrateuch were reworked into a crystallized covenant theology by priestly traditionalists." (*Canaanite Myth*, 343 [see above, n. 5]); and "A New Conquest was described in terms of the language of the old conquest of Israel's Epic (e.g. Isaiah 34). A new Exodus was described in the language of the old Exodus, and with bold mythological language which dissolved both the old and new Exodus into the language of the battle of Yamm or Leviathan, dragon of chaos (e.g., Isa 51:9–11)" (*Canaanite Myth*, 345).

In summing up the case against the presumed existence of the "epic" in biblical literature not only in its present form but also in its precanonical antecedents, we would add one further general remark. The epic must be considered the specific expression of a congenial societal *Gestalt*.[58] A culture which does not present itself in a *Gestalt* conducive to the emergence of "epic," will not create, adopt, or preserve the epic genre. Its presence cannot be presumed merely on grounds of intellectual speculations but can only be empirically discerned in those societies which did in fact produce "epics" and in which this genre had a definite *Sitz im Leben*. It cannot and should not be reconstructed where its existence cannot be tangibly established. With reference to the epic as a specific literary genre, Israel presents to us a deep societal structure which is quite different from those of her neighbors.[59] The cosmological epic requires a rich background of myth for its development: Israel certainly lacked such a background, having rejected myth from the very outset.

The historical epic has been demonstrated to have flourished in societies which nurtured specific values and a clearly circumscribed societal ethos in which "individual honor and fame" played a central role. But as Rauber has shown, even during the days of the judges and the early kings— Israel's "heroic age"—that ethos and those values were foreign to Israelite society.[60] Comparativists generally and biblical comparativists especially should be encouraged to pay heed to differences between cultures and not to concentrate solely on similarities lest their particular structures become distorted. Adequate attention must be given to the interpretation of the dissimilarities from other cultures of the Ancient Near East, not only in the realm of religion, which made biblical civilization the peculiar and particular phenomenon it is. All in all our analysis leads us to answer in the negative the question posed by Mowinckel and echoed by Cassuto: "Hat es ein biblisches Nationalepos gegeben?" Biblical Israel did not produce, nor did it foster, the epic genre. Charles Conroy[61] comes to a similar conclusion in a

58. See S. C. Humphreys, "Transcendence and Intellectual Roles: The Ancient Greek Case," *Deadalus* 104 (1975) 91–118.

59. This difference is not sufficiently appreciated by D. Damrosch, who fully subscribes to the idea that myth and history merged in ancient Israel, resulting in an epic (*The Narrative Covenant: Transformations of Genre in the Growth of Biblical Literature* [San Francisco: Harper & Row, 1987] 32–87).

60. D. F. Rauber, *Genre* 3 (1970) 330ff. (see above, n. 48).

61. C. Conroy, "Hebrew Epic: Historical Notes and Critical Reflections," *Biblica* 61 (1980) 1–30.

lucid essay in which he surveys the state of the art. In conclusion he urges "a prudent reserve or, perhaps better, a temporary silence concerning the term 'Hebrew epic' in a discussion of the pre-JE state of Pentateuchal traditions."[62]

V

The negative answer leaves us with a new question. Did the ancient Israelite literati simply forgo the employment of the epic, thus robbing themselves of a prominent and effective vehicle for the dramatic depiction of cosmological and historical events, or did they compensate for the loss by innovating or especially developing other literary forms for the same purpose?[63]

We have already proposed above that the singular prominence of narration in biblical literature appears to be more than incidental and rather points to a concerted effort to make the "narrative" a substitute literary tool for the "epic." I fully concur with Schneidan's thesis that the total rejection of the pagan world view resulted in "the birth of a new kind of historicized fiction, moving steadily away from the motives and habits of the world of legend and myth,"[64] to which I add, "and epic." Biblical narration is indeed distinguished by certain characteristics which are usually adduced as signifiers of the epic: it is highly dramatic, using a style in which verbs, viz., words of action, outnumber words of description, nouns, adjectives, and adverbs. The dramatic effect is heightened by the closely circumscribed scene of action in respect to place as well as in respect to time.[65] This results in the stringing of vignettes when it comes to describing events that occurred over a protracted period or in different locations. The fully integrated "novel," a comprehensive piece of narration, is the exception rather than the rule. Thus the biblical narrative is admirably adjusted to the purpose of

---

62. See further J. Van Seters, *In Search of History: Historiography in the Ancient World and the Origins of Biblical History* (New Haven: Yale University Press, 1983) 224–27. For a different view, see L. M. Pakodzy, "Zur Frage" (above, n. 4).

63. Neither Conroy nor van Seters considers this question at all.

64. H. Schneidau, *Sacred Discontent* (Baton Rouge, LA: Louisiana State University Press, 1977) 215, after R. Alter, *The Art of Biblical Narrative*, 25ff. (see above, n. 53).

65. See S. Talmon, דרכי הסיפור במקרא (Jerusalem: Hebrew University, 1965) 50–69; "The Presentaion of Synchroneity and Simultaneity," in this volume, pp. 112–33.

recording events in lively fashion, just as is the epic. However being conceived in straightforward prose style and therefore devoid of "poetic" features which characterize the epic (such as *parallelismus membrorum* which makes for a certain rhythm), the narrative or novel is not suited for recitation in a cultic setting for which rhythm and "poetic-mythical" language appear to be a *sine qua non*.

The rejection of the epic and the unsuitability of narrative for employment in the cult created a void which called for amends, although the need was probably less pressing in the Israelite worship than it would have been in the pagan cults. The Israelite sacrificial service was distinguished, in the words of Y. Kaufmann, by the "holy silence" which reigned in the sanctuary.[66] Although some verbal accompaniment of the sacrificial acts was without doubt the norm, it never crystallized into a full-fledged liturgy of any kind and was considered secondary to sacrifice. This assumption is buttressed by the fact that biblical literature does not exhibit any definite "order of prayer," breviaries, or even any fixed prayer texts. We also note an almost complete absence of prayer legislation, which is further accentuated by the abundance of laws and statutes pertaining to sacrifices of various sorts found in all legislative codices and literary strata in the Bible. All this leads to the conclusion that biblical Israel had not instituted "prayer service," at least not until the later stages of the Second Temple Period.[67]

However it still remains true that we find in the Bible verbalized expressions of reverence which were a constitutive though secondary element of public and possibly also of private worship: psalms, incantations, and recitations of God's mighty deeds in history and cosmogony. As said, it stands to reason that these recitations had lost much if not all of the coercive force with respect to the deity with which they are imbued in pagan-polytheistic cults. There the underlying belief in the efficacy of sympathetic magic makes the worshiper expect that prayer and incantation would directly affect the gods and make them react favorably to his needs and requests.

Having discarded magic and having rejected the literary genre in which the pagan conception of the man-god relationship was principally expressed, viz., the epic, ancient Israel was hard-pressed to devise new literary forms to

66. Kaufmann, *History*, 2/1.476–77 (see above, n. 15).
67. For a fuller treatment of this issue, see S. Talmon, "The Emergence of Institutionalized Prayer in Israel in Light of Qumran Literature" (*WQW*, 200–243).

fill the resultant void in the established pattern of worship. Like their pagan counterparts, the Hebrew writers were well aware of man's urge to recount God's mighty deeds in thankful recognition. At the same time the retrospective account of God's acts in history gave recurring expression to the basis of the covenant between God and his people and constituted a request that God would work again such acts of succor and salvation in the present time. These rosters of divine interventions in the past (predominantly in Israel's history but also pertaining to creation and the cosmos) were couched in what appears to be a new, particularly biblical genre the "historiographical psalm." To the best of my knowledge this *Gattung* has not been identified as such. The songs, which in my consideration represent it, were usually subsumed under some other more widely attested genre. This type of the "historical"[68] or preferably "historiographical psalm" is best recognized in the cluster of Psalms 105, 106, and 107:1–22, which on the strength of the opening formulae "Give the Lord thanks and invoke him by name" (Psalm 105) and "It is good to give thanks to the Lord" (Psalms 106 and 107), are considered Thanksgiving Psalms of the "Hallel" type[69] or are defined separately as "hymn,"[70] "penitential prayer,"[71] "national confessions of sins,"[72] or "Lehr und Trost-Psalmen."[73] Others have highlighted the "didactic" element in these psalms, notwithstanding their "hymnal" character. Mowinckel,[74] like others, points out the historic content of these psalms and draws special attention to the circumstance that the Chronicler included Ps 105:1–15 and 106:47–48 together with 96:1b–13a in the psalm which he inserted in his compilation (1 Chronicles 16). Mowinckel explains this selective quotation by the employment of this composition in the cult, "on one of the days of the harvest festival, or on some festal day on a special historic

---

68. M. Dahood, *Psalms III* (AB 17A; Garden City, NY: Doubleday, 1970) 51.
69. C. A. Briggs, *The Book of Psalms* (ICC 2; Edinburgh: Clark, 1925) 330–331, 343, 348, 358; W. O. E. Oesterley, *The Psalms* (New York: Macmillan, 1939) 2.445, 452.
70. M. Buttenwieser, *The Psalms* (Reprint; New York: Ktav, 1969) 805; M. Dahood *Psalms III* (see above, n. 68) 80; G. Quell, *Das kultische Problem der Psalmen* (BWAT N. S. 11; Berlin: Kohlhammer, 1926) 100, 108.
71. Buttenwieser, *The Psalms*, 823; H. Graetz, *Kritischer Commentar zu den Psalmen* (Breslau: Schottlaender, 1883) 2.565.
72. Dahood, *Psalms* (see above, n. 68) 67.
73. Graetz, *Psalmen* (see above, n. 71) 558.
74. S. Mowinckel, *The Psalms in Israel's Worship* (trans. D. R. Ap-Thomas; Oxford: Blackwell, 1962) 2.112.

occasion," since the people felt the urge to express what they wanted to say "by choosing and putting together parts of canonical psalms."[75]

Mowinckel's attempt to discover the *Sitz im Leben* of these psalms in specific festivals, especially of the harvest periods, which is in line with his approach generally, can be questioned. However this issue does not require discussion in the present context. What is important is his correct observation that the historic content of this or another psalm made it suitable for employment in Israelite worship. Yet neither he nor any other scholar considered the proposition that the "historiographical" psalm was fostered by the Hebrew writers as a convenient substitute for the pagan epic to take its place in the Israelite cult. In addition to the above-mentioned psalms (105, 106, 107), others such as Psalm 78 also fulfill this task. Their main thrust lies in the enumeration or recitation of historic events which are recorded in prose style in diverse historiographies. The psalmodic form adjusts such rosters to the requirements of the cultic setting, without being concerned that the historical account is also intended to serve didactic purposes, is meant as a "penitential prayer," or has a wisdom character like Psalm 78 which is justifiably compared with the "Song of Moses" (Deuteronomy 32).

I am quite aware of the fact that the proposed existence of the genre "historiographical psalm" calls for further investigation, and its definition requires refinement, but I would nevertheless maintain that together with the biblical prose narrative the historiographical psalm took the place of the epic which had been purged from the repertoire of the biblical writers.[76]

---

75. Ibid., 200.
76. This is a much deeper and more incisive process than the one envisaged by Cross, who opines that "The festal context of the latter [i.e., the "ritual conquest"] with its celebration on Zion in the royal cultus involves the transformation of the theme of the old hymns and the Epic" (*Canaanite Myth*, 174 [see above, n. 5]).

THE PRESENTATION OF SYNCHRONEITY AND SIMULTANEITY IN BIBLICAL NARRATIVE

I

The biblical author, not unlike any other author, found himself in a predicament when he faced the logistic problem of how to present intelligibly two episodes which occurred synchronously under different circumstances and in different geographical settings, but nonetheless were intimately bound up with each other with regard to the historical or dramatic events portrayed in them. Recording such episodes one after the other would result in the impression that they came about in a chronological sequence and not simultaneously. Such an arrangement would thus distort the "historical truth."

Several techniques suggest themselves for escaping from this predicament. One was adopted by the author of the book of Kings. He achieved the dovetailed presentation of synchronous events which happened in the southern kingdom on the one hand and in the northern kingdom on the other by having recourse to a system of staggered cross-references by which important events in the history of the one are related to specific dates in the chronology of the other. This well-known procedure does not require detailed discussion. A few examples will suffice to illustrate this strategy: "In the twentieth year of the reign of Jeroboam king of Israel, Asa became king of Judah (1 Kgs 15:9). . . . Nadab son of Jeroboam became king of Israel in the second year of Asa king of Judah" (15:25). Or "It was in the thirty-first year of Asa king of Judah that Omri became king of Israel (16:23). . . . Ahab son of Omri became king of Israel in the thirty-eighth year of Asa king of Judah" (16:29), etc.

Such a procedure is applicable only when the author can make use of a fairly well-defined chronological system such as can be applied in the portrayal of the period of the monarchy. It cannot work at all with regard to stretches of time for which this basic requirement is lacking, as, e.g., for the Period of the Judges, and consequently also the book of Judges. Here we can observe the distorting impact of a simplistic juxtaposition of historical events which in fact were not consecutive, but rather were concurrent in some cases and partially overlapping in others. The author's failure, or possibly his inability to capture the variety of chronological relationships between the recorded facts in a proper historiographical schema results in the reader's almost automatically and mechanically adding up the sum total of years given for the individual judges. It follows that the period of the judges becomes enlarged to an extent which cannot be accommodated in any chronological framework between the conquest of Canaan and the establishment of the monarchy. The sum total of the figures given for the individual judges adds up to 390 or 410 years, depending on whether the traditions concerning the rule of Samson (Judges 15–16) are considered two parallel accounts of his one term of office which lasted "20 years," or whether (and this is the less likely interpretation) they are taken to represent two consecutive terms of office, each of 20 years' duration (15:20 and 16:31). Samson's judgeship would thus add up to 40 years. In either case neither a period of 410 nor of 390 years can be accommodated within the time span of 150, or at the most 200, years which independent chronological calculations based on biblical and extrabiblical data permit us to give to the era of the judges.

A similar situation seems to obtain in the list of kings who ruled in Edom prior to the emergence of a monarchical regime in Israel (Gen 36:31–39; 1 Chr 1:43–51a). The term שופט used in the book of Judges, and the term מלך in the Edomite list, are in fact synonymous and do not reflect different political concepts and institutions.[1] The fact that not one of these "kings" is the son of his predecessor, and no two ruled in the same city, proves decisively that the roster does not reflect a line of successive rulers hailing from one dynasty. It can be safely concluded that, as is the case with the Israelite "judges," the terms of office of some of the Edomite "kings" at least in part run contemporaneously. This circumstance is altogether obliterated by the present arrangement which lines them up one after the other: "Bela son of Beor reigned in Edom, and his city was named Dinhabah. Bela died, and in

---

1.   See S. Talmon, "'In Those Days There Was No King in Israel,'—Judges 18–21," *KCC*, 39–52; "Kingship and the Ideology of the State," *KCC*, 26–31.

his stead[2] reigned Joab son of Zerah of Bozrah. When Joab died, Husham of Teman reigned in his stead," etc. (Gen 36:31ff.).

Another way by which an author or an arranger of an extensive historical narrative could avoid the pitfalls inherent in the consecutive stringing of synchronous events was to make their overlapping become visually apparent by recording the facts in parallel columns. The columns would be separately consecutive for a sequence of synchronous occurrences and would become intermittent for the presentation of partially overlapping or altogether diachronic events. Such an arrangement would invite the reader to divide his attention but at the same time would help him appreciate the proper diachronic or synchronous relations between the events recorded. This technique, however, could be employed only in written records and could not be used in oral presentation.

The simple principle of dividing a page or the surface of any writing material was indeed known in the Ancient Near East, where it was successfully employed in bilingual or trilingual inscriptions. But to the best of my knowledge, it was never applied in narrative or historiographical literature. For the oral or written presentation of synchronous events, biblical authors, revisors, and redactors required an uncomplicated technique which would permit narration to flow smoothly and would not destroy the dramatic effect of biblical storytelling by thoroughly chopping up its internal coherence. The simplest method by which to indicate synchroneity is the employment of technical terms or special syntactical structures, such as: בעת ההיא (e.g., Judg 14:4, et al.); ויהי בעת coupled with an infinite verb (e.g., 1 Sam 18:19); ויהי ב... with an infinite (e.g., Judg 13:20; 1 Sam 4:18) or a finite verb (e.g., 1 Sam 7:10); ויהי כאשר with a finite verb (e.g., Gen 27:30); עד between two finite or infinite verbs (e.g., Judg 3:26; 1 Sam 14:19); והנה preceding or coming between two verbs (e.g., Judg 4:22; 19:22; 1 Sam 9:14); et sim.

A somewhat more artistic device for expressing the synchroneity of two events in a "linear" text is the $yqtl$-qtl syntactical structure. In essence it is based on the employment of an identical verb in the parallel cola of one sentence, instead of the prevalent procedure of having two synonymous or antinomous verbs serve in the two half-verses. In such instances the biblical writers, apparently following a practice which had also served Ugaritic

---

2. The translation adopted by the NEB, "he was succeeded by," appears to imply uninterrupted direct continuity and thus may lead to a mistaken interpretation of the Edomite political system.

authors, would achieve variation in the parallelistic structure by using in the first colon the verb in the imperfect with consecutive *waw (w-yqtl)* preceding the substantive and in the second the perfect form *(qtl)* following upon the substantive.[3] This arrangement can be found not only in the adjacent cola of one verse, but also in "distant parallels." It is usually taken to serve as a means for achieving a measure of diversity in the otherwise reiterative parallelism.[4] However, it would appear that when the two verbal forms in the *yqtl-qtl* structure refer to two different events, they often are also intended to express synchroneity. The following examples will suffice to illustrate the point.

In the story of the concubine at Gibeah (Judges 19), the author makes the arrival of the Levite (with his servant and his פילגש)[5] coincide with the return of the "old man" who arrived in Gibeah from the fields at nightfall by having recourse to the *yqtl-qtl* pattern:

Judg 19:15: ויבא וישב ברחוב העיר
19:16: והנה איש זקן בא מן מעשהו מן השדה

This structure is intended to put in relief the simultaneous occurrence of the two events which on the surface are not related but in actual fact constitute together the basis for the ensuing dramatic developments.

In the Cain and Abel episode, the enmity of the elder brother was aroused by God's rejection of his sacrifice and acceptance of his younger brother's. The Hebrew text puts into relief the synchroneity of the two events, which possibly occurred in different locations, by reporting them in the *yqtl-qtl* pattern, which cannot be rendered adequately in English because of the lack of the required formal equivalents.

Gen 4:3–5: ויבא קין מפרי האדמה מנחה לה׳
והבל הביא גם הוא מבכרות צאנו ומחלבהן
וישע ה׳ אל הבל ואל מנחתו
ואל קין ואל מנחתו לא שעה

3. See, e.g., Gen 1:5; 15:10; 48:14; Judg 7:25; 11:17; 20:32; 1 Sam 13:2; 1 Kgs 2:35; Esth 2:18, et al.
4. See S. Talmon, "The Textual Study of the Bible: A New Outlook," *QHBT,* 9–26 and bibliography adduced there.
5. LXX^AB: καὶ εἰσῆλθον.

Contrary to the masoretic division of the passage into three verses, we should divide it into only two, each containing three cola, arranged in chiastic parallelism, A=B=C ‖ C=B=A, with additional internal chiasms within the cola:

ויבא קין ‖ הבל הביא
וישע ה׳ ‖ לא שעה

The dovetailing presentation of the events, combined with the *yqṭl-qṭl* structure, implies the simultaneity of the separate actions of Cain and Abel and of God's concomitant responses.

At times the *yqṭl-qṭl* structure also suggests simultaneity by employing different verbs, but verbs which give expression to one and the same notion. The following example may serve as an illustration of this pattern. In the report of Jeroboam ben Nabat's cult and calendar reform,[6] the book of Kings records that Jeroboam made "two calves of gold. . . . One he set up at Bethel, and the other he put at Dan" (1 Kgs 12:28–29), viz., in the *Grenzheiligtümer* at the southern and northern borders of his newly constituted realm. The simultaneity of these actions which occurred in two geographically different locations is highlighted by the employment of one verb, שים, in the *yqṭl* and the other, נתן in the *qṭl* form:

1 Kgs 12:29:   וישם את האחד בבית אל ואת האחד נתן בדן

Although שים and נתן are etymologically distinct, a large number of idioms and parallel passages prove that biblical authors considered these verbs to be pragmatically interchangeable.[7] Next to שים שלום (Num 6:26), we find נתן שלום (Lev 26:6; cp. Num 25:12; Hag 2:9; 1 Chr 22:9); next to אשימך שממה (Isa 43:16), הנותן בים דרך (Ezek 35:9; cp. 5:14); שממות עולם אתנך (Jer 6:8), אף אשים במדבר דרך (Isa 43:19). In parallelismus membrorum: גביר שמתיו לך שום תשים עליך מלך . . . לא תוכל לתת עליך (Gen 27:37); ואת כל אחיו נתתי לו לעבדים ‖

---

6.   See S. Talmon, "The Cult and Calendar Reform of Jeroboam I," *KCC*, 113–39.

7.   The same pertains to the Greek verbs τιθήναι and διδόναι, by which שים and נתן are rendered in the LXX. The phenomenon requires a more detailed discussion than can be offered here. For the present, see S. Talmon, "The Textual Study of the Bible" (above, n. 4) 340–43.

איש נכרי (Deut 17:15); ‏ותן לו תודה‏ . . . ‏בני שים נא כבוד לה׳‏ (Josh 7:19), et sim. We shall have occasion to adduce below further examples of this technique.

II

At this juncture a discussion of what H. W. Wiener termed "resumptive repetition" appears to be in order. Wiener first employed the term in his attempt to separate and delineate two historical accounts which, in his view, were interwoven in the present complex Judg 2:11–1 Kgs 2:46.[8] He describes the function of the "resumptive repetition" thus: "An important formal trace of compilation which meets us in many of the O. T. narratives gives useful help in the work of disentangling the early material. It may be called the practice of resumptive repetition. When an editor desired to incorporate something, he frequently inserted it, and then resumed the original narrative, repeating the last sentence before the break with more or less accuracy. Much was presented in this way that in our time would be placed in footnotes. Sometimes, however, the adoption of this method is equivalent to saying, 'According to another source the course of events was as follows.'" [9]

Curt Kuhl took up Wiener's idea after almost a quarter of a century in a short paper entitled "Die 'Wiederaufnahme—ein literarkritisches Prinzip?"[10] Kuhl elaborated on Wiener's definition and collected further instances of the *Wiederaufnahme* (his German equivalent of the English "resumptive repetition"), preponderantly from the book of Ezekiel.[11] It would appear that Wiener's and Kuhl's treatment of the issue failed to make a deeper impact on the literary study of the Bible. References to the *Wiederaufnahme* in scholarly publications are not more numerous than those to the "resumptive

---

8. H. M. Wiener, *The Composition of Judges II 11 to 1 Kings II 46* (Leipzig: Hinrichs, 1929).
9. Ibid., 2.
10. It would appear that C. Kuhl subscribed to and emulated Wiener's idea (Kuhl, *ZAW* 64 [1952] 1–11) after having reviewed the latter's above-mentioned book (see ibid., p. 9, n. 1) in *TLZ* (54 [1929] col. 346). Kuhl also attempted to explain the textual expansion in the Greek of Dan 3:24 by this device. See his "Die drei Männer im Feuer" (BZAW 40 [1930] 163).
11. The "Wiederaufnahme" or "resumptive repetition" is found in practically all books of the Bible but is more prevalent in narrative and historiographical literature (Kuhl, *ZAW* 64 [1952] 3).

repetition."[12] Scholars apparently were not convinced that the above technique indeed was a *literarkritisches Prinzip* and not just a haphazard occurrence in some texts which could be ascribed to this or that editor. The failure of Wiener and Kuhl to achieve adequate recognition of the value of the resumptive repetition for an objective analysis of a fair number of diverse biblical texts may be attributed in part to their overly sketchy and overly restricted presentation of the case. Both conceived of the resumptive repetition exclusively as a tool used by "compilers" for combining two, or possibly more, originally independent narrative complexes, i.e., as a technique which pertains to the secondary stage of "inlibration."[13] They considered it a most valuable aid for detecting in the present literary weave of a biblical book or literary unit the seams which disclose the joining together of diverse "sources," or a secondary stitching into the basic fabric of additional materials which post fact had come to the attention of the "editor." We shall presently attempt to show that by defining the resumptive repetition or *Wiederaufnahme* exclusively as a technique pertaining to editorship, an entirely different dimension of this device remains unobserved, namely its application to the structuring and the analysis of a narrative which relates two or more events synchronously occurring in different locales.[14]

It should be stressed that it is precisely this distinction (between viewing the resumptive repetition as an "editor's" rather than an "author's" technique) which marks the difference between modern scholars and some traditional Jewish exegetes who preceded Wiener and Kuhl in the discernment of this device. In the discussion of some biblical narrative texts, medieval commentators, e.g., Shelomo Yitzhaki (Rashi),[15] Nachmanides, Abarbanel, Bekhor Shor,[16] and possibly others, already remarked on this technique and even defined it in terms which are surprisingly similar to, even identical

---

12. One of the few exceptions is I. L. Seeligmann ("Hebräische Erzählung und biblische Geschichtsschreibung," *TZ* 18 [1962] 302–25).

13. I believe this term was only used orally by the late H. Wolfson to describe the assembling and integrating of traditions and sayings into a "book."

14. The pattern of "resumptive repetition" shows some similarity to the *inclusio*, although the two serve different literary purposes. See, for the present, S. Talmon and M. Fishbane, "Aspects of the Literary Structure of the Book of Ezekiel" (*Tarbiz* 42 [1972] 27–41 [Heb.]); idem, "The Structuring of Biblical Books—Studies in the Book of Ezekiel" (*ASTI* 15 [1976] 129–53); further Talmon, "'The Navel of the Earth' and the Comparative Method" (in this volume, pp. 50–75).

15. See, e.g., his comments on Josh 11:22 and 14:15.

16. See, e.g., their comments on Gen 9:32 and 10:10.

with, the ones to which Wiener and Kuhl had recourse. However, in their sometimes harmonistic attempts to explain an obvious discontinuity in narratives which they discussed, those traditional exegetes referred to the pattern *en passant,* and did not systematize their *ad hoc* exegetical insights. Thus they could not formulate an underlying principle.

Their procedure is exemplified by Rashi's comment on Exod 6:30, ויאמר משה לפני ה׳ הן אני ערל שפתים ואיך ישמע אלי פרעה:

> He [the author of Exodus] had made this statement previously [6:12] and repeated it here, ושנה עליו, because he had interrupted the subject matter [by splicing in the genealogical roster 6:14–25]. This is a customary device, וכך היא השיטה, like one who says, "Let's return to the former matters," נחזור אל הראשונות.

Similarly, Nachmanides[17] is seemingly baffled by the reiteration in Exod 1:1 of the introductory phrase, "These are the names of the Israelites who entered Egypt with Jacob," which here, as already in Gen 46:8, precedes a roster of Jacob's offspring. He correctly explains this circumstance as disclosing the writer's intention to link Gen 46:8–27 with Exod 1:1–5. By resuming in the latter passage the subject matter of the former, the text arches over the intervening account of Jacob's trek and sojourn in Egypt and the events which developed after his death (Gen 46:28–50:26), all of which deflect the reader's attention from the principal account. Nachmanides' comment runs as follows:

> He [i.e., the writer] *resumes* [sic, יחזור] where he had interrupted his presentation [namely in Gen 46:7], "He brought all his descendants to Egypt," [immediately] after which it is said [written], "These are the names of the Israelites who entered Egypt" [46:8]; and this very verse he *reiterates* here, ואותו הפסוק בעצמו הוא שהחזיר בכאן. Although these are *two books, the narrative* is composed of matters which [should] come one after the other. When he [i.e., the writer] referred there to Jacob's sons, he gave only a short account of [the fate of] his grandsons and all his offspring [46:9–27a] and *resumed* the main issue, והחזיר הכלל, when he said [46:27b], "Thus the house of Jacob numbered seventy when it entered Egypt" [cp. Exod 1:5a].

---

17. His commentary is quoted from the edition by H. D. Shewel (Jerusalem: Kiryah Ne'emanah, 1962).

The gist of Nachmanides' observation is that Jacob's genealogy should have been placed in the first chapter of Exodus, where it should come after either v. 5 or v. 6. When for unspecified reasons the list was appended to the account of Jacob's descent into Egypt (Gen 46:7), the arranger[18] of the Pentateuch (i.e., Moses) made sure to restore the correct historical perspective by again picking up the thread in Exod 1:1 by means of a resumptive repetition.

Nachmanides then adduces another example to illustrate the biblical writers' manner of linking similar passages which in the present text of the Bible are disjointed but in essence are bound up in one narrative and/or historical-chronological sequence:

> The same pertains to [the end of] Chronicles [2 Chr 36:22–23] and the book of Ezra which continues [שהשלים] Chronicles, "In the first year of Cyrus king of Persia, when the word of the Lord spoken through Jeremiah was fulfilled, . . . thus spoke Cyrus king of Persia. . . ." He *reiterated* those two verses verbally, ואותם שני פסוקים בלשונם החזיר, at the beginning of the book of Ezra [1:1–2] to [re]connect the account. Since they are two books, he continued the report of the first [i.e., Chronicles], on the events which preceded the building of the temple, in the second [Ezra], which records what happened from the time of the building onwards. A similar situation obtains with regard to the two books Genesis and Exodus.

Nachmanides then expressly rejects Ibn Ezra's different interpretation of the Genesis-Exodus case and defines Rashi's remarks as "aggadic." Recognizing the homiletic value of those comments, Nachmanides still insists that "the connecting of the verses [Exod 1:1 and Gen 46:8] by a conjunctive *waw* must be explained as I have done."

Nachmanides actually perceived that the chronological order of events requires the book of Ezra to be placed after Chronicles. This arrangement is in fact extant in some Hebrew MSS which represent the main Palestinian masoretic tradition, as, e.g., the famous Aleppo Codex.[19]

18. I adapted this term for the biblical setting from the rabbinical reference to R. Meir as the arranger or compiler of the Mishnah, מסדר המשנה. It is meant to highlight the fact that the composers of the biblical books conceived of their task as being limited to putting together the material before them in an orderly fashion rather than rewriting it and impressing on it their personal stamp as an "editor" is wont to do. (See Talmon and Fishbane, *Tarbiz* 42 [1972] 27–41.)

19. A facsimile edition of this codex was published by the Hebrew University Bible Project. In the Aleppo Codex the book of Chronicles evidently opened the collection of the Hagiographa. Consequently, Chronicles was preserved when in 1947 the marauders who attacked the Aleppo synagogue threw the iron strongbox in which the Codex was kept into the fire. But only the parts closest to the walls of the box were destroyed by the intense heat. As a re-

In these, as in other instances,[20] Nachmanides is seemingly concerned with resumptive repetition as a structural and not as a stylistic device, viz., with an arranger's or editor's rather than with an author's technique. But we should bear in mind that such a distinction betrays a critical attitude to biblical literature which can in no way be taken to represent the view of a premodern exegete like Nachmanides. He would hardly differentiate between two types of writers who had had a hand in the creation and the preservation of biblical literature. Without necessarily subscribing to a traditional harmonistic conception of each separate canonical "book," we must nonetheless realize that a definite continuity of literary maxims and techniques appears to obtain in the various phases of the growth of the Bible, from creative authoring, compiling, revising, and editing, to the final stage of its textual transmission.[21] *Mutatis mutandis* these techniques were employed by diverse classes of literati who were active at various stages of the literary process. Against this background the resumptive repetition as an author's device can best be appreciated. The author safeguarded the linear continuity of the narration and at the same time permitted the listener or the reader to become aware of the synchroneity of the events related by cutting the thread of a story at a convenient (or even not quite so convenient) juncture. He would then splice in other matters of a different narrative character and resume the first account by means of repeating the verse, phrase, or even the word, at which the cutoff had occurred.

It should be stressed that we use the term "literary technique" comprehensively in reference to a stylistic feature which can be shown to have been widely employed by diverse biblical writers over an appreciable length of time and therefore cannot be viewed as an idiosyncrasy of one or another author. In consequence the discovery and circumscription of this and similar

sult the entire Pentateuch, with the exception of the last ten pages (Deut 28:17–34:12) and Ezra-Nehemiah, are now missing in the codex, since these books constituted its outer ends. (See I. Ben Zvi, "The Codex of Ben Asher," Textus 1 [1968] 1–17; S. Talmon, "Ezra-Nehemiah," IDBSup, 317–28.)

20. See further his comment on Gen 6:9–10. Nachmanides correctly says that the superscription "this is the genealogy of Noah" (v. 9a) should have been followed immediately by the reference to his sons in v. 10. The major part of v. 9, in which Noah's righteousness is described, constitutes an insert and is extraneous to the genealogical material. Therefore he (i.e., the biblical writer) "resumed [the issue], החזיר, with 'Noah begat three sons' because he had interrupted, הפסיק, his account to state that 'Noah was a righteous man,' etc., for which reason God bade him to [build] the ark."

21. See my remarks in QHBT, 327ff.

tools of literary craftsmanship may provide more objective means for tracing
the composition and literary history of a given unit or "book" and possibly of
the canon as a whole. This is true because their very technical nature is better suited to objectivity than appears to be the case with other historico-
critical methods, which to a degree are based on subjective criteria.

III

In the ensuing discussion no systematic distinction will be established,
but some broad lines of differentiation will be observed. Cases of complete
or almost complete concurrence within a restricted frame of time will be
considered under the heading "simultaneity"; when a more extensive time
element is involved which necessarily results in only a partial overlapping,
"synchroneity" or "contemporaneity" will be used.

Stylistic resumptive repetition differs from the above-mentioned specific
biblical terms which indicate that two events occurred at one and the same
time, such as בעת ההיא, ויהי כאשר, et sim., in that it does not involve a special technical term. It must, rather, be considered a means of bringing the
synchroneity of events to the reader's attention by indicators which are woven in the very fabric of the narrative. In analyzing the actual utilization of
this device, I shall present some of the examples, as it were, "in reverse,"
first recording the repetition and then linking it back to the "temporary"
break in the narrative which it is intended to resume.

(1) The first case to be studied involves the contemporaneity of events
which occurred in altogether different geographical settings.

Gen 39:1:	ויוסף הורד מצרימה ויקנהו פוטיפר סריס[22] פרעה שר הטבחים איש
	מצרי מיד הישמעאלים אשר הורדהו שמה
37:36:	והמדנים מכרו אתו אל מצרים לפוטיפר סריס פרעה שר הטבחים

22. The prevalent translation "eunuch" (NEB), "eunuqe" (SB), which follows the Greek
σπάδοντι φαραω, is not borne out by the connotations of סריס in Hebrew or cognate
languages and introduces a completely unwarranted nuance into the narrative under
review. The Aramaic translations render it correctly, רבא דפרעה, followed by the
Einheitsübersetzung—"Hofbeamter."

122

Seemingly bracketed by the doubled reference to the sale of Joseph is the independent and self-contained tale of Judah and Tamar, which takes up the whole of chapter 38.[23]

The splicing of the Judah-Tamar episode into the Joseph cycle was already discerned in the Midrash and is regarded there as indicative of similarities and dissimilarities in the fate of Judah and Joseph, the eponyms of the two future rival kingdoms, Ephraim and Judah.[24] Some medieval commentators recognized the fact that an issue of chronological sequence was involved. Thus Rashi (ad Gen 39:1): "[The writer] returns [here] to the preceding story [of Joseph] which he had interrupted in order to link Judah's 'descent' [38:1] with the sale of Joseph, thus to explain that because of this misdeed [his brothers] brought him [Judah] down from his greatness [or seniority]." Seforno (ad 38:1) states more explicitly that the two events were synchronous, whereas Abarbanel (ad loc.) has the sale of Joseph precede "Judah's descent." The clearest grasp of the chronological difficulties involved is that of Ibn Ezra (ad loc.), who takes the Judah-Tamar episode to have preceded the sale of Joseph because the span of time presupposed in it cannot be compressed into the 22 years which elapsed between the sale of Joseph and Jacob's trek to Egypt (Gen 46:1ff.). By having recourse to the method of cutting the sale story at Gen 37:36 and resuming it at 39:1 after the insertion of chapter 38, the author (or possibly the arranger of the book of Genesis) escapes the pitfall of deferring the presentation of the Judah-Tamar episode until after the completion of the Joseph cycle, an arrangement which would have thrown his account out of kilter, chronologically speaking.

The two bracketing verses are not completely identical. However, the differences are well within the acceptable limits of stylistic-textual variation. The clause in 37:36 may be considered a compressed version of its counterpart in 39:1, or vice versa, the latter an expanded version of the former. One further observes a partial inversion of components in the two verses

23. Both the masoretic section system and the chapter division correctly identify the Judah-Tamar episode as a separate unit.

24. *Gen. Rab.* 85, 1 (ed. Theodor-Albeck, p. 1030, lines 1–3). It is worthy of remark that the well-thought-out structure of the Joseph cycle shows the recurrence of some aspects or motifs of the Judah-Tamar tale in the episode of Joseph and Potiphar's wife: both narratives revolve on an amorous affair of a not-quite-legitimate, or altogether illegitimate nature, between a Hebrew and a foreign woman, with the woman taking the initiative. In both cases the facts, or the alleged facts, are brought to light by the female protagonist who adduces as evidence personal effects which belong to the male, a staff and a seal in one instance and a garment in the other.

which almost amounts to "chiastic distant parallelism."[25] Viewed from the angle of biblical stylistics, the reference to "Ishmaelites" in 37:36 as against the mention of "Midianites" in 39:1 is but an instance of legitimate variation and should not be construed as proof that the redactor of Genesis has welded together different "strands" or "sources," as is widely held.[26] In the present context, as also in other settings,[27] the designations "Ishmaelites" and "Midianites" are devoid of any ethnic connotation but are coterminous, both being equivalent to "caravan traders."

(2) Our next example is a case of the "synchroneity" of two events which occurred in practically the same locale. 1 Samuel 18 is generally considered to be of a composite nature. While differing on details of analysis, commentators are agreed that vv. 17–28 should be deemed a unit which is set apart from the surrounding text on two counts: internally by subject matter, David's planned marriage with Saul's elder daughter Merab and his actually wedding the king's younger daughter Michal;[28] and structurally by the *Ringkomposition* or *inclusio,* viz., the reiteration of vv. 14–16 in vv. 28–29, which, however, can also be taken as a resumptive repetition. It appears that within the complex of vv. 17–27, the Merab story (vv. 17–19) should be separated from what follows (vv. 20–27). It may be further suggested that this latter block is composed of two parallel-running episodes: Michal's love for David, and Saul's planning to utilize his daughter's attachment to bring about David's death at the hand of the Philistines. The splicing of the narratives is achieved by splitting the Michal component and inserting the report on Saul's evil intentions between the resulting brackets:

25.　See *QHBT*, 358ff.

26.　The *Midr. Gen. Rab*, loc. cit., solved the apparent difficulty by harmonistically proposing that a series of sales had taken place: from the brothers to the Ishmaelites, from them to the Midianites, and from the latter to Potiphar.

27.　Cp., e.g., the Gideon narrative (Judges 6–8), in which the enemy of Israel is predominantly referred to as Midian. However, next to this designation there is the reading "Midian and Amalek" (Judg 6:3), which the LXX has preserved in 7:1 as well. In 8:10 the enemy is called בני קדם, and in 6:33 and 7:12 all three designations are present, מדין ועמלק ובני קדם, not necessarily as a result of conflation. See M. Anbar, "Changement des noms des tribus nomades d'un même événement" (*Biblica* 49 [1968] 221–32).

28.　The setting of the story is reminiscent of Jacob's marrying the two daughters of Laban, with an interesting inversion of circumstances.

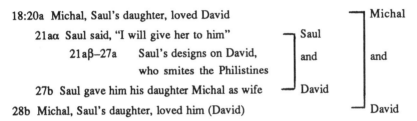

18:20a Michal, Saul's daughter, loved David

   21aα Saul said, "I will give her to him"

       21aβ–27a   Saul's designs on David,
                    who smites the Philistines

   27b Saul gave him his daughter Michal as wife

28b Michal, Saul's daughter, loved him (David)

The synchroneity of the two events is underlined by the application of the *yqṭl-qṭl* pattern in distant parallels.

1 Sam 18:20:   את דוד . . . ותאהב מיכל

18:28:   ומיכל[29] . . . אהבתהו

(3) Another court scene which displays a similar structure deals with the murder of David's son Amnon by his half brother Absalom (2 Sam 13:28–39). The author is at pains to present the concurrent events in Amnon's house where the murder took place and in the king's palace where David is informed of Absalom's deed and his ensuing flight. The required synchroneity is achieved by splitting the portrayal of Absalom's flight and sandwiching in the scene at David's court between the two parts.

13:28–33:   The report of Amnon's murder

34a: *(yqṭl)* ויברח אבשלום

34b–36:   David's other sons bring the news to their father in his palace

37a: *(qṭl)* ואבשלום ברח

(4) A somewhat similar two-strain narrative seems to be present in the Joseph story. The dramatic effect of Joseph's disclosing his true identity to his brothers is heightened by the reference to his crying out so loudly that his

---

29.   A detailed literary analysis of this episode may be found in J. P. Fokkelman, *Narrative Art and Poetry in the Books of Samuel* ([3 vols.; Assen/Maastricht: Van Gorcum, 1986–1990] 2.209–47).

lament was heard, not only in his chambers where he had closeted himself with his brothers, but also in the royal palace.

Gen 45:2: ויתן את קלו בבכי וישמעו מצרים וישמע בית פרעה

This had a twofold follow-up:

45:3–15: Joseph entreats his brothers to come to Egypt and sends word to his father to this effect.

Simultaneously

17–20: Pharaoh is filled with sympathy and permits, or rather commands, Joseph to arrange for his father's and brothers' transfer from Canaan to Egypt. This account is introduced by a variant reiteration of 45:2 in

45:16: והקל נשמע בית פרעה לאמר באו אחי יוסף

The resumptive repetition technique is especially helpful in the portrayal of battle scenes when the author wishes to inform the reader of activities going on "simultaneously" in the opposing camps, or in different parts of one and the same camp.

(5) A very persuasive instance of the second type can be found in the report of Saul's first battle against the Philistines. The story begins in 1 Sam 13:5 and is continued, after an insert (13:19–22), in chapter 14. While Saul and his men prepare for battle, Jonathan, the king's son, decides on a foray against the enemy, assisted only by his armor-bearer. The author must now present two connected but nevertheless separate matters: the scene in Saul's camp and Jonathan's act of bravery. He achieves the effect of simultaneity by cutting off the account of Jonathan's feat in 14:1a by means of a reference to the Philistines' post, מצב פלשתים אשר מעבר הלז, which the enemy had set up to hold the pass at Michmash (13:23b). The account is resumed in 14:6a with the synonymous reference to מצב הערלים האלה, and comes to an end in 14:15 (or possibly 14:16).

1 Sam 14:1: ויהי היום ויאמר יונתן בן שאול אל הנער נשא כליו
לכה ונעברה אל מצב פלשתים אשר מעבר הלז

Between the two parts of the Jonathan episode, 14:1 and 14:6–15 (16), the author inserted a vignette of Saul's camp, ושאול יושב בקצה הגבעה (14:2), which on its part is then continued in 14:17, ויאמר שאול לעם אשר אתו, after Jonathan's foray has come to an end.

As an aside the author adds an important piece of information, "But he [Jonathan] did not tell his father" (v. 1b; cp. vv. 24–30; 36–45), to prepare the reader for future developments, and a reference is made to the priest Ahijah son of Ahiṭuv (v. 3a) as a prolepsis of future matters which will be related in 14:17–19. The insert closes with an affirmation to the effect that none of the Israelites knew of Jonathan's departure either (v. 3b).

Another insert offers a description of the terrain which Jonathan has to cross (vv. 4–5). This elaboration does not bear directly on the issue of "simultaneity" but illustrates in its own way the literary mechanism of "splicing in."

After all this, the narrator returns to Jonathan and his aide-de-camp, resuming that episode by repeating the opening statement in 14:1 with only slight changes.[30]

| 1 Sam 14:6: | ויאמר יהונתן אל הנער נשא כליו |
| | לכה ונעברה אל מצב הערלים האלה |

Then the author gives a detailed account of Jonathan's bravery and of his victory over the Philistine outpost (vv. 6–15).

After that the other thread concerning Saul and his army is spun out (vv. 16–26). And finally, the Jonathan episode is resumed with a reference to Jonathan's ignorance of Saul's command that none should eat on that day (v. 27), which echoes the repeated assertion that neither Saul nor the people had knowledge of Jonathan's scheme and feat (vv. 1b and 3b). Chart A clearly shows that the interweaving of chronologically parallel strands is the dominant structural element in the overall account.

(6) A similar situation obtains in the report of Saul's last war against the Philistines. Here too the author intended to present the events as occurring

---

30. The fuller spelling יהונתן (cp. v. 8) is used here rather than the apocopated spelling יונתן which prevails throughout the pericope (chap. 14; cp. 13:22); the added designation בן שאול (14:1) is dropped and the Philistines' post is referred to by מצב הערלים (cp. 14:8, האנשים) rather than by מצב פלשתים (13:23; 14:1a, 4, 11) or המצב (14:15).

13:15^b	ויפקד שאול את העם הנמצאים עמו כשש מאות איש
13:16^a	ושאול ויונתן בנו והעם הנמצא עמם ישבים בגבע בנימן
13:16^b	ופלשתים <u>חנו במכמש</u>
13:17–18	ויצא **המשחית** <u>ממחנה</u> פלשתים שלשה ראשים
	הראש אחד יפנה אל דרך עפרה אל ארץ שועל
	והראש אחד יפנה דרך בית חרון
	והראש אחד יפנה דרך הגבול הנשקף על גי הצבעים המדברה
13:23	ויצא <u>מצב פלשתים</u> אל מעבר מכמש
14:1	ויאמר יונתן בן שאול אל הנער נשא כליו
	לכה ונעברה אל מצב פלשתים אשר מעבר הלז
14:2	ושאול יושב בקצה הגבעה
a	והעם אשר עמו כשש מאות איש
14:3 b	ואחיה בן אחטוב . . . בשלו נשא אפוד
14:4–5	ובין המעברות אשר בקש יונתן לעבר על מצב פלשתים
	שן הסלע מהעבר מזה ושן הסלע מהעבר מזה
	ושם האחד בוצץ ושם האחד סנה
	השן האחד מצוק מצפון מול מכמש והאחד מנגב מול גבע
14:6–14	ויאמר יהונתן אל הנער נשא כליו
	לכה ונעברה אל מצב הערלים האלה . . .
	ותהי המכה הראשנה אשר הכה יונתן ונשא כליו כעשרים איש
14:15	ותהי חרדה <u>במחנה</u> בשדה ובכל העם <u>המצב</u> **והמשחית** חרדו גם המה
14:16	ויראו הצפים לשאול בגבעת בנימן והנה ההמון נמוג וילך והלם
14:17 a	ויאמר שאול לעם אשר אתו
14:18 b	ויאמר שאול לאחיה הגישה ארון האלהים
14:46	ויעל שאול מאחרי פלשתים ופלשתים הלכו למקומם

CHART A — 1 SAMUEL 13–14

synchronously in the Philistine camp on the one hand and in the Israelite camp on the other. In 1 Sam 27:1–4 he had begun to relate David's flight before Saul into Philistine territory. Quite logically he linked this item with the story of David's vassalship to Achish, King of Gath (27:5–12; 28:2). Then he portrayed the problematic situation in which Achish and David find themselves when the Philistines march against Israel (29:1–11). Into this continuous account he inserted the self-contained Witch of Endor episode (28:5–25), thus signifying that it occurred at the very time of Achish's altercation with the other Philistine leaders over David's admissibility into their camp. The reiteration

1 Sam 28:1:	ויהי בימים ההם ויקבצו פלשתים את
	מחניהם לצבא להלחם בישראל
29:1:	ויקבצו פלשתים את כל מחניהם אפקה
	וישראל חנים בעין³¹ אשר ביזרעאל

circumscribes the inserted, chronologically parallel account of Saul's encounter with the Witch of Endor and reestablishes the disrupted continuity of the David-Achish tale.

In the case under consideration, the employment of the resumptive repetition pattern is especially sophisticated. We may speak here of a double-barrelled resumption, since 28:1 is also taken up in 31:1, which introduces the continuation of the report on the Israelite camp cut off in 28:25.[32] Significantly however, the resumption in 31:1 connects with the first half of 28:1, whereas the second half of that verse continues the David-Achish strand. The ensuing chart visually displays this pattern of insert and repetitive resumption occurring in the five-chapter narrative:

31. The MT reads בָּעַיִן without identifying the spring in question. Its widely accepted identification as ʿEn-ḥarod is based on the prominence of that water source in the tale of Gideon's battle against the Midianites (Judg 7:1ff.). However, the adjacency to the "Witch of Endor" episode bestows some merit on the LXX reading: Αενδωρ.

32. The additional reiteration in 1 Sam 28:4, את שאול ויקבץ בשונם ויחנו ויבאו פלשתים ויקבצו כל ישראל ויחנו בגלבע, was necessitated by the introduction of the mention of Samuel's death and Saul's abolition of witchcraft. This flashback serves at the same time as a prolepsis of central features in the witch of Endor episode (28:9, 11–20).

The Philistines		Israel	
28:1a	The Philistines make ready to attack Israel		
28:1b–2	Achish and David		
	28:3 Flashback and Prolepsis		
28:4a	Resumption: The Philistine camp	The Israelite camp	28:4b
		Saul's fright of the enemy	28:5–6
		Saul and Witch of Endor	28:7–25
29:1a	Resumption: The Philistine camp	The Israelite camp	29:1b
29:2–5	The Philistines and Achish		
29:6–10	Achish and David[33]		

(7) In the wake of his encounter with Achish, David left the Philistines, and the author again bisects his story to make room for the splicing in of two more synchronous events.

29:11b:	ופלשתים עלו יזרעאל
30:1–31:	David defeats the Amalekites
31:1a:	ופלשתים נלחמים בישראל
31:1b–7:	Saul's defeat and death, which occurred when David fought the Amalekites

This is another instance of the recurring employment of the repetitive resumption in the comprehensive framework of the composite narrative which runs from 27:1 to 31:7 (or possibly to 31:13).

(8) Some of the above examples show that the technique of repetitive resumption readily lends itself to intricate structuring in cases which require the integrated presentation of a variety of contemporaneous, synchronous or simultaneous events. The diverse aspects of the technique can be summarized, to a degree, by an analysis of the following instance. In 1 Samuel 2 the author was faced with the necessity of relating synchronous events in the house of Eli, in which on the one hand, Eli's sons were involved, and on the

33. For a full treatment of the literary structure of this passage, see Fokkelman, *Narrative Art,* 555–95 (see above, n. 29).

	Samuel	Eli's Sons	
2:11	וַיֵּלֶךְ אֶלְקָנָה הָרָמָתָה עַל בֵּיתוֹ וְהַנַּעַר הָיָה מְשָׁרֵת אֶת ה'	וּבְנֵי עֵלִי בְּנֵי בְלִיַּעַל לֹא יָדְעוּ אֶת ה'	2:12
2:18	וּשְׁמוּאֵל מְשָׁרֵת אֶת פְּנֵי ה' נַעַר חָגוּר אֵפוֹד בָּד	Here follows an account of their misbehavior. They violated established norms when people came to offer sacrifices.	2:13–17
2:19–21a	Additional information on Samuel's family.		
2:21b	וְהַנַּעַר שְׁמוּאֵל גָּדֵל עִם ה'		
2:26	וְהַנַּעַר שְׁמוּאֵל הֹלֵךְ וְגָדֵל וָטוֹב גַּם עִם ה' וְגַם עִם אֲנָשִׁים	Eli scolds his sons for their wrongdoings but to no avail.	2:22–25
3:1a[34]	וְהַנַּעַר שְׁמוּאֵל מְשָׁרֵת אֶת ה' לִפְנֵי עֵלִי	A divine messenger visits Eli, reprimands him for not keeping his sons under control, and prophesies a bad end for his house.	2:27–36

At this juncture the two narrative strands are interwoven: Samuel has a vision of the disastrous future of Eli's house. Eli compels him to reveal to him what he has seen (3:2–18).[35]

| 3:19a | וַיִּגְדַּל שְׁמוּאֵל וַה' הָיָה עִמּוֹ | | |

34. The relation between 3:1 and 2:26 on the one hand, and between 2:21 and 2:18 on the other, is marked by "distant chiasm."
35. This passage is most probably a doublet of the preceding announcement of the divine messenger who appeared to Eli.

CHART B — 1 SAMUEL 2–3

131

other hand, Samuel. The parallelism of the narratives makes the reader aware of the glaring disparity between these two parties. This disparity begins to show soon after Samuel's arrival at the Shiloh sanctuary and results in an overt competition over the inheritance of Eli's office as Israel's acknowledged leader. The introduction (1 Sam 2:11–12) thus serves concomitantly as a prolepsis of future developments which will occur at the end of Eli's days (chaps. 4–8). In the case under review, one finds several intersections in the narrative concerning Samuel. At such junctures parts of the report concerning Eli's sons are spliced in. The cutoff is always indicated by the repeated reference to Samuel's serving at the sanctuary and his growing steadily in stature. In order to enhance the visual impression of simultaneity or synchroneity, it appears advisable to arrange the two strands in parallel columns (see Chart B).

IV

We stated at the outset that the problem of presenting synchronous events in the linear medium of written literature, and similarly also in oral recitation, confronted not only biblical authors and arrangers, but constitutes a challenge to writers at all times. The technique of splicing a report and resuming the initial thread of a narrative after the insertion of a parallel tale certainly cannot be considered an exclusive achievement of the ancient Hebrew literati. Rather, it should be be viewed as a device which is intimately bound up with narrative literature per se. It presumably was born out of the limitations which inhere in the very character of storytelling and the restrictions which arise from the nature of the one-dimensional material on which tales are committed to writing. This problem can be solved satisfactorily only by a two- or three-dimensional presentation of synchronously or simultaneously unfolding events. As already said, one way of achieving the desired results would be writing down concurrent details in parallel columns. In essence this practice was actually known to Ancient Near Eastern writers and employed by them, as the phenomenon of the two-column arrangement of bilingual inscriptions proves. Another way of making sure that the simultaneity of concurrent events is preserved in their dramatic presentation is by having recourse to a divided or revolving stage. The very conception of putting on drama in this form and the "narrational" advantages that result from it may be likened, *mutatis mutandis,* to the literary device of "splicing and resuming." However, such means of "dramatized simultaneity" are likely to develop in cultures which, unlike biblical culture, are given to the visual presentation of epics and narratives. This strategy is fully exploited by modern play writers. In incipient forms it was known to classical and medieval dramatists and employed by them. However, these, and similar techniques, presumably were not available to the biblical writers or were not considered by them to be suited to their purposes.

The techniques of presenting synchroneity in Classical Greek literature were in fact traced in a most intricate fashion by Thaddaeus Zielinski.[36] Some type of "repetitive resumption" was probably known to Ancient Near Eastern (especially Ugaritic) authors, foremost in Mesopotamia, and possibly also in Egypt. From here arises the obvious question, whether biblical writers, whose intimate knowledge of (at least parts of) these literatures is beyond doubt, did in fact emulate scribal maxims and techniques forged by their non-Israelite predecessors and contemporaries. However this question requires a separate, detailed investigation.

---

36. See T. Zielinski's study, "Die Behandlung gleichzeitiger Ereignisse im antiken Epos" (*Philologus: Zeitschrift für das klassische Alterthum,* Supplementary Vol. [Leipzig, 1899/1901] 407–49). I was able to avail myself of only the first part of this study, and I do not know whether other parts were ever published. See also J. Gaisser, "Digression in the Iliad and the Odyssey" ([*Harvard Studies in Classical Philosophy* 73; Cambridge, MA: Harvard University Press, 1969] 1–43).

POLEMICS AND APOLOGY IN BIBLICAL HISTORIOGRAPHY: 2 KINGS 17:24–41

I

Scholars generally concur in the opinion that the report in 2 Kings 17 on the last days of the northern kingdom and the fate of the land after the conquest of Samaria by the Assyrians is to be distinguished from the present textual framework and should be viewed as a separate entity. Irrespective of its ascription to this or another author, redactor, or reviser, it is taken to be a self-contained unit. At the same time it is the common view that chapter 17 is not of one cloth but is constituted of sundry smaller components. The picture which emerges from its analysis poses several questions with regard to the identity of the authors of the diverse components, the identity of the compilers or editors whose hands had been at work in bringing about the present combination of texts and their aim. In some instances the wording of especially prominent verses and collocations also calls for an investigation. Some scholars apply to the analysis of the text under review (as to the entire book of Kings) the techniques which the sources school perfected in the study of the Pentateuch.[1] Others maintain that, being a work of historiography proper, the book of Kings should be subjected to different modes of critical analysis and that subsequently these modes could possibly be applied to the study of other biblical books, including the Pentateuch.

The criticism leveled against the established sources theory and a proposition for a novel approach were succinctly summarized by A. Jepsen: "The sources analysis of the book of Kings was carried out for too long in the shadow of the critical analysis of the Pentateuch. . . . From this resulted that no generally accepted uniform solution of the problems was found with respect to either the Pentateuch or the other books. . . . Should therefore not an attempt be made to approach the sources analysis from an altogether dif-

---

1. These matters are explicated in all major commentaries and do not require a discussion in detail. Some points will be brought under closer scrutiny.

ferent starting point . . . which might lead to clearer results?"[2] However, it appears that in practice, Jepsen's attempt and the conclusions at which he arrived are not superior to those his predecessors had presented.[3] They certainly did not settle the differences of opinion which prevail among commentators and exegetes regarding the structure and composition of 2 Kings 17.

It would seem that the lack of scholarly consensus on 2 Kings 17 results in part from an insufficiently accurate definition of the textual unit to be investigated and of its constituent subunits and from their identification in accord with established models. Moreover not enough thought is given to the processes of amalgamation by which the diverse components were combined and ultimately achieved their present literary form, i.e., to aspects of *Tradierungsgeschichte*. Lastly, with some noteworthy exceptions, only cursory attention was given to historical circumstances and religious convictions which facilitated the emergence of the above textual unit as preserved in the MT and which to some degree a close reading can still elicit from the text. Endeavoring to rectify some of these deficiencies, the ensuing discussion will be based on an analysis of the structure of 2 Kings 17, which aims at defining more succinctly the different literary subunits which can still be discerned in the present textual web, without having recourse to analytical techniques which had evoked Jepsen's criticism. Once the major components have been defined, I shall try to trace the process of their incorporation into the larger framework. I will then depict how chapter 17 as a whole was integrated into the book of Kings. It is hoped that this investigation will lead to the identification of the circles that formulated the text as handed down and to gauge the motivations of the tradents who infused the pericope into the book of Kings.

2. A. Jepsen: "Die Quellenanalyse des Königsbuches hat allzu lange im Schatten der Pentateuchkritik gestanden. . . . Die Folge ist, dass weder für den Pentateuch noch für die anderen Werke eine einhellige Lösung gefunden ist, die allgemein anerkannt wäre . . . Ob da nicht einmal der Versuch gemacht werden darf, überhaupt die alttestamentliche Quellenkritik von einem anderen Ausgangspunkt her anzupacken, der nicht so umstritten ist, und, wenn man von bisherigen Vorurteilen absieht, die sich aus der Pentateuchkritik ergaben, (vrgl. Noth, Überlieferungsgeschichtliche Studien, S. 52) eher zu einem klaren Ergebnis führt, das dann vielleicht auch für weitere Schriften Bedeutung hat" (*Die Quellen des Königbuches* [Halle: Niemeyer, 1953] 3).

3. Jepsen distinguishes the following strands in 2 Kings 17: 17:1—Anfangsnotiz; 17:3–6 (=18:9–11)—Notiz; 17:2, 21, 23b—Berichte über kultisches Verhalten; 17:7–20, 22, 23a, 34–40—RII (nebistische Redaktion); 17:24–33, 41—Späterer Zusatz (chronistischer Bericht).

II

The overall extent of the composite unit under review within the framework of 2 Kings can be fairly securely established by the discernment in it of the structuring technique known as *Wiederaufnahme*, or *resumptive repetition*. This technical device seemingly was employed by biblical authors and redactors (or arrangers) who were faced with the task of splicing into a comprehensive composition independent or semi-independent but nevertheless related narrative strands. The discernment of *resumptive repetition* proffers an objective criterion for determining still-discernible "joints" in the present fabric of a given text. Being a professional scribal technique, it was used by a wide range of biblical literati at various times. Thus it is bound to turn up in practically all biblical books. Its use can in no way be connected with any specific religious or ideational trends such as modern scholarship takes as constituting the warp and woof of the *literarhistorische Quellen*. The discernment of *Wiederaufnahme* in the analysis of a biblical composite text concerns purely literary-technical phenomena, in the restricted sense of the term, unaffected by ulterior considerations of a theological or ideational nature. The proper application of *Wiederaufnahme* analysis can provide a new point of departure in the investigation of the composition of biblical books, such as Jepsen attempted, although without achieving convincing results.

The *Wiederaufnahme* consists of the verbatim or nearly verbatim repetition of a word cluster, varying in range, at the two intersections at which an independent segment was wedged into a comprehensive textual framework. The main narrative thread, broken to accommodate the insert, is eventually resumed with what amounts to a textual echo of the phrase which immediately preceded the caesura. The technique was described and exemplified in detail by C. Kuhl, who introduced the term *Wiederaufnahme* into the historical-critical analysis of biblical literature, predominantly of the book of Ezekiel,[4] elaborating on Wiener's earlier application of the *resumptive repetition* to the structure of the book of Judges.[5] Neither of these scholars took note of their predecessors, such as Rashi, Nachmanides, and Abarbanel, who had entertained the very same notion, but without presenting it systemati-

---

4.   C. Kuhl, "'Die Wiederaufnahme'—ein literarkritisches Prinzip?" *ZAW* 64 (1952) 1–11.
5.   H. W. Wiener, *The Composition of Judges II 11 to Kings II 46* (Leipzig: Hinrich, 1929).

cally. In their exegesis of complex biblical passages, the medieval commentators sometimes used the formula חזר אל העניו הראשון, "he [the author] returned [after the insert] to the first matter at hand," employing in fact the precise Hebrew equivalent (חזר אל) of the terms *Wiederaufnahme* and *resumptive repetition*. It is to be deplored that neither the pioneering work of the medieval exegetes, nor that of modern scholars effected a more widespread attention to this ancient scribal device in the endeavor to clarify the processes which had been at work in the formation of the biblical books in their transmitted form.[6]

The isolation of *Wiederaufnahmen* in the attempt to determine the exact extent of the interpolation in 2 Kings 17 produces results which differ considerably from those generally proposed by commentators. Scholars mostly concur in the identification of chapter 17 in toto as a secondary interpolation into the already stabilized text of 2 Kings. In thus delineating the inserted unit, they were guided by the chapter division. However, here, as in many other instances, the reliability of the chapter division is open to criticism, since it does not tally with text analysis based on literary considerations.

Some scholars posit the caesura after 2 Kgs 17:6, defining the insert to extend from v. 7 to the end of the chapter (v. 41).[7] In this instance the suggested division was triggered by the apparent "annals-character" of 17:1–6, which agrees with an intrinsic feature of the book of Kings but is conspicuously absent from the "insert." While I concur with the view that the insert ends with 17:41, I propose that its true beginning is to be located at 17:5. The historical report which begins in 17:1 and breaks off after 17:4 is continued, after another lengthy insert (18:1–8), in 18:9a, as will yet be explicated. It is generally recognized that the ensuing account of Samaria's last days in 18:9b–11 is a parallel of the notation in 17:5–6, which exhibits, however, a significantly different wording in that it lacks the synchronisms of 18:9–10 (see below). The chronistic continuity of passages 17:1–4 and

---

6. For a somewhat more detailed discussion of *resumptive repetition* and further illustrations of its applications, see S. Talmon, "The Presentation of Synchroneity and Simultaneity in Biblical Narrative" (in this volume, pp. 112–33) and A. Berlin, *Poetics and Interpretation of Biblical Narrative* ([Sheffield: Almond, 1983] 126–29 and 43–82).

7. See commentaries.

18:9–11 (12)[8] and the partial overlap of 17:5–6 with 18:9–11 is made manifest by the following chart.[9]

18:9–11		17:1–6
		בשנת שתים עשרה לאחז מלך יהודה 1
		מלך הושע בן אלה בשמרון על ישראל
		תשע שנים
		ויעש הרע בעיני ה' 2
		רק לא כמלכי ישראל אשר היו לפניו
		עליו עלה שלמנאסר מלך אשור 3
		ויהי לו הושע עבד וישב לו מנחה
		וימצא מלך אשור בהושע קשר 4
		אשר שלח מלאכים אל סוא[10] מלך מצרים
		ולא העלה מנחה למלך אשור כשנה בשנה
		ויעצרהו מלך אשור ויאסרהו בית כלא
ויהי בשנה הרביעית למלך חזקיהו	9	
היא השנה השביעית להושע בן אלה מלך ישראל		
עלה שלמנאסר מלך אשור		ויעל מלך אשור בכל הארץ 5
על שמרון ויצר עליה		ויעל שמרון ויצר עליה שלש שנים
בשנת שש לחזקיהו וילכדה מקצה שלש שנים	10	
היא שנת תשע להושע מלך ישראל		בשנת התשיעית להושע 6
נלכדה שמרון		לכד מלך אשור את שמרון[11]
ויגל מלך אשור את ישראל אשורה	11	ויגל את ישראל אשורה
וינחם בחלח ובחבור נהר גוזן וערי מדי		וישב אתם בחלח ובחבור נהר גוזן וערי מדי

The synchronisms of Hoshea's reign with the regnal years of Ahaz and Hezekiah of Judah prove that 17:1–4 and 18:9–11 are constituent parts of the historiographical disposition which characterizes the book of Kings. And the references to the twelfth year of Ahaz in 17:1, as to Hezekiah's fourth and sixth regnal years in 18:9–10, leave no doubt that 18:9a indeed resumes the historical report on the last days of Samaria which began in 17:1 and broke off in 17:4, and brings it to its finale, the deportation of Israel (LXX: τὴν Σαμαρειαν) by the Assyrian king.

8. Verse 17:12 evidently is not part of the original chronistic notation, but rather a parenetic conclusion from the editor's hand, whether the Deuteronomist's or the Chronicler's (see below).

9. We are not concerned here with the doubtful accuracy of the dates and synchronisms recorded in these passages. For an overview of the problem and the solutions offered, see H. Tadmor, "Chronology" (*EncMiq* 4.245–310, esp. 286–89, 302).

10. The spuriousness of this personal name was proven by H. Goedicke ("The End of 'So, King of Egypt,'" *BASOR* 171 [1963] 64–66) and buttressed by W. F. Albright (ibid.).

11. Assyrian sources ascribe the conquest of Samaria to Sargon II. See H. Winckler, *Die Keilschrifttexte Sargons* ([Leipzig: Pfeiffer, 1889] 1.147ff.) and *ANET* (284ff).

Disregarding for the present the annals piece, 18:1–8, which directly precedes the resumptive repetition and which undoubtedly is an integral part of the historiographical framework of Kings (see below), we can now examine the comprehensive insert which is bracketed by 17:3–4 and the resumption in 18:9 and which extends from 17:5 to 17:41. The composite nature of this enclave is obvious. The discernment of a resumptive repetition again proves to be of help in drawing the dividing lines between its respective units: the common opinion that vv. 7–23a form a distinct unit derives support from the recurrence of the phrase ויגל ישראל את אשורה at its beginning (v. 6αβ) and with some variation at its end, ויגל ישראל מעל אדמתו אשורה (v. 23b). These two statements frame the pericope 17:7–23a as the complementary components of an *inclusio*. The conclusion is buttressed by the employment at the very end of the pericope (17:23bβ) of the formula עד היום הזה, which will require further attention.[12]

III

The annalistic notation in 2 Kgs 17:5–6, which in the above analysis was isolated from the preceeding text (vv. 1–4), reads: "The king of Assyria invaded the whole country; he marched up to Samaria . . . deported [the people of] Israel to Assyria, and settled them in Halah and Habor, Nehar Gozan and the cities of Media" [LXX: καὶ Ορη Μήδων.][13] This factual account does not contain any of the formulaic references to the misdeeds of Samaria's rulers which abound in the book of Kings and are presented there as the causes of setbacks and disasters which befell their realm. This conspicuous absence requires an explanation. It is further put in relief by the

---

12. The repetitions of the formula in 17:34a and 41b serve as an *inclusio* which marks off one more subunit. Resultingly, the text part between the above two units, viz., 17:24–33, is recognized as an additional component woven into the comprehensive insert 17:24–41. The complexity of that insert is enhanced by various glosses and iterations which cannot be traced here in detail and which in any case do not materially affect our main argument.

13. L⁺: ἐν ορ(ι)οις = Syr (also in 18:11); *Tg. Neb.* = MT. The reading הרי (for MT ערי) which may still be reflected in the MT of 1 Chr 5:26 והרא (missing, however, in the LXX and Syr) is preferred by J. A. Montgomery (*Kings* [ICC; Edinburgh: Clark, 1951] 477–78) and other commentators. But see W. Rudolph, *Chronikbücher* ([HAT, series 1, vol. 21; Tübingen: Mohr, 1955] 50). The same interchange occurs in reverse in 2 Kgs 23:16, MT: בהר, LXX: ἐν τῇ πόλει; 2 Chr 21:11, MT: בהרי יהודה, LXX: ἐν πόλεσιν Ιουδα. See further S. Talmon, "הר *har*" (*TWAT* 2.467 = *TDOT* 3.434).

presence of a rather qualified disapproval of Hoshea's reign in the antecedent verse (17:2), "He did what was wrong in the eyes of the Lord but not like the kings of Israel before him," which we deem to differ in origin from the ensuing text unit, 17:5–6. Scholars did in fact pay attention to the surprisingly attenuated censure of Hoshea, which sets him off to advantage against his peers, but did not provide a satisfactory explanation for it. Thus B. Stade, as quoted by J. A. Montgomery:[14] "The pre-Exilic editor of Kings must . . . have read in the sources at hand notices of Hoshea that presented him in a more favorable light than his predecessors."[15] Similarly, A. Jepsen can find no obvious reason for the apparent more lenient criticism of Hoshea in 17:2 and like most commentators does not give a single thought to the even more surprising absence of any disapproval of his reign in vv. 5–6.[16] J. Gray offers the rather curious explanation that "his [Hoshea's] comparative virtue according to Deuteronomistic principles was a virtue of necessity," since "the political involvements . . . left him no time for religious matters."[17]

Furthermore, such criticism is also absent from the parallel version of that notation in 18:9–11. However, there the severe judgment which the book of Kings routinely passes on Ephraimite kings surfaces in the added comment (v. 12) which spells out the cause of Samaria's downfall: "because they did not listen to the voice of YHWH their God and transgressed his covenant, all that Moses YHWH's servant had commanded and did not listen or keep it." This verse is clearly a condensed echo of the extensive hortatory passage in 17:7–23, and serves as a redactional link for 18:9–11 (together with 18:1–8) with that parenetic pericope.[18]

The doubling of the account of the conquest of Samaria, together with the evident deviation of 17:5–6 from the conceptual framework of the book of Kings, suggest that this latter chronistic notation was quoted from a northern source. It may well be a fragment of Ephraimite annals which the editor of Kings inserted into his work for reasons which can no longer be ascertained.[19] It should be mentioned that J. Gray considered the possibility that

14. Montgomery, Kings, 464–65.
15. B. Stade, Ausgewählte akademische Reden (Giessen: Ricker, 1899) 208.
16. Jepsen (Quellen, 61): "Worin das scheinbar etwas günstigere Urteil über Hosea begründet ist, 17,2, ist nicht ohne weiteres deutlich."
17. J. Gray, I and II Kings (OTL; London: SCM/Philadelphia: Westminster, 1977) 641.
18. 2 Kgs 17:11–12 actually may be considered an inverted Wiederaufnahme of 17:22–23. 18:11 repeats 17:23bα, and 18:12 echos 17:22–23a.
19. Quotations of non-Judean or for that matter of extra-Israelite materials are not an exceptional feature in biblical literature. E.g., the Edomite Chronicle (Genesis 36) and the (anti-)

"vv. 3–6 could conceivably be drawn from the Annals of Israel,[20] at least up to the siege of Samaria in v. 5." But in the end he rejects this hypothesis: "the fact of the capture of the city, and the deportation to certain places in Mesopotamia and the Iranian escarpment in v. 6 cannot come from such a source, and, in fact, we may question whether state archives were kept recording the intrigues of Hoshea in the last precarious years of Israel, the last three of which were occupied with the final desperate resistance of Samaria."[21] This latter argument is utterly unconvincing, as Gray must have recognized: "Behind vv. 3–5 there is a nucleus of recorded historical facts, as is suggested by the similarity of vv. 5–6 to 18:9–11. The latter passage is a citation, probably from the Annals of Judah,[22] which could not allow such a significant event to pass unnoticed. We suggest that where the two passages agree, the primary source is the *Israelite one* [my italics], and where they differ, namely in Hoshea's Egyptian intrigues, stated to be the occasion of his removal three years before the fall of Samaria (vv. 3–4), the source is the *Annals of Judah.*"[23] Closer attention to the presence of *Wiederaufnahme* in 2 Kings 17–18 and to stylistic and linguistic peculiarites which show up not only in 17:3–6, but also in vv. 24 and 29–31 (see below), give credence to the hypothesis that these verses are indeed remnants of an Ephraimite Chronicle, possibly of the ספר דברי הימים למלכי ישראל. The presumed Ephraimite origin of 17:5–6 is supported by the absence of any synchronizing formula of Hoshea's last years with the regnal years of the contemporaneous Judean king Hezekiah. This omission was indeed noted by scholars, who refer to it however only *en passant* rather than attempting to explain it.

Some characteristics of this fragment of an Ephraimite chronicle allow us to isolate other pieces of a similar nature in the text complex 17:7–41,

Moabite War Song (Num 21:27–30) were most likely quoted from an Edomite source and from the probably non-Israelite sayings or songs of the משלים respectively.

20. Viz., from ספר דברי הימים למלכי ישראל, which the author of Kings recurrently quotes as a source from which he drew information on the history of Ephraim (1 Kgs 14:19; 15:31; 16:5, 14, 20, 27; 22:39; 2 Kgs 1:18; 10:34; 13:8, 12; 14:15, 28; 15:11, 15, 21, 26, 31).

21. Gray, *Kings*, 639.

22. ספר דברי הימים למלכי יהודה (1 Kgs 14:29; 15:7, 23; 22:46; 2 Kgs 8:23; 12:20; 14:18; 15:6, 36; 16:19; 20:20; 21:17, 25; 23:28; 24:5).

23. Gray further terms 17:24–28 an "addendum to the Annals of Israel on the Assyrian resettlement of Israel . . . possibly from an account by a priest of the restored cult of Bethel" (p. 650). He equally suspects "from the absence of any criticism of the Bethel cult, that vv. 29–34a (in chap. 17) are not from a Deuteronomistic hand, but from a local priestly authority, which was responsible probably for vv. 24–28" (*Kings*, 638–39).

which are "factual" accounts and do not exhibit any synchronizing formulae or disparaging remarks concerning the northern kingdom, sparked by their authors' theological principles. We can dispose immediately of two typically parenetic passages which abound in exactly this type of recrimination, viz., 17:7–23 and 17:34–41. Once these parts are extracted, we are left with section 17:24–33, which in the present text arrangement is set apart as a unit by its enclosure between two mentions of the formula עד היום הזה (vv. 23b and 34a). But even within this pericope two heterogeneous strata can be discerned: one hortatory-interpretative, the other factual. The former consists of vv. 25–28 and vv. 32–33. Rather than giving a straightforward historical account, its author is at great pains to discredit the foreign population whom the Assyrians transferred to Samaria, insisting that they adhered to a *cultus mixtus* consisting of an essentially pagan nucleus thinly disguised by a transparent Yahwistic veneer (2 Kgs 17:32–33 and 17:41):

ויהיו יראים את ה׳ . . . ויהיו עשים להם בבית הבמות את ה׳ היו יראים ואת אלהיהם היו עבדים
ויהיו הגוים האלה יראים את ה׳ ואת פסיליהם היו עבדים

The author never tires of informing his readers that this objectionable situation did not change and that it was operative "until this day" (vv. 34a, 41), that is to say until his own times.[24]

In contrast, vv. 24 and 29–31 may be seen as the continuation of the chronistic notation in 17:5–6. In combination, the recovered "factual" passages in 2 Kings 17 form a historical account of assumedly Ephraimic provenance, though seemingly lacking a suitable introduction.[25] The basic text of this northern document can approximately be reconstructed as follows:

---

24. This understanding of the formula עד היום הזה was convincingly proven by B. Childs ("A Study of the Formula 'Until This Day,'" *JBL* 82 [1963] 279–92). See further: H. Schulte, ". . . Bis auf diesen Tag": *Der Text des Jahwisten, des ältesten Geschichtsschreibers der Bibel* (Hamburg: Reich, 1967).

25. Verses 3–4, which like vv. 5–6 stand out from the overall historiographical framework by the absence of parenetic and synchronistic formulae may possibly be seen as such an introduction.

17:5 ויעל מלך אשור בכל הארץ ויעל שמרון ויצר עליה שלש שנים

6 בשנת התשיעית להושע לכד מלך אשור את שמרון

ויגל את ישראל אשורה וישב אתם בחלח ובחבור נהר גוזן וערי מדי

24 ויבא מלך אשור מבבל ומכותה ומעוא ומחמת וספרוים

וישב בערי שמרון תחת בני ישראל וירשו את שמרון וישבו בעריה

25aα ויהי בתחלת שבתם שם

29 ויהיו עשים גוי גוי אלהיו... גוי גוי בעריהם אשר הם ישבים שם

30 ואשי בבל עשו את סכות בנות ואנשי כות עשו את נרגל ואנשי חמת עשו את אשימא

31 והעוים עשו נבחז ואת תרתק והספרוים שרפים את בניהם באש לאדרמלך וענמלך אלהי ספרים.

2 Kings 17:5	[Then] the king of Assyria invaded the whole land, marched against Samaria, and besieged her three years.
6	In the ninth year of Hoshea, the king of Assyria captured Samaria, deported [the people of] Israel to Assyria, and settled them in Halah and Habor, Nehar Gozan, and the cities [LXX: mountains] of Media.
24	[Then] the king of Assyria brought [people] from Babylon and Cuthah, Avva, Hamath, and Sepharvaim and settled [them] in the cities of Samaria in place of the Israelites. They took possession of Samaria and dwelled in her cities.
25aα	When they first settled there
29	each nation worshipped its own gods, each nation in the cities in which they had settled:
30	the men of Babylon worshipped Succoth Benoth, the men of Cuth[ah] worshipped Nergal, and the men of Hamath worshipped Ashima.
31	The Avvites worshipped Nibhaz and Tartak, and the Sepharvites burn their children in the fire [as sacrifice] for Adrammelech and Anammelech, the gods of Sepharvaim.[26]

The above analysis leads to the separation of three major strands which are interwoven in the text complex 2 Kgs 17:1–18:12:

(a) Two annalistic notations, 17:1–4 and 18:1–11. The passages have many characteristics in common with the historiographical framework of the book of Kings and can be comfortably integrated into it. Particularly closely associated with that framework is the passage 18:1–8, in which the ascent of Hezekiah to the throne of Judah is synchronized with Hoshea the Israelite's third year of reign. This notation interrupts the account of Samaria's last days which otherwise would run continuously from 17:1 to 18:11. It was placed at this juncture, since in 18:9 Hoshea's seventh year is synchronized with Hezekiah's fourth regnal year.

26. For an identification of these towns and the local deities, see G. R. Driver, "Geographical Problems" (*FS B. Mazar* [EI 5; Jerusalem: IEJ, 1958] 8–20) and R. Zadok, "Geographical and Onomastic Notes" (*JANES* 8 [1976] 113–26).

(b) Parenetic and hortatory materials: 17:7–22, 25–28, 32–41; 18:12. While these texts evidently share a common ground, further analysis is required for establishing in detail their literary homogeneity.

The polemical tone of these passages highlights the Judean author's or redactor's manifestly partisan interpretation of events pertaining to Samaria. Thus they are of special importance for the elucidation of the historical setting in which the final redaction of the comprehensive pericope, 17:1–18:12, was carried out (see below).

(c) Fragments of an independent chronistic account of an assumedly Ephraimite provenance, viz., 17:5–6, 24, 29–31.

IV

The "Ephraimite Chronicle" requires some discussion before an attempt to date 2 Kings 17 can be made. The distinctiveness of this chapter rests not only on literary, structural, and ideational considerations. It also shows in other particularities, especially in the references to the cultic customs of the foreign peoples whom the Assyrian conquerors settled in the territory of the former northern kingdom which was integrated into their province system. The basic facts are recorded *sine ira*. In vv. 29a and 30–31 we are told that "they [the foreigners] worshipped each nation its own gods" (29a). This general statement is then broken down in a more detailed roster in which the pagan deities of the diverse peoples are severally specified (vv. 30–31). But since "foreigners" are involved, their worship of pagan deities does not evoke the author's criticism, nor does he refer to the reputedly "syncretistic" nature of these cults, in which vestiges of homage to YHWH were infused into their idol worship.

The accusation of syncretism is the very pivot of the "Lions episode" (vv. 25–28), which requires some attention. It tells of attacks of lions on the foreign settlers,[27] who perceive this calamity as a sign that YHWH's wrath was kindled by their ignorance of how to worship him:

27. This tale has to it the ring of a tradition which may have been native to Bethel. It is fashioned upon a basic lion-motif which recurs in other prophetic narratives set in that very territory (1 Kgs 13:24–32; cp. 2 Kgs 23:16–18; 1 Kgs 20:35–36).

וישלח ה' בהם את האריות ויהיו הרגים בהם. ויאמרו למלך אשור לאמר הגוים אשר
הגלית ותושב בערי שמרון לא ידעו את משפט אלהי הארץ וישלח בם את האריות והנם
ממיתים אותם כאשר אינם ידעים את משפט אלהי הארץ (26–17:25b).[28]

When the king of Assyria is informed of the settlers' predicament, he orders
an exiled Israelite priest to be returned to the land, so as to instruct the foreigners in the customs and rites of the local deity, וירם את משפט אלהי הארץ.
His command is promptly carried out, and the priest settles in Bethel.[29]

S. Paul has drawn attention to an Assyrian cylinder inscription which
commemorates Sargon's founding of his new capital at Dur-Šarrukin
(Khorsabad) and which describes an apparently similar event in practically
identical terms. Attempting to "Assyrianize" the population of the city
which attracted deportees from all over the empire, Sargon commissioned
"Assyrians, masters of every craft, as overseers and supervisors to teach
(them) [the foreign settlers] correct instruction in serving the gods and the
king, *ana šuḫuz ṣibitte palāḫ ili u šarri*." Paul suggests that this Akkadian expression is an antecedent of the biblical collocation וירם את משפט אלהי הארץ.[30]
The linguistic similarity is indeed striking. But I doubt that the Bethel
episode, like the Dur-Šarrukin inscription, attests to a "characteristic of Sargon's general administrative policy," namely the "normalization of internal
religious (and political) affairs in key cities," as Paul opines.[31] Neither
Bethel nor Samaria can be put on an equal footing with Khorsabad. It is a far
cry from Sargon's intention to "Assyrianize" the population of his capital to
a presumed effort on his part to "Israelize" the foreign deportees whom the
Assyrians had implanted in the former Ephraimite territory. Furthermore the
cylinder inscription credits Sargon with initiating the Assyrianization of the
foreigners in the capital because of manifest political and religious considerations. In contrast, in the biblical account the king's action is prompted by
the intervention of unnamed agents to ward off a fairy-tale attack of lions,
which is part of the "hortatory-parenetic" Judean component in 2 Kings 17

28. Cp. the very similar phrases כי לא ידעו דרך ה' משפט אלהיהם (Jer 5:4); ועמי לא ידעו את
(Jer 8:7); and in contrast, כי המה ידעו דרך ה' משפט אלהיהם משפט ה' (Jer 5:5).
29. We are not concerned here with the textual problem which arises from the use of singular
next to plural forms in this verse.
30. S. Paul, "Sargon's Administrative Diction in II Kings 17:27," *JBL* 88 (1969) 73–74.
31. H. Tadmor had previously pointed out the linguistic similarity between the Hebrew phrase in
2 Kgs 17:27 and the Akk. collocation in Sargon's cylinder. But unlike Paul he did not draw
any further conclusions from this fact. (See Tadmor, "Temple and Royal City in Babylonia
and Assyria," העיר והקהילה [Jerusalem: Israel Historical Society, 1968] 200–201.)

(see above). Therefore the phrase וירם את משפט אלהי הארץ should probably be taken as a conscious imitation by a Judean author of the Akkadian expression *ana šuḫuz ṣibitte palāḫ ili* but is altogether devoid of the latter's specific historical ramifications.[32]

By setting aside the tale of the lions and the priest(s) (vv. 25–28) as a non-factual insert, v. 29 which follows immediately upon it is rejoined with v. 24, and the "factual annals-nucleus" can be identified as consisting of vv. 24, 29–31. Concomitantly the continuity of the lions episode is restored. The opening phrase of v. 32, ויהיו יראים את ה׳, picks up the thread where it was cut in v. 28, ויהי מורה אתם איך ייראו את ה׳, harks back to 25aβ, לא יראו את ה׳, and leads up to the crucial argument in v. 33 which utterly discredits those "people," proving that their professed adherence to Israel's God is mere lip service intended to serve as a cover-up for their disdainful syncretism: את ה׳ היו יראים ואת אלהיהם היו עבדים כמשפט הגוים אשר הגלו אתם משם, "they paid homage to the Lord while at the same time they served their own gods, according to the custom of the nations from which they had been carried into exile [viz., to Samaria]."

Within the small annals-nucleus (vv. 24, 25aα, 29–31), there is also an editorial gloss which can still be detected: v. 29b contains a statement which ostentatiously links the foreign cults with "the בית הבמות which the Samarians had made [or: built]." The reference can only be to the central northern sanctuary or sanctuaries which Jeroboam I (ben Nebat) had established in Bethel and Dan (1 Kgs 12:25–33; 13:1, 33–34). The statement which is echoed in v. 32, ויעשו להם מקצותם כהני במות ויהיו עשים להם בבית הבמות, must be ascribed to the author of the "Lions episode" or to the editor who inserted that episode into the present context. Like that tale, it purports to link the renewal of the cult at the site of the ancient Israelite sanctuary at Bethel with the introduction into it of pagan cultic practices. At the same time, that gloss in v. 29b foreshadows the argument developed ensuingly that the combination of the two disparate cult patterns resulted in a seemingly Yahwistic (but in reality pagan) religion which the descendants of the foreign settlers still practiced in the redactor's times, ויהיו הגוים האלה יראים את ה׳ ואת פסיליהם היו עבדים גם בניהם ובני בניהם כאשר עשו אבתם הם עשים עד היום הזה (v. 41, cp. vv. 32–34a).

---

32. A Hebrew equivalent of *palāḫ ili* is present in the Ephraimite annals-nucleus in the phrase ויהיו עשים גוי גוי אלהיו (17:29, cp. vv. 30–32). Hebrew עשה equals Aram. פלח and Akk. *palāḫ* (see below).

The alleged religious and cultic interpenetration is quite plausible. Such processes of acculturation are often at work whenever and wherever population changes occur. A prime example of the syncretistic fusion of cults, in reverse as it were, can be oberved in the history of the Israelite religion after the conquest of Canaan (see, e.g., Judg 2:11–17). Israelite shrines were established on former Canaanite cult sites, and polytheistic pagan practices and concepts infiltrated Israelite monotheism, leaving indelible traces in biblical literature. Then, as after the fall of Samaria, the new arrivals gained the upper hand on the political scene, but at the same time the cult and culture of the autochthonous population penetrated deeply into the conquerors' religious beliefs and practices, blurring their original distinctiveness almost to the point of obliteration.

However in the case under review, the notation in 17:29b is most probably not an integral part of the original Ephraimite document, but rather an editorial comment. In content it clashes with the immediately following statement that the newcomers individually established their native cults, "each nation in the cities in which they had settled." That is to say, the foreigners set up a variety of shrines, transferring to their new abode the cults to which they had adhered in their diverse homelands. In contradistinction the phrase "בית הבמות which the Samarians had built" (v. 29b) certainly refers to the distinctly Ephraimite *temenos* at Bethel. There Jeroboam I had established the בית במות, a singular "high-place-temple," which the local hierarchy conceived as "the royal Temple, sanctuary of the realm" (Amos 7:13), equal in prestige to the royal Temple of Jerusalem. Bethel was highly esteemed in the northern kingdom, just as the Temple of Jerusalem was considered in Judah the central and ultimately the only legitimate shrine.

In the original report on Jeroboam's cult reform (1 Kgs 12:31–33),[33] the term בית במות[34] is used in the singular to emphasize the uniqueness of the

---

33. See S. Talmon, "The Cult and Calendar Reform of Jeroboam I," *KCC*, 113–39.

34. The use of that very term in the Mesha Inscription (line 27), אנכ. בנתי. בת. במת. הרס. כי. הא., is usually understood as a reference to a city thus named, which is identified with במות (Num 21:19ff.) and במות בעל (Num 22:41; Josh 13:17; See H. Donner and W. Röllig, *KAI* [Wiesbaden: Harrassowitz, 1964] 2.178). However, there is room for conjecturing that Mesha boasts of having rebuilt the central Moabite temple. A reflection of the destruction of this major shrine is possibly contained in Isa 15:2 in a badly preserved text: עלה הבית ודיבן הבמות לבכי. The original reading may have been: עלה [באש] בית הבמות ודיבן לבכי (cp. Num 21:28). A reference to that main Moabite במה is possibly also present in Isa 16:12, where במה parallels מקדש, and in Jer 48:35.

Bethel structure. Burney[35] altogether misses the significance of the term by stating that in בית במות "בית" is a collective, as in II.17.29, 32, בבית הבמות, of the temples of the various cults at Samaria. IK 13.32; II.23.19, plur., בתי הבמות." He is followed by Montgomery:[36] "The houses of the high-places may refer simply to the rock-hewn sacred precincts as at Gezer, which were themselves 'houses of deity'"; and "for the composite pl. phrase cf. II 17[29.32] and see GK §124r: per contra בתי הבי 13[32]." However, in reality the plural, בתי הבמות (1 Kgs 13:32), originally referred to (each of) the twin-temples at Bethel and Dan (12:29–30) which served as *Grenzheiligtümer* at the southern and northern boundaries of the Ephraimite kingdom.[37] The imposing cultic structure which A. Biran excavated at Dan gives witness to the exceeding importance of the site.[38] This grandiose temple was not just another of the many high places in the northern (2 Kgs 17:9; Ezek 6:6; Hos 10:8; Mic 5:9–14; 2 Chr 34:6–7; et al.) and for that matter in the southern kingdom (Jer 2:28; 11:13; 2 Chr 21:11;[39] et al.). The sanctuary at Dan was in fact the twin of the royal temple at Bethel and like it מקדש מלך ... ובית ממלכה[40] (Amos 7:13; cp. 1 Kgs 3:4 and Josh 10:2).[41] However in all its subsequent biblical mentions, the reading בתי במות attests to the Judean writers' and revisers' predisposition to undermine the singularity of the northern *Reichsheiligtum* in Bethel and to relegate it to the status of merely another במה.[42] This biased presentation certainly distorts the northerners' understanding of the unique status of the Bethel shrine, which has deep roots in the biblical tradition (Gen 12:6ff; 13:1–4; 28:10–22; 35:1–15; Judg 20:17–28; et al.).

---

35. C. F. Burney, *The Book of Judges with Introduction and Notes* ([London: Rivingtons, 1918] 178).

36. Montgomery, *Kings*, 257–59.

37. See S. Yeivin, "דן," *EncyMiq* 2.678–83, esp. 683.

38. See A. Biran, "ואולם ליש שם העיר לראשונה," *All the Land of Naphtali: The Twenty-fourth Archaeological Convention* (Jerusalem: IES, 1966) 21–32.

39. MT: עשה במות בהרי יהודה [יהורם] גם הוא; LXX: ἐν πόλεσιν Ιουδα. See above, n. 13.

40. It is of interest to note that B. Mazar made use of this honorific title of the Bethel (and Dan) sanctuary to highlight by it the unique status of the Jerusalem Temple in the realm of Judah. (See B. Mazar, "ירושלים—מקדש מלך ובית ממלכה," *Judah and Jerusalem: The Twelfth Archaeological Convention* [Jerusalem: IES, 1957] 25–32.)

41. Together these royal twin temples were comprehended under the designation במות ישחק ומקדשי ישראל (Amos 7:9).

42. This tendency shows clearly in the avoidance of the telling term בית במות in the report of the destruction of the Bethel sanctuary in Josiah's counter-reform: וגם את המזבח אשר בבית אל הבמה אשר עשה ירבעם בן נבט אשר החטיא את ישראל גם את המזבח ההוא ואת הבמה נתץ (2 Kgs 23:15; cp. 1 Kgs 12:31–33). The special status of הבמה at Bethel surfaces already in 1 Sam 10:3–5 and then in Ezek 20:29.

The predominance of Bethel is reflected in one other editorial comment: "and they [i.e., the foreigners, or possibly the remaining Ephraimites][43] appointed for themselves from among their peers [or nobles][44] במות priests, ויעשו להם מקצותם כהני במות, who officiated בבית הבמות" (17:32). This comment is a slightly reworded quotation of a distinctive statement in the report on the steps taken by Jeroboam I, aimed at solidifying his rebellion against the Davidic house and the Temple of Jerusalem: "He made [built] the בית במות and made [appointed] priests מקצות העם (1 Kgs 12:31; cp. v. 32 and 13:33).

The above analysis leads to the conclusion that the references to the Ephraimite calf cult which allege the proliferation of בית/בתי במות in Samaria, before and after the fall of the northern kingdom, evidence a sustained bias of Judean editors. Therefore the tendentious allusion in 17:29b is patently a secondary insertion into the wording of a document which factually related the implantation of foreign settlers and their cults in former Ephraimite territories. As said,[45] the original text may have read as follows (17:24, 25, 29a, 30, 31):

ויבא מלך אשור מבבל ומכותה ומעוא ומחמת וספרוים וישב בערי שמרון [46] תחת בני ישראל
וירשו את שמרון וישבו בעריה ויהי בתחלת שבתם שם . . . ויהיו עשים גוי גוי אלהיו . . .
גוי גוי בעריהם אשר הם ישבים שם ואנשי בבל עשו את סכות בנות [47] ואנשי כות עשו את נרגל
ואנשי חמת עשו את אשימא והעוים עשו נבחז ואת תרתק והספרוים
שרפים את בניהם באש לאדרמלך וענמלך אלהי ספרוים

V

A closer look at this Ephraimite document reveals two linguistic particularities which set it apart from the surrounding text and which confer upon

---

43. Thus Montgomery: "A good priest came and reformed his compatriots' religion" (*Kings*, 473).

44. For this understanding of (מקצות)ם, see Talmon, "The Cult and Calendar Reform of Jeroboam I" (*KCC*, 115–18). In a forthcoming paper I endeavor to show that this connotation of מקצותם persisted in late biblical and early postbiblical Hebrew.

45. See above, pp. 142–43.

46. Cp. Ezra 4:10: ושאר אמיא די הגלי אסנפר רבא ויקירא והותב המו בקריה די שמרין; LXX: ἐν πόλεσιν τῆς Σομορων; Rashi: "In the cities around Samaria." Similarly several modern commentators.

47. Cp. Amos 5:26.

this short piece a linguistic singularity unparalleled in any other biblical text:

(a) The verb עשה is employed six times in vv. 29–31 with a signification which is unique to this context, differing perceptibly from its prevalent connotations in Biblical Hebrew, in which it defines a variety of activities, all equivalent to *facere*, "make, manufacture, fashion, execute, produce," et sim. Under the comprehensive meaning "to make" can be subsumed the more specific collocation "make gods or idols," in which עשה is mostly coupled with a direct object (e.g., Judg 18:24, 31; 1 Kgs 14:9). Somewhat similar is the expression עשה זבחים, "bring offerings" or "sacrifice," usually combined with an indirect object (Exod 10:25; 1 Kgs 12:27; cp. Jer 44:19, et al.). On the strength of this prevalent use of עשה את, most lexica,[48] commentators, and translations render עשים, "they were making" (17:28, 32, 34, 41), עשו, "they made" (17:29–30, 41), taking the plastic representations of the gods, i.e., the idols, to constitute the direct object of these predicates. While this translation suitably renders עשו in the gloss ויניחו בבית הבמות אשר עשו השמרנים (v. 29b) in the other occurrences of עשה in 17:29–31, it produces misleading results. The last item in that roster of pagan cults clearly describes a specific sacrifice offered to the deities named, "the Se-pharvites burn their children in the fire for Adrammelech and Anammelech, the gods of Sepharvaim" (v. 31b), and does not refer to the making of images of these deities. The parallelism of this line with the preceding lines engenders the conclusion that there also עשה connotes the worship of these deities and not the manufacture of their idols.[49] Therefore ואנשי בבל עשו את סכות בנות ואנשי כות עשו את נרגל should be rendered, "the Babylonians wor-shipped Sukkot Benot, the Cuthites worshipped Nergal," etc. And indeed in this context *Tg. Neb.* regularly renders עשה by עבד, used especially in reference to idol worship,[50] or by פלח, which has the same connotation. The term was correctly understood by the medieval commentator David Kimchi. In his comments on אשר עשו השמרנים, "which the Samarians had built" (v. 29b), and ויהיו עשים להם בבית הבמות, "they were making [their sacrifices] in the בית הבמות" (v. 32), Kimchi employs the very same verb: זה ישראל

48. See, int. al., *GB*[17], 623; KB, 740; BDB, 794; *TWAT* 6.416
49. The medieval lexicographer Ibn Ğanâḥ understood עשה in this context to mean "set up": עניגו לקיחה והקמה. See his ספר השרשים ([ed. W. Bacher; Berlin: Itzkowski, 1896] 388, 552).
50. See M. Jastrow, *Dictionary of the Targumim, the Talmud Babli and Yerushalmi, and Midrashic Literature* (New York: Title Publishing Company, 1943) 2.1034–35.

הכהנים היו (v. 29b); שהיו בשמרון ובאותם בתי הבמות שעשו הם הניחו... אליהם עושים להם עבודתם וקרבנותיהם בבמות (v. 32). In contrast, in the roster of the foreign cults he renders עשה by the Hebrew root עבד, which signifies "worship": כן היה שם ע"ג שהיו עובדים בארצם, "They adhered there [i.e., in Samaria] to the same pagan worship to which they had adhered in their countries [of origin]."[51]

This employment of עשה in 2 Kgs 17:29a, 30–31 differs decidedly from its use in seemingly identical biblical formulae which describe the actual manufacture of idols. The difference becomes especially prominent when we compare our text with the traditions pertaining to the making of the golden calf, after which Jeroboam ben Nebat fashioned the calf or the calves which he set up in Bethel (and Dan).[52] In all these instances עשה has as its direct object the nouns עגל מסכה (Exod 32:4, 8; Deut 9:16; Neh 9:18) and עגלי זהב (1 Kgs 12:28; cp. 2 Kgs 10:29; 2 Chr 13:8)[53] or in conformity with the "break-up pattern," simply עגל (Exod 32:19, 20, 24, 35; Deut 9:21; 1 Kgs 12:32; Hos 8:5) or מסכה (Deut 9:12; Hos 13:2, cp. Ps 106:19; further Exod 34:17; Lev 19:4).

The particular use of עשה in 2 Kgs 17:29a, 30–31 appears to be a specifically Ephraimite linguistic trait.[54] It possibly mirrors an Akkadian prototype. Akk. *epēšu* exhibits a semantic range similar to Hebrew עשה. Collocated with *pān* or *ana* and the name of a deity or with *ilāni*, "gods," in general, it may connote "perform a ritual" or "worship."[55] Special mention should be made of the expression *palāḫ ili* in the Khorsabad Cylinder (see above, p. 145).

---

51. It appears that among modern scholars only B. L. Levine captured the correct meaning of the passage: "There . . . [in 2 Kgs 17:30] it is reported that the men of Cuth . . . עשו Nergal, that is to say that they worshipped him [פלחו לו]" (See "נרגל," *EncMiq*, 5.924).

52. In the report of the reforms of Jeroboam I, עשה further describes the making/building of the בית במות (1 Kgs 12:31) and its altar (12:33), the installation of priests מקצות העם (12:31, 32; 13:33), and the observation of the *Sukkot* festival on the fifteenth day of the eighth instead of the seventh month (12:32, 33).

53. In the tale of Micah's Sanctuary, presumably that same idol is referred to by פסל ומסכה (Judg 17:4; 18:14, 17, 18) or פסל (18:20, 30, 31).

54. It could be, however, that it surfaces in Jer 3:16, where עשה is used together with זכר and פקד, terms which also connote "worship."

55. See "*epēšu*, 2f3," (*CAD*, 229). The concurrence of this connotation in Akk. *epēšu* with the unusual employment of Hebrew עשה in 2 Kings 17 was noted independently by my colleague H. Tadmor. In this concurrence of the Hebrew and the Akkadian verbs, a possible mediating role of Aramaic cannot be ruled out.

The proposed interdependence of עשה in 2 Kgs 17:29a, 30–32 and Akk. *epēšu* engenders the surmise that the restored "Ephraimite Chronicle" may well have had an Assyrian antecedent. If so, it may be presumed that the "factual" report of the events which befell Samaria before and after the conquest by the Assyrians, which differs perceptibly from the historiographical framework of the book of Kings, was originally worded in Akkadian but was handed down in an Ephraimite-Hebrew translation.

(b) This supposition derives support from the other linguistic particularity of the editorial comment embedded in 17:29, viz., the use of the toponym "Samarians," which is a hapax legomenon in the Hebrew and the Aramaic biblical onomasticon. It should be stressed that in this instance we are not concerned with a presumed Ephraimite piece of history-writing but rather, as said, with a Judean redactional insert. However in view of the overall concern of 2 Kings 17 with Ephraimite history, and as the result of a possible linguistic cross-fertilization, that very short Judean piece appears to exhibit a unique reflection of an Assyrian term. The use of the toponym "Samarians" in the phrase בית הבמות אשר עשו השמרנים is the only instance in the Bible in which the (Israelite) inhabitants of the northern kingdom or of its capital, Samaria, are referred to in this manner.[56] This singularity is especially striking since toponyms derived from the names of countries and cities abound in biblical literature.[57]

The absence from the biblical onomasticon of the toponym "Samarian(s)" is particularly conspicuous in postexilic books, including their Aramean portions, where we encounter adjectival constructs like מלך שמרון (1 Kgs 21:1; 2 Kgs 1:3, et al.), שער שמרון (1 Kgs 22:10; 2 Kgs 7:1), but never שמרני or שמרנים. Even Sanballat, the commander of the חיל שמרון in Nehemiah's days (Neh 3:34), is never called שמרוני[58] but is referred to by the appellation חרני (Neh 2:19), derived from the nom. loc. חורון.

---

56. See Montgomery, *Kings*, 471.
57. To adduce only a few instances: אדומי (Deut 23:8; 1 Sam 21:8; 22:9, 18; 1 Kgs 11:14) and אדומים (1 Kgs 11:1, 17; 2 Kgs 16:6; 2 Chr 25:14; 28:17); אפרתי (Judg 12:5; 1 Sam 1:1; 1 Kgs 11:26) and אפרתים (Ruth 1:2); גבע(ו)ני (Neh 3:7; 1 Chr 12:4) and גבענים (2 Sam 21:1–9), et sim.
58. Also in the Elephantine Papyri he is mentioned as סנאבלט פחת שמרון. See A. Cowley, *Aramaic Papyri of the Fifth Century B.C.* ([Oxford: Clarendon, 1923] 113, papyrus 30, line 29). The same holds true for the Wadi Dâliyeh papyri. See F. M. Cross, "Papyri of the Fourth Century B.C. From Dâliyeh" (*New Directions in Biblical Archaeology* [ed. D. N. Freedman and J. C. Greenfield; Garden City, NY: Doubleday, 1969] 42): בן [סנא]בלט פחת שמר[ן].

It is of interest that also in postbiblical sources the appellation שמרונים is usually avoided, even in reference to the Samaritans of the Second Temple Period. Ben Sira refers deprecatingly to "the foolish people that dwells in Shechem" (Sir 50:26) rather than choosing a designation derived from the city name Samaria. A similar usage is reflected in one component of the double Greek translation of 2 Kgs 17:32, which Burney considers to mirror the original reading, while, in his opinion, the MT represents "the restoration of an imperfect text upon the lines of 1 Kgs 12:31."[59] The LXX and Luc. render the passage in question (17:32):

καὶ ἦσαν φοβούμενοι τὸν κύριον. καὶ κατῴκισαν τὰ βδελύγματα
αὐτῶν ἐν τοῖς οἴκοις τῶν ὑψηλῶν ἃ ἐποίησαν ἐν Σαμαρείᾳ ἔθνος
ἔθνος ἐν πόλει ᾗ κατῴκουσιν ἐν αὐτῇ . . .

The translation seems to reflect the MT of 17:29, with the telling difference that שמרונים, which is used there in reference to the builders of the בית הבמות is rendered here by the circumscription ἃ ἐποίησαν ἐν Σαμαρείᾳ, which can be retroverted to read: אשר עשו בשמרון.

I tend to assume that the unique appellation שמרונים (2 Kgs 17:29) is possibly another indication of the influence of the Assyrian geopolitical terminology on biblical writers. It probably originated in a direct quote from an Assyrian original. I do not take שמרנים to stand for the Assyrian province Samerina, as some commentators suggest,[60] but rather as a designation of the Israelite kingdom of Samaria. The Assyrians had introduced this designation in the days of Adad-Narari III, i.e., approximately 800 BCE. In the stela from Tel Al-Rimah (1.8), Adad-Nirari refers to the king of Israel as *ia-'a-su sa-me-ri-na-a-a*, i.e., "Ia'asu the Samarian." He similarly designates the

---

59. Burney, *Judge* (337 [see above, n. 35). Burney's preference for the LXX over the MT is put in doubt by Montgomery (*Kings*, 471).

60. See, e.g., Gray, *Kings* (652, 654). We have no reason for assuming that cuneiform *sa-me-ri-na-a-a*, like שמרנים, is meant to give expression to the fact that the kingdom of Samaria had been turned into the Assyrian province Samerina, as A. Malamat proposed in a discussion of Adad-Nirari's stela ("On the Akkadian Transcription of the Name of King Joash," *BASOR* 204 [1971] 37–39). Instead we should consider the biblical term שמרנים a one-time reflection of the toponym "Samarian," introduced by Adad-Nirari and later used by Tiglath Pileser III in reference to Menachem of Israel, which, however, did not gain for itself a permanent place in the biblical onomasticon. See M. Weippert, "Jau[a] mār Ḥumri: Joram oder Jehu von Israel?" (*VT* 28 [1978] 113–18).

Phoenician kings "the Tyrian"[61] and "the Sidonian" (1.9).[62] The toponym "Samarian," which is applied here to the Israelite king, constitutes a departure from the patronymic *bīt-ḥumri*, by which name Adad-Nirari's grandfather Shalmanesser III referred to Jehu, who had in fact annihilated the house of Omri.

VI

Having identified in 2 Kings 17 the remains of an assumed Ephraimite document, we will now consider the question of how it was adjusted and annotated when it was incorporated into the present framework. We will try to establish the identity of the revisers and possibly determine the historical conditions which triggered the inclusion of the comprehensive enclave in the book of Kings.

The key factor in our deliberations on these issues appears to be the editor's manifest intention to derogate a "syncretistic" form of YHWH worship still operative in his own days which he obviously rejects. His polemical presentation is aimed at the descendants of those foreign syncretists whom the Assyrians had implanted in Samaria, who still lived in the northern parts of the land of Israel, and whom he wishes to discredit in the eyes of his readers, most probably his Judean contemporaries. The polemic certainly did not originate shortly after the destruction of Samaria, since the Judeans then showed a rather conciliatory attitude toward the inhabitants of the northern territories. King Hezekiah attempted to bring about a reconciliation of the erstwhile Ephraimites with Judah and succeeded in his attempt, at least to some degree (2 Chronicles 30). The prophets Jeremiah and Ezekiel seem-

61. Cp. the biblical nomenclature צר/צרים (1 Kgs 7:14 = 2 Chr 2:13; Ezra 3:7; Neh 13:16; 1 Chr 22:4); צידני (Judg 3:3; Ezek 32:30); and ציד(ו)(נים (Deut 3:9; Josh 13:4, 6; Judg 10:12; 18:7; 1 Kgs 5:20; 11:5, 33; 16:31; 2 Kgs 23:13; Ezra 3:7; 1 Chr 22:4) et al.

62. See S. Page, "A Stela of Adad-Nirari III and Nergal-Ereš from Tell al Rimah," *Iraq* 30 (1968) 139–53; idem, "Joash and Samaria in a New Stela Excavated at Tell al Rimah," *VT* 19 (1969) 483–84; H. Cazelles, "Une nouvelle stèle d'Adad-Nirari III d'Assyrie et Joas d'Israel," *CRAIBL* (1969) 106–14; A. Jepsen, "Ein neuer Fixpunkt für die ausserbiblische Chronologie der israelitischen Könige," *VT* 20 (1970) 359–61; J. A. Soggin, "Ein ausserbiblisches Zeugnis für die Chronologie des JᵉHÔᵓĀŠ/JÔᵓĀŠ, König von Israel," *VT* 20 (1970) 366–68; H. Tadmor, "A Note on the Saba'a Stele of Adad-Nirari III," *IEJ* 19 (1969) 46–48; M. Haran, "מלכות אפרים בשעת דמדומים", תקופות ומוסדות במקרא (Tel Aviv: Am Oved, 1972) 236.

ingly show a preference for the remnants of Ephraim over Judah. A conflict over political, religious, and cultic matters did indeed develop during the reign of Josiah, who destroyed the high places of Samaria including the central sanctuary in Bethel (2 Kgs 23:16–20). But nothing in the reports about his reform would explain the polemics against the "northern syncretists" which permeate the account in 2 Kings 17. Therefore I cannot subscribe to M. Cogan's theory that "the destruction of Jerusalem (586 BCE) may serve as the *terminus ad quem* for our polemic."[63] Cogan argues that "late pre-exilic Judah, the reign of Josiah in particular provides an appropriate setting for attention to be focused upon the Israelite kingdom and its inhabitants, former and present."[64] There is little in the text of 2 Kings 17 which would substantiate such a claim or the assumption that 2 Kings 17 turns against "the Israelite exiles, who by their continued idolatry, forfeit any rights to their former inheritance," denying them legitimacy; and that "their exile is proof of rejection." This interpretation of 2 Kings 17 derives from the ascription of the polemics to a deuteronomistic redactor, and the resulting dating of the passage to the time of Josiah.

I propose that chapter 17 was incorporated into the book of Kings at a considerably later stage in Israelite history, after the destruction of Jerusalem, and actually after the return from the exile. Judging by his pronounced anti-Ephraimite attitude and some linguistic and stylistic peculiarities, it may be presumed that the writer was himself a returnee and that he was closely associated with the author/editor of the book of Ezra (see below) or else with the Chronicler,[65] with whom he shares an illuminating, identical stylistic/linguistic feature: The present composite passage, 2 Kgs 17:1–6, exhibits another case of a *Wiederaufnahme*. ויעל מלך אשור (v. 5) is a resumptive repetition of עליו עלה שלמנאסר מלך אשור (v. 3) which proves that the reference to Hoshea's conspiracy with Egypt and his refusal to pay tribute and his ensuing arrest by the king of Assyria (v. 4) is a secondary insert into the originally shorter text. It cannot go unnoticed that exactly the same

---

63. M. Cogan, "Israel in Exile: The View of a Josianic Historian," *JBL* 97 (1978) 40–44.

64. In this understanding of the historical setting of 2 Kings 17, Cogan was preceded by medieval commentators such as Kimchi (see his comments ad loc. and on 2 Kgs 23:19) and Abarbanel (ad 23:18).

65. For this differentiation between the author/editor of Ezra (Nehemiah) and the Chronicler, see S. Japhet, "The Supposed Common Authorship of Chronicles and Ezra-Nehemiah Investigated Anew" (*VT* 18 [1969] 330–71) and S. Talmon, "Ezra and Nehemiah" (*IDBSup* [1976] 317–18).

structure and the very same choice of terms turn up in the Chronicler's account of Egyptian King Shishak's campaign against Rehoboam of Judah, "because of his disloyalty to God," כי מעלו בה׳ (2 Chr 12:2b), and because "he forsook God's Torah," עזב את תורת ה׳ (v. 1a), as Hoshea "did what was wrong in God's eyes," ויעש הרע בעיני ה׳ (2 Kgs 17:2a). The Chronicler's opening statement, "In the fifth year of Rehoboam's reign Shishak king of Egypt attacked Jerusalem," בשנה החמישית למלך רחבעם עלה שישק מלך מצרים על ירושלים (2 Chr 12:2a; cp. 2 Kgs 18:9, השנה השביעית להושע בן אלה מלך ישראל עלה שלמנאסר מלך אשור על שמרון) is repeated in 2 Chr 12:9, ויעל שישק מלך מצרים על ירושלים, exactly as ויעל מלך אשור בכל הארץ (2 Kgs 17:5) is a *Wiederaufnahme* of עליו עלה שלמנאסר מלך אשור in 17:3. And as in 2 Kings 17 the resumptive repetition shows v. 4 to be an insert, so the prophetic tale of Shemaiah the prophet in 2 Chr 12:5–8 is set apart by the *Wiederaufnahme* as a secondary intrusion into the original text. This hypothesis is fully proven by the absence of both the prophetic insert and the resumptive repetition in the parallel account of the Rehoboam-Shishak episode in 1 Kgs 14:25–28.[66]

2 Kings 17 in fact reflects one of the latest stages in the editorial processes which affected the book of Kings. The postexilic author of this text is bent on preventing the integration into his own community of groups in the population of the land who had not shared in the experience of the exile which had revolutionized the religious attitudes of the returnees. The members of the reconstituted Judean body politic took upon themselves by oath "to obey God's law given by Moses the servant of God, and to observe and fulfill all the commandments of God our Lord, his rules and his statutes," ובאים באלה ובשבועה ללכת בתורת האלהים אשר נתנה ביד משה עבד האלהים ו̲ל̲ש̲מ̲ר̲ ו̲ל̲ע̲ש̲ו̲ת̲ א̲ת̲ כ̲ל̲ מ̲צ̲ו̲ת̲ ה̲׳ א̲ד̲נ̲י̲נ̲ו̲ ו̲מ̲ש̲פ̲ט̲י̲ו̲ ו̲ח̲ק̲י̲ו̲ (Neh 10:30). In contrast 2 Kings 17 presents the local inhabitants of northern Israel as still clinging to the disreputable Ephraimite version of Yahwism which the prophets had condemned and which in addition had been contaminated by the syncretism of the foreigners whom the Assyrians had settled in Samaria. Their descendants at first proposed to join the returnees' community in the rebuilding of the Temple in Jerusalem, professing their adherence to YHWH and asserting that they "seek," i.e., "revere" him like the returned exiles and "offer him sacrifices" (Ezra 4:1–2). But the author of the parenetic pericope in 2 Kgs 17:32–41 completely voids their claim and alleges that "until this

---

66. See Berlin, *Poetics,* 126 (above, n. 6).

very day . . . they do not pay homage to God, do not keep his rules and his statutes which he enjoined upon the descendants of Jacob,"[67] . . . עד היום הזה

אינם יראים את ה׳ ואינם עשים כחקתיו וכמשפטיו וכתורה וכמצוה אשר צוה ה׳ את בני יעקב

(v. 34), winding up his remonstrance with the accusation "like fathers like sons," כאשר עשו אבתם הם עשים עד היום הזה (v. 41). While both 2 Kgs 17:34 and Neh 10:30 use deuteronomistic stereotypes (cp. Deut 8:11; 11:1; 26:17; 30:16; 1 Kgs 2:3; 8:58, int. al.), the choice of such pointedly similar phraseology appears in this instance to be intentional.

It is remarkable that in Ezra 4:1–2 the petitioners are not referred to by the comprehensive designation "peoples of the land," עם/עמי הארץ/צות (Ezra 3:3; 4:4; 9:1, 2, 11, 14; 10:2, 11; Neh 9:22, 24, 30; 10:29, 31, 32) or גויי הארצות (Ezra 6:21), which prevails in Ezra-Nehemiah, but rather by the more specific term "adversaries of Judah and Benjamin, צרי יהודה ובנימין. The authors' insistence on presenting their own group as being composed of Judeans (Ezra 2:1; 5:1; 6:14; Neh 1:2; 5:1; 7:6; 13:23) and Benjaminites (Ezra 1:5; 10:9; Neh 11:4–9, 31–35; 12:31–34) leaves room for the identification of the petitioners as northern Israelites. There is a kernel of truth in their claim that they had been serving the God of Israel and had brought him sacrifices. The traditions which tell of the acceptance of the Jerusalem cult in the days of Hezekiah by "men from Asher, Manasseh, and Zebulun" (2 Chr 30:11)[68] and of "men from Shechem, Shiloh, and Samaria," who came up to Judah in the days of Gedaliah of whose murder they had no knowledge, "carrying offerings and frankincense to bring to the house of God" (Jer 41:5), reveal the attachment of some northerners to the Jerusalem Temple. The association of these northeners with the Jerusalem Temple and additional considerations of a political and economic nature may have induced some returnees to advocate their acceptance into the

---

67. The patently faulty MT reading כחקתם וכמשפטם resulted from a *lapsus calami*, the contraction of יו to final ם, as, e.g., 1 Sam 21:14, MT: ויתהלל בידם; LXX: ἐν ταῖς χέρσιν αὐτοῦ; Ezek 25:9 may contain a doublet: מהער(יו)ם מעריו. See F. Delitzsch, *Lese-und Schreibfehler im Alten Testament*, etc. ([Berlin/Leipzig: DeGruyter, 1920] 120–21) and cp. R. Weiss, "Ligatures in the Hebrew Bible [נו=ם]" (*JBL* 82 [1963] 188–94).

68. Montgomery (*Kings*, 473) opines that the priest who returned to Bethel (2 Kgs 17:26–28) actually "reformed his compatriots' religion" (not that of the transplanted foreigners) and "that his party had the benevolent assistance of Hezekiah." This interpretation is hardly plausible since Hezekiah aimed at reuniting the population of former Ephraim with Judah, with the Jerusalem Temple serving as the common and only cultic center, thus to restore the status quo ante the schismatic reform of Jeroboam I. See S. Talmon, "The Cult and Calendar Reform of Jeroboam I" (*KCC*, 123–28).

newly constituted community. Foremost among the advocates may have been priests who had an obvious interest in increasing the numbers of the faithful who would sustain the service in the rebuilt Temple (Hag 2:10–14). The author of the passage (Ezra 4:1–3) objected to this tendency. He disqualified the petitioning "adversaries of Judah and Benjamin" by putting in their mouths words which ostentatiously disclose their non-Israelite origins, viz., their descent from the "foreigners" whom the Assyrians had settled in conquered Samaria. It does not require great powers of discernment to detect the writer's hand in the penning of the statement: "we have been sacrificing to him [to whom this temple is dedicated] since the days of Esarhaddon the king of Assyria who brought us up here" (4:2). These words amount to an admission of their being non-Israelites. In the mouths of the petitioners they are incongruous, since they defeat their professed purpose. But the statement makes excellent sense coming from the pen of an antagonistic author who, like Haggai, wanted to support those returnees who were determined to reject the approaches of the "contaminated" inhabitants of northern Palestine.[69]

The objection to the admittance of the local petitioners into the returnees' community raised by the writer of Ezra 4, who implicitly bases himself on the "historical" report in 2 Kings 17, is echoed in the pronouncements of the postexilic prophet Haggai. Any contact with "these people, העם הזה . . . הגוי הזה, he warns, will perforce result in the contamination of the

69. For a more detailed discussion of this passage, see S. Talmon, "מסורות במקרא על ראשית תולדות השומרונים" (*Eretz Shomron: The Thirtieth Archaeological Convention, September 1972* [Jerusalem: IEJ, 1973] 23–33 = idem, "Biblische Überlieferungen zur Frühgeschichte der Samaritaner," *Gesellschaft und Literatur in der Hebräischen Bibel: Gesammelte Aufsätze* [Neukirchen: Neukirchener Verlag, 1988] 1.138–51). I take this opportunity to correct a mispresentation of my views in M. Cogan's paper (*JBL* 97 [1978] 40 [see above, n. 62]). He ascribes to me the statement that "The population of the land of Ephraim was entirely exchanged after the destruction: the autochthonous Israelite community in toto was deported and the land filled with foreign people who were transferred there." Similarly, B. Oded states erroneously that like Torrey, I "take the biblical scribe's picture of total deportation as . . . starting point" and argue "that the deportations were so extensive that the Israelite 'remnant' constituted no more than an insignificant element in the population structure of the Assyrian provinces" ("II Kings 17: Between History and Polemic," *Jewish History* 2 [1987] 39). The truth is that in my Hebrew essay (p. 27, and in the German translation as well, p. 143), I said the exact opposite. I stressed that this is what the Judean editor of 2 Kings 17 wants us to believe, adding that "this view has no basis whatsoever in historical reality, אולם לדעה זו אין יסוד במציאות ההיסטורית, and that in actual fact "the number of Ephraimites deported, as the number of foreigners exiled to the land of Samaria, was by necessity restricted."

returnees' faith and cult, purified by the very experience of exile: all they (those people) do and wherever they offer sacrifices will cause defilement כן כל מעשה ידיהם ואשר יקריבו שם טמא הוא (Hag 2:14).[70] Like clean comestibles and potions (meat, bread, wine, and oil), which by mere contact with a source of ritual uncleanliness will become defiled (Hag 2:11–13), so the Temple which the returnees are about to rebuild will be defiled if those foreign syncretists who falsely profess to serve Israel's God are allowed to be partners in its restitution and thereby to become members of the returnees' community.

The allegedly "old source" which a postexilic editor inserted into 2 Kings 17 is thus made the ideological *point d'appui* for the total rejection by the Judean returnees of the population that remained in the territory of one-time Samaria, "the adversaries of Judah and Benjamin," צרי יהודה ובנימין (Ezra 4:1–3), because they adhered to a defiling (Hag 2:10–14) *cultus mixtus,* from the time that their non-Israelite forebears were implanted in Samaria by the Assyrians (2 Kgs 17:24ff.) "to this very day," עד היום הזה (2 Kgs 17:34, 41). Thus this late insert into the book of Kings is another example of the use of historical texts for political propaganda.[71]

---

70. I fully subscribe to the interpretation of Haggai's question which on the surface is a request for a ruling on cultic matters, as a simile which pertains to the factions involved, the returnees, and the local population, as proposed by D. J. W. Rothstein (*Juden und Samaritaner* [BWAT 3; Leipzig: Hinrichs, 1908]). For the prevalent application of both העם and הגוי to the returnees' (as yet) "impure" community, see P. R. Ackroyd, "Studies in the Book of Haggai" (*JJS* 3 [1952] 5–6); H. G. May, "'This People' and 'This Nation' in Haggai" (*VT* 18 [1968] 190–97); and commentaries, most recently C. L. Meyers and E. M. Meyers, *Haggai, Zechariah 1–8* ([AB 25B; Garden City, NY: Doubleday & Co., 1987] 57–58).

71. Some pertinent illustrations of such procedures are given, int. al., by H. A. Hoffner, Jr. ("Propaganda and Political Justification in Hittite Historiography," *Unity and Diversity: Essays in the History, Literature and Religion of the Ancient Near East* [ed. H. Goedicke and J. J. M. Roberts; Baltimore: Johns Hopkins University, 1975] 49–62); P. Machinist ("Literature as Politics: The Tukulti-Ninurta Epic and the Bible," *CBQ* 38 [1976] 455–82); and M. Brettler ("The Book of Judges: Literature as Politics," *JBL* 108 [1989] 395–418).

ESCHATOLOGY AND HISTORY
IN BIBLICAL THOUGHT

I

The eschatological vision of Christians and Jews and their expectations of the future have their roots in the Hebrew Bible. However, it must be stressed that the subsequent development of these ideas in postbiblical Jewish and Christian theology (beginning with the New Testament) did not necessarily proceed in complete dependence upon or in absolute agreement with the concept which prevails in the Hebrew Bible. Rather, the concept of eschatology and the hope for the future in postbiblical Judaism and in Christianity were subjected to modifications by which they were completely transformed.

A few brief observations are offered here with the aim of clarifying the concept of *eschatology*, since this concept is differently understood and variously interpreted in different cultures and philosophies. One may say in general that in Christian faith and dogma, eschatology is predominantly centered upon an outlook inspired by faith in the ultimate fulfilment of the salvation process. Theologians, anthropologists, specialists in the sociology of religion, and historians who live in the world of Christian ideas have also applied this concept to the expectations for the future entertained by societies of antiquity and by primitive societies up to the present day. Thus, for example, they describe as eschatological the Cargo Cults practiced among several peoples in the South Pacific region. These cults, which came into existence mainly after the First World War, express a hope for the future that envisages the appearance of a Messiah-like savior who will prepare the way for a political and religious renaissance of the currently afflicted society. The expected future always involves victory over "the enemy," usually represented as white men, as well as a superabundance of the commodities most highly prized by the islanders. War, death, and a renewal of national life play a salient part in these visions.[1] We do not find in them, however, any trace of the devout, spiritual self-commitment by individuals or community that forms the alpha and omega of the hopes for the future embodied in the religions based on biblical revelation. It is a flight from their experience of the present evil which they are powerless to confront, into the realm of wishful thinking that the Cargo Cults and similar conceptions manifest.[2] Their beliefs lack the positive values which form the foundation and central pillar of the expectations for the future held by Jews and Christians. This determining factor being absent, it may be questioned whether the term *eschatology* can legitimately be applied to dreams of future bliss such as those which find their expression in the Cargo Cults.

In a similar manner "the teaching concerning last things"—I stress *last things*—has been retroactively transplanted from the interpretation of Christian faith and dogma into the Hebrew Bible. Here, however, the circumstances are different from those pertaining to the Cargo Cults. The profound dependence of New Testament literature upon the imagery and thought content of the Hebrew Scriptures is evident. Therefore, one might take the view that an inference can unreservedly be drawn from the earlier writings of the Hebrew Bible and applied to the image of an eschatological era in early Christian literature. This would also warrant the application by Christians of the term *eschatology* to the expectations for the future enter-

---

1.   See, int. al., K. T. Preuss, *Tod und Unsterblichkeit im Glauben der Naturvölker. Sammlung gemeinverständlicher Schriften* (Gebiet der Theologie und Religionsgeschichte 146; Tübingen: Mohr, 1930); H. Petri, "Das Weltende im Glauben australischer Eingeborener," *Paideuma, Mitteilungen zur Kulturkunde* 4 (1950) 349–62; A. Lommel, "Der 'Cargo Kult' in Melanesien: Ein Beitrag zum Problem der Europäisierung der Primitiven," *Zeitschrift für Ethnologie* 78 (1953) 17–63; P. Worsley, *The Trumpet Shall Sound: A Study of 'Cargo' Cults in Melanesia* (London: Macgibbons Kee, 1957); S. L. Thrupp, ed., *Millennial Dreams in Action: Studies in Revolutionary Religious Movements* (New York: Schocken, 1970); Y. Talmon, "Millenarian Movements," *European Journal of Sociology* 7 (1966) 159–200 (with ample references to pertinent literature). See also N. Cohn, *The Pursuit of the Millennium: Revolutionary Messianism in Medieval and Reformation Europe and Its Bearing on Modern Totalitarian Movements* (New York: Harper, 1961), esp. pp. 1–32; M. Eliade, *Le mythe de l'éternel retour* (Paris: Gallimard, 1969) = *The Myth of the Eternal Return* (New York: Pantheon, 1954).

2.   To some degree this also applies to the biblical hope for an ideal aeon in history, which was transferred into metahistory as a result of recurring disappointments. The historical hope was then turned into *eschatological vision*. See M. Buber, "Introduction" (*Kingship of God* [trans. R. Scheinmann; London: Allen & Unwin, 1967]).

tained by the biblical Israelites. These expectations could then be described as the "fulfilment of salvation history at the end of days."

This transference of the eschatology concept could be defended by arguing that in portraying the conceptual universe of the ancient Israelites from which we are separated by an interval of more than two millennia, we must necessarily have recourse to linguistic images with which we are familiar. I can no more escape from my vocabulary than I can escape from my skin. Allow me to clarify this hypothetical argument by means of a few examples.

Since Max Weber introduced the term *charisma*, borrowed from the New Testament, into the study of the Old Testament, it has been widely used in reference to the leaders of biblical Israel who were imbued with divine spirit.[3] Writers also apply to the social structures of the Ancient Near East expressions and concepts that are a legacy of Classical Greece, the Roman Empire, or the Middle Ages. It has even become quite common to talk of a "primitive democracy" in Mesopotamia and in biblical Israel[4] or to employ terminology borrowed from the medieval feudal system to describe Israel's societal institutions.

Here, however, we should sound a warning.[5] Different cultures cannot simply be fitted into a single linguistic or conceptual framework. If we proceed by way of sweeping generalizations, we run the risk of either diluting originally precise terms by using them in a transferred sense, or of trimming the peculiar features of phenomena which are specific to other cultures (primitive, ancient-oriental, or Far Eastern) in order to adjust them to our own comprehension, thereby violating their particular identity. The problem was in fact recognized and taken into consideration by some scholars. Dis-

---

3.   M. Weber, *Ancient Judaism* (trans. H. H. Gerth and D. Martindale; Glencoe, IL: Free Press, 1952); H. H. Gerth and C. W. Mills, trans., *From Max Weber: Essays in Sociology* (London: Kegan Paul, 1947), chaps. 9, 10.

4.   The concept was applied by T. Jacobsen to Mesopotamian polity and thereafter also to biblical Israel (See Jacobsen, "Primitive Democracy in Ancient Mesopotamia," *JNES* 2 [1943] 159–72; idem, *Toward the Image of Tammuz and Other Essays on Mesopotamian History and Culture* [Cambridge, MA: Harvard University Press, 1970] 157–70; C. Umhau Wolf, "Traces of Primitive Democracy in Ancient Israel," *JNES* 6 [1947] 98–108; R. Gordis, "Primitive Democracy in Ancient Israel," *A. Marx Jubilee Volume* [Philadelphia: JPS, 1950] 347–96; et al.) A dissenting opinion was expressed by P. A. H. de Boer ("Israel n'a jamais été une democracie," *VT* 5 [1955] 227, n. 2). See further S. Talmon, "The Judean ʿAm Haʾareṣ in Historical Perspective" (*KCC*, 68–78); idem, "Kingship and the Ideology of the State" (*KCC*, 9–38).

5.   See S. Talmon, "The Comparative Method in Biblical Interpretation," in this volume, pp. 11–49.

cussing the concept of *eschatology* under scrutiny here, G. von Rad says, "In contrast to the ever more general and accordingly more colourless linguistic use of the *eschatological*, warning voices have been raised, rightly demanding that the term remain a precise one which may be used only to denote a definite, well-marked phenomenon."[6] But in everyday practice, exegetes, theologians, and historians of religion often do not heed this warning.

It need hardly be stressed that the elucidation of the concept *eschatology* in relation to the Hebrew Bible should be based mainly on insights obtained from the Hebrew texts themselves. Inferences from other sources should be used only on a limited scale, if at all, and even then *mutatis mutandis* with the necessary adaptation to the thought climate that pervades the Hebrew writings. In other words: the entire complex of Israelite literature with the values contained in it must be viewed in itself, within its own framework of characteristic features, and not be assessed merely as a precursor of postbiblical Jewish and Christian ideas.[7]

Let us begin with a truism: In the biblical text there is no exact Hebrew equivalent of the Greek word ἐσχατολόγια in the sense of "teaching about last things." However, from this we do not necessarily draw the conclusion that the ancient Israelites lacked the views and concepts denoted by this Greek term.[8] The presence or absence of these views from the Hebrew Scriptures can be determined only by a thorough investigation of the contents of relevant texts that must go beyond a mere linguistic analysis.

This undertaking is beset by great difficulties. It cannot be stressed often enough that the Hebrew Bible is not just a book but, in Martin Buber's words, "a Book of books."[9] The generic title *biblia* refers to an anthology, a collection of writings which grew and accumulated over more than a millennium and presents to the reader both a longitudinal section (diachronic) and

6. "Gegenüber einem immer allgemeiner und demgemäss immer blasser werdenden Sprachgebrauch vom Eschatologischen erhoben sich aber warnende Stimmen, die mit Recht forderten, dass der Begriff präzis bleiben müsse und nur auf ein bestimmtes, markantes Phänomen angewendet werden dürfe" (G. von Rad, *Theologie des Alten Testaments* [München: Kaiser, 1960] 2.127).

7. See my remarks concerning this issue in "The Concept of Revelation in Biblical Times," in this volume, pp. 192–215.

8. Similarly, Biblical Hebrew has no equivalent for the Greek noun ἀποκάλυψις. See R. Rendtorff, "Die Offenbarungsvorstellungen im Alten Israel" (*Offenbarung als Geschichte* [ed. W. Pannenberg; Göttingen: Vandenhoeck & Ruprecht, 1963] 21ff.).

9. "Biblia, Bücher, so heisst ein Buch aus Büchern" (M. Buber, "Der Mensch von heute und die jüdische Bibel," *Die Schrift und ihre Verdeutschung* [ed. M. Buber and F. Rosenzweig; Berlin: Schocken, 1936] 13).

a cross section (synchronic) of the literature that came into existence during that period, in its manifold variety of genres and forms. At the same time, this anthology reflects the spiritual panorama of Israel from the *Landnahme* in Canaan until some two centuries before the destruction of the Second Temple and the loss of political sovereignty in the year 70 CE.[10]

A living culture such as that of biblical Israel is not static. It develops and changes in the course of time both as a result of internal stresses and through the influence of external forces. This is true also of the expectations for the future expressed in the Hebrew Bible. Hence it follows that it is almost impossible, as von Rad demands, to isolate and extract from the Hebrew Bible that "characteristic phenomenon" to which the concept *eschatology* legitimately could be applied.[11]

Another peculiarity of biblical literature stands in the way of such an attempt. We do not find in the Hebrew Bible efforts to present systematically the concepts that served the Israelites as guidelines in speculative thought or in their actual life. It seems that the ancient Hebrews rejected from the outset the compulsion that is involved in any attempt at systematization. Rather, it would appear that they conceptualized by "association" in a manner which we might consider nonmethodical. They reacted predominantly *ad hoc* and *ad rem* to stimuli that arose out of history. This applies to biblical anthropology and sociology as well as to theology, to cite only a few major aspects of the biblical marketplace of ideas.[12] Thus, for example, they were content to define only a few basic principles concerning kingship, such as are articulated in the "King's Law" (Deut 17:14–20), which certainly did not suffice for an adequate circumscription of the monarchical institution.[13] The reader and the scholar are therefore obliged to piece together a mosaic of idea-fragments extracted from the texts so as to make them form a meaning-

---

10. I have discussed the gradual emergence of what ultimately came to be known as the *Canon of (Hebrew) Scriptures* in "Heiliges Schrifttum und Kanonische Bücher: Überlegungen zur Ausbildung der Grösse Die Schrift im Judentum" (*Mitte der Schrift? Ein jüdisch-christliches Gespräch: Texte des Berner Symposions vom 6.–12. Januar 1985* [Judaica et Christiana 11; Bern: Lang, 1987] 45–80).

11. G. von Rad, *Theologie* (see above, n. 6) 127.

12. See S. Talmon, "Literary Motifs and Speculative Thought," *HSLA* 16 (1988) 150–68; idem, "Har and Midbār: An Antithetical Pair of Biblical Motifs," *Figurative Language in the Ancient Near East* (ed. M. Mindlin, M. J. Geller, and J. E. Wansbrough; London: SOAS, 1987) 117–42.

13. See my remarks on this issue in "Kingship and the Ideology of the State" (*KCC*, 9–38); and " 'The Rule of the King': 1 Samuel 8:4–22" (*KCC*, 53–67).

ful whole. It is inevitable that in such attempts one should have recourse to texts that reflect more tersely and precisely than others the thoughts that one wishes to systematize. Accordingly, the prophetic books and the Psalms have a specially strong attraction for theologians and historians of ideas, for in them the religious dimension dominates to an extent which is scarcely attained in other biblical books and genres. This pertains also to Christian *Old Testament eschatology*,[14] which is extrapolated mainly from the Prophets and the Psalms.[15] But even if a real concept of eschatology could be proven to inhere in these texts, it could not legitimately be used as a master key for the entire Hebrew Bible. The spirit of ancient Israel manifests itself in the historical writings, in wisdom literature, and in the legal codes no less than in the Prophets and the Psalms. And this literature contains hardly any traces of a "real eschatology."

II

We shall now examine in short what the term *eschatology,* understood as the "teaching about last things," stands for. An exhaustive treatment of the problem would be out of place here, nor is it required. But it may be useful in this context to quote Alfred Jepsen's comment:

> The Old Testament also knows an expectation for the future and speaks of what is about to happen. The question has been extensively discussed whether this expectation can be termed eschatology. According to one's understanding of the concept, all, some or none of O. T. statements about the future, fall within this category. If eschatology describes only a new world era, the end of the present historical epoch, then one must be cautious in employing this term; but if eschatology refers to a future in this history, to a

---

14. The literature on this issue is too voluminous to be adduced here. But mention must be made of the basic study of S. Mowinckel, "Das Thronbesteigungsfest Jahwäs und der Ursprung der Eschatologie" (*Psalmenstudien* [Oslo: Universitetsvorlaget, 1922], vol. 2, esp. pp. 211–324). See also H. D. Preuss, ed., *Eschatologie im Alten Testament* (Darmstadt: Buchgesellschaft, 1978).
15. This limitation shows, e.g., in the study of C. Kayatz-Bauer, "Exegetische Information über Eschata, Fortschritt und gesellschaftliches Engagement," (*Eschatologie und geschichtliche Zukunft: Thesen und Argumente* [Essen: Fredebeul & Koenen, 1972] 5.89–118).

turning-point in it, one may surely apply the concept to the O. T., and so, of course, if the term eschatology is to embrace all statements about the future.[16]

Such an extension of the application of the term would, however, lead to a dilution of its content and render it meaningless. Jepsen is therefore quite right when he says:

> Thus more important than airing the issue of terminology is the depiction of the peculiar structure of O. T. statements about the future, in all their diversity and modifications. They do not form a unified system. . . . We therefore include here within the term Eschatology all statements about the future without thereby making any pronouncement regarding the applicability of the concept eschatology to all these expectations.[17]

The Greek word ἐσχατολόγια, the teaching about last things, presupposes a capacity for abstract thinking and a sense of chronological perspective that appear to go beyond the bounds of ancient Israelite thought. It is therefore not suprising that, as we have said, the Hebrew Bible has no single lexical equivalent for the Greek concept expressed by the one word ἔσχατον. The notion of an *absolute last* or an *absolute end* seems to be far removed from biblical thinking. Biblical man thought impressionistically. In space he recognized a relative *before* and *behind* as seen from the standpoint of the speaker, onlooker or agent, but no absolute *foremost* or *hindmost* referring to extremities independent of the person concerned. *Backwards* and *forwards* can point in opposite directions in one and the same situation. This difference in the expression of chronological and spatial relationship, often perplexing to someone accustomed to more precision in the relative location

16. "Auch das AT kennt eine Zukunftserwartung, spricht von dem, was geschehen wird. Es ist viel darüber verhandelt worden, ob man die Erwartung als Eschatologie bezeichnen darf. Je nachdem, wie man den Begriff versteht, fallen alle, einige oder keine der at. Zukunftsaussagen darunter. Wenn E. nur ein neues Weltzeitalter umschreibt, das Ende der gegenwärtigen Geschichtseposche, wird man in der Anwendung diese Begriffes zurückhaltend sein müssen; wenn E. sich aber auf die Zukunft dieser Geschichte, eine Wende in dieser Geschichte bezieht, dann darf man den Begriff E. im AT verwenden; ebenso natürlich, wenn E. alle Zukunftsaussagen umfassen soll" (Alfred Jepsen, "Eschatologie," *RGG* 2.655).

17. "So ist wichtiger als diese terminologische Frage die eigenartige Struktur der at. Zukunftsaussagen, in all ihrer Mannigfaltigkeit und allem Wechsel darzustellen. Sie bilden kein einheitliches System. . . . So werden unter dem Stichwort E. hier alle Zukunftsaussagen zusammengefasst, ohne dass damit über die Anwendbarkeit des Begriffes E. auf alle diese Erwartungen etwas ausgesagt werden soll" (ibid.).

of objects in time and space (first, last), can be illustrated by the following examples.[18]

(a) Noah, the first viniculturist, "drank some of the wine, became drunk and lay naked in his tent" (Gen 9:20–21). Out of respect for their father, his sons Shem and Japheth covered him with a garment to avoid seeing him naked. The scene is described as follows (v. 23): "They walked backwards, אחרנית . . . and their faces were backwards, אחרנית." Here the word *backwards* describes the sons' position in relation to their father, referring simultaneously to their faces and to their backs. The indication of direction is thus not absolute but relative.

(b) A similar expression may be observed in the account of Jacob's meeting with his brother Esau (Genesis 33), whom he had craftily deprived of his father's blessing (Genesis 27). With good reason Jacob feared that a conflict might ensue. He therefore placed his concubines, Bilhah and Zilpah, and their children at the head of the column where they would be most exposed to a possible attack. His principal wives, Leah and Rachel, he kept in the background, with Rachel, his favorite, and her son Joseph bringing up the rear (Gen 33:2). In relation to the concubines and their children who were in front—ראשנה, i.e., "the first"—Leah, Rachel, and their children were together "the last"—אחרנים. Since Biblical Hebrew has neither a comparative nor a superlative to describe chronological (later, latest) or spatial relationships (farther back, farthest back), it lacks an adequate expression to describe the position of Leah and her children relative to Rachel and her son Joseph. It could also be that the narrator did not intend to indicate the actual end of the column. His main concern was to describe the position of Jacob's principal wives, for whom the concubines served as safety bumpers, so to speak, and then to stress the especially safe position of Rachel and her son who were further shielded by Leah and her children. Therefore he could only indicate their relative positions by saying, "He [Jacob] placed Leah and her children last, אחרנים, and Rachel and Joseph אחרנים (Gen 33:2), using exactly the same Hebrew word in both clauses

The same relativity also characterizes the ancient Hebrews' concept of time. The recording of events in a series is often not *linear:* it does not proceed from an absolute starting point and lead to an absolute end. It is based on references to *earlier* or *before, later* or *afterwards,* in relation to

---

18. A full exposition of this issue will be presented in a separate publication.

some prominent midpoint in time, the point of departure important to the *dramatis persona* involved, rather than to absolute poles. Here are some examples.

(a) Qoheleth maintains that for everything on earth there is a precedence. What appears to be "(absolutely) new," חדש, only appears to be so because of our short memory but in fact "has already existed long ago, before our time" (Qoh 1:10). He then illustrates his contention by stating that those who live in the present time do not remember "the first," i.e., former, generations, אין זכרון לראשנים; nor will "the last," i.e., future, generations be remembered by those who come after them, וגם לאחרנים שיהיו לא יהיה להם זכרון עם שיהיו לאחרנה (Qoh 1:11). The vocables ראשנים, אחרנים, and לאחרנה do not define stages in an absolute chronological scale but rather designate past and future segments of time to which the "speaker" relates from his vantage point in the present.

(b) Equally, the postexilic prophet Zechariah refers to his predecessors, prophets like Amos, Hosea, Isaiah, and Jeremiah who were active before the destruction of the First Temple, as הנביאים הראשנים (Zech 1:4; 7:12). Zechariah himself, together with Haggai and Malachi flourished after the return from the Babylonian exile, i.e., after a critical cut-off point in time. They are considered to be among the נביאים אחרונים. Translating these Hebrew terms "first" and "last" prophets is imprecise, since this rendition suggests an absolute chronology. The correct equivalents are "former" and "later" (prophets). The "former" ones were themselves preceded by seers like Samuel, Nathan, Ahijah, and Gad (1 Samuel *passim;* 2 Samuel 7, 12, 24; 1 Kings 1, 11, 14, et al.). Likewise the "later" ones looked forward to the coming of their successors. The book of Malachi, which closes the collection of biblical prophetic writings, ends by proclaiming the coming of the prophet Elijah at some unspecified point in the future "before the onset of the great and terrible day of YHWH" (Mal 3:23–24). Thus the last of the later, i.e., of the postexilic prophets, is himself entered into a series in which he is relatively but not absolutely the last.

(c) A similar comprehension of time is reflected in the words of Haggai, who compares the postexilic temple, הבית הזה האחרון, with Solomon's preexilic temple, designated הראשון (Hag 2:9). Here הבית האחרון undoubtedly designates not the last but the later, i.e., the Second Temple, which could in principle be followed by a third and even a fourth. Indeed, the Qumran community, which arose in the second century BCE, awaited the rebuilding of a temple in the "New Jerusalem,"[19] in accordance with their views, so divergent in many other respects from those of mainstream contemporary Judaism.

(d) Another illustration of אחרון, connoting "later" or more precisely "next" in relation to the "present," may be found in the "Praise of the Capable Wife," אשת חיל (Prov 31:10–31). Taking care of the needs of her husband and children (31:11, 23), she also "keeps her eye on the doings of her household" (31:27) and makes sure that everyone of its members is properly fed and clad (31:14, 15, 21, etc.). Therefore, she "can afford to laugh at tomorrow" (NEB),[20] ותשחק ליום אחרון (31:25), fully satisfied that she has stored ample provisions not only for the present day but also for an uncertain tomorrow. If we translated יום אחרון "last day," we would invest the phrase with a sense of "finality" and thus would miss altogether the very tangible, down-to-earth praise that the wise author of the couplet wishes to bestow upon the אשת חיל.

(e) The temporal connotation "next" rather than "last," which often attaches to אחרון, as shown, is brought into full light in passages in which an accompanying synonymous explanatory expression evidences this specific meaning of the term. The precision becomes especially prominent when אחרון is employed in lists or accounts of a generational character. Some telling examples are:

(1) Deut 29:21: ואמר הדור האחרון ‖ בניכם אשר יקומו מאחריכם
The next generation ‖ Your sons who follow you (NEB).
La génération future ‖ Celle de vos fils qui se léveront après vous (SB).
Eine spätere [besser: die kommende] Generation ‖
Also eure Söhne, die nach euch erstehen" (EÜ).

(2) Ps 78:6: למען ידעו דור אחרון ‖ בנים יולדו יקמו ויספרו לבניהם
That it may be known to the next generation,[21]
To sons born [to you], who will arise and tell it to their sons.[22]

19. Y. Yadin, ed., *The Temple Scroll* (Jerusalem: IEJ/Hebrew University, 1984).
20. Similarly R. B. Y. Scott (*Proverbs and Ecclesiastes* [AB 18; Garden City, New York: Doubleday, 1965] 186), "She happily looks forward to the morrow" and "Elle rit au jour à venir" (SB [Paris: Cerf, 1961] 846). W. McKane (*Proverbs* [OTL; Philadelphia: Westminster, 1970] 261) renders the phrase less precisely, "She laughs at the uncertain future," as do B. Gemser (*Sprüche Salomos* [HAT, first series, 16; Tübingen: Mohr/Siebeck, 1937] 84); H. Ringgren and W. Zimmerli (*Sprüche/Prediger* [ATD 16/1; Göttingen: Vandenhoeck & Ruprecht, 1980] 118): "Sie lacht des künftigen Tages"; and EÜ ([Stuttgart: Katholische Bibelanstalt, 1980] 1404): "Sie spottet der drohenden Zukunft."
21. Einheitsübersetzung: "Das kommende Geschlecht." The translation "future generation" (NEB) or "la génération qui vient" (SB) obfuscates the intended sense of immediacy.
22. Viz., "to your grandchildren."

In the following instance, the same connotation attaches to אחר, which should either be seen as a synonymous vocable of אחרון, or as its abbreviation :

(3) Joel 1:3:   עליה לבניכם ספרו ובניכם לבניהם ובניהם לדור אחר
Tell it to your sons [children] and your sons to their sons,
And their sons to the next generation.[23]

III

This relative system of dating events according to their coming in time before or after a fixed middle point, instead of in relation to an absolute beginning and end, seems to account for the fact that biblical language shows no equivalent for the Greek ἔσχατον in the sense of an "absolute last."

The most pregnant passages cited in the endeavor to establish an "Old Testament eschatology" are generally characterized by Hebrew expressions which in Greek are rendered by ἔσχατον. The question must be asked whether this rendering accurately reflects the intrinsic meaning of the Hebrew terms. The conceptual content of these terms cannot be determined adequately by their etymological derivations, much less by having recourse to ancient translations. These non-Hebraic tools are often impaired by the translators' conceptual field of vision, which does not match the conceptual world of the biblical authors. Hence, the inquiry must concentrate on the Hebrew Bible itself and establish its findings by intertextual comparisons. This is the surest approach for obtaining reliable and precise semantic information about the expressions under review.

Such presumably "eschatological" texts are often marked by the use of one of the following three expressions:

(a) From the time of Amos, the first "missionary prophet," we find in biblical literature the concept of יום ה', "the Day of YHWH" or the "Day of the Lord" (Amos 5:18–20), sometimes also designated היום ההוא, "that day," as in Mal 3:23. The translation often given, "the Last Day" or "the Day of

---

23.   Here the (formulaic?) reference extends over four generations. The precision is again lost in the loose NEB translation of the last stich, "Let them pass it on from generation to generation," which SB correctly renders, "à la génération qui suivra, " and EÜ, "dem folgenden Geschlecht."

the Last Judgment," has christological overtones. In the wake of this translation an eschatological character was attributed to "that day." It was seen
as marking the end of the historical world. The interpretation of this concept
by von Rad and others caused the term to be understood as an expression of
an ancient, even archaic, Israelite longing for the end of time, which was
adopted by Amos. But in the biblical context "that Day" is conceived as a
future stage in time when Israel will take revenge on the nations who oppressed her. At the same time this revenge was regarded as the execution of
divine punishment. Amos, it is said, gave a new dimension to this national
dream of vengeance, investing it with prophetic morality: on that day God
will sit in judgment over all evildoers, but primarily over the sinners among
his own people.[24] The motif of יום ה׳ appears only in prophetic literature and
finds scarcely any echo in historiography, legal literature, or biblical poetry.
Therefore M. Weiss questions the antiquity of the concept and surmises that
the idea originated with Amos and subsequently found an answering echo in
prophetic circles and only in prophetic circles.[25]

(b) קץ is frequently used in apocalyptic visions in the books of Ezekiel
and Daniel (Ezek 21:30, 34 [LXX: 21:25, 29]; Dan 8:7, 19; 11:13, 27, 35,
40; 12:4, 9; 2 Chr 21:19) in conjunction with the qualifying terms עת,
"period," and מועד, "time." This combination proves that קץ alludes to a
fixed and predetermined point in time, at the end of a period but not necessarily at the End of Time. This interpretation is borne out by the employment
in Ezekiel 7 of בא הקץ in a ring-composition with the synonymous phrases
בא היום and בא העת, all pointing to an imminent event, עתה (7:3), הנה באה
(7:6, 10), to a "day (which) is near," קרוב (7:8; cp. 7:12). In these instances
the translation of the phrase by "the hour of final punishment" (NEB) is in-
accurate and misleading.

The philological and literary analysis proves that the concepts considered under (a) and (b) do not refer to an End of Time but rather to a divinely
appointed crisis, a turning point in history, i.e., a point within historical time
and not a post- or supra-historical date. The fact that the end envisaged here

---

24.   A concise summary of the issue is provided by W. S. McCullough ("Israel's Eschatology
      from Amos to Daniel," *Studies on the Ancient Palestinian World* [ed. J. M. Wevers and
      D. B. Redford; Toronto: University of Toronto Press, 1972] 86–101).

25.   See M. Weiss, "The Origin of the 'Day of the Lord' Reconsidered," *HUCA* 37 (1966)
      19–71.

lies within historical time must be especially emphasized, since this recognition gives important information about the biblical hopes for the future.

The time gap which extends between the present time of the author, or of the *dramatis personae* to whom he addresses himself, and the date of the expected future crisis is somewhat more precisely indicated by:

(c) The expressions אחרית הימים, or אחרית השנים are generally rendered "End of Time" or "End-of-the-World years." But once again a study of biblical philology suggests that the word אחרית, like the etymologically cognate word אחרון, often equals "descendants," denoting the next or the third generation.

A prophetically foreseen turn of Israel's fate, whether propitious or condemnatory, is often said to occur in a period of time which is predominantly termed אחרית הימים, and once אחרית השנים (Ezek 38:8). The expression is mostly translated "End of Time," "End of Days," etc., or "End-of-the-World Years" and is thus invested with a metahistorical signification.[26] But a survey of pertinent passages suggests that אחרית, like אחרון, often connotes "offspring/descendant," more precisely, the next generation or the one after it. As was shown in reference to אחרון/אחר, this connotation becomes fully apparent when אחרית is juxtaposed with intratextual or contextual explanatory synonyms or vocables of a similar meaning.

The following selected instances exemplify this particular use of אחרית:

(1) Jer 31:17:   ויש תקוה לאחריתך . . . ‖ ושבו בנים לגבולם

The text is best translated, "There is hope for your descendants . . . your sons will return to their land" (cp. v. 16), much like the renditions of SB, "Il est un espoir pour ta descendance . . . ils vont revenir, tes fils, sur leur terre," and EÜ, "Es gibt eine Hoffnung für deine Nachkommen. . . . Die Söhne werden zurückkehren in ihre Heimat," rather than translated as in the NEB, "You shall leave descendants after you. . . . "[27]

26. See J. Carmignac, "La notion d'eschatologie dans la Bible et à Qumrân," *RevQ* 7 (1969) 17–39; H. Kosmala, "At the End of the Days," *ASTI* 2 (1965) 27ff.; H. Seebass, "אחרית," *TWAT* 1.224–28.

27. The phrase יש תקוה לאחריתך is used in Prov 23:18 and 24:14 in a break-up pattern: כי אם יש אחרית ‖ ותקותך לא תכרת.

(2) Job 42:12–13: וה' ברך את אַחֲרִית איוב מראשיתו . . . ויהי לא שבעַנה בָנִים ושלוש בָּנוֹת

The context and pertinent parallels suggest the following somewhat free translation of this text: "YHWH blessed Job with a second set of children more than [he had blessed him] with the first," rather than "blessed the end of Job's life more than the beginning" (NEB), "bénit la condition nouvelle de Job plus encore que l'ancienne" (SB), or "segnete die spätere Lebenszeit Ijobs mehr als seine frühere" (EÜ).

(3) Ps 109:13: [28]יהי אחריתו להכרית ‖ בדור אחר ימח שמם
May his offspring[29] be cut off;
In the next generation may his name[30] be extinguished.[31]

(4) Deut 32:20: אראה מה אחריתם ‖ כי דור תהפכת המה ‖ בנים לא-אמֻן בם
Let me see what their descendants[32] [are like];
They are a mutinous generation,
Sons who are not to be trusted.

The proposed synonymity of אחרית with בנים (and בנות), "children," is put in full light when both terms are mentioned in juxtaposition with the parent generation, as in:

(5) Ezek 23:25: אפך ואזניך יסירו ואחריתך בחרב תפול
המה בניך ובנותיך יקחו ואחריתך תֵּאָכֵל באש

In an oracle of doom, the prophet threatens the inhabitants of Judah that the Babylonians will destroy the kingdom[33] and will surely vent their rage against old and young alike. They will put parents to the sword together with their children. The term אחרית in the phrases ואחריתך בחרב תפול and ואחריתך

28. אחר equals אחרון (see above). LXX: μιᾷ resulted from a misreading of אחד for אחר. שמם is probably a miswritten שמו.
29. NEB: "his line"; SB: "sa descendance"; EÜ: "Nachkommen."
30. Viz., "his family."
31. Cp. Ps 37:37–38. I have discussed this motif in "*Yād Wāšēm*: An Idiomatic Phrase in Biblical Literature and Its Variations" (*Hebrew Studies* 25 [1984] 8–17).
32. That is to say the offspring of the children of Israel, who in the preceding verse are called God's "sons and daughters." The renditions "their end" (NEB), "ce qu'il aviendra d'eux" (SB), and "was in Zukunft mit ihnen geschehen wird" (EÜ) miss the point.
33. Here called Oholibah.

תֵּאָכֵל בָּאשׁ is explained by the interspliced hendiadys בניך ובנותיך, "your children."[34]

(6) Amos 4:2:　כי הנה ימים באים עליכם ונשא אתכם בצנות ‖ ואחריתכן בסירות דוגה

> Days are coming when you will be carried away in [fish] baskets,
> And your daughters [dragged away] with [fish] hooks.[35]

The pale LXX rendering of ואחריתכן by καὶ τοὺς μεθ' ὑμῶν, "those who are with you," is inferior to *Tg. Neb.*'s correct translation ובנתכון, "your daughters," which is echoed in the commentaries by Kimchi, בניכן ובנותיכן, "your sons and daughters"; Ibn Ezra, הבן שיעמוד אחרי כן, "the son who will then arise"; and Rashi, who bases his understanding of the term on Dunash ibn Labrat's comment: "We found that a man's offspring can be called אחריתו, as in Dan 11:4."[36] The intrinsic sense of the phrase is lost in translations such as, "et jusqu'aux dernières" (SB), "und was dann noch von euch übrig ist" (EÜ), and "your remnant,"[37] which S. Paul surprisingly adopts in his most recent commentary, "the very last one of you."[38]

(7) Num 23:10b:　תמת נפשי מות ישרים ותהי אחריתי כמהו

The preceding reference to the "multitudes of Israel" in the first hemistich (23:10a) suggests that the second should be translated:

---

34. The MT refers המה to the enemy who will "take your sons and daughters." But המה בניך could possibly be connected with the first stich as an interpretative apposition to the preceding ובנותיך; ואחריתכן would then explain the usage of that very term in the second stich.
35. סירות is a fem. form of סירים, "thorns" (Isa 34:13; Hos 2:8; Nah 1:10). See especially Qoh 7:6, כקול הסירים תחת הסיר, where by way of paranomasia the laughter of a fool is likened to the "crackling of [burning] thorns under a pot."
36. Cp. NEB, "your children," and H. W. Wolff, *Dodekapropheton 2* ([BKAT 16/2; Neukirchen-Vluyn: Neukirchener Verlag, 1975] ad loc.).
37. H. W. Wolff, *Joel and Amos* (Hermeneia; Philadelphia: Fortress, 1977) 204.
38. S. Paul, *Amos* (Hermeneia; Minneapolis: Augsburg Fortress, 1991) 128–35. Cp. J. L. Mays, *Amos* (OTL; London: SCM, 1969) 71. T. H. Robinson and F. Horst (*Die Zwölf Kleinen Propheten* [HAT Erste Reihe 14; Tübingen: Mohr/Siebeck, 1954] 84) offer what appears to be the worst possible translation, taking אחריתכן to mean "your behind": "da trägt man euch fort mit Haken und euren Hintern mit Fischangeln." Cp. E. Hammershaimb (*The Book of Amos: A Commentary* [trans. J. Sturdy; New York: Schocken, 1970] 66–67): "The women are compared with the corpses of animals which are dragged away with a hook in the nose and in the back."

Num 23:10b: May I die an honorable death, and may my offspring be like theirs [Israel's].

The connotation of אחרית in the texts adduced above prompts the conclusion that the expression אחרית הימים[39] in most instances signifies the appreciably close occurrence of future events in the course of history. In Deut 31:29 this signification of אחרית הימים is made explicit by an intratextual explanatory reference to a situation which can be expected to arise after the death of Moses, the *dramatis persona*.[40]

(8) Deut 31:29:   כי ידעתי אחרי מותי כי השחת תשחתון וסרתם מן הדרך אשר צויתי אתכם
וקראת אתכם הרעה באחרית הימים כי תעשו את הרע בעיני ה'

Like other leaders of biblical Israel, Moses is apprehensive lest after his death the people transgress the commandments he has taught them (cp., int. al., Josh 24:1–15; 1 Sam 12:6–17). Therefore, he ends his farewell speech (31:24–29) by admonishing Israel to keep God's laws, threatening transgressors with divine punishment:

> For I know that *after my death* you will do much evil
> and turn aside from the way which I told you to follow,
> and *in [those] days to come* disaster will befall you,
> because you will be doing what is wrong in the eyes of YHWH.

In the parallelistic structure of this verse, the plain sense of the A-phrase, אחרי מותי, in the first stich, illuminates intratextually the seemingly opague B-phrase באחרית הימים, in the second stich.[41] The text does not speak of metahistorical "Last Days" or the "End of Time" when the deplorable state of affairs of which Moses warns his contemporaries could materialize. It speaks, rather, of an imminent future phase in history, actually the days of their אחרית, their children or grandchildren (cp. Gen 49:1–27).[42]

---

39. Equally אחרית השנים (cp. Ezek 38:8 with 38:16).
40. Cp. with Balaam's speech above (Num 23:10), in which אחריתי is explicated by מות.
41. Similarly, the Aramaic term אחרית יומיא (Dan 2:28) is explicated in the ensuing verse by אחרי דנה, "after this." Daniel interprets Nebuchadnezzar's dream as pertaining to events which will soon come about.
42. When the angel Michael reveals to Daniel "what will happen to your people באחרית הימים" (Dan 10:14a), a wider panorama is envisaged. But this vision also is set in the frame

The results of this linguistic inquiry, which can be corroborated by further examples, suggest that in the Hebrew Bible, hope for the future within the framework of history predominates over the idea of an eschatological future set in metahistory. This does not necessarily mean that in biblical literature no vestiges of a concept which transcends history are found. But the analysis of the above texts that pertain to the future indicates that they refer to an imminent event or turning point in history.

The concept that visions of the future are history-bound fits perfectly into the framework of the biblical world of ideas in general.[43] Actual history is seen to extend over some seven to eight generations: three to four before, and three to four after the time of the speaker or author (Jer 27:7). This prospective and retrospective view of history finds an expression in literary motifs. The tradition of three generations of patriarchs and matriarchs may serve as an example. Jacob descends into Egypt with "his children and his children's children" (Gen 46:6–7; cp. Judg 12:14; Jer 29:6; 1 Chr 8:40). Whoever lives to see children and grandchildren is regarded as blessed. "He who leaves an inheritance to grandchildren" (Prov 13:22) is proverbially happy. They are the pride of the grandfather (Prov 17:6). Especially distinguished is the man to whom are granted great-grandchildren in his lifetime, as were Joseph (Gen 50:23) and Job (Job 42:16). Whatever lies beyond this period of time is not precisely defined but is rather described as "distant past" or "forever" and "to eternity."

Thus we read in Ezek 37:25, "They will dwell in the land that I gave to my servant Jacob, in which their fathers lived; they shall dwell in it, they, their children and their children's children *forever*, and my servant David will be their king [prince] *forever*," and in Ps 132:12, "If your children keep my covenant and my testimony that I shall teach them, also their children shall sit *forever* upon your throne" (cp. Jer 35:6; 1 Chr 28:8; also 2 Kgs 17:41).[44] We find the same idea expressed in proverbs and rhetorical figures threatening punishment that will extend beyond the sinner's lifetime. Con-

---

of historical time by means of another term which highlights the precise meaning of אחרית הימים, viz., "those days to come," עוד חזון לימים (10:14b).

43. The biblical concept of history will be discussed in a separate study.

44. It can also be argued that the term עד עולם, which is usually translated "forever" or "for all eternity," in fact relates to a restricted period of time. See E. Jenni, *Das Wort* leolam *im Alten Testament* (Berlin: Töpelmann, 1953); P. A. H. de Boer: "Leolam, à jamais connote dans l'Ancien Testament et dans les textes extrabibliques où on la rencontre une longue durée de vie. Il n'est en aucun cas question d'une vie éternelle" (*VT* 5 [1955] 226).

sider for example Jer 2:9, "Wherefore I will yet plead with you, says YHWH, and with your children's children will I plead." The God of Israel is a jealous God "visiting the guilt of the fathers upon the children, upon the third and upon the fourth generation" and shows his love to his faithful ones "even to the thousandth generation" (Exod 20:5; 34:7; Num 14:18; Deut 5:9; Ps 103:17).

IV

Against this background we can now attempt to define in broad outline the content of biblical hopes for the future. The results of this endeavor will be a composite picture, since they derive from texts culled from various strata of biblical literature. For this reason the presentation cannot be systematic, neither in pinpointing specific conceptions in definite periods of the biblical era, nor in tracing a presumed development of the concept of the future during biblical times. Only a few basic elements in the vision of the future can be ascertained to appear in most, though not all, relevant biblical texts and which, notwithstanding their differences, can be reduced to a common denominator. The resulting mosaic will necessarily remain incomplete.

In view of the fact already demonstrated that biblical visions for the future are set within the framework of history, it is understandable that they are characterized by a trend which foresees the restoration of past glories: the expected reconstitution of a situation which has already been experienced and which became "idealized" by its depiction in utopian hues. They express the belief that the hoped-for *turning point in time* (not the *End of Time*) will culminate in a situation that is an infinitely better image than one already encountered in the historical past. This visionary picture reflects the notion that hope is the memory of the past translated into the future, a longing to relive past history without the disappointments which marred the former times and without the flaws which disfigure the present.

Martin Buber has summarized the two-layered character of Israel's hope for the future with impressive brevity:

"Eschatological" hope—in Israel, the "historical people par excellence" (Tillich), but not in Israel alone—is first always historical hope; it becomes eschatologized only through growing historical disillusionment. In this process faith seizes upon the future as the unconditioned turning point of history, then as the unconditioned overcoming of history. From this point of vantage it can be explained that the eschatologization of those actual-historical ideas includes their mythicization. . . . Myth is the spontaneous and legitimate language of expecting, as of remembering, faith. But it is not its substance. . . . The genuine eschatological life of faith is in the great labour-pains of historical experiences—born from the genuine historical life of faith; every other attempt at derivation mistakes its character.[45]

"Eschatology as a function of historical experience"[46] shares a common base with the expectation of the rise of a future Anointed One: restoration, shot through with threads of utopian idealization.[47] It is an incontestable fact that in postbiblical Jewish and Christian thought, eschatology and messianism became inextricably intertwined. This was not the case, however, at the outset, in the conceptual universe of biblical Israel. As already mentioned it is impossible to chart objectively, on the strength of unambiguous data in the Hebrew writings, the course of development which the concepts then took. Nevertheless one can propound the thesis that in the earlier strata of ancient Israelite literature, *eschatological* and *messianic* visions occur independently of one another.[48] The prototype of an eschatological vision—better defined a *vision of later times*—is contained in the books of two representatives of the first generation of missionary prophets, Isaiah (2:2–4) and Micah (4:1–5).[49] These passages do not contain any mention of a messianic figure. The same is true of other texts already referred to above. By contrast, passages that do contain a vision of an Anointed One, such as Jer 23:5–6 (or 5–8), refer exclusively to the expected scion of the house of David, i.e., to a royal figure. Showing no features of an eschatological universalism, they

45. Buber, "Preface," *Kingship of God* (see n. 2 above).
46. V. Maag, "Eschatologie als Funktion des Geschichtserlebnisses," *Saeculum* 12 (1961) 123–30.
47. G. Scholem, "Toward an Understanding of the Messianic Idea in Judaism," *The Messianic Idea in Judaism and Other Essays on Jewish Spirituality* (ed. N. N. Glatzer; New York: Schocken, 1971).
48. For the relationship of these two types of visions, see S. Talmon, "Biblical Visions of the Future Ideal Age" (*KCC*, 140–64).
49. We do not need to consider here the question of whether Micah quoted from Isaiah or vice versa, or whether both depended on a common source. For a discussion of the issue see, int. al., H. Wildberger, *Jesaja 1–12* ([BKAT 10/1; Neukirchen-Vluyn: Neukirchener Verlag, 1965] 76–81); O. Kaiser, *Das Buch des Propheten Jesaja, Kapitel 1–12* ([ATD 17; Göttingen: Vandenhoeck & Ruprecht, 1981] 61–64); H. W. Wolff, *Dodekapropheton 4: Micha* ([BKAT 14/4; Neukirchen-Vluyn: Neukirchener Verlag, 1982] 87–92); D. R. Hillers, *Micah* ([Hermeneia; Philadelphia: Fortress Press, 1984] 51–53).

quite clearly reflect historical experience (cp. Jer 22:1–5 with 1 Kgs 5:6–8; 10:28–29; and Deut 18:16–17 with 1 Sam 8:11).

Two main strands of expectation for the future can be distinguished clearly in biblical texts. If one wishes to apply to them the term *eschatology*, while taking the aforementioned considerations into account, one could speak of a *situation-eschatology* on the one hand and a *Messiah-eschatology* on the other. The fusion of the two concepts can in fact be observed in the biblical writings, but it finds its clearest expression in Christian messianic eschatology. This is partly to be explained by the fact that the expectation of an *Endzeit* in Christian belief arose out of the picture of an actually experienced *Vorzeit*, charged with the values and the image of an *Endzeit*, in which the *eschaton* had already been realized in history, as it were. The concretization of the messianic idea in the person of Jesus enabled believers to pass through the gates leading into the eschatological Kingdom of God. The ensuing recognition that what had been regarded by the faithful as marking the End of Time was not in fact the final event caused the relegation of the End of Time to an era beyond the scope of history. Concurrently, the prototypical model of the *Vorzeit* was lifted from the history of biblical Israel and was now identified in the early Christian epoch. Thus it was *ent-historisiert*. The eschatological image became separated from historical patterns.[50]

A development, similar in many respects, can be observed in post-biblical Jewish expectations of the future in which the messianic idea assumed a central place. G. Scholem defined the unhistorical character of postbiblical Jewish messianism as follows:

> The magnitude of the Messianic idea corresponds to the endless powerlessness in Jewish history during all the centuries of the exile, when it was unprepared to come forward onto the place of world history. There's something preliminary, something provisional about Jewish history; hence its inability to give of itself entirely. For the Messianic idea is not only consolation and hope. Every attempt to realize it tears open the abysses which lead each of its manifestations *ad absurdum*. There is something profoundly unreal about it. . . . Thus in Judaism the Messianic idea has compelled a *life lived in deferment*, in which nothing can be done definitively, nothing can be irrevocably accomplished: One may say, perhaps, the Messianic idea is the real anti-existentialist idea.[51]

---

50. See S. Talmon, "Types of Messianic Expectation at the Turn of the Era," *KCC*, 202–24; idem, "Biblical Visions of the Future Ideal Age," *KCC*, 140–64.

51. G. Scholem, "Toward an Understanding" (see above, n. 47), 35.

This description does not apply to the expectations of the future contained in the Hebrew Bible. The faith of ancient Israel is characterized by a realism and activism which are manifest in ideas about the future as well, a time expected to supervene upon radical revolution in world affairs. The prototypical era upon which the hoped-for future is modeled, is derived from biblical historiographies and from the books of the prophets of the First Temple Period and the restoration period after the Babylonian Exile. The ideas and beliefs about society and politics which inhere in this historical pattern are expressed in prophetic oracles of woe and solace, as well as in songs of psalmists. The line of thought which inspires all these biblical authors and also pervades their visions of the future, reflects the historical conditions of the Davidic-Solomonic era. The hope for a restoration of that period purged of its shortcomings in actual history, idealized, and to some extent transfigured in a utopian manner, supplied the basic contours of the Coming Days. It could be said that in the biblical picture of the future the restorative orientation has its foundations in the historical books, while the utopian superstructure was inspired by the writing of the prophets and the psalmists.

V

Hope for the future is marked by an expected *Renewal of the Covenant* contracted by the God of Israel with his people.[52] This renewal is indeed regarded as a fresh beginning, but not as the establishment of an entirely *New Covenant*.[53] The Hebrew expression ברית חדשה must be understood relatively, not absolutely.[54] It propagates the principles of the covenant that God had previously contracted and recontracted with Israel at various stages in history. This is a basic element in biblical Covenant Theology: the covenant relationship between God and his people is a constant factor, which however needs to be renewed from time to time. Crises in the nation's history require a renewal of the ברית.[55] New conditions necessitate its reaffirmation. The

---

52. See M. Weinfeld, "ברית," *TWAT* 1.781–808.
53. See H. Weippert, "Das Wort vom Neuen Bund in Jeremiah XXXI, 31–34," *VT* 29 (1979) 336ff.; C. Westermann, *Genesis I* (BKAT 1; Neukirchen-Vluyn: Neukirchener Verlag, 1974) 633ff.
54. See above, pp. 167–68.
55. This is a major theme in the theology of the Qumran Covenanters, especially stressed in CD.

covenant that God will reestablish with Israel in the future is seen as one more link in the chain which began with the covenant between God and man at the time of creation.

This truth is suggested by Hosea. In his presentation of the future ברית, he has recourse to images and expressions borrowed from the creation story: "On that day will I make a covenant . . . with the beasts of the field, and with the birds of heaven, and with the creeping things of the earth" (Hos 2:20). The passage echoes the words with which God established his (new) Covenant with Noah: "God spoke to Noah and his sons, saying, 'Behold, I establish my covenant with you and with your descendants after you; also with every living creature that is with you, birds, cattle, and every beast of the earth with you; all that came out of the ark, everything that lives on the earth'" (Gen 9:8–10; cp. 9:12–17). On their part these words hark back to the Covenant God established with Adam (Gen 1:26–30). The Covenant with Noah, the new Adam, symbolizes the new creation of the world after the flood, when creation had relapsed into תהו ובהו in the Flood.

That covenant is also taken up by Jeremiah in his vision of the future (Jer 31:31–37). After the Flood, God had promised Noah that he would never again destroy the world (Gen 8:21; 9:9–15). He set the rainbow among the clouds in the sky as an everlasting sign that he would always maintain the cosmic order he had created. As long as the world lasts, (the sequence of) seed time and harvest, frost and heat, summer and winter, day and night would never again cease (Gen 8:21ff.). The Covenant with Noah for eternity, ברית עולם (Gen 9:16; cp. CD iii 4; 1QH iii 11–12; iv 22; 1QM xvii 3), means that the rhythm of nature is assured forever.[56] For Jeremiah this irrevocable law is the foundation of the future renewal of the covenant, the ברית חדשה, which God will make with Israel and Judah (Jer 31:31; cp. CD vi 19; viii 25, 31; 1QpHab ii 3): "Thus says the Lord, who provides the sun for light by day and the moon and the stars for light by night, who calms the sea when its waves roar. Just as this order will never be shaken, so will Israel never cease to exist as a nation before God" (Jer 31:35–36).

These prophetic pronouncements, almost quotations, should not be viewed as mere literary or stylistic devices. By lifting phrases from the wording of the *Primeval* ברית and applying them to the *Future* ברית, Hosea and Jeremiah point to the basic element common to both: the old order has not

---

56. See S. Talmon, "Prophetic Rhetoric and Agricultural Metaphora," *Storia e tradizioni d'Israele: Studi in onore di J. A. Soggin* (Brescia, Italy: Paideia, 1991) 267–79.

been superseded; rather, it needs to be revitalized.[57] What appears at first glance to be only a literary repetition actually emphasizes an association of ideas connecting the subject matter of the quotation with that of the passage quoted. The textual connection expresses, as by a catchword, a profound connection of ideas.

The awaited renewal of the ברית signifies not merely a reestablishment of the Primeval Covenant. Its portrayal by the prophets culminates in the presentation of an ideal situation which prominently features the hope for universal peace and for a new political and social order that will embrace all mankind. This universalism can be traced to the Creator's equally all-embracing Covenant with Adam and with Noah. The visionary-utopian coloring that the prophets give the picture effectively stresses the universalist feature still more strongly. But even in this grandiose representation of the future we can also recognize elements derived from the actual history of Israel.

To support our thesis we must refer back to the assumption that the Hebrew Bible sets forth a concept of God's *renewing* his covenant with Israel at various stages in history. A brief explanation will clarify this point. The pre-Israelite covenant with humanity, personified severally in Adam and Noah, is followed by the special Covenant with Abraham (Gen 15:18; 17:1–14; cp. CD xii 11), Isaac (Gen 17:15–19; 26:1–5), and Jacob (Gen 28:13–15; 35:9–15; cp. 32:23–31; 48:3–4). It is retrospectively described in a comprehensive review as the *Covenant with the Patriarchs* (Exod 6:2–8; Deut 4:31; Jer 34:13; Mal 2:10; Ps 105:3–10; cp. CD viii 17–18; xiii 6; xiv 8). In the Revelation at Sinai the covenant is extended to all Israel, redeemed from Egyptian bondage (Exod 34:10; Deut 5:2). At that time God reinstated the *Covenant with the Ancients,* the Patriarchs—ברית ראשונים (Lev 26:45; cp. CD i 4; vi 2)—as a *Covenant with the Nation.* By this renewed covenant, Israel, while still a young nation (Ezek 16:8, 59–63), is sanctified, chosen, and separated from all other peoples (Exod 19:5; 24:8; 34:27; Deut 7:6; Dan 11:28–30). This covenant was also made "forever" (Exod 31:12–17; 34:10; Lev 24:8; Deut 4:23; 29:9ff.; cp. Judg 2:1; 2 Kgs 17:35; Isa 24:5; 55:3; Jer 32:40; Ezek 16:60; Ps 89:35). Now the "Tables of the Covenant" and the "Ark of the Covenant" serve as symbols of God's pact with his people (Num

---

57. Cp. M. Buber, "Leitwortstil in der Erzählung des Pentateuch," *Die Schrift und ihre Verdeutschung* ([ed. M. Buber and F. Rosenzweig; Berlin: Schocken, 1936] 211–38).

10:33; 14:44; Deut 10:8; Jer 3:16), as the rainbow in the clouds bears witness to the Primeval Covenant with humanity.

There is also the recurring tradition of a divine covenant with certain distinguished persons. Like the Patriarchs before them they are recognized as representatives of the entire people. Thus were Moses, Exod 24:7–8, and Aaron, the ancestor of the priestly house, whose special status is ratified by a "covenant of salt," ברית מלח עולם (Num 18:19; cp. Lev 2:13).

These considerations allow a better understanding of the nature and function of the covenant which God made "forever" with David and his house (2 Sam 23:5; 2 Chr 21:7). The permanence of the covenant with David and his descendants, as seen by Jeremiah, is no less irrevocable than the order of the universe which the Creator laid down after the Deluge (cp. Jer 33:19–21 with 25–26 and Gen 9:8–16; cp. 8:21–22). Now the "tabernacle" (2 Sam 7:6) and the "house" built to honor God's name (7:13) symbolize the ברית. But although everlasting, the covenant must be renewed from time to time. This will always occur after a crisis suffered by the house of David, as under Asa (2 Chr 15:12), Joash (2 Kgs 11:17), Hezekiah (2 Chr 29:10), and Josiah (2 Kgs 23:3; 2 Chr 34:21). Like the covenants with the patriarchs, or with Moses and Aaron, the Covenant with David is not merely in the nature of a divine promise made exclusively to him and his house. The contract God made with the ruler includes Israel as a whole. The concept of the Davidic dynasty as the representative of the entire people is expressed unequivocally in phraseology and imagery that relate to the royal house as well as to the people of Israel. In this case also the similarity of wording must be understood as an indication of the symmetry between people and king.[58]

The renewal of the covenant with the people, in the form of the ברית with David, had become necessary because of the revolution in the social and political structure of Israel: the transition from the system of periodically appointed שופטים, reflected in the book of Judges, to the hereditary monarchy. With the foundation of the Davidic dynasty the People of Israel became a *Nation* with its own characteristic polity.[59] The radically different sociopolitcal conditions were not covered by the Covenant with the Patriarchs, nor by the Covenant with the People at Sinai. For this reason it needed

---

58. See Talmon, "Kingship and the Ideology of the State," *KCC*, 12–13.
59. See idem, "The Biblical Concept of Jerusalem," *Journal of Ecumenical Studies* 8 (1971) 300–316.

ratification by means of the Covenant with David, whereby the God of Israel endowed historical facts with a *legal* basis anchored in faith. On the face of it, the postexilic Returnees' Contract with God, in its wording relates only to certain aspects of religious and civil life. But in reality it reflects a comprehensive Renewal of the Covenant (Ezra 10:3; Neh 10:1–40 with reference to chap. 9). The terminology employed in these passages—כרת, ברית, אמנה—establishes quite clearly the "covenantal" character of this contract. It is a further link in the chain of renewals of which the prophets speak (Jer 31:31–37; Hos 2:20).[60] In the face of the expected loss of all religious paraphernalia and instruments of statehood (Hos 1:3–5; 3:4; Jer 25:8–11; 26:4–6, et al.), the prophets saw the renewed covenant symbolized in the people's change of heart, the new heart on which would be inscribed the stipulations of the ברית, God's Torah (Jer 31:33–34; cp. Hos 2:16–25).

This was also the nature of the New Covenant into which the Qumran community would enter. The members of this community considered themselves to have returned "from the Wilderness of the Nations" and thus identified themselves as the Returnees from the Babylonian Exile.[61] Their Covenant Renewal, ברית חדשה, is an expression of their closeness to God and their gratitude for the grace he had shown them. The covenant confirmed their status as the Remnant of the Righteous. According to their view, Israel, after having been destroyed by the Babylonians in 586 BCE, was given a new lease on life in their community (CD i 1–8):

> Now hearken all ye that know righteousness, and consider the works of God, for He hath a dispute with all flesh and He will execute judgment upon all that despise Him. For when they sinned in that they forsook Him, He hid His face from Israel and from His sanctuary and gave them to the sword. But when He remembered the covenant of the forefathers, He caused a remnant to remain of Israel and gave them not up to be consumed. And [at the predestined turning point] in [of] the epoch of wrath, three hundred and ninety years after He had given them into the hand of Nebuchadnezzar, king of Babylon, He [once again] visited them [turned to them]; and He caused to grow forth from Israel and Aaron [i.e., from the royal house of David and from the priestly house of Aaron] a root of cultivation to possess His land and to wax fat in the goodness of His soil.[62]

60. See Weinfeld, *TWAT* 1.781–808 (above, n. 52).
61. See S. Talmon, "The New Covenanters of Qumran," *Scientific American* 225/5 (1971) 76ff.; idem, "Between the Bible and the Mishnah," *WQW*, 21–52.
62. C. Rabin, ed., *The Zadokite Documents* (Oxford: Clarendon, 1954) 3.

Viewed against this background, the concept of ברית חדשה, taken from the Hebrew Bible to denote the New Testament, in all probability was orginally understood as a Renewal of the Covenant. This interpretation of the concept is of great importance for the understanding of the term in its biblical and early postbiblical setting.[63]

VI

These thoughts concerning the meaning and the development of the covenant idea are offered as a further illustration of the ancient Israelites' understanding of their history. The digression seems to be justified, since the New, or rather, Renewed Covenant occupies a central postion in biblical expectations for the future ברית, again established by God and explicitly or implicitly linked to a point of reference in historical experience. This is a fact of decisive importance. In the past the "eternality" of the Covenant that God contracted with Adam, Noah, the people of Israel, and David was repeatedly called into question because of the shortcomings of the human partners. By contrast, such failures are categorically excluded from the vision of a future covenant.[64] In retrospect, the Covenant with Adam and Noah, and certainly that with the Patriarchs, is invested with *historical* significance. Also the creation of the world is looked upon as an historical fact.[65] But it is the ברית with the people and above all the ברית with David that constitutes the central feature in the covenantal relationship which God established with all Israel. The *Vorstellung* of the future is expressed in images and phrases taken from the portrayal of the political, social, and religious situation previously experienced during the reigns of David and Solomon. This is clearly demonstrated by the opening lines in Jeremiah's vision of the days to come:

> Behold the days are coming, says YHWH, when I will fulfill the promise I made to the
> House of Israel and the House of Judah: In those days and at that time I will cause a

---

63. The text of CD viii 8–12 should also be viewed from this angle and interpreted accordingly. An exhaustive study of this question is a desideratum, which cannot, however, be undertaken within the scope of this paper.

64. See Weippert, *VT* 29 (1979) 336ff. (above, n. 53).

65. See S. Talmon, "The Biblical Understanding of Creation and the Human Commitment," *The Second Annual F. Neumann Symposium Ex Auditu* 3 (1987) 98–119.

185

shoot of righteousness to spring forth from David.[66] He shall practice justice and righteousness in the land. In those days Judah shall be saved and Jerusalem[67] shall dwell securely.... For thus saith YHWH: David shall never lack a male descendant to sit on the throne of the House of Israel; and the Priests and Levites shall never lack a descendant to stand in my presence and offer burnt-offerings, to burn meal-offerings and offer sacrifices every day (Jer 33:14–18).[68]

The reference to the political security of Israel and Judah is an unmistakable reprise of the statement that serves as the summation of the Solomonic era, "Judah and Israel lived in security, every man under his vine and his fig tree from Dan to Beer-Sheba, throughout the days of Solomon" (1 Kgs 5:5), which is clearly echoed in prophetic visions of the "days to come" (See Mic 4:5 and Joel 4:20; cp. Lev 26:5, et al.). At that time the Temple in Jerusalem was built and the forms of temple service established to which Jeremiah refers in his words of promise. In short, the historical epoch of David and Solomon is regarded as the *Vorzeit,* and its image is projected into the portrayal of the hoped-for future situation. Therefore, the future cannot be considered as absolutely *new*. It is indeed radically different from the past actually experienced in that it promises a new start and will be free from the blemishes of the past. But in essence the situation envisaged to arise after the expected turning point is conceived in historical terms. The vision remains earthbound. It is transfigured, but not altogether removed from comprehensible reality. God promises to renew his covenant with *regenerated humanity,* with his *regenerated people* in a *recreated world*. On the foundation of this renewed covenant the individual and the community will build up a pure life, free from sin.

The ideal picture of the future mainly focusses on "natural" or "ascriptive" units: family, clan, nation. The family remains the basis of society, as in the actual historical world. The relationship between fathers and sons will not be marred anymore by the tensions which marred it in historical times: "Behold, I will send you Elijah the prophet before the coming of the great and terrible day of YHWH. He will turn the heart of the fathers toward the[ir] children and the heart of the children toward the[ir] fathers" (Mal 3:23–24). Peoples and nations will persist in their various frameworks

66. Cp. CD i 7.
67. "Jerusalem" possibly signifies "Israel" (see Jer 33:17).
68. The passage Jer 33:14–26 is missing in the LXX. However, for our purpose it is immaterial whether the prophecy indeed originated with Jeremiah or whether it was secondarily ascribed to him.

of statehood after the expected turn of time. But the relations between them will be regulated by justice and not decided upon by violence and war. There are references to "elective" groups of faithful ones, to whom God will show his favor when he punishes sinners. These "faithful" are now seen as the chosen ones *within* Israel, his special possession, not the entire people of Israel whom God had chosen from all peoples at Sinai and made his own (cp. Mal 3:13–22, esp. v. 17 with Exod 19:5–6). But the chosen appear only in postexilic books, i.e., in the later or latest parts of biblical literature. These passages evidence the beginning of a process of internal disintegration—a schism which will become fully visible in Israel two or three centuries later.[69]

In the portrayal of future time, little attention is given to the individual. The ideas of redemption, resurrection, and life after death play but a minor part. They emerge only in the latest strata of biblical literature, especially in the latter part of the book of Daniel which is regarded its latest component (2d century BCE). Even there such ideas are not fully elucidated. An unequivocal reference to resurrection and life after death appears only in Dan 12:1–2: "At that [future] time your people shall be spared, all those whose names are written in the [my] book [cp. Mal 3:16]. Of those who lie sleeping in the dust of the earth, many will awake, some to everlasting life, some to shame and everlasting disgrace." We must not deduce from this isolated statement that by that time biblical Israel had developed a definite concept of life after death. It can at best be regarded as the seed from which the doctrine of the resurrection grew in the post- and extra-biblical world of ideas.[70]

In the Hebrew Bible the view prevails that death is indeed man's end. The psalmist's enemies ask: "When will he die and his name perish?" (Ps 41:6). Here *name* is clearly a figurative synonym for children.[71] The author of the book of Job compares a dead man with a flower which blooms and then withers, or with a felled tree that can never again put forth shoots (Job 14:1–9). He asks, "Once a man is dead can he come back to life?" (Job

---

69. See S. Talmon, "The Emergence of Jewish Sectarianism in the Early Second Temple Period," *KCC*, 165–201.

70. See idem, "Die Wertung von 'Leben' in der Hebräischen Bibel," *Der Herr des Lebens: Jüdische und christliche Interpretationen in der Ökumene* (Arnoldshainer Texte 39; Frankfurt/M: Haag & Herchen, 1985) 15–30 = *Juden und Christen im Gespräch: Gesammelte Aufsätze* (Neukirchen-Vluyn: Neukirchener Verlag, 1992) 2.48–60.

71. Idem, *Hebrew Studies* 25 (1984) 8–17 (above, note 31).

14:14) or "Man? He dies and lifeless he remains; man breathes his last and then where is he?" (14:10). The writer is not content with rhetorical questions but states explicitly, "Man, once in his resting place, will never arise again; there is no awakening from [that] sleep" (14:12; cp. 3:13; Isa 43:17; Ps 41:9; 88:4–8, et al.).

The theme of the finality of death, which frees man from his pains on earth, occupies a central position in the view of the author of the book of Job. It is placed at the very beginning of the dialogue series (chap. 3), as if it were a motto. This thought reverberates through biblical wisdom literature and is echoed in the pessimism of the Preacher: "Every creature originates from dust and returns to dust. Who knows if the spirit of man mounts upward, or if the spirit of the beast goes down to the earth?" (Qoh 3:20–21).[72] The anticipatory answer is given in 3:19 (cp. 9:2–3): "The fate of men and beasts is identical: one dies, the other too. . . . The living know at least that they will die. The dead know nothing, nor is there any more reward for them; their memory is forgotten" (cp. Qoh 9:5). "There is no achievement, no planning, nor knowledge, nor wisdom in Sheol, where you are going" (9:10; cp. 10:14).

Similar thoughts permeate texts which express the Preacher's attitude toward death: "A live dog is better than a dead lion" (Qoh 9:4). Biblical man, wishing to avoid or to delay death, tries to persuade God that man's death also redounds to his disadvantage: in the netherworld one cannot praise God; the dead cannot celebrate him; they that go down into the pit cannot hope to attain his truth (Isa 38:18). In the shadows of the netherworld God's miraculous deeds are eclipsed; in the land of oblivion his divine justice and countenance are unknown. No miracles can be worked for the dead; those who lie in their graves cannot praise God (Ps 88:11–13). In these texts, to which others could be added (cp., e.g., Qoh 5:14–15), there is no hint of hope for "life after death." After death man is "gathered unto his fathers," as are Abraham (Gen 25:8), Ishmael (Gen 25:17), Isaac (Gen 35:29), Jacob (Gen 49:29–33), Aaron (Num 20:24), and Moses (Num 27:13; Deut 31:16). The phrase may well refer to burial in a family vault (2 Kgs 22:20). Good men "lie with their fathers." Thus Jacob (Gen 47:30; 49:29), Moses (Deut 31:16), David (2 Sam 7:12; 1 Kgs 11:21), Solomon (1 Kgs 11:43; 2 Chr 9:31), and likewise the later kings of Judah and Ephraim (1 Kgs 14:20, 31;

---

72. This skeptical statement is "revised" in what is considered to be an appendix to the original collection of proverbs: "Before the dust returns to the earth [to be] as it had been, and the breath [soul] to God who gave it" (Qoh 12:7).

15:8, 24; 16:6, 28, et al.). The same applies to the rulers of other nations, except those who, possessed by wanton hubris (Isa 14:18), treated Israel with special cruelty (Ezek 32:28–32).

Thoughts about death rarely go beyond the state of interment. Biblical authors declare with pessimistic or realistic resignation that after death man returns to dust (Gen 3:19) and becomes the prey of worms (Isa 14:11; Job 7:5; 17:14; 21:26; 25:6). There is no attempt at philosophical or theological speculations on the question of what lies beyond the threshold of death. When such thoughts are expressed in phrases like "to be gathered to one's fathers" or "to rest with one's fathers," they point to the survival of the community (family, clan, or nation) and not to an expected resurrection of the individual. These phrases testify to an awareness of solidarity which makes possible a hope for the future but without dwelling on the idea. Such hope is concentrated on the offspring, who are to fill the void on earth left by the departure of their forebears. The individual dies and becomes nought; the community continues to exist and therefore has a future.

Individual man lives in one dimension. He cannot reach out beyond his own lifetime. The community has two temporal dimensions: a synchronic and a diachronic. Communal life promotes an awareness of history which extends from the present backward into the past and forward into the future. The biblical injunction "remember, call to mind" your past (Deut 5:15; 8:2; 15:15, et al.) and God's mighty deeds in history (Exod 13:3; Deut 8:18; Ps 143:5), as God remembers his covenant (Gen 9:15; Lev 26:42, 45; Ezek 16:60)—this is the soil from which the watchword springs: you may, indeed you should, hope.

The future epoch in general can be divided into two stages. It begins with the Day of Reckoning: God wages war against the nations who have sinned against Israel and passes judgment on the evildoers in Israel and on all mankind. This is the יום ה', the time of divine judgment. The concept springs from man's recollection of God's deeds in historical experience. The collective memory preserves the remembrance of critical junctures in the past at which God intervened in the course of events, took the side of the righteous and the oppressed, and waged war against evildoers and oppressors, who are mostly represented as Israel's enemies. This stage of chastisement is the precondition for the dawn of salvation which will then appear for the righteous remnant of Israel and the righteous of all nations. The yearned-for perfect world will succeed the imperfect world of history, just as formerly the world of history replaced the antediluvian creation that had gone astray (Gen 6:13–22; 9:8–17).

It is my thesis that this two-staged picture of the unfolding future is also conceived as a retrojected reflection of historical experience under David and Solomon. In the portrayal of the future cosmic conflict, one can perhaps discern traces of David's war-ridden days, while in the portrayal of the ensuing era of bliss, Solomon's peaceful reign, the *pax Salomonica* is reflected. Thus the picture of the future corresponds in its essential features to the social and political conditions which obtained during the period of David and Solomon, when Israel was one nation.

It would take us too far afield to cite further texts which prove that the biblical authors, including the prophets, employ concepts, ideas, and verbal images that are taken over directly from the historical books or paraphrase models found there. They borrow them, thereby to describe the ideal world that lies beyond the turning point of time. The prophets, who were mostly opposed to the social and religious trends of their own day and severely criticized the people and their king, do not offer any alternative societal or political structure. King and people remain the bases upon which the hoped-for renewed world order is to rest. The future Anointed One is still regarded as a king, a successor of David, sprung from his royal house.

The prophets extended their vision of the future in depth and breadth to form a panorama that embraces the entire cosmos. The God of the universe, who reigns as supreme judge in Jerusalem (Isa 2:3–4; 51:4–5; Mic 4:2–3), will bring about the final reconciliation of all creation: between different creatures and between creatures and man (Isa 11:6–8; 65:25); between man and nature (Isa 65:17ff.; Ezek 34:25ff.; Hos 2:23–25; Joel 4:18, et al.); between man and man; and between nation and nation (Isa 2:4–5; Mic 4:3).

VII

In summary, it is obvious that the biblical vision of the future has its roots in actual conditions previously experienced in history. Even in the utopian, unprecedented aspects of this vision, points of topical reference can be discerned. The center of gravity is bound to earth. There is indeed a supraterrestrial, suprahistorical dimension but only in ancillary form. In visions of the future found in apocalyptic literature and then in the spheres of

Christian thought and postbiblical Jewish tradition, the sublime aspects are expanded and intensified and assume a decisive significance. In these later writings the biblical vision of the future, originally drawn from history, becomes *eschatological*.

The pivotal factor, in the biblical picture of the future as well as in ancient Israel's attitude toward history, is humanity's responsibility. It is the duty of every individual to bring the ideal future time into being in his own community by his righteous conduct in actual life. In this idea we observe a principle of education and self-discipline. Humanity is required to improve themselves and their environment, to nurture in themselves and in their contemporaries a life stance which will make them capable of internalizing the concept of the ideal aeon and thus be prepared for its realization at a time not precisely defined. Progress toward the turning point in history must necessarily be gradual. Therefore, the process leading up to its achievement is seen as an evolutionary transformation of the universe. There are indeed biblical texts that speak of God's future intervention in history, which is to usher in the supra- or meta-historical epoch. Such texts are found mainly in the later parts of biblical literature, in which an incipient apocalypticism makes its appearance: Ezekiel's Gog of Magog Oracle (Ezekiel 38–39) and his vision of the Valley of Dead Bones (Ezekiel 37), the prophecy of a future cosmic upheaval which closes the book of Zechariah (chap. 14), and the prophecies of final judgment and retribution in Joel 3 and Malachi 3. But more than depending upon such a revolutionary cataclysm, the achievement of the ideal aeon depends upon the conduct of humanity, which, if inspired by God's commandments and sustained by divine grace, will lead to a purer life of the individual and of society in the course of history. People must be stirred to the depths of their beings to recognize clear-sightedly their own shortcomings and the depravity of their society and then to devote themselves to the task of remedying these defects. The ways and means for achieving this goal are given in the norms rooted in faith and made evident in the Torah—the Teaching, combined with tenets derived from historical experience. The realization of the utopian ideal future can be furthered by approximating its image to historical models and extracting from them their inherent positive values. The acceptance of responsibility for the (even though only partial) realization of the ideal future in the present makes humanity God's partner in the creation of a new and better world founded on biblical precepts and prophetic revelation.[73]

73. See M. Buber, *Paths in Utopia* (trans. R. F. C. Hull; London: Routledge & Kegan Paul, 1949).

THE CONCEPT OF REVELATION
IN BIBLICAL TIMES

I

The acknowledgement of the "God who reveals himself to Man" is the central pillar of biblical faith. All exegetes and theologians are agreed on this principle, for which Martin Buber produced the following concise definition:

> Biblia, books, is the name of a book, of a book composed of many books. It is really one book, for one basic theme unites all the stories and songs, sayings and prophecies contained within it. The theme of the Bible is the encounter between a group of people and the Lord of the world in the course of history, the sequence of events occurring on earth.[1]

It can likewise be regarded as a matter of general agreement that the characterization of the Jewish and the Christian faiths as religions founded on revelation springs orignally from the Hebrew Bible which they hold in common—even if revelation is an element in the self-understanding of every religion.[2]

Within the limits of these basic concepts, and also with regard to the interpretive methodology to be employed in determining the ancient Israelites' understanding of revelation from the biblical texts, we can scarcely distin-

1. "Biblia, Bücher, so heisst ein Buch, ein Buch aus Büchern. Es ist aber in Wahrheit ein Buch. All diese Erzählungen und Gesänge, Sprüche und Weissagungen sind vereint durch das Grundthema der Begegnung einer Menschenschar mit dem Namenlosen, den sie, seine Anrede erfahrend und ihn anredend, zu benennen wagte, ihre Begegnung in der Geschichte, im Gang des irdischen Geschehens" (M. Buber, "The Man of Today and the Jewish Bible," *On the Bible: Eighteen Studies by Martin Buber* [ed. N. N. Glatzer; New York: Schocken, 1968] 1, originally published as "Der Mensch von heute und die jüdische Bibel," *Die Schrift und ihre Verdeutschung* [ed. M. Buber and F. Rosenzweig; Berlin: Schocken, 1936] 13).
2. C. M. Edsman, "Offenbarung, 1. Religionsgeschichtlich," *RGG³* 4 (ed. K. Galling; Tübingen: Mohr, 1960) 1597.

guish a specifically Jewish approach from a specifically Christian one. Within these limits, the divergences in the concept of revelation observable in scholarly literature on the Hebrew Bible, in the strict sense of the word, rest not so much upon the contrast between an explicitly Christian as opposed to an explicitly Jewish approach, as on the dissimilar state of scholarship which Rolf Knierim attributes to three basic factors:

(1) A certain "presupposition of a religio-phenomenological, religio-psychological and theological character, which conditions the scholar's view of the Old Testament texts."

(2) A central and all-pervasive "message to be discovered in the Old Testament by means of exegesis which then permits the entire corpus to be interpreted in a consistent and uniform manner."

(3) A markedly different "application of exegetical methods."[3]

When questions are raised about the form and content of biblical revelation, the situation changes completely. In considering these questions the interpreter works from a perspective inevitably influenced by his particular beliefs and dogmas. Not even the sincerest endeavor on the part of a scholar to let himself be guided in his inquiry by the modes of early Israelite thought can free him from the influences emanating from his self-identification as a Christian or a Jew. The decisive factor is that whereas for the Jew the books of the Hebrew Bible (the *Tanakh*) are the sole source for the understanding of the biblical concept of revelation, for the Christian these books represent only one part of his Bible (the Old Testament), whose revelation-concepts for him attain their full flowering and their essential, ultimate crystallization only in the New Testament. In the eyes of a Jewish Bible scholar, the forms and content of the revelation which marks the New Testament can be traced only indirectly and, in any case, only in some aspects to the Hebrew Bible. As is the case with other theological concepts and ideas, their postbiblical development did not proceed in complete dependence on the notions set forth or implied in the Hebrew Bible, nor in full harmony with them. The

3.   R. Knierim, "Offenbarung im Alten Testament," *Probleme biblischer Theologie: G. von Rad zum 70. Geburtstag* (ed. H. W. Wolff; München: Kaiser, 1971) 206ff.: (1) Ein bestimmtes "Vorverständnis, etwa religionsphänomenologischer, religionpsychologischer oder theologischer Art, unter dem die alttestamentlichen Texte gesichtet werden." (2) Ein zentrales und durchgängiges "Anliegen, das man aufgrund der Exegese im Alten Testament findet und von dem man dann die Gesamtheit der Texte einheitlich interpretieren kann." (3) Eine ganz unterschiedliche "Verwendung exegetischer Methoden."

later (i.e., the postbiblical) stages in the development of the biblical faith show a bifurcation between a Christian and Jewish understanding of "revelation in biblical times" which resulted from the specific conditions of theological training in the two religions.

About a decade before Knierim, Rolf Rendtorff[4] similarly assessed the state of research:

> Today the word 'revelation' has become a distinguishing mark in theological usage. This is also apparent in recent presentations of Old Testament theology, in which it is frequently and variously employed. Here it is remarkable how little consensus there is in discussion of revelation.[5]

While Knierim's essay goes beyond the subject of specifically Old Testament exegesis, Rendtorff arrives at his conclusions from the viewpoint of an Old Testament scholar:

> A theology of the Old Testament which takes its bearings from Old Testament thought *itself* [my italics] must always start from the Israelite understanding of history and Israel's historical metamorphoses.

His views relate in particular to those concepts of revelation in ancient Israel which can be established on the basis of an analysis (or rather his analysis) of the Old Testament Scriptures:

> It has . . . become manifest that for ancient Israel, YHWH could be perceived through his deeds in history and that it was through them that he revealed himself.[6]

4.   See R. Rendtorff, "Die Offenbarungsvorstellungen im Alten Israel," *Offenbarung als Geschichte* (ed. W. Pannenberg; Göttingen: Vandenhoeck & Ruprecht, 1963) 21ff., esp. 41 = *Gesammelte Studien zum Alten Testament* (ThB; Munich: Kaiser, 1975) 39–59.

5.   "Das Wort 'Offenbarung' ist heute im theologischen Sprachgebrauch zu einer gängigen Scheidemünze geworden. Das zeigt sich auch in den neueren Darstellungen der alttestamentlichen Theologie, in denen es vielfältig begegnet. Dabei ist aber auffallend, wie uneinheitlich das Reden von Offenbarung ist" (ibid., 21). See also R. Schäffler, "Der Offenbarungsbegriff—die Frage nach Kriterien seines sinnvollen Gebrauches" (*Offenbarung im Denken Franz Rosenzweigs* [Essen: 1979] 9–75, esp. 70ff.).

6.   "Eine Theologie des Alten Testaments, die sich am alttestamentlichen Denken selbst orientiert, wird immer vom israelitischen Geschichtsverständnis und seinen geschichtlichen Wandlungen ausgehen müssen. . . . Es ist . . . deutlich geworden, dass für das Alte Israel

There will be more to say about this definition of *revelation* as history which is directed explicitly at the Hebrew Bible and its significance for the understanding of the biblical belief in revelation.[7]

On the other hand, Knierim regards inquiry into the Old Testament concept of revelation not as a self-contained problem but as preliminary to a theological inquiry extending far beyond the framework of Old Testament studies proper. This would involve an examination of

> what the foregoing discussion can contribute to the solution of such longstanding and thorny problems as the relation between 'natural' and 'special' revelation, the revelation of Deity and of the Divine Name, the recognition of God in historical and ontological categories, of God as perceived in word and in deeds, of certainty and faith.[8]

Posing such questions implies certain premises which suggest an existential and predominantly Christian theological objective. Similar premises, though admittedly far less explicit, transpire also in the final passage of Rendtorff's essay:

> A theology of the Old Testament which is founded on Old Testament thinking . . . must nonetheless take into account the fact that at the time of the closing of the Old Testament canon, the history of YHWH's dealings with Israel and the world was not

Jahwe in seinen geschichtlichen Taten erkennbar wird, dass er sich ihnen als er selbst erweist" (Rendtorff, "Die Offenbarungsvorstellungen," 40–41). This does not imply that this concept of revelation was confined to Israel. Bertil Abrektson has shown that "the Old Testament idea of historical events as Divine Revelation must be counted among the similarities not among the distinctive traits: it is part of the common theology of the Ancient Near East" (*History and the Gods: An Essay on the Idea of Historical Events as Divine Manifestations in the Ancient Near East* [Lund: C. W. K. Gleerup, 1967] 114). See further J. Barr, "Revelation in History" (*IDBSup* [Nashville: Abingdon, 1976] 649–746); W. R. Irwin, "Revelation in the Old Testament" (*The Study of the Bible Today* [ed. H. R. Willoughby; Chicago: The University of Chicago Press, 1947] 247–67).

7. The idea that in the Old Testament God reveals himself chiefly in historical acts is frequently accentuated in modern scholarship. This is shown in the literature cited by Rendtorff, to which can be added the references given by Albrektson and Barr. But the volume edited by W. Pannenberg (with R. Rendtorff, T. Rendtorff, and U. Wilckens) sparked a specially intensive discussion both in biblical scholarship and systematic theology, so that the term *revelation as history* offers a good starting point for a reconsideration of the problem (*Offenbarung als Geschichte* [see above, n. 4]).

8. "Was das Gesagte für so alte und spannungsgeladene Verhältnisprobleme wie das von 'natürlicher' und 'spezieller,' von Gottes- und Namensoffenbarung, von Erkennen Gottes in geschichtlichen und ontologischen Kategorien, von Gott in Wort und in der Tat, von Gewissheit und Glauben austrägt" (Knierim, "Offenbarung," 235).

considered to have run its course; on the contrary, the latest writings in the Old Testament look forward to the ultimate revelation of YHWH.[9]

Even in a sincere attempt to understand the ancient Israelite concept of revelation solely in the light of Old Testament thought, the introduction of christological dogmas can lead to conclusions which are unacceptable to scholars whose roots are in Judaism. This applies, e.g., to the theses propounded by W. Pannenberg:

> Revelation takes place not at the beginning of revealed history but at its end. . . . The universal revelation of God's divinity is not yet realized in the history of Israel, but only in the fate of Jesus of Nazareth, insofar as this anticipates the end of all history.[10]

Studies of the ancient Israelite concept of revelation, which are based on linguistic and humanistic foundations and employ a common methodology make it possible for Jewish scholars to cooperate in elucidating the problem. But when these studies are made to yield Christian dogmatic assertions, such a procedure must lead to a point beyond which Christians and Jews will necessarily go their several ways in their efforts to understand the Old Testament belief in revelation and to grasp its existential import.

II

After these introductory remarks, I can now set about the task of tracing the outlines of a Jewish view on the concept of revelation held in biblical times. Please note that I am presenting *a* Jewish view—not *the* Jewish view.

---

9. "Eine Theologie des Alten Testaments, die sich am alttestamentlichen Denken selbst orientiert . . . wird aber auch voll in Ansatz zu bringen haben, dass in der Zeit des Abschlusses des alttestamentlichen Kanons die Geschichte Jahwes mit Israel und der Welt nicht als abgeschlossen verstanden wurde, sondern dass gerade die spätesten alttestamentlichen Schriften die endgültige Offenbarung Jahwes noch vor sich sahen" (Rendtorff, "Die Offenbarungsvorstellungen," 41).

10. "Die Offenbarung findet nicht am Anfang, sondern am Ende der offenbarten Geschichte statt. . . . Die universale Offenbarung der Gottheit Gottes ist noch nicht in der Geschichte Israels, sondern erst im Geschick Jesu von Nazareth verwirklicht, insofern darin das Ende alles Geschehens vorweg ereignet ist" (W. Pannenberg, "Dogmatische Thesen zur Lehre von der Offenbarung," *Offenbarung als Geschichte* [see above, n. 4] 91–114, esp. 95ff. and 103ff.).

Considering the linguistic, literary, and spiritual peculiarities of the biblical writings, which I shall mention later, and having regard for the rich diversity of the intellectual world of postbiblical Jewry, it would be a rash undertaking to offer a presentation of the concept of revelation in biblical times which would claim to be universally valid. I shall therefore merely set out some thoughts which reflect the attempt of a student of the Hebrew Bible to draw upon traditional Jewish exegesis, so as to shed light upon the concept of "revelation in biblical times." Some results of this inquiry concur with central issues elaborated by the "revelation-as-history" school. But I shall strive to attain my aim by a method of exegesis which differs essentially from that currently prevailing in Old Testament studies.

The biblical canon can be considered an anthology of ancient Hebrew writings, which contains a selection of works created over a period of about a thousand years (from the twelfth to the second century BCE). Thus the Hebrew Bible affords us a view of the ancient Israelite world of ideas in this entire period. This is surely not surprising. A similar situation can be observed in regard to other fields of belief and thought.[11] None of the ancient Israelite authors has given us a systematic or comprehensive account of a theory of sociology,[12] of literature, or of biblical theology. Nowhere in the Hebrew scriptures can we find a philosophical, phenomenological, or theological attempt to give what may be called a scholarly definition of revelation.[13] Whatever principles the reader or observer can derive from the Hebrew Scriptures rest upon an assemblage of reports, mostly short and not detailed, about revelations experienced by specially chosen individuals or by the people as a whole, and upon the attempt, based on this collection, to organize the separate narratives into one conceptual complex.[14]

Further, it must be borne in mind that the collection of Hebrew biblical writings is by no means homogeneous. The revelation-narratives contained in

11. Cp. my short observations regarding "Eschatology and History in Biblical Thought," in this vol., pp. 160–91.
12. See S. Talmon, "Kingship and the Ideology of the State," *KCC*, 9–38.
13. The absence of any attempt at systematization is also a feature of postbiblical Jewish thinking, as is evident from the conceptual universe of the sages. The fact has been stressed that among the approximately 3000 Greek loanwords in rabbinic literature, no philosophical-technical terms occur, not even attempts to render such Greek terms into Hebrew or Aramaic. See S. Lieberman, *Greek in Jewish Palestine* (New York: JTSA, 1972). Not until the Middle Ages did Jewish philosophers embark upon systematic thought and its appropriate formulations, for which purpose they evolved the required vocabulary.
14. See S. Talmon, "Literary Motifs and Speculative Thought," *HSLA* 16 (1988) 150–68.

them arose at various times and stem from a range of cultural milieus. They are familiar to us through reports which were probably not composed by the subjects of revelatory experiences, but were handed down orally and committed to writing at a later period. We must therefore reckon with the possibility that we do not possess any authentic firsthand accounts of actual revelation but only traditional versions formulated in retrospect and colored by subsequent interpretation. These facts are generally known and recognized. However, they must be underlined at the outset of our reflections, even though mentioning them may be considered carrying coals to Newcastle.

The most striking feature of present-day biblical scholarship is manifest in the indefatigable efforts to define and demarcate precisely the various literary and historical components, not merely of the entire canon, but of each single book and often of the several sections of a book. Regarding the issue under scrutiny, scholars are not content to disentangle the components imbodied in the "larger units" which have come down to us; by rearranging them, they attempt to construct a literary sequence which will offer a clear picture of the ancient Israelites' concept of revelation. The apparent discrepancies in the biblical descriptions of revelations are attributed to different intellectual circles of Israelite literati and then are integrated into a developmental scheme. On the strength of the analysis and the reconstruction based on it, various notions of revelation are extracted from the various sources and documents. These notions, it is claimed, are reflected in the particular vocabulary which distinguishes one tradition stratum from another. Thus for example the terminology employed to describe revelation in the Priestly Document (P) is distinguished from that of the Deuteronomist (D) and both of these from the Elohist (E) and the Jahwist (J). Since these various sources or strata of literary activity can supposedly be dated (even though there is not unanimity on the precise dating), the attempt is made to classify and arrange the documents according to a scale of values by means of which the development of the conception of revelation from "primitive" to more advanced stages in the biblical period can be assessed.[15]

This endeavor is understandable. It accords with present-day thought patterns which are marked by an urge to arrange and classify a search for models and schemas in which thoughts and the thought process can be grasped and made comprehensible. In this tendency one recognizes the intel-

15. See Rendtorff, "Die Offenbarungsvorstellungen."

lectual heritage of the classical world, transmitted by medieval philosophy (including scholasticism), which in modern science manifests itself in the urge to discover "structures" in the intellectual sphere.

The ancient Hebrew, however, and perhaps the ancient Semites in general, do not appear to have been subject to such a compulsive urge to systematize; they seem, rather, to have shied away from such a tendency, if indeed it played a part at all in their way of thinking.

Judged by the standard of modern patterns of thought, the biblical authors can be described as "non-methodical." I would suggest that this characteristic is evidenced also by the absence of any attempt to set a common theological denominator to the revelations recorded in the Bible. Each revelation reported in the Scriptures resulted from an ad hoc impetus. The biblical narratives describe each one as a separate event without attempting to derive them from or to trace them back to a common principle.

III

It would take us too far afield to recapture in detail the scholarly discussion concerning revelation in the Old Testament. It suffices to refer to the extensive surveys offered by Rendtorff, Pannenberg, Barr, and others. I would like only to deal briefly with a few aspects of the problem which in my view demand a fresh scrutiny and in this connection to suggest some theses based upon a Jewish approach to the biblical concept of revelation.

Man's experience of God in revelatory situations is depicted in the Hebrew Bible in recurring word pictures or formulae which can nonetheless express fine shades of meaning. In this context three verbs play a specially prominent role:

(1) גלה, chiefly used in the reflexive niphᶜal conjugation with God as subject, נגלה, or in the hitpaᶜel form, התגלה;[16]

(2) ראה, either in the active paᶜal (qal) conjugation, with man as subject, or in the passive or reflexive form נראה, referring to God as the agent of revelation.

(3) ידע, mainly in the niphᶜal form, נודע, which is to be understood as a reflexive.[17]

16.   See H. J. Zobel, "גלה," *TWAT* 1.1021–31.
17.   See J. G. Botterweck, "ידע," *TWAT* 3.486–512.

As already stated, modern scholars of the literary-historical school adduce these various modes of expression as proof of the assumption that they originate from different sources and reflect diverging biblical concepts of revelation. In a brief summing-up of the theory currently prevailing, Rendtorff remarks:[18] "Revelation in the strict sense of the word . . . generally means God's self-revelation. . . . But there are various ways in which one can speak of YHWH's self-revelation or self-disclosure. The oldest and most original use of the term occurs when we are told that the Deity 'shows himself.' The niph⁽c⁾al of ראה is the term used for such divine revelations," which bear a cult-etiological character. This term is frequently used by J, sometimes independently of the cult-etiological schema, in which case it is connected with a divine promise, but "never for . . . a cultic theophany." Ultimately "the notion of YHWH's self-revelation was considered altogether inappropriate."[19]

The Priestly Document substitutes ידע, "to know" for ראה, "to see." This is evident when the wording of the revelation to the patriarchs (Gen 17:1; 35:9 [J]) is compared with the description of the revelation granted to Moses (Exod 6:3 [P]): "Here the term *noda*⁽c⁾ is opposed to *nir'ah*." According to Rendtorff, here voicing the scholarly consensus,

> There can be no doubt that, bearing in mind the very precise language patterns of the Priestly Document, this was done quite deliberately. The visible appearance of YHWH is assigned to a provisional stage; with Moses a new phenomenon emerges: YHWH allows himself to be perceived *als er selbst.*[20]

But is this really the case? Is the Priestly Document so deliberately worded that every phrase in it builds upon clear antecedent thought processes, as one would expect from a modern exegete or theologian? Does not

18. "Als Offenbarung im strengen Sinne wird . . . allgemein die Selbstoffenbarung Gottes verstanden. . . . Aber es finden sich verschiedene Weisen vom Sich-Zeigen oder Sich-Kundtun Jahwes zu reden. . . . Der älteste urtümlichste Sprachgebrauch begegnet dort, wo es heisst, dass die Gottheit 'sich zeigt.' Das Niphal von ra'ah ist der Terminus für solche Gotteserscheinungen" ("Die Offenbarungsvorstellungen," 23ff.).

19. "Nirgends für . . . eine kultische Theophanie. Schliesslich ist der Begriff des Sich-Zeigens Jahwes überhaupt als unangemessen empfunden worden. Cp. Pannenberg, "Dogmatische Thesen," 7–20 (see above, n. 10).

20. [Es] kann nicht zweifelhaft sein, dass das in dem durchreflektierten Sprachgebrauch der Priesterschrift sehr bewusst geschieht. Das Erscheinen Jahwes wird einer vorläufigen Stufe zugewiesen; mit Mose beginnt etwas Neues: Jahwe gibt sich *als er selbst* zu erkennen" (Rendtorff, "Die Offenbarungsvorstellungen," 25).

such a view imply that the compiler or redactor of the Priestly Document, and like him the authors of the other sources, was subject to the drive towards systematization which, as already mentioned, weighs heavily upon present-day scholarship? Is it methodologically correct to ignore completely the concept referred to above, גלה, "to reveal [oneself]," just because it does not quite fit into the schema of ideas to which biblical literature is harnessed? The Greek verb ἀποκαλύπτειν from Hebrew גלה, does not have a theological connotation; on the contrary it is used with the "basic meaning 'to uncover or reveal,' generally in a secular sense. This corresponds to the common usage of גלה, where the secular sense also prevails. Where it does appear as a theological term, it rests on no uniform conception and is thus not a suitable starting point for inquiry."[21]

It is correct to say that in Biblical Hebrew both גלה and ראה occur mainly in secular contexts. In many cases they have a distinctly concrete meaning: גלה, "disclose or uncover," and ראה, "see," can both refer to sexual taboos and to offenses against them (e.g., Exod 20:26; Lev 18:6–19; 20:18–21; Deut 27:20; 2 Sam 6:20; Isa 47:2; Jer 13:22; Ezek 23:18–19) or in a figurative sense to the uncovering of the nakedness (meaning "weakness") of a country (Gen 42:9, 12). Thus גלה and ראה appear as synonymous expressions in parallelism (e.g., 2 Sam 22:16 = Ps 18:16; Isa 47:3; Ezek 16:36–37; 23:29; cp. also Gen 9:21–23) that are employed as alternatives in passages dealing with secular and sexual themes (cp. Lev 20:11, 17) and also in contexts which describe revelation (Isa 40:5; cp. Num 24:3–4, 16–17). Viewed against this background, the combination of both verbs in the description of a revelation in 1 Sam 3:21 (cp. v. 7) is of importance, even if it is a case of the conflation of two readings.[22] Similarly, the allusion in Gen 35:7 to the theophany experienced by Jacob at Bethel (Gen 28:16) by the employment of the verb (ה)נגלו is quite in accordance with biblical language. Only if one ignores this linguistic usage and subjects the text to the rules laid down by

21. "[In der] Grundbedeutung aufdecken, enthüllen, wobei der profane Sprachgebrauch dominiert. Das entspricht dem Befund von *galah,* bei dem auch der profane Gebrauch überwiegt. Wo es als theologischer Terminus erscheint, liegt ihm keine einheitliche Vorstellung zugrunde, so dass es als Ausgangspunkt der Untersuchung ungeeignet ist" (ibid.; cp. Pannenberg, "Dogmatische Thesen," 12).

22. See S. Talmon, "Double Readings in the Masoretic Text," *Textus* 1 (1960) 144–84. According to Rendtorff the occurrence of both verbs together in 1 Sam 3:21 is due to an editor's correction ("Die Offenbarungsvorstellungen," 25, n. 17).

the literary-critical method can one maintain that "according to the prevailing usage *nir²ah* should have been expected here."[23]

The double use of גלה and ראה in a secular physical sense on the one hand and with a transcendental sacral connotation on the other accords with customary biblical language patterns and cannot be regarded as exceptional. The same phenomenon can be observed in the case of ידע, "to know, discern." It seems to be highly questionable whether the proposition can be sustained that the increasingly frequent use of this verb of cognition, especially in P, should be attributed to a more refined concept of revelation. In the light of what has been said about גלה and ראה, I would refrain from overloading this usage with theological or philosophical overtones.

Just as גלה alternates with ידע, so does ראה, even though their semantic range does not completely overlap. The two verbs occur as synonyms in parallelism (e.g., Deut 29:2–3; 33:9; Isa 5:12–13; Qoh 8:16) and in freer syntactical constructions (e.g., Gen 18:21; Lev 5:1; 1 Sam 18:28; Isa 6:9). They can alternate in parallel passages (cp. Josh 24:31; Judg 2:7) and often occur together in a hendiadys (cp. 1 Sam 14:38; 18:28; 23:22–23; 1 Kgs 20:7, 22; 2 Kgs 5:7; Isa 29:15;[24] 41:20; 44:9; Jer 2:19; 5:1; Qoh 6:5; Neh 4:5).[25]

Like ראה and גלה, ידע too can refer to sexual intercourse and can thus bear a purely physical meaning (cp. Gen 4:1, 17, 25; 19:5, 8; 38:16, 26; Num 31:18, 35; Judg 11:39; 19:22, 25; 21:11, 12; 1 Sam 1:19; 1 Kgs 1:4; perhaps also Gen 2:9, 17; cp. Isa 7:14–16). Like גלה, "to disclose, uncover," ידע can bear the similar meaning, "to reveal, show [oneself]." One must consider the possibilities that the description of God's covenant with Israel in words borrowed from the erotic and marital relationship between man and woman[26] served as a connecting link between the secular and physical meaning and the range of connotations associated with "revelation." At any rate, ידע and ראה, like ידע and גלה, are used together in passages describing revelation (e.g., Num 12:6). In a few cases all three verbs occur together, e.g., in the description of the mighty deeds by which YHWH reveals himself to the world. "YHWH has made known [הודיע] his salvation; he has revealed [גלה] his righteousness [power] in the sight of the nations. . . . All the ends of

---

23. "[Dass] man [hier] nach dem sonstigen Sprachgebrauch *nir'ah* erwarten könnte" (Pannnenberg, "Dogmatische Thesen"). Cp. further Deut 4:35.

24. מי ראו ומי יודענו appears to echo Lev 5:1: והוא עד או ראה או ידע.

25. See S. Talmon, "Synonymous Readings in the Textual Traditions of the Old Testament" (ScrHier 8; Jerusalem: Magnes, 1961) 340–42.

26. As is well known, the Song of Songs has likewise been interpreted allegorically.

the earth have seen [ראה] the salvation of our God" (Ps 98:2–3).[27] A similar constellation emerges if 1 Sam 3:7 is viewed together with 3:21. This is surely legitimate, since both verses refer to Samuel's acting as a prophet of YHWH: "Samuel did not yet know [ידע] YHWH, and the word of YHWH had not yet been disclosed to him [גלה]" (v. 7)[28] YHWH "appeared [נראה] in Shiloh, because he had revealed [הגלה] himself there to Samuel according to his word" (v. 21). One can also compare the passage in which the heathen Balaam is presented, or presents himself, as a seer to whom God reveals himself: "Word of him who hears God's [אל] speech, who obtains knowledge [ידע] from the Most High [עליון],[29] and beholds [ראה = חזה] visions [of, or from] the Almighty [שדי], prostrate but with eyes unveiled [גלה]" (Num 24:16; cp. 24:4 and 22:22–34).

The foregoing linguistic investigation, though of necessity brief, casts doubt upon the thesis that the verbs ראה and גלה indicate an "indirect" manifestation of God by "primeval creative or historic deeds," whereas נודע/ידע refers to a "direct self-revelation."[30] According to Zimmerli the distinguishing mark of the latter is the "formula of self-presentation—I am YHWH,"[31] which is the answer to man's question about the identity of the divine being whom he has experienced. This theological hypothesis is hardly tenable when set against a literary and linguistic analysis of the relevant texts.

The semantic equivalence of the several expressions denoting revelation in Biblical Hebrew usage would suggest that the use of ראה and ידע in Exod 6:3 can possibly be attributed to a customary stylistic idiom rather than to a calculated word choice by the author of the Priestly Document which was triggered by theological considerations: "I *appeared* to Abraham, Isaac and

---

27. Zobel suggests that the parallelism of גלה and ידע in the hiph'il הודיע in Ps 98:2 has no precedent ("גלה," *TWAT* 1.1023).

28. This linguistic parallel, which proves a similarity of content, has not been noted by the exegetes, nor has it influenced the literary-historical school of analysis at all. (See Rendtorff, "Die Offenbarungsvorstellungen," 25, and the commentaries.)

29. The use of the construct state, וידע דעת עליון, should be understood as equivalent to an accusative, not a genitive (cp. דעת אלהים, Hos 4:1; 6:6; Prov 2:5). Instead of "who knows the thought of the Most High," the phrase might be rendered, somewhat freely: "who possesses divine knowledge."

30. See Pannenberg, "Dogmatische," 7ff., 91ff.

31. W. Zimmerli, "Ich bin Jahwe," in *Geschichte und Altes Testament: Festschrift für A. Alt* (Tübingen: Mohr, 1953) 179–209; idem, "Das Wort des Göttlichen Selbster-weises (Erweiswort): eine prophetische Gattung," *Mélanges bibliques, rédigés en l'honneur de André Robert* (Paris: Bloud et Gay, 1957) 154–64; idem, *Ezechiel* (BKAT; Neukirchen-Vluyn: Neukirchener Verlag, 1979) 55ff.

Jacob as El Shaddai, but I did not make myself *known* to them by my name YHWH." If the term נודע is *apposed* to נראה and not *opposed* to it, as the sources school assumes,[32] then perhaps the divine name should not be regarded as a substitute which replaces the epithet El Shaddai that had prevailed in patriarchal times, but rather as an additional designation of God which comes to be considered the divine name *par excellence* after the revelation at the burning bush. This is Buber's understanding of the pericope:

> The section which deals with the Revelation at the Burning Bush (Exod 3:1–4:17) cannot be regarded as a compilation from varying sources and documents. All that is needed is to remove a few additions, and there appears before us a homogeneous picture; any apparent contradiction can be accounted for by the fact that the text has not been fully understood. The style and composition of this section show that it is the fruit of a highly cultivated dialectic and narrative art; but certain of the essential elements of which it is composed bear the stamp of early tradition. . . . When Moses came to the Midianites, he entered the range of life of the Fathers; and he senses the apparition he now sees as being that of the God of the Fathers. As YHVH had once gone down with Jacob to Egypt (Gen 46:4), so has he now gone from Egypt to Midian; possibly with Moses himself, who was obviously under his protection like Jacob of old. At all events Moses perceives who it is that appears to him; he recognizes him. That was what had happened in the days of the Fathers too. Abraham had recognized YHVH in the El 'Elyon of Melchizedek, YHVH had permitted himself to be seen (Gen 16:7, 13) by Abraham's concubine, the Egyptian maid Hagar, as the spirit of a desert spring— seemingly one of those divinatory springs at which something can be "seen" during sleep. What happens here, as it had appeared there, is from the point of view of religious history an identification. The God brought with and accompanying a man is identified with the one known previously to be found at this spot; he becomes recognized in him.[33]

This would explain the fact that (El) Shaddai also occurs subsequently among the divine names not only in texts in which we can descry non-Israelite elements, such as the Balaam episode (Num 24:4, 16) and in the book of Job (*passim*), but also in biblical passages which are beyond all doubt authentically Israelite. One such example is Ruth 1:20–21; more weighty instances are to be found in the prophetic books, e.g., Isaiah (13:6 = Joel 1:15), Ezekiel (1:24; 10:5), and in the Psalms (68:15; 91:1).

32.   Rendtorff, "Die Offenbarungsvorstellungen," 25. See also I. L. Seeligmann, "Erkenntnis Gottes und historisches Bewusstsein im alten Israel," *Beiträge zur Alttestamentlichen Theologie: FS W. Zimmerli zum 70. Geburtstag* (ed. H. Donner, R. Hanhart, and R. Smend; Göttingen: Vandenhoeck & Ruprecht, 1977).

33.   M. Buber, *Moses: The Revelation and the Covenant* (New York: Schocken, 1958) 39, 44–45.

IV

This is actually the traditional Jewish view. Traditional exegesis unreservedly rejects the analysis, almost axiomatically assumed in present-day
Bible scholarship and theology, which assigns various concrete expressions
of the God-idea to separate identifiable strands in the Hebrew Bible, and
with it the associated demarcation of revelation-concepts which can be distinguished from one another in respect of the modes of divine manifestations, their content and imagery. Such a separation of the sources in biblical
literature was entirely unacceptable to Jewish exegetes who are considered
"pre-critical," such as S. D. Luzatto and D. Hoffmann,[34] not to speak of the
medieval commentators. Scholars trained in the critical method, such as
Benno Jacob, Umberto Cassuto, and M. H. Segal,[35] also categorically refuse
to divide the concepts of the biblical belief in God and revelation into the
particular formulations of the Elohistic, Jahwistic, Priestly, Deuteronomistic,
Prophetic, or Chronistic schools. The various names and epithets of God and
the various forms of divine revelation and their multifarious content are regarded not as expressions of different concepts of Deity, but as manifestations of the sole God, who reacts to man's deeds in many different ways and
allows himself to be perceived by men in sundry modes of revelation,[36]
"who does not remain within his (transcendental) being and essence but descends into actuality at particular times and places."[37]

The forms of divine revelation are congruent to man's world. At different
times and in different situations, God reveals himself under different names
and in different manifestations. The patriarchs experienced him under the
name El Shaddai. The same God revealed himself to Moses under the name
YHWH (Exod 6:3). According to biblical tradition he was invoked by this
name even in earliest times (Gen 4:26; 16:13; 21:33), but from the days of

---

34. D. Hoffman, *Die wichtigsten Instanzen gegen die Graf-Welhausensche Hypothese* (Berlin:
Itzkowski, 1904).
35. B. Jacob, *Das erste Buch der Tora: Genesis* (Berlin: Schocken, 1934), esp. "Anhang-
Quellenscheidung," 949–1049; U. Cassuto, *The Documentary Hypothesis* (trans. I. Abrahams; Jerusalem: Magnes, 1961); M. H. Segal, *The Pentateuch: Its Composition and Authorship, and Other Biblical Studies* (Jerusalem: Magnes, 1967) 1–172.
36. On this point see F. Rosenzweig, "Die Einheit der Bibel," *Die Schrift* (see above, n. 1),
46–51.
37. "Der nicht in seinem Sein, in seinem Wesen verharrt, sondern sich ins da-Sein, in die
Anwesenheit herniedemeigt" (F. Rosenzweig, "Der Ewige," *Die Schrift*, 208; cp. 194).

Moses, YHWH became the principal name of the God of Israel. The Midrash *Exod. Rabbah* takes the famous verse Exod 6:3 as the starting point for a summary of the significance of the various divine names. The following saying is attributed to Rav Abba bar Memel (a Palestinian Amora of the first generation):

"I am named according to my deeds. At times I am invoked as אל שדי, at times as אלוהי צבאות, as אלהים, or as השם. When I sit in judgment over men, I am called אלהים; when I go forth to fight against the wicked, my name is צבאות; when I suspend a man's punishment for his sinful acts, I am called אל שדי; when I have pity on my world, I am supplicated as השם. . . . I am named according to my deeds."[38]

This brief enumeration in the midrash of the divine designations current in the Bible could be extended by adding several other names and compounds used to denote the God of Israel: השם is identified with אלהים (1 Kings 18 *passim*, esp. v. 39; cp. Ps 72:18; 84:9–13; 100:3) and with אל אלהים (Josh 22:22; Ps 50:1), to mention only a few. Traditional Jewish exegesis naturally rejects the claim that this rich nomenclature can be taken as evidence for the existence of synchronous or diachronous literary strands or strata which can be distinguished from one another. In actual fact, even with the tools available to modern scholarship, such an analysis cannot be carried out consistently or convincingly.[39]

By insisting on the unity of God in the multiplicity of his epithets, the midrash puts clearly in relief essential features of man's experience of God as recorded in the Bible:

38. See the discussion of this issue by E. E. Urbach (*The Sages: Their Concepts and Beliefs* [trans. I. Abrahams; Jerusalem: Magnes, 1975] 37ff.); see further N. Leibowitz on Exod 6:3, עיונים חדשים בספר שמות (Jerusalem: World Zionist Federation, 1970).

39. The problem does not need to be aired here. The state of the art is set out in recent introductions to the Old Testament, e.g., O. Eissfeldt, *Einleitung in das Alte Testament = The Old Testament: An Introduction* (trans. P. R. Ackroyd; New York: Harper & Row, 1965); O. Kaiser, *Introduction to the Old Testament: A Presentation of Its Results and Problems* (trans. J. Sturdy; Oxford: Blackwell, 1969); J. A. Soggin, *Introduction to the Old Testament: From Its Origin to the Closing of the Alexandrian Canon* (trans. J. Bowden; London: SCM, 1976); R. Smend, *Die Enstehung des Alten Testaments* (Stuttgart: Kohlhammer, 1978); G. Fohrer, *Einleitung in das Alte Testament = Introduction to the Old Testament* (trans. D. E. Green; Nashville, TN: Abingdon, 1968); and B. Childs, *Introduction to the Old Testament as Scripture* (Philadelphia: Fortress, 1980).

(1) The possibility that Divinity can be experienced in various concretizations is categorically rejected. In rabbinical, as in biblical thought, this rejection is obviously aimed against polytheistic religions. It can, however, also be understood as a total denial of views, which would explain the diversity of God's self-revelation in biblical tradition as indicating various concepts of Deity, such as form the basis of theories propounded by modern scholarship. The various manifestations of God in Israel's history should not be construed as evidence of a concept of Deity which was modified and developed in course of time, nor do they indicate differing views which were held in Israel simultaneously at some given period. It is only God's ability to adapt his manifestations to men's differing situations which gives rise to a rich variety of forms by which he reveals himself in the life of the individual and in the history of Israel.

(2) The various names by which the biblical God makes himself known are to be understood as verbalizations of his deeds in the world. They offer man the possibility of harmonizing his experience of God at any given time with his varied experiences in life, without putting in question God's uniqueness and oneness.

(3) God who reveals himself can be experienced in an almost bewildering profusion of anthropomorphic representations. At the same time, he is *inconceivable* and *beyond compare* with any created being: "With whom will you compare God? What shape will you attribute to him?" (Isa 40:18; 44:8; 45:14; cp. Exod 15:11; Deut 3:24; 2 Sam 22:32 = Ps 18:32; Ps 71:19 and esp. 89:7; 1 Chr 17:20; 2 Chr 6:14).[40] This utterance undermines the very essence of idolatry and the magical practices associated with it. A God who cannot

40. In statements about the incomparability of God and the impossibility of representing him in material form, various names of the Deity are employed. They cannot therefore be assigned to a particular literary stratum but must be regarded as the common property of biblical faith as such. In this respect they differ from motifs and figurative expressions which are invariably associated with one or the other epithet (See M. Z. Segal, "The Divine Names, El Elohim, YHWH in the Biblical Books," *Tarbiẓ* 9 [1939] 123–62 [Heb.]; idem, *Tradition and Criticism: Collected Essays in Biblical Research* [Jerusalem: Kiryat-Sefer, 1957] 31–47 [Heb.]).

be represented (Isa 44:10; 45:22; 46:9; etc.) in concrete form cannot be manipulated by men.[41]

These contrasting statements about God—who, while being inconceivable and transcendant, rules over the world of men and yet is, or can be, in continual communication with men—present an almost unbridgeable dichotomy. But exegetes and theologians must accept the full strain of this tension. It cannot be resolved by attributing its genesis to different initially independent concepts of revelation which were held contemporaneously or successively and were merged with each other only at a comparatively late stage in the development of biblical literature. Knierim rightly observes:

> The fact . . . that the God who reveals himself as YHWH is always the same does not necessarily mean that his manifestations can always be recognized within one and the same context of perception or in the same concrete experience. The context of perception is flexible and subject to change. If the Old Testament speaks unsystematically . . . of an interpenetration and apposition of various modes of manifestations (cp. many psalms), this is of theological significance, since thereby God's revelation as YHWH is essentially attested in every possible kind of concrete experience. Therefore the multifariousness of vocabulary in the various literary genres and *Sitze im Leben* must be accorded a theological value.[42]

Certain basic guidelines can indeed be indicated which are common to all or most of the situations in which God makes himself known to man. But the multiplicity of the forms of revelation should not be subsumed under one common denominator in our excessive eagerness to compress them into a system. The tension which comes to light in the traditions must be understood as a special characteristic of biblical faith. It appears that just this tension reveals an essential factor in the conceptual universe of ancient Is-

---

41. See M. Weber, *Das antike Judentum: Aufsätze zur Religionssoziologie* (Tübingen: Mohr, 1921) 3.233–34, 279–80, 411–12 = *Ancient Judaism* (trans. C. Gerth and D. Martindale; Glencoe, IL: Free Press, 1952) 220–22, 262–63, 400.
42. "Die Tatsache . . . dass der sich in seiner Identität als Jahwe offenbarende Gott immer derselbe ist, bedeutet, deshalb noch nicht, dass auch die Art des Offenbarwerdens immer und nur in ein und demselben Verstehenskontext oder derselben Wirklichkeitserfahrung erkannt wird. Der Verstehenskontext ist flexibel, Veränderungen unterworfen. Wenn darum das Alte Testament unsystematisiert . . . von einem Ineinander und Beieinander von verschiedenen Weisen (vgl. viele Psalmen) redet, so ist dies theologisch bedeutsam, weil dadurch grundsätzlich das Offenbarwerden Gottes als Jahwe in jeder möglichen Art von Wirklichkeitserfahrung bezeugt wird. An diesem Punkt muss denn auch die Mannigfaltigkeit im Wortfeld, in den verschiedenen Gattungen und Sitzen im Leben, theologisch ernstgenommen werden" (Knierim, "Offenbarung," 226).

rael.[43] It must be taken into account in any study of the biblical concept of revelation. This diversity reflects the linkage of the revelation-experiences with historical events and the extent to which such experiences were conceived of as being anchored in the historical reality of a living community.

V

The Midrash *Exod. Rabbah* 6:3 offers an excellent starting point for a consideration of the Jewish concept of biblical revelation which extends beyond what is specifically Jewish and is of universal heuristic value. The basic declaration, "I am known by my deeds" anchors "revelation" in "dynamic tangibility," in nature, extra- or supra-natural events, and especially in the experience of the people of Israel. This understanding disposes of the distinction commonly drawn in modern theology between "revelation in creation" and "revelation in history"; between revelation in nature and supra-natural miracles.[44] All divine activity is "actuality" and therefore history, beginning from the very creation of the world. At that stage, God could not reveal himself directly to man, since man had not yet been created, but only indirectly, in the individual phenomena of creation and in the totality of the cosmos: "His works are great, beyond all reckoning, his marvels past all counting" (Job 9:10; cp. Jer 10:12–13; Amos 4:13; 5:8; 9:5–6; Job 38–39; et al.). Once man had been created, revelation in various forms was directed towards him: towards Adam and Noah in the primeval age which preceded the history of Israel; then towards the patriarchs, the prophets, and the entire nation. What God reveals, however, is never his *identity*, but rather his *actions* in the universe and in history.

God's essential nature, his identity, remained hidden even from Moses. Notwithstanding the exceptional "familiarity" between YHWH and Moses which biblical tradition emphasizes (Deut 34:10), the relationship between God and the archetypal prophet (Deut 18:15, 18) was not evenly balanced. YHWH "knows [Moses] by name," i.e., in his very being (contrast Exod 6:3). He appeared to him "in [full] view," מראה, in his "form," תמונה (Num 12:8). But not even to Moses did YHWH reveal himself. Moses' appeal,

---

43. G. Scholem, *Zur Kabbala und ihrer Symbolik* (Zürich: Rhein, 1960) 119; E. E. Urbach, *The Sages* (see above, n. 38), 37ff.
44. See Knierim, "Offenbarung" (above, n. 3), 224.

"Let me behold your presence, כבוד, i.e., "yourself," is unreservedly refused: "You cannot see my face [פנים], for man may not see me and live [cp. Judg 6:22–23; 13:22]. . . . As my כבוד passes by, I will put you in a cleft of the rock and shield you with my hand until I have passed by. Then I will take my hand away and you will see my back; but my פנים must not be seen" (Exod 33:13–23; cp. 1 Kgs 19:11–13; Job 9:11; et al.). In this context, כבוד and פנים, "presence" and "face," are used synonymously. Both words describe or, perhaps better, circumscribe the "personality" of YHWH.

It must be stressed that in Biblical Hebrew the synonymity with כבוד constitutes only a partial aspect of the semantic content of פנים. This noun has a wider range of meaning. In other figurative expressions, פנים is equated with the concrete noun פה, "mouth."[45] The partial synonymity of פנים, in some of its aspects with כבוד and in others with פה, enabled the biblical authors to express by the word פנים, in one context the impossibility of perceiving YHWH and in another to indicate by it a special intimate relationship between God and man. Thus the immediate relation of YHWH and Moses is conveyed in the statement that God speaks to him פה אל פה, "mouth to mouth" (Num 12:8) or פנים אל פנים, "face to face" (Exod 33:11). In these phrases פנים like פה refers to the immediacy of their encounter (Gen 32:31; Ezek 20:35), not to the "essential nature" of those taking part in the encounter, and therefore should not be understood as implying "self-revelation" or "self-proclamation."[46] Since in these texts the special content of פנים is determined by its parallelism with either כבוד or פה, whereby various overtones of the word are being brought into play, it follows that the statements "YHWH spoke to Moses face to face" (Exod 33:11) and "you cannot see my face" (Exod 33:20) are only an apparent contradiction. What this means is that even in the direct verbal exchange in which Moses took part, the identity of YHWH remained hidden from him.

Divine revelation is thus not, as modern scholarship often describes it, a matter of "self-disclosure"[47] or "self-revelation."[48] It is always an "act of power," (*Machterweis*), as Rendtorff rightly emphasizes.[49] At the center of

45. On this see S. Talmon, "The Textual Study of the Bible—A New Outlook," *Qumran and the History of the Biblical Text* (ed. F. M. Cross and S. Talmon; Cambridge, MA: Harvard University Press, 1975) 350ff.
46. Zimmerli, "Ich bin Jahwe" (see above, n. 31), 179–209.
47. Pannenberg, "Dogmatische Thesen," 8.
48. K. Barth, "Das Christliche Verständnis der Offenbarung," *ThEx* N.S. 12 (1948) 3–35.
49. Rendtorff, "Die Offenbarungsvorstellungen," 32–33.

the revelation is "God who acts," the *spiritus agens* of all that exists. This phrase, coined by G. E. Wright,[50] has lost none of its significance and validity, even though it may require certain adjustments and refinements, as suggested by Albrektson and Barr.[51] Revelation in the Hebrew Bible is the occasional breakthrough, in particular cases the occasional crossing of the dividing line, which otherwise absolutely separates man from God.[52] It is a concrete manifestation of God's immanent presence in the world, especially in the historical events which affect his people Israel. Revelation is a visible manifestation of his acts, in the past as in the present, and has a determining impact on the future. God reveals himself to man not for his own sake in an act of *Selbstvorstellung*, but for man's sake. The emphasis is on the recipient of the revelation, not on its initiator. In this we perceive its being directed towards man and more particularly towards his people (which characteristic is a prominent feature of the Israelite conceptual universe).

In the final analysis, it is not the chosen individual to whom the revelation is addressed, but rather the entire community. The individual serves as an intermediary between it and God. In full accord with this statement is the fact that mantic, ecstatic and meditative elements are of secondary importance in biblical accounts of revelation and do not constitute their intrinsic features. The divine message incorporated in the revelation is essentially meant for the community. Therefore revelation can be the medium for proclaiming basic principles which make demands upon the community, influence its way of thinking and determine its path in history. In most cases revelation is given *ad hominem, ad hoc,* and *ad rem.* But there is always in the background a much broader scene, the history of Israel or of mankind in general.

This statement can be confirmed by a mere fleeting glance at some traditional accounts of revelation. Adam and Noah (the second Adam) experienced divine revelation (Gen 3:9ff.; 7:1ff.; 9:1ff.) as representatives of humanity in an era which preceded Israel's history proper and with which the

---

50. G. E. Wright, *God Who Acts: Biblical Theology as Recital* (SBT 8; London: SCM, 1952); idem, *The O.T. against Its Environment* (SBT 2; London: SCM, 1950); idem, *The Old Testament and Theology* (New York: Harper & Row, 1969); cp. Y. Kaufmann, *The Religion of Israel: From Its Beginning to the Babylonian Exile* (trans. and abbr. by M. Greenberg; Chicago: University of Chicago Press, 1960) 70–72, 99ff.; et al.

51. Albrektson, *An Essay;* Barr, "Revelation in History," 649–746 (see above, n. 6).

52. Knierim, "Offenbarung," 212–13; T. C. Vriezen, *Theologie des Alten Testaments in Grundzügen* (Wageningen/Neukirchen: Neukirchener Verlag, 1956) 198 *et saepius*.

biblical narrator prefaces the course of that history. Even at that primeval stage, revelation is not conceived as an intimate personal communication but instead serves the purpose of promulgating enactments which impose obligations upon mankind. The "public" aspect of revelation emerges still more clearly in the patriarchal traditions, which can be regarded as paradigmatic for revelations later addressed to especially chosen persons. The traditions about Abraham (Genesis 15, 18, et al.) and Jacob (Gen 28:10–22; 32:25–33)[53] contain a greater proportion of mantic and mythical elements than those relating to the pre-Israelite ancestors of humanity, Adam and Noah. This can be seen as a prolepsis of characteristics which mark the prophetic narratives and also occur occasionally in traditions about "missionary" prophets. But in all these revelations addressed to individual persons, the community directedness remains the decisive element. Hence the manner in which revelation is intertwined in the course of Israel's history. This is most emphatically true of the revelations attributed to Moses and the classical prophets. Y. Kaufmann puts this very aptly: The self-understanding of the biblical missionary prophets "is rooted in the belief in a continuous revelation. . . . The foundation of Israelite prophecy is belief in revelation in history."[54]

This interpretation of the biblical concept of revelation is diametrically opposed to the thesis propounded by K. Barth of the *Uniqueness of Divine Revelation* in the person of Christ, which is cited with approval by Pannenberg:

> The uniqueness of [that] revelation is implied in its strict understanding as self-revelation. . . . When one speaks of several revelations, one no longer thinks of revelation in the strict sense of the word. To assert a plurality of revelations means to discredit each single one of them. The *Gestalt* of the divine manifestation then ceases to be the sole adequate expression of the one who reveals himself.[55]

---

53. Isaac plays a subordinate part in this, as in other respects.
54. Y. Kaufmann, תולדות האמונה הישראלית (8 vols; Tel Aviv: Devir, 1938) 1.730 .
55. "Die Einzigkeit der Offenbarung [ist] in ihrem strengen Begriff als Selbstoffenbarung bereits beschlossen . . . Sowie man von mehreren Offenbarungen redet, denkt man schon keine Offenbarung in strengem Sinne mehr. Die Behauptung einer Mehrzahl von Offenbarungen bedeutet die Diskreditierung jeder einzelnen von ihnen. Die Gestalt der göttlichen

One is led to assume that the definition of "revelation" presented here is not based on an analysis of relevant central traditions of the Hebrew Bible but is, rather, derived from a christological dogma and is adjusted to it. Barth's thesis claims the phenomenon of revelation (in the sense of self-revelation) exclusively for the Christian faith and thereby categorically negates the legitimacy of employing the term with reference to other religions. Such an assertion surely must be considered untenable by the historian, sociologist, or phenomenologist of religion. It is sufficient to quote the brief summary offered by C. M. Edsman:

> Revelation is part of the self-understanding of every religion as being a creation of divine and not human nature. . . . Although it is always risky to transfer concepts taken from the sphere of one religion to another. . . . Barth's characterization of Christian revelation, from the purely phenomenological aspect, applies also to corresponding experience, effects and concepts of non-Christian religions.[56]

Rigorous insistence on Barth's thesis can only lead to the result that in respect of their understanding of revelation in the Hebrew Bible, the Jewish interpreter and his Christian colleague stand at a parting of the ways.

VI

The essential nature and purpose of revelations experienced by individual persons—their community directedness and the function of their recipients as "intermediaries"—is most clearly displayed in the Sinai Theophany. This event must be considered in close connection with the Exodus from Egypt. Within the scope of the present discussion it is of no consequence whether the Exodus and the Sinai traditions were originally independent units and were only later combined, or whether they were included *ab initio* in a single body of tradition, a question often raised among Old

---

Manifestation ist dann in keinem Falle der einzig adäquate Ausdruck des Offenbarenden" (Pannenberg, "Dogmatische Thesen" [above, n. 10], 9–10).

56. "Offenbarung gehört zum Selbstverständnis jeder Religion, eine Schöpfung göttlicher und nicht menschlicher Art zu sein . . . Obgleichen es immer gewagt ist Begriffe aus einem Religionskreis auf einen anderen zu übertragen . . . dürfte die Charakterisierung der christlichen O[ffenbarung] durch Barth rein phänomenologisch auch auf entsprechende Erlebnisse, Wirkungen und Vorstellungen nichtchristlicher Religionen zutreffen" (C. M. Edsman, "Offenbarung," *RGG³* 4.1597).

Testament scholars. In the endeavor to gauge the biblical understanding of revelation, the decisive fact is that the ancient Israelite authors regarded those traditions as being of one cloth.[57] This is how it has been understood by Jewish exegetes from remote antiquity down to the present day.[58] The Sinai Theophany and the Exodus tradition together frame a most formative epoch in the history of Israel and of the biblical faith. Only when these two events are seen as complementary experiences can it be said that "The fundamental fact of Old Testament faith is the liberation of Israel from the house of bondage . . . it is by this act that God made himself known to Israel."[59] The revelation transmitted by Moses to the people of Israel in Egypt and during the Exodus becomes at Sinai a first and unique revelation whereby YHWH makes himself known directly to all Israel. Only thus can we explain the fact that the formula פנים אל פנים, first applied only to Moses (Exod 33:11; cp. Deut 34:10), is used in the retrospective account of the Sinai theophany in Deut 5:4 to describe YHWH's encounter with his people: "Face to face [פנים אל פנים] YHWH spoke to you on the mountain out of the fire."

This account of a divine revelation experienced by all Israel marks the dividing-line between two epochs in the history of biblical revelation.[60] It stands between the traditions of revelations experienced by chosen personalities, such as are recorded in the book of Genesis, and those vouchsafed to the prophets, which characterize the later books of the Bible. The Sinai Theophany is the foundation upon which rests the entire subsequent biblical concept of revelation. In Buber's words:

> [It] could be the verbal trace of a natural event, i.e., of an event that took place in the world of the senses common to all men and fitted into connections that the senses can perceive. But the assemblage that experienced this event experienced it as revelation vouchsafed to them by God and preserved it as such in the memory of generations, an enthusiastic, spontaneously formative memory. Experience undergone in this way is not self-delusion on the part of the assemblage; it is what they see, what they recognize and perceive with their reason, for natural events are the carriers of revelation, and revelation occurs when he who witnesses the event and sustains it experiences the revelation it contains. This means that he listens to that which the voice, sounding forth from his

57. Leibowitz, עיונים, ad loc. (see above, n. 38).
58. See Segal, *The Pentateuch*, 36; U. Cassuto, *The Book of Exodus* (trans. I. Abrahams; Jerusalem: Magnes, 1967); Leibowitz, עיונים, ad loc.
59. G. S. Henry, *A Theological Word Book of the Bible* (ed. A. Richardson; London: SCM, 1950) 196–97.
60. Kaufman, תולדות (see above, n. 54), 1.722.

event, wishes to communicate to him its witness, to his constitution, to his life, to his sense of duty.[61]

The revelation gave Israel objective laws which were embodied in the subjective commandments of YHWH. The revealed law is the basis of the Covenant proclaimed at Sinai, which YHWH contracted with his people, and which was henceforth to determine Israel's path in history and prove its value there.[62] This idea runs like a crimson thread through all strata and sources of biblical literature. It finds its basic expression in the preface to the Sinai theophany in Deut 4:9–14: "Take good care . . . not to forget the things which you have seen with your own eyes. . . . You came near and stood at the foot of the mountain. The mountain was ablaze with fire to the very skies: there was darkness and cloud, ערן, and thick mist. . . . At that time YHWH charged me to teach you statutes and laws which you should observe in the land into which you are passing to occupy it."

Thus covenant, law, and revelation develop into subcategories of history. The institutions growing out of covenant and law testify to the immanent revelation of God in history. The fusion of the Exodus experience with the Revelation at Sinai produces in Israel a new phenomenon: *History as Revelation.*[63]

61. [Sie] ist die Wortspur eines natürlichen, d.h. eines in der den Menschen gemeinsamen Sinnenwelt geschehenen und ihren Zusammenhängen eingefügten Ereignisses, das die Schar, die es erfuhr, als Gottes Offenbarung an sie erfuhr und so in einem begeisterten, willkürfrei gestaltenden Gedächtnis der Geschlechter bewahrte. Dieses so-erfahren aber ist nicht eine Selbsttäuschung der Schar, sondern ihre Schau, ihre Erkenntnis und ihre wahrnehmende Vernunft, denn die natürlichen Ereignisse sind die Träger der Offenbarung, und Offenbarung ist geschehen, wo der Zeuge des Ereignisses, ihm standhaltend, diesen Offenbarungsgehalt erfuhr, sich also sagen liess, was in diesem Ereignis die darin redende Stimme ihm, dem Zeugen, in seine Beschaffenheit, in sein Leben, in seine Pflicht hinein sagen wollte" (Buber, "Der Mensch von heute und die jüdische Bibel," in *Die Schrift* (see above, n. 36), 25–26 = "The Man of Today and the Jewish Bible," *On the Bible* (see above, n. 1), 9.

62. See J. Baillie: "Revelation is always given us through events" and "All revelation is given through history" (*The Idea of Revelation in Recent Thought* [New York: Columbia University Press/London: Oxford University Press, 1956] 78, 132); L. Köhler: "Dass Gott sich durch seine Werke, seien es die der Natur, seien es die der Geschichte, offenbart, ist ein durch ungemein viele Beispiele belegtes *Theologoumenon*" (*Theologie des Alten Testaments* [Tübingen: Mohr, 1936] 4).

63. Cp. E. Jacob: "Yahwe est le Dieu de l'histoire et l'histoire est son plus sur moyen de revelation" (*La tradition historique en Israel: Études théologiques et religieuses* [Montpellier: Faculté de Théologie Protestante, 1946] 12).

THE DESERT MOTIF IN THE BIBLE
AND IN QUMRAN LITERATURE

I

The study of the desert motif has played an important role in biblical research since K. Budde introduced it into the discussion. Budde's rather cautious and fairly balanced presentation of the desert as a formative factor in what he termed "The Nomadic Ideal in the Old Testament"[1] unloosed a veritable spate of publications which further developed the ideas he had proposed. Budde had taken as his point of departure a presentation of the Rechabites as the proponents of a religious belief that conceived of the God of Israel as a typical god of the desert. Presumably in order to recreate the original experience of this deity, the Rechabites adhered to a mode of life that retained the principles of a desert society,[2] thus to avoid the contamination of the pure Yahwistic religion by pagan beliefs and cultic customs, which in Israel had set in with the Conquest of Canaan. Drawing into the discussion the genealogical notice in 1 Chr 2:55, which connects the Rechabites with the Kenites[3] and also the theory that Israelite faith emanated from a Kenite Yahwism, Budde concluded that the Rechabites not only faithfully adhered to the ancient desert religion, but that they purported to serve as its missionaries.[4] According to Budde the prophets, and especially Hosea, reject this oversimplified concept of YHWH as a desert god. But he nevertheless agrees that the desert plays a decisive role in Hosea's idea of Israel's future purification and that indirectly the primitive *desert ideal* left its impression on the prophet's message.

1. K. Budde, *New World* (1895) 4.726–45. Republished in German as "Das nomadische Ideal im Alten Testament," *Preussische Jahrbücher* 88 (1896) 57–79.
2. Jer 35:6–10; 2 Kgs 10:15–16.
3. See my remarks on this passage in *IEJ* 10 (1960) 174–80.
4. Cp. also R. de Vaux, *Les Institutions de l'Ancient Testament* (Paris: Cerf, 1958) 1:21–23 = *Ancient Israel: Its Life and Institutions* (trans. J. McHugh; New York: McGraw Hill, 1961) 14–15. A bibliographical survey on the issue under review can be found in this work (pp. 519–20).

This opening, the hint at an idealization of the desert in Hosea's preaching, was fully exploited by P. Humbert.[5] In Humbert's analysis, the *desert* is for Hosea the ideal period in Israel's history.[6] In the prophet's teaching it also crystallizes into the goal toward which he strives to guide the nation: "Retour aux conditions de la vie de l'époque mosaïque, tel est . . . le programme d'avenir d'Osée."[7] In Humbert's interpretation this will be a return to the classical setting of Yahwism: "La désert est la patrique classique du yahvisme."[8] Thus the desert was introduced into the basic concepts of the Israelite faith as a factor of major importance. Now the desert ideal achieved the proportions of a veritable avalanche. It dominated discussions of the history of Israel and its religion. Under its impact YHWH was portrayed as a demonic desert deity, an image which originated in the primitivity of pre-Israelite nomads and was allegedly perpetuated as an idea and as an ideal in the period of the settlement and in prophetic teaching.

Eduard Meyer, a careful historian, advocated an even wider application of the desert concept in the analysis of Hebrew religion and history than K. Budde and P. Humbert had proposed.[9] But the peak of the trend toward the desert ideal was reached with the publication of J. W. Flight's paper, "The Nomadic Idea and Ideal."[10] Not only does Flight subscribe wholeheartedly to the theory that the prophets elevated the *nomadic idea* to a *nomadic ideal,* but he further votes for the adoption of this ideal as a beacon for religious orientation in the present: "The note which needs to be

---

5. P. Humbert, "Osée, le prophète bedouin," *RHPR* 1 (1921) 97–118; "La logique de la perspective nomade chez Osée et l'unité d'Osée 2, 4–22," *Festschrift für Karl Marti* (BZAW 41; Giessen: Töpelmann, 1925) 158–66.
6. E. Sellin puts it thus: "Für die vorexilischen Propheten ist die Wüstenzeit die Idealzeit, die 'Normalzeit'" (*Das Zwölfprophetenbuch* [KAT 12/2; Leipzig: Scholl, 1930] 236).
7. Humbert, "La logique," 162.
8. Humbert, *RHPR* 1 (1921) 106.
9. E. Meyer, *Die Israeliten und ihre Nachbarstämme,* with supplements by Bernhard Luther (Halle: Niemeyer, 1906) 129–41 (repr. Darmstadt: Wissenschaftliche Buchgesellschaft, 1967).
10. J. W. Flight, "The Nomadic Idea and Ideal in the Old Testament," *JBL* 42 (1923) 158–226. At about the same time, M. Soloweitschik published in Hebrew a discussion of the role presumably played by the desert in the history of Israel and in its *Weltanschauung* ("המדבר בתולדותיו והשקפת עולמו של עם ישראל," *Debir* 2 [1923] 16–45). Independent of Budde and his followers, whose publications he does not mention, Soloweitschik arrives at conclusions similar to theirs. He presents the desert as the "birthplace of true Yahwism" (p. 30) and as an idealized concept in classical prophecy (pp. 31–40). However, Soloweitschik carefully notes the modulations and the developmental aspects of the desert idea which become apparent in different strata of biblical literature.

struck in Christianity today is one which corresponds fundamentally to that which the prophets sounded in their day when they advocated a return to the nomadic ideal in the broadest sense. [Mark the definition: "broadest sense." S.T.] It is a call back to the essential spiritual simplicity of faith and life which God has revealed in the life and person of his son Jesus Christ."[11]

One can hardly fail to recognize the somewhat unexpected turn that the desert ideal took in the process of scholarly discussion. What had started out as an analysis of one theme in the ancient Hebrews' thought and literature ended up by becoming the expression of the quintessence of biblical religion.

It must be stated in all fairness that scholars sometimes have taken a more balanced view of the role that the desert played in biblical thought.[12] H. P. Smith hesitantly but correctly observed that "the ideal of the Hebrew writers for themselves was agricultural."[13] However, the impact of the desert ideal theory was not really overcome. There results an ambiguity which clearly shows in R. de Vaux's discussion of the issue. He notes that "our oldest biblical texts show little admiration for nomadic life . . . that nomadism itself is not the ideal." But he nevertheless agrees that in the prophetic books "we do encounter what has been called the 'nomadic ideal' of the Old Testament. . . . They [the prophets] condemn the comfort and luxury of urban life in their own day (Amos 3:9; 6:8, etc.) and see salvation in a return, at some future date, to the life of the desert, envisaged as a golden age (Hos 2:16–17; 12:10)."[14] The Rechabites are represented, without material evidence, as "the best-known group to organize a return to the desert and to the nomadic ideal." Because of his associations with the

---

11. Flight, *JBL* 42 (1923) 224 (see above, n. 10). See also U. W. Mauser's summary in *Christ in the Wilderness:* "Thus, the wilderness becomes the image of a spiritual condition and the miraculous watering of the parched land a figure of the Spirit which restores life in man" ([SBT 39; London: SCM, 1963] 52).

12. See, e.g., C. Barth, "Zur Bedeutung der Wüstentraditionen" (VTSup 15; Leiden: E. J. Brill, 1966) 14–23.

13. H. P. Smith, *Religion of Israel* (New York: Scribners, 1914) 12. Flight quotes this statement but does not heed the warning note (*JBL* 42 [1923] 158–226 [see above, n. 10]). See also the caveat entered by A. Causse: "Sans doute convient-il de ne pas exagérer, autant que l'on fait Budde et les critiques qui l'ont suivi, le rôle de l'idéal nomade dans l'histoire d'Israël et dans le développement du prophétisme" (*Du groupe ethnique à la communauté religieuse* [Paris: Alcan, 1937] 74).

14. De Vaux, *Ancient Israel,* 14 (see above, n. 4).

Rechabites, Jehu is dubbed "the 'wilderness' king," and Jeremiah is pronounced their "later sympathizer."[15]

The discussion of the reputed desert ideal has recently gained new impetus in the wake of the discovery of the Qumran Covenanters' literature. It is generally maintained that within the spiritual framework of the community which produced these documents, we can observe the desert idea not only in the form of a sought-for ideal, but also as a theological concept in operation, that is, as an historic actuality. De Vaux concisely summarizes this approach: "We shall encounter this mystique [sic] of the desert again in the last days of Judaism, among the sectaries of Qumran, when Christian monasticism still lies in the future."[16]

II

I propose to challenge the desert ideal thesis on two counts. First, the assumed existence in biblical society of a reform movement that advocated a "return to the original nomad status" and informed prophetic teaching (supposedly represented by the Rechabites) is based on historical premises and on sociological comparisons that cannot be upheld. In the historical times that are reflected in biblical literature, Israel never can be defined as a true nomad society. "Nowhere in the Bible are we given a perfect picture of tribal life on the full scale."[17] Nor is there found an indication that in the biblical period the Israelite tribes proper ever passed through a stage of true nomadism.[18] (Splinter groups such as the Midianites, Kenites, Kalebites, and others who attached themselves to Israel require a separate treatment.) Already in patriarchal times Israelite society bears the imprint of semisettled

15. G. H. Williams, *Wilderness and Paradise in Christian Thought* (New York: Harper, 1962) 17. See also Meyer, *Die Israeliten*, 136 (see above, n. 9).

16. De Vaux, *Ancient Israel*, 14 (see above, n. 4); also W. F. Albright, "Primitivism in Western Asia," *A Documentary History of Primitivism and Related Ideas* (ed. A. O. Lovejoy et al.; Baltimore: Johns Hopkins University, 1935) 1.429–31.

17. De Vaux, *Ancient Israel*, 12 (see above, n. 4).

18. If tribal units of the patriarchal era such as the Benjaminites could directly be associated with nomadic and seminomadic groups in Mesopotamia of the Mari Age, the picture of early Hebrew society as presented in the Pentateuch could be amplified and possibly its development be further retraced. However this vexing problem lies beyond the scope of the present paper. For a discussion see J. R. Kupper, *Les Nomades en Mesopotamie aux temps des rois de Mari* (Paris: Les Belles Lettres, 1957).

life in which only occasional reflections of nomadic life can be discerned. In fact, if we accept the definition proposed by Cyrus Gordon, who conceives of the patriarchs as "merchant-princes,"[19] the often-suggested comparison of the patriarchal groups with pre-Islamic bedouin society becomes altogether misleading. Says Gordon: "It is surprising in retrospect that the patriarchs could ever have been considered unsophisticated nomadic sheikhs."[20] Quite the contrary, it certainly can be stated that in the pentateuchal traditions the patriarchal groups are motivated by an "agricultural orientation," even though they did not attain the status of a fully sedentary society. The patriarchal stories reflect the very same ideals that in the post-Exodus traditions crystallize in the hope of a permanent settlement in thePromised Land of Canaan. It is immaterial for the issue under review whether these ideals are indeed rooted in an early Israelite socioreligious philosophy or whether their ascription to the forefathers is a mere anachronism, a retrojection into pre-Exodus days of post-settlement authors' concepts.[21]

Once the patriarchal era is excluded, we are left with the period following upon the Exodus and preceding the Conquest of Canaan as the possible matrix of the image on which the reputed desert ideal was patterned. Historically and sociologically this hypothesis appears to be untenable. Whatever may in reality have been the length of time that the Israelites spent in the desert, the ideological compression of the Desert Trek into one stereotyped (or schematic) generation, forty years (Deut 2:7; Ps 95:10, etc.), proves that it was considered to have been of minor impact on the sociohistorical development of Israel.[22] Furthermore, even in that comparatively

19. C. H. Gordon, "Abraham and the Merchants of Ura," *JNES* 17 (1958) 28–31; see also idem, "Abraham of Ur," *Hebrew and Semitic Studies Presented to G. R. Driver* (ed. D. Winton Thomas and W. D. McHardy; Oxford: Clarendon, 1963) 78–84; W. F. Albright, "Abram the Hebrew: A New Archaeological Interpretation," *BASOR* 163 (1961) 38–40. See D. J. Wiseman, "They Lived in Tents," *Biblical and Near Eastern Studies in Honor of L. W. LaSor* ([ed. G. R. Tuttle; Grand Rapids: Eerdmans, 1978] 197): "This picture of the patriarchs is hardly one of even the 'enclosed nomadism' characteristic of the Mari documents or of the Middle Bronze Age or of the wider ranging nomadism of the first-century Arameans."

20. C. H. Gordon, "Hebrew Origins in the Light of Recent Discovery," *Biblical and Other Studies* (Studies and Texts: Philip W. Lown Institute of Advanced Judaic Studies, Brandeis University 1; Cambridge: Harvard University Press 1963) 10.

21. In any case the question cannot be decided due to the lack of proper evidence, as may be learned from Eduard Meyer's unconvincing attempt to come to a conclusion (*Die Israeliten*, 129–32, 138–41 [see above, n. 9]).

22. See S. Talmon, "Har and Midbār: An Antithetical Pair of Biblical Motifs," *Figurative Language in the Ancient Near East* (ed. M. Mindlin, M. J. Geller, and J. E. Wansbrough; London: University of London, School of Oriental and African Studies, 1987) 136–37.

short period, which is undoubtedly portrayed against a desert setting, the tribes of Israel are not presented as living in the organizational pattern of a typical nomad society. It is interesting to observe that the main characteristics of desert life and of desert society, as they were abstracted from an analysis of the pre-Islamic Arab tribes, find little expression in the pentateuchal books that record the Desert Trek. "Tribal solidarity, desert hospitality and blood vengeance,"[23] insofar as they are reflected in Hebrew biblical literature, are mirrored in the accounts of Israel's sedentary history as recorded in the former and latter prophets, rather than in the pentateuchal accounts of the Desert Trek. The few cases of "bedouin hospitality" that de Vaux adduces to bear out the presumed nomadic character of the patriarchal society[24] in fact prove the opposite. Abraham's reception of the three men at Mamre (Gen 18:1–8), Lot's welcoming of the three angels (Gen 19:1–8), and the hospitality extended by Laban to Eliezer (Gen 24:29–33) at best can be viewed as relics of nomadic mores in a predominantly sedentary society. The same may be said of the custom of blood feud, which underlies the establishment of Cities of Refuge (Num 35:9–15; Deut 19:1–13). This juridical institution can become operative only in a sedentary society (Joshua 20, et al.) at a stage when blood vengeance as an acclaimed means of retribution has lost legal recognition. It is worthy of remark that only one case of executed blood vengeance (2 Sam 3:22–27)[25] and none of a successful retreat to a City of Refuge is actually recorded in biblical historical traditions.[26] The sagas of Cain (Gen 4:13–16) and of Lamech (Gen 4:23–24) are set in hoary antiquity and cannot reflect on patriarchal, not to mention later concepts. "Tribal solidarity" plays an insignificant role in Israelite history. The massacre of the Shechemites by Simeon and Levi may etiologically reflect a feud raid by these tribes on the territory of Shechem (Genesis 34). But their action is met with outright disapproval by the biblical authors (Gen 34:30–31, probably also 49:5–7) and cannot be construed as a demonstration

---

23. Causse, *Du groupe ethnique,* 15–31; S. Nyström, *Beduinentum und Jahwismus* (Lund: Gleerup, 1946).
24. De Vaux, *Ancient Israel,* 10 (see above, n. 4).
25. Unless the attack of Simeon and Levi on the town of Shechem in punishment for the rape of their sister Dinah by its prince's son is so regarded (Gen 34:25–29). But this case is atypical.
26. The custom that allowed the accidental killer to seek safety at an altar (Exod 21:14) must be discussed separately from the institution of cities of refuge. Joab, who availed himself of that custom, did so at his peril (1 Kgs 2:28–34; but see 1 Kgs 11:15–16). Adonijah's flight to the altar does not result from a juridicial issue (1 Kgs 1:50–53). See M. Greenberg's discussion of "The Biblical Conception of Asylum," *JBL* 78 (1959) 125–32.

of tribal mores. Again, the rallying of the sons of Levi to help Moses in the Golden-Calf episode (Exod 32:26) at best reflects guild solidarity, ideologically and etiologically reinterpreted. Korah's rebellion and the insurrection of Datan and Abiram, in which were involved only some components of the respective ethnic units (Num 16:1–35), clearly prove that even in the trek stage the presumed tribal solidarity did not become auomatically operative. It proves in fact that it was already in the process of disintegration.[27]

Summing up, we may say that in the pentateuchal portrayal of Israelite society in the desert period, the reflection of phenomena that are characteristic of the later sedentary social structure is much more accentuated than is the reverberation of presumed ancient desert ideals in literature that mirrors the historical milieu of Israel as a sedentary society.[28] Altogether we note in the Bible a dearth of firsthand information on desert conditions and true nomad life. In view of the foregoing discussion this cannot cause any surprise. Whenever such information is offered and whenever desert life is reflected in biblical imagery, these instances give witness to a deep-seated aversion to such conditions, a great fear of, not a longing for them. We shall yet give some further attention to this matter.

Second, little support can be derived from our sources for the attempted presentation of desert life as a social ideal and of the Desert Trek as an ideal period in the conceptual framework of the biblical writers. The representatives of the bedouin in biblical typology are Cain,[29] Ishmael, and to a certain degree Esau. Neither the one nor the other can be presented as the biblical writers' ideal type by any stretch of the imagination. Wresting a precarious livelihood from the desert as hunters (Gen 21:20; cp. 25:27), dispersed over vast arid areas (Gen 25:18), and being in daily combat with others whose livelihood depends on the same meager resources (Gen 16:12; cp. 27:3–4) certainly was not the vision of the early Israelite. Nomadism is con-

---

27. Max Weber stresses correctly that "collections of ancient Israelite laws show no trace of genuine Bedouin right, and the tradition holds that the Bedouins [lege: "nomads"] were the deadly enemies of Israel. Eternal feud ruled between Yahwe and Amalek. Cain, the ancestor of the Kenite tribe, bearing the 'sign of Cain,' that is the tribal tattoo, was a murderer condemned by the Lord to vagrancy and only the frightful harshness of blood revenge was his privilege. For the rest, Israelite custom hardly ever suggests Bedouin elements" (*Ancient Judaism* [trans. and ed. H. H. Gerth and D. Martindale; Glencoe, IL: Free Press, 1952] 13, cp. 36–49, 61–63; see also the editors' comment, p. xvii).

28. See M. Delcor, "Quelques Cas de Survivance du Vocabulaire Nomade en Hébreu Biblique," *VT* 25 (1975) 307–22.

29. See Weber's comment, quoted above.

ceived as a regression from a higher status in society, not as a desirable goal toward which to progress. Cain, the one-time farmer, the fratricide who undid the cosmic order established by divine decree (Gen 9:5–6), was ousted from sedentary civilization to become again a roaming bedouin (Gen 4:11–12).[30] Nomadism is a punishment, the widerness the refuge of the outlaw.

Also, the Rechabites cannot be adduced in evidence of the presumed prophetic desert ideal. Their nonagricultural mode of life is a reality, not a motif; an occupation (cp. 1 Chr 4:38–41; 5:18–22; 7:20–21), not a vocation. They may have resisted the course of cultural development that affected all Israel. But nowhere in the Bible are we told of an effort on their part to propagate their ideals with missionary zeal. Jehu, who for a season joins forces with them (2 Kgs 10:15–17), is not a "desert king,"[31] nor is Jeremiah a desert prophet. By way of a simile, the prophet sets up the Rechabites before the nation as an example of steadfastness. But the *tertium comparationis* lies in their adherence to the command of their ancestor (1 Chr 2:55),[32] not in the contents of that command. Jeremiah has no admiration for the primitive forms of Rechabite life, nor for the ideas that may underlie it,[33] but for the tenacity with which they observe man-decreed laws, whereas Israel flagrantly transgresses divinely appointed ordinances.[34]

The desert and the desert period are not conceived in the Bible as intrinsically valuable, but originally and basically as a punishment and a necessary transitory stage in the restoration of Israel to its ideal mode of life. The ideal is an organized, fully developed society with a deep appreciation of civilization, settled in the cultivated Land of Israel. The *desert* motif that occurs in the Old Testament expresses the idea of an unavoidable transition period in which Israel is recurrently prepared for the ultimate transfer from

---

30. Rabbinic tradition further denigrates Cain: He was not Adam's offspring but rather the fruit of Eve's cohabitation with the snake. He became the personification of evil. The "daughters of man," whose copulation with the בני אלהים produced the pre-deluge נפילים, were Cain's descendants, ultimately causing the destruction of creation by the flood, etc. (*Pirqe R. El.* 21–22).

31. Thus Williams, *Wilderness*, 17 (see above, n. 15); similarly earlier Meyer, *Die Israeliten*, 137–38 (see above, n. 9).

32. See S. Talmon, "1 Chronicles 2:55," *IEJ* 10 (1959) 174–80.

33. Correctly observed by W. Eichrodt (*Theologie des Alten Testaments* [part 2/3; Berlin: Evangelische Verlagsanstalt, 1933] 245 = *Theology of the Old Testament* [trans. I. A. Baker; Philadelphia: Westminster, 1961]).

34. See F. S. Frick, *The City in Ancient Israel* (SBLDS 36; Missoula: Scholars Press, 1977) 214–17; P. P. Seidensticker, "Propheten-Söhne-Rechabiter-Nasiräer," *Studium Biblicum Franciscanum*, Liber Annus 10 (1959–60) 101–5.

social and spiritual chaos to an integrated social and spiritual order. The *Trek-in-the-Desert* motif represents on the historical and eschatological level what *creatio ex nihilo*, the transfer from chaos to cosmos, signifies on the cosmic level.[35]

Whenever the desert motif seems to attain the status of a self-contained positive value, this attribution results, as will be shown, from variational developments of the initial theme by way of the infusion into it of other, originally unrelated themes. In essence the process may be described as a *mixing of motifs*, which introduces new subsidiary elements into the *desert* motif with a concomitant mutation of its original significance.

III

Without adopting the overemphasis that marred the discussion of the desert theme in biblical literature, it can yet be said that the analysis of the desert motif does indeed give us an insight, sometimes by way of negative proof, into some fundamental and extremely fruitful religious and social ideas which informed the conceptual universe of biblical Israel. The analysis reveals the exceeding tenacity with which this motif was perpetuated in diverse stages of biblical literature and in the Qumran writings and was then infused into Christian imagery, albeit with a fundamentally different significance.[36]

This leads to one more point of interest in reference to the biblical desert motif. It appears that this motif is especially well suited for submission to an analysis which will bring out poignant features and characteristics of the motif as a literary theme, illustrating the functions, developments, and mutations of a motif in a given literary framework. Though we are concerned only with one specific motif in biblical literature, some typical processes and developments that will emerge in our analysis are transferable to other motifs in biblical, and *mutatis mutandis*, also in extrabiblical literature. Therefore it is imperative that we concern ourselves with the definition of the term *motif*, since it is the desert motif that is the subject of our inquiry.

---

35. Cp. Jer 31:31–40.
36. For this development, which will not be discussed here, see Williams, *Wilderness* (above, n. 15).

The term *motif* seems to have been used first in English in 1848 or 1850 in application to the field of visual art. In 1851 *motive* is defined in a handbook for painters as "the principle of action, attitude and composition in a single figure or group." By 1860 John Ruskin is speaking of "a leading emotional purpose, technically called its motive" in "any great composition." Then *motif* is used in 1887 in the realm of musical theory to describe "the sort of brief recurring fragment in the operas of Richard Wagner (1813–1893), which Wagner called a Grundthema." Within a year or two, *motif* as a term for a recurrent theme or subject in a work of art was well integrated into the current vocabulary, and in 1897 the term was applied in a literary analysis of the biblical book of Ruth.[37]

Since then individual scriptural motifs were often investigated. However, little was done by way of defining the literary phenomenon so described and mapping out the field in which it can be fruitfully employed in biblical research. This lack of proper definition sometimes results in the employment of other literary categories, such as *Gattung,* toward the classification of materials which in fact should be subjected to motif analysis.[38]

Decidedly more satisfactory is the situation in the field of New Testament studies. The Lund school of theology, led by A. Nygrén and G. Aulén, successfully investigated the dominant literary motifs in order to establish analytically the actual contents of the Christian faith crystallized in these motifs.[39] P. L. Berger thus summarizes the role of motif in the Lund method: "The concept of the religious motif, which can be used with advantage in any phenomenological approach to religion, outside as well as inside the Christian tradition, refers to a specific pattern or gestalt of religious experience, that can be traced in a historical development."[40] Elaborating on this definition, we suggest to define *motif,* with special application to Hebrew biblical literature, as follows:

A literary motif is a representative complex theme that recurs within the framework of the Hebrew Bible in variable forms and connections. It is rooted in an actual

---

37. See "Motif, Motive," *A New English Dictionary* 6.695.
38. A case in point is R. Bach, *Die Aufforderungen zur Flucht und zum Kampf im alttestamentlichen Prophetenspruch* (WMANT 9; Neukirchen-Vluyn: Neukirchener Verlag, 1962).
39. Anders Nygrén, *Agape and Eros* (trans. P. S. Watson; London: SCM, 1953/Chicago: Chicago University Press, 1982); Gustaf Aulén, *The Faith of the Christian Church* (revised ed.; trans. Eric H. Wahlstrom; Philadelphia: Westminster, 1960).
40. P. L. Berger, "The Sociological Study of Sectarianism," *Social Research* 21 (1954) 477.

situation of anthropological or historical nature. In its secondary literary setting, the motif gives expression to ideas and experiences inherent in the original situation and is employed by the author to reactualize in his audience the reactions of the participants in that original situation. The motif represents the essential meaning of the situation, not the situation itself. It is not a mere reiteration of the sensations involved, but rather a heightened and intensified representation of them.

In view of the composite quality of a motif, its adaptability to new settings, and its compatibility with other themes, its ultimate configurations may be far removed from the initial form. Therefore often a minute analysis will be required when one assays to establish their connection and derivation and to retrace the intermediate stages of development.

Because of its complexity[41] a literary motif cannot be fully evaluated in isolation. It must be viewed against the background of other synonymous and antonymous themes with which it can be linked in recurring and modifiable patterns. This apposition and opposition will help to clarify the focal meaning of a motif under review and to delineate the limits of its significance within a given body of literature.

IV

We can now proceed to apply the proposed definitions above to the analysis of the מדבר motif. At this stage of the investigation, the Hebrew term מדבר is to be preferred to the English term *desert,* since *desert* narrows the more comprehensive connotation of מדבר to the meaning of "parched wilderness."[42] The notion of *wilderness* can be expressed in Biblical Hebrew by a number of functionally synonymous terms, such as ציה, שממה, שמה, ישימון, etc., to which allusions will be made but which will not receive a detailed treatment in our discussion.[43]

Our preoccupation with מדבר as a motif removes from direct scrutiny all of the 267 occurrences of the term in the Bible that refer to the real physical phenomenon. Our focal interest lies in those passages in which מדבר is used in a secondary setting as a literary theme. However, before turning to the

---

41. In this complexity we may perceive one of the fundamental features in which "motif" differs from literary "image," which usually is of a simpler nature.

42. No certain etymological derivation of מדבר has been proposed. For a concise summary of suggestions, see S. Talmon, "מדבר *midbā r,* ערבה *ᶜarābāh,*" *TWAT* 4.663–66.

43. For a more complete discussion of these terms, see ibid., 660–95.

motif plane, we must determine in rough outline the major aspects of מדבר in reality, since these aspects serve as the bases of the figurative employment and therefore will help in establishing its significances.

מדבר can be divided into two major classes of connotations, one basic, the other derivative, which on their part fall into several subgroups: (1) the spatial connotation in references to the geophysical phenomena; (2) the temporal connotation in references to a specific historical situation.

Three main subgroups of the spatial-geophysical connotation can be discerned. We shall not present them here in full detail, and we note that the demarcation lines between them are not fixed or static.

(1) מדבר describes agriculturally unexploited areas, mainly in the foothills of southern Palestine, which serve as the grazing land par excellence for the flocks and the cattle of the semisedentary and the sedentary agrarian population. In this context the term is often synonymous with ערבה, and like it may be translated "steppe." The majority of occurrences of the vocable מדבר in the Bible will come under this heading. Here are some illustrations:

Gen 36:24: These are the sons of Zibeon: Aiah and Anah. This is the Anah who found the ימים in the מדבר when he was tending the asses of his father Zibeon.[44]

1 Sam 17:28: And whom have you left to look after those few sheep in the מדבר?

2 Chr 26:10: He built [watch]towers in the מדבר and hewed out many cisterns, for he had large herds, both in the *shephelah* and in the plain.[45]

This connotation points to the derivation of the noun מדבר from דבר, "to drive out." The root may be connected by way of metathesis with רבד and רבץ, technical terms that describe the grazing of flocks. For example, in Isa 13:20–21, "There no Arab [herdsman] shall pitch his tent, no shepherds fold, יַרְבִּצוּ, their flocks there.[46] But desert animals, צײם, will graze, וְרָבְצוּ, there.[47]

44. A useful summary of biblical wilderness terminology may be found in A. Schwarzenbach, *Die geographische Terminologie im Hebräischen des Alten Testamentes* ([Leiden: E. J. Brill, 1954] 93–112).

45. Further reference may be found in 1 Sam 25:4, 21. In Num 14:33 we should read with the Vulgate תעים instead of the masoretic רעים and translate: "And your children shall wander in the wilderness for forty years." Thus the parallelism with Num 32:13 is retained.

46. RSV: "will make their flocks lie down there."

47. RSV: "But wild beasts will lie down there"; NEB: "There marmots shall have their lairs."

We shall translate this connotation of מדבר with "drift-land," or in short, "drift."[48]

The focal aspects of the drift setting show (a) in the anthropological sphere, descriptions of the fate of man (and his belongings, e.g., flocks) vis-à-vis an unaccommodating nature; (b) in the sociological sphere, the presentation of the various aspects of shepherd society; (c) in the ecological sphere, the description of tent-life phenomena.

(2) The geographical setting of the "drift," in the borderland between cultivated land and desert, causes the term מדבר to become a designation of the comparatively thinly inhabited open spaces adjacent to settlements of a temporary (מחנה), relatively fixed (נוה),[49] or altogether stable nature (village or town). These spaces are viewed as an extension of the encampment or the settlement and are not considered an integral part of it. The distinction is of an ecological character as well as a sociological one.

As an extension of the מחנה, מדבר is used for example in Exod 16:10: "While Aaron was speaking to the whole congregation of the Israelites, they looked toward the מדבר, and behold, the glory of God appeared in the cloud" (cp. Num 24:1).

The term connotes the space adjacent to a נוה in Isa 27:10, where Israel in the stage of its destruction seems "like a solitary, fortified, בצורה [better נצורה, 'besieged'] city, a forsaken and desolate encampment, נוה, like a drift, מדבר, wherein cattle graze."

Very common is the designation of the outskirts of a permanent settlement as its מדבר. We find the term used this way with reference to Beersheba (Gen 21:14), Beth-aven (Josh 18:12), Engedi (1 Sam 24:1–2), Damascus (1 Kgs 19:15), Tekoa (2 Chr 20:20), et al. It is this connotation that is mirrored in the Qumran term מדבר ירושלים.[50]

(3) מדבר is also employed to denote the true desert, the arid zones beyond the borders of the cultivated land and the drift, as for example in

48. *Drift* is meant to recapture the connotation of "drive (livestock) out into the open pasture" inherent in מדבר. It approximates "range," defined as an open region over which livestock may roam and feed." In German the word *trift* carries a similar meaning.

49. For a discussion of the diverse aspects of biblical נוה and its Akkadian counterpart *nawûm*, see J. Bottéro and A. Finet, *Archives Royales de Mari* ([Paris: Imprimeric Nationale, 1954], 15.237); M. Noth, *Die Ursprünge des alten Israel im Lichte neuer Quellen* ([Cologne and Opladen: Westdeutscher Verlag, 1961] 16); D. O. Edzard, "Altbabylonisch *nawûm*" (*Zeitschrift für Assyriologie*, N.S. 19 [1959] 168–73). Also Y. Amir, "מדבר" (*EncMiq* 4.674–78).

50. See below, p. 251.

2 Sam 17:27–29; 2 Kgs 3:8–9. This meaning is correctly retained in English as "wilderness."

We can be brief in highlighting the focal aspects of מדבר-wilderness in biblical literature. The wilderness is a place of utter desolation: a vast void of parched earth with no streams or rivers to provide sustenance for plants and wildlife, except for a very few species (Jer 2:24). It is a place unfit for human habitation (Jer 9:11; cp. 50:39–40; 51:41–43; Job 38:26), the few wandering nomads (ערבים) being the only exception (Jer 3:2; 9:25).

This מדבר-wilderness is the scene of utter cruelty, beast against beast and man against man (Lam 5:9). It is perilous to enter the vast tracts, which are traversable by only a few paths or byways, often barely recognizable. However, due to its remoteness from settled land and its terrifying desolation, the wilderness becomes the chosen refuge of outlaws and fugitives, who may prefer an off-chance of surviving in exceedingly adverse circumstances to the calamities which are certain to befall them from the hands of their pursuers. Hagar flees into the desert to escape the anger of Sarah (Gen 16:6–14). In the wilderness her son Ishmael becomes the prototype of the marauding bedouin: "He lived in the wilderness and became a bowman" (Gen 21:20). David takes to the Judean desert in his flight before Saul: "Men who were in distress or in debt or discontented gathered round him, and he became their chief" (1 Sam 22:2). By repairing to the מדבר, Elijah tries to save his soul when Jezebel plans to kill him: "He was afraid and ran for his life. When he came to Beer-sheba in Judah, he left his servant there. But he himself went a day's journey into the wilderness" (1 Kgs 19:3–4). This utilization of the מדבר as a refuge by one who had been forced out of his society may have been conducive to the crystallization of a new concept yet to be discussed, the desert as the locus of a seemingly voluntary retreat.

It has already been said that there are comparatively few references to "wilderness-reality" in scripture. This dearth seems to reveal the relatively unimportant role that the wilderness or the desert proper played in the life of the Israelites in biblical times. Those references that there are pertain mainly to the arid tracts in the deep south of Palestine and the Sinai Peninsula. Thus מדבר recurrently becomes a component of the designation of these particular areas, such as מדבר סיני, מדבר פארן, מדבר צין, et sim. That region in its wider extent is also referred to as desert *par excellence,* with the definite article: המדבר or המדבר הגדול.

The predominant characteristics of מדבר-wilderness in biblical literature evidence the ancient Israelite's unfamiliarity with and his loathing of the desert. This was the attitude of the city-dweller, the farmer, the semi-sedentary shepherd, even of the donkey-nomad, who may have traversed the desert on beaten tracks but would not voluntarily venture into its depth. This attitude differs glaringly from that of the true camel-nomad, the bedouin, to whom the desert is home.

(4) The connotation of מדבר as a barren, awe-inspiring, howling wilderness is intimately related to yet another category of a rather specific brand of "reality." In the Bible some residues may be found of a mythical concept of *wilderness,* which is much more fully developed in ancient Semitic mythology,[51] as in postbiblical midrashic literature. "In Arabic and Accadian folklore, the desert is the natural habitat of noxious demons and jinns."[52] In Ugaritic myth the natural habitation of Mot, the god of all that lacks life and vitality, "is the sun-scorched desert, or alternatively, the darkling region of the netherworld."[53] Mot is the eternal destroyer. He periodically succeeds in vanquishing Baal, the god of fertility and life, and thus reduces the earth temporarily to waste and chaos. It may be due to this identification in Canaanite myth of desert and darkness with Mot that any equation of YHWH with the wilderness is anathema to the biblical writers. "Have I been a wilderness to Israel like a land of [thick] darkness"[54] demands YHWH, "[so that Israel has reason to reject me]?" (Jer 2:31).

These mythical visions of מדבר-wilderness are mirrored in biblical passages in which the desert is presented as being populated by phantom-like creatures, together with the scanty animal population. Thus, while tending asses that were grazing in the מדבר, Zibeon's son Anah found the ימים (Gen 36:24), whom the midrash identifies as demonic beings.[55] "There the desert owls shall dwell, and there satyrs [שעירים] shall gambol" (Isa 13:21). Also in early Arab tradition "the wilderness is replete with such demonic beings. Whoever spends his life there as traveller must not fear them; the desert

51. A. Haldar, "The Notion of the Desert in Sumero-Accadian and West-Semitic Religions," *UUÅ* 3 (1950) 1–70.
52. T. Gaster, *Thespis* (revised ed.; New York: Doubleday, 1961) 132, n. 19.
53. Ibid., 125.
54. NEB: "Have I shown myself inhospitable to Israel like some wilderness of waterless land?"
55. Cp. E. Ben Yehudah, "ימים," *Thesaurus Totius Hebraitatis* 4.2056, n. 2.

dweller must become the wolf's friend and fraternise with the Ghul."[56] The presence of such monsters in fact indicates that a tract of land has been reduced to the primeval state of chaos: "An unknown, foreign and unoccupied territory (which often means 'unoccupied by our people') still shares in the fluid and larval modality of chaos."[57] Such will be the future fate of Edom: "Horned owl and bustard shall make their home in it, screech-owl and raven shall haunt it. He [God] has stretched across it a measuring line of chaos and a plummet of confusion" (Isa 34:11). "Wild beasts shall consort with jackals, satyr [שעיר] shall encounter satyr; there the night hag [לילית] shall repose and find for herself a resting place" (Isa 34:14).[58] מדבר plays a prominent role in Psalm 29, which brims with mythical creation terminology in a historicized setting: "The voice of the Lord flashes forth flames of fire. The voice of the Lord makes the wilderness, מדבר, writhe; the Lord makes the wilderness of Kadesh writhe. . . . The Lord sits down on his throne, למבול;[59] the Lord sits enthroned as king forever."[60]

This mythic aspect of מדבר was retained in the ritual of driving out a goat (שעיר) to Azazel in the wilderness (ארץ גזרה) as an atonement offering (Lev 16:5–10, 21–22) and subsequently became permanently associated with the rites of the Day of Atonement (Lev 16:29). We shall have occasion to suggest that these mythical undertones of מדבר possibly influenced some developments of the desert motif in the Bible.

The connotations of מדבר in the geophysical reality ("drift," "wilderness") determine the secondary literary employment of מדבר-language in the Bible. The "drift" and "wilderness" connotations in the main trigger literary imagery that is based predominantly on the figurative employment of "typical," not "one-time specific," מדבר-reality. Generally speaking, turning "reality" into an "image" involves a transfer from the original setting onto an altogether different plane. Usually the image serves to achieve a concretization of abstract ideas and relationships.

---

56. J. Wellhausen: "Die Wüste ist voll von diesen Spukgestalten. Wer sein Leben als fahrender Mann dort zubringt, darf sich vor ihnen nicht grauen; ein Wüstenbruder muss mit dem Wolf befreundet und mit der Ghul vertraut sein" (*Reste arabischen Heidentums* [2d ed.; Berlin: Reimer, 1897] 149–50).

57. M. Eliade, *The Sacred and the Profane* (New York: Harper, 1961) 31.

58. Cp. Jer 4:23–26.

59. For this interpretation of מבול, see Y. N. Epstein, "מבול (תהלי כ״ט י)," *Tarbiẓ* 12 (1942) 82.

60. Ps 29:7–10; cp. further Isa 42:11–13; 50:2; Job 38:25–26.

Again there is no need to go into much detail. Such מדבר-imagery is the stock-in-trade of biblical prophets and psalmists. Some examples will suffice.

(1) The "leader-led" relationship, e.g., between king and nation or God and nation, is often portrayed as the dependence of a flock on the shepherd: "I will gather together the remnant of Israel; I will herd them like sheep in a fold, like a flock in its pasture" (Mic 2:12). A most intricate employment of the image, abounding in details, is found in Ezekiel 34. Verses 20–25 are one illustration:

> Therefore, thus says the Lord YHWH to them, "Behold I myself will judge between the fat sheep and the lean. Because you push with flank and shoulder and butt all the weak ones with your horns till you have scattered them abroad, I will save my flock; they shall be ravaged no more; I will judge between sheep and sheep. I will set up over them one shepherd, my servant David, and he shall pasture them; he shall pasture them and become their shepherd. . . . I will make with them a covenant of peace and rid the land of wild beasts so that they may dwell securely in the open pastures, מדבר, and sleep in the woods" (cp. Isa 40:10–11; Jer 23:1–6).

(2) The ecological aspects of the drift are recaptured especially in tent-imagery. Steadfastness and security are likened to a well-anchored tent: "Look upon Zion, city of our feasts. Your eyes will see Jerusalem, a quiet habitation, a tent that shall never be shifted, whose pegs shall never be pulled up; nor any of its ropes be snapped" (Isa 33:20). Failure and death, on the other hand, are compared to an uprooted tent: "My dwelling is pulled up and taken from me like a shepherd's tent" (Isa 38:12; cp. Jer 10:20; Job 4:21). The spreading out of tent sheets to accommodate an increased population portrays a situation of the previously barren woman who has been blessed with offspring: "Enlarge the capacity of your tent, let the curtains of your habitation be spread wide; hold not back, lengthen your ropes, and drive in [strengthen] your pegs" (Isa 54:2).

The dusky beauty of a suntanned maiden conjures up the image of the shepherds' pitch-black goathair tents. "I am dark but lovely, O daughters of Jerusalem," says the Shulamite, "like the tents of Kedar, like the tent-curtains of Solomon" (Cant 1:5).

Notwithstanding the reference to Kedar, a typical desert tribe, the last-mentioned image derives from the drift context. Wilderness imagery never expresses beauty, success, or security. Quite to the contrary, it spells abject fear, destruction, and desolation, which the Israelite perceived in desert reality (Isa 14:17; Zeph 2:13–14, et al.).

(3) A ruler in his downfall is compared to a vinestock transplanted from fertile ground to the wilderness: "Your mother was like a vine in a vineyard,[61] planted by the waterside, fruitful and luxuriant, for there was water in plenty. It had stout branches [fit] for [making] scepters for rulers. It grew tall into the thick foliage. . . . But it was torn up in anger and thrown to the ground. . . . Its strong branches were blighted, and fire burned it. Now it is replanted in the wilderness, in a dry and thirsty land. It has no strong branch anymore [to make] a scepter for [those who] rule. This is a lament, [for] she [your mother] became a lament" (Ezek 19:10–13). The fate of such a plant in the desert is certain: it will wither. Like it is the man who puts his trust in human beings and not in God: "He shall be like a shrub in the desert and shall not see any good come.[62] He shall dwell in the parched places of the wilderness, in an uninhabitable salt land" (Jer 17:6). The cruelty of humans in their deprivation is like that of "ostriches in the wilderness" (Lam 4:3) or of "wild asses in the desert . . . scouring the wilderness for food" (Job 24:5).

(4) Yet, as in reality, the desert also can equal "refuge": "Flee, save yourselves," is the prophet's advice to the Moabites. "Be like a wild ass in the desert" (Jer 48:6). And the psalmist "would wander far away and find shelter in the wilderness, to find refuge [from his enemies]," who are like "the raging wind and tempest" (Ps 55:8–9).

This fact gives rise to an incipient positive image which derives from "wilderness-language," namely the employment of *desert* to symbolize "retreat," as in Jeremiah's famous lament: "Oh that I could have in the wilderness a wayfarer's lodging place that I might leave my people and depart from them" (Jer 9:1). This theme was not further developed in biblical literature. Even in the Jeremiah passage the "positive" aspect is subsidiary. The prophet is not drawn into the desert to meditate there, as it were, and come face to face with God. He does not seek there communion with God.

---

61. Reading בכרם or בכרמך for MT בדמך.

62. יראה probably equals ירוה, and טוב connotes מים. The image is the antithesis of the one adduced in Jer 17:8: יהיה כעץ שתול על פלגי מים ועל יובל ישלח שרשיו, "He shall be like a tree planted by the waterside that stretches its roots along the streamlets." The supposed interchange, רוה-ראה, requires a separate discussion. It appears to underly 2 Sam 13:5 as well (השקה ‖ הראה); (שבע ‖ רוה/ראה) Ps 60:5; cp. Job 10:15 (רוה/ראה); Isa 53:11, (אכל ‖ רוה/ראה); cp. 71:20; Qoh 2:1 (נסך ‖ ראה), cp. Ps 4:7 (נס[ך] ‖ ראה); Qoh 2:24 (הראה ‖ אכל ושתה).

All he longs for is to dissociate himself from his fellowmen who hate and persecute him.

V

So far we have dealt with perspectives of מדבר in its overall spatial-geophysical connotation. We can now turn to its temporal-historical connotation. In a rather large number of its occurrences in biblical literature, מדבר serves as a designation of the clearly circumscribed period that followed upon the Exodus and preceded the Conquest of Canaan. This period roughly falls into two unequal stretches of time.

(1) The one, spanning the first two years, includes the events from the crossing of the Red Sea to the Sinai theophany and to what immediately follows upon it.

(2) The other extends from that point in time when Israel is encamped in the Paran Desert to the War against the Midianites, which is the last skirmish against desert people, after which Israel enters the territories of the Transjordanian nations. This period encompasses most of the remaining thirty-eight years.

These are the years of the Desert Trek proper, the wanderings which were imposed upon Israel as a divine punishment for their sins and for their doubting God's power to lead them safely into the Promised Land (Deut 2:14–16). The episodes of this period are surveyed comprehensively in what may be called "The Book of Israel's Failings," which comprises Num 11:1–31:20 (or possibly 31:54) with the exclusion of 26:1–30:17, which appears to be a self-contained unit that was secondarily spliced in. The "Book of Israel's Failings" is editorially clearly set apart.[63] The incidents related in this

---

63. The preceding section of Numbers ends with the "War Song of the Ark" (Num 10:35–36), which in rabbinic tradition is considered a separate book and is singled out by a prefixed and an appended inverted letter *nun*. The "Book of Israel's Iniquities" terminates before the insert with the statement ויהי אחרי המגפה (25:19a). The Masoretes indicated a break in the verse here by closing it with an *ʾetnaḥ* instead of the regular *sôf pāsûq* and noting a *pisqâh beʾemṣaʿ pāsûq*. This device signals a peculiarity in the transmitted text. See S. Talmon, "*Pisqâh Beʾemṣaʿ Pāsûq* and 11QPsᵃ" (*Textus* 5 [1966] 11–21 = *WQW*, 264–72). The half-verse 25:19a actually connects with וידבר ה' אל משה לאמר (cp. 26:1). Here the thread of the basic narrative is retied. Thus, taken together, 25:19a and 31:1 bracket out the insert 26:1–30:17.

book and its atmosphere have decisively determined the image of the desert period in subsequent biblical literature.[64]

We now have to establish the themes and ideas which could be derived from the account of the historical Desert Trek and the moods and reactions which this account could be expected to evoke in the audience that was exposed to it. The encounter was achieved either by a direct reminiscent recital of the story, most probably in a cultic setting, or else by employing the trek experience as a literary motif. Such secondary employment requires a historical and sociological disengagement from the historical trek situation and an ontological perspective toward desert conditions. Therefore, it can cause no surprise that figurative desert-language is not used at all in the historical portions of the Pentateuch or in biblical historiography. Here, as in legal literature, *desert-language* refers to the thing itself, not to its image. Also in Wisdom Literature, which in essence is nonhistorical, the Desert Trek does not serve as a source for literary motifs. There are, however, some instances of מדבר-imagery which are anchored in the wilderness aspect, as in Job 1:19; 24:5, or in the creation-myth setting, as in Job 38:25–26.

The Desert-Trek motif makes its first appearance in the deuteronomistic attempt to recapture the quintessence of that "historical" experience and to present it as the typological crystallization of the immanent relation between the people and God (Deuteronomy 32; cp. Psalms 78 and 106). The desert motif is preponderantly employed in the books of the preexilic prophets and in the book of Psalms. Thus it can be stated that the מדבר theme is in fact concentrated in biblical literature that pertains to the First Temple Period. With the end of the monarchy, the employment of the desert motif abates, possibly due to the reexperience of actual wilderness-desolation conditions (see, e.g., Mal 1:2–3). In postmonarchical literature it is replaced by new themes that represent similar ideas and notions and emanate from events and situations that are set in the period of the monarchy, such as the destruction of cities and the exile of the settled population.

Two major themes emerge from the traditions pertaining to the desert period in Israel's history.

---

64. Note that out of 42 occurrences of the term מדבר in Numbers, 25 are found in these 12 chapters, against 17 in the remaining 22.

(1) In the first part of this period, it is dominated by the Sinai theophany in which YHWH reveals himself to Israel and establishes a covenant with his people.

(2) The second part of the period is characterized by two mutually complementary strands of significance that run throughout the account: God provides Israel with sustenance and guides his people in the chaotic wilderness. In his benevolence he shields them from danger, although the desert period as such is by definition a period of punishment for Israel. But the people, stubborn and without remorse, continue flagrantly to disobey God and to kindle his anger. Worse than the future days of the judges, the desert period is typified by Israel's wickedness, by an uninterrupted sequence of transgressions. It lacks even the relieving moments of temporary repentance which ameliorate the biblical verdict on the times of the judges.

It is my thesis that the theme of *disobedience and punishment* is of much greater impact on the subsequent formulation of the desert motif in biblical literature than is the conception of the desert as the locale of divine revelation and of YHWH's love for Israel. The idealization of the desert that scholars perceived in the writings of some prophets derives from an unwarranted isolation of the *revelation-in-the-desert* theme from the preponderant *transgression-and-punishment* theme with which it is closely welded in the pentateuchal account of the Desert Trek.

(3) The widespread opinion that "the pre-exilic prophets for the most part [sic] interpreted the forty years as a period when God was particularly close to Israel, when he loved his chosen people as the bridegroom his bride,"[65] in the last count rests on the slender evidence of two passages, Hos 2:16–17 and Jer 2:2, which are discussed out of their setting in the wider context of the prophets' message. A closer analysis of this theme, viewed in relation to other concepts and motifs in biblical and especially in prophetic literature, indicates that they are of minor importance. In no way can they be construed to serve as the nucleus of a reputed desert ideal. The experience of a theophany in the desert is not an intrinsic feature of prophecy as such, but rather a particular instance in the life of *some* prophets. Nor can it be presented as a fundamental characteristic of Israel's God, as has been proposed. One witnesses, in fact, attempts to establish a phenomenological relationship between the Yahwistic faith and the desert. The conclusion pre-

---

65. Williams, *Wilderness*, 15–16 (see above, n. 15).

sented by Max Weber as a result of empirical studies that a provenance from the borderland between desert and cultivated land is characteristic of the biblical prophets,[66] is formulated as a phenomenological axiom in a geography of religion.[67] The desert is elevated to the position of an especially "geeignete Offenbarungsstätte des wahren Gottes."[68] "Beduinentum und Jahwismus" are conceived of not only as historically related but as existentially consanguineous phenomena which were most fruitfully mated in the prophetic experience of the desert deity YHWH in his natural setting.[69] Such a regional determinism cannot be squared with the prevailing prophetic idea of YHWH as an omnipresent deity who defies any geographical or conceptual circumscription.[70] Therefore, it appears that in revealing himself in the desert, whether to the prophet as an individual or to his people as a group, YHWH accommodates himself to the actual habitat of the recipients of this revelation. What the Temple is to the priests, to Jeremiah, Ezekiel, and to Isaiah—citizens of the metropolis—the desert (or drift) is to Moses and Amos the herdsmen, and to Elijah who also lived in the מדבר, the borderland between "Kulturland und Wüste." Elijah does not go into the desert in search of God, as said, but out of fear of Jezebel. That he experiences a theophany in the wilderness is coincidental, not predetermined by YHWH's desert character.

Thus we may assume that initially the theophany in the desert does not reveal the nature of YHWH but rather the existential setting of the men who experienced him there. Being a *historical* deity and not a nature god, and being the exclusive god invested with geographically and otherwise unrestricted power, he was not bound to reveal himself in a specific location but could permit people to experience him in their own existential framework. It is for this reason that in the limited historical period of the Trek in the Desert, the desert is the exclusive locale of divine revelation. With the Conquest of Canaan the Israelite concept of YHWH became charged with new images. It may well be that in the first stage, during the conquest of the

66. "Grenzgebiete des Kulturlandes im Übergang zur Wüste" (Weber, *Ancient Judaism*, 206–7 [see above, n. 27]).
67. G. Lanczkowski, *Altägyptischer Prophetismus: Ägyptologische Abhandlungen* (Wiesbaden: Harrassowitz, 1960) 4.52–57.
68. R. Kittel, *Gestalten und Gedanken in Israel* (Leipzig: Quelle und Meyer, 1926) 42.
69. S. Nyström, *Beduinentum und Jahwismus* (Lund: Gleerup, 1946). See also R. T. Anderson: "It is most likely that Yahweh was originally a desert deity" ("The Role of the Desert in Israelite Thought," *JBR* 27 [1959] 43).
70. This was correctly stressed by Budde, *New World*, 4.734 (see above, n. 1).

central mountain ridge, YHWH was identified as a "mountain deity." In this identification we may perceive a variation on the image of the pre-Conquest times, with its specific attachment to Mount Sinai and Mount Horeb.[71] This concept lingers on into monarchical times among surrounding nations, like the Arameans, who continue to conceive of Israel's God as אלהי הרים (1 Kgs 20:23), just as the *desert-god* image lingers on in Israel proper. After the establishment of the monarchy, the conception of YHWH as the royal ruler of an orderly universe overshadows all previous notions. It becomes the dominant motif in Israel's religion and is carried over into prophetic visions of the future, in which neither the desert god nor the mountain god has a stake.[72]

VI

We can now consider the desert motif in conjunction with other biblical motifs. This is especially important in view of the twofold signification that we discerned in the account of the Desert Trek. The figurative employment of the trek traditions mirrors the two diverging aspects in the God-Israel relation that characterize the days of the desert wanderings: on the one hand divine grace; on the other hand Israel's failings which engender punishment. The reinforcement of one or the other aspect is achieved by infusing into the trek motif new images and allomotifs that are anchored in מדבר-language in the wider sense of the word.

Thus Jer 2:6 exhibits a fusion of the historical trek theme as an expression of God's benevolence and guidance with the partly mythical *wilderness-desolation* theme. After first calling attention to the Exodus experience and the ensuing wanderings in the מדבר, "They did not ask, 'Where is YHWH who brought us up from the land of Egypt, who led us in the *midbar*,'" the prophet then continues in a new vein, "in a land of deserts and pits, in a land of drought and deep darkness, in a land where no one ever passes through, where no human lives" and thus introduces the howling wilderness aspect. Similarly in Ps 78:52 the notion of divine protection that inheres in the trek motif is combined with the *shepherd* image that has no roots in the historical account but derives from the drift context: "Then he led his people out [from Egypt] like sheep and guided them in the מדבר like a

71. Cp. Deut 4:10; 1 Kgs 8:9; Mal 3:22 and also Judg 5:5; Ps 68:9, etc.
72. See S. Talmon, "הר har, גבעה gibʿāh," *TWAT* 2.478–83 = *TDOT* 3.442–47.

flock." Hosea introduces an altogether new element into the trek motif, which is then further developed by Jeremiah. These modifications deserve special attention, since they triggered the emergence of the desert ideal already referred to.

The predominant motif of the first three chapters of the book of Hosea portrays YHWH's steadfast affection for Israel in terms of the unfailing love of a husband for his wayward wife.[73] As punishment for her unfaithfulness, the wife is deprived of her material comforts and reduced to abject poverty. Her husband leads her out of the luxury and plentitude that the land affords and takes her back into the מדבר (Hos 2:12–16). The hardship she experiences should cause her to repent, to mend her ways, and thus prepare her for a renewed and everlasting fidelity toward her husband. From "there [the מדבר] I will restore her vineyards, turning the Valley of Curse into a Gate of Hope" (Hos 2:17–18). עמק עכור brings to the mind of the writer's audience the incident in the days of the *Landnahme*, when עכן בן כרמי[74] "took of the חרם." His trespassing of the divine command resulted in Israel's defeat at the hands of the people of Ai (Josh 7:1–15). Because he brought trouble on Israel, "God [brought] trouble on his head: ויאמר יהושע מה עכרתנו יעכרך ה׳" (Josh 7:25). He is killed by stoning, and the place where he is executed "is called עמק עכור to this day" (7:26). In the new *Landnahme*, the Valley of Curse will be turned into the Gate of Hope. On the plane of the "nation," this process is viewed as a reenactment of the Desert-Trek period, which had served Israel as a transition from enslavement in Egypt to a free covenant relationship with God in Canaan. Accordingly Hosea's taking his wife back to the wilderness is not an aim *per se*. Rather, like the historical trek through the desert, it serves as punishment and as a *rite de passage* toward the true goal, the reestablishment of the wife-Israel in the Land of Canaan.[75]

The transition aspect of Hosea's desert motif is obviously derived from the account of the historical Desert Trek. However, the *marital-love* image

---

73. In this precise form the motif is present only in the first three chapters of the book, as Y. Kaufmann correctly observed (תולדות האמונה הישראלית [Tel Aviv: Dvir, 1945] 3/1.93–95).

74. The father's name is evidently echoed in Hosea's words, ונתתי לה את כרמיה משם (Hos 2:17).

75. A statement like that of Mauser's, "Thus a return to the wilderness is also a return to the Grace of God," misconstrues the signification of the Hosea passage (*Christ in the Wilderness*, 46 [see above, n. 11]).

has no roots in the desert account,[76] which uses other imagery to conceptualize YHWH's attachment to Israel—for example the *parent eagle-fledglings* image (Exod 19:4; Deut 32:11). But it turns up as an independent motif in the first chapter of the book of Hosea. Therefore it can be surmised that the fusion of these two initially unrelated themes, the trek motif and the love motif, originated with the author of this book. However the already observed cases of a combination of trek themes and drift imagery make one look for a traditional *love-cum-*מדבר motif, in which מדבר signifies "drift" or "wilderness."

Two possible sources come to mind. One is found in Canticles. A major theme of this collection of poems is the romantic attachment of youthful lovers on the drift. The maiden in search of her beloved among the shepherds and their flocks is portrayed as "coming up from the drift [מדבר] like a column of smoke from burning myrrh and frankincense" (3:6).[77] Again she is seen "coming up from the drift leaning upon her beloved" (8:5). It may be conjectured that Hosea infused an independent love-on-the-drift theme into the equally independent trek motif and thus created the quite uncommon motif combination *love-in-the-historical-desert-period*.

The other source that suggests itself is more remote than the first but has one additional factor in common with Hosea's employment of the motif combination: it pertains to divine love in the מדבר, in the setting of a Canaanite myth. There is in the Baal and ʿAnat cycle a rather outspoken and crude description of Aliyan Baal's mating with a heifer in the דבר, the name of a region which presumably was pasture or possibly desert land:[78]

---

76. The midrash retrojects this theme into the Sinai episode. Moses thus addresses the people on the morning of the theophany: "Arise from your sleep; the bridegroom is at hand and is waiting to lead his bride under the marriage canopy" (*Pirqe R. El.* 41; *Midr. Cant.* 1:12; 5:3; *Deut. Rab.* 3:12; ʾAg. Ber. 41:126). Cp. L. Ginzberg, *The Legends of the Jews* ([New York: IPS, 1955] 3.92).

77. The attribution of the metaphor to the maiden is to be preferred over its attribution to Solomon's litter (RSV).

78. C. H. Gordon, *Ugaritic Manual* (AnOr 35/2; Roma: Pontificium Institutum Biblicum, 1955) 149; idem, trans., *Ugaritic Literature* (Roma: Pontificium Institutum Biblicum, 1949) 42.

Aliyan Baal hearkens
He loves a heifer in *dbr*[79]
   A young cow in the fields of *šḥlmmt*
He lies with her seventy-seven times
   [Yea   ] eighty-eight times (67:5:18–22).

Arṣ dbr in the Ugaritic myth is part of the netherworld, the domain of Mot. It is inhabited by his helpmates, just as in some biblical references the מדבר is the abode of demons (Isa 13:21–22; 34:11–14). It stands to reason that in the Hosea motif a revised Canaanite mythological theme, divine love on the drift (or possibly "in the wilderness") was wedded with the historical *wilderness-trek* motif.[80] Such an interpretation lends a new dimension to this latter motif. Far from being the "normal" or "ideal" habitat of YHWH, the wilderness that is the realm of Mot, the ruler of the netherworld, is forced to yield to the supreme power of Israel's God. Where the Canaanite fertility god Baal failed because his power is limited to agricultural areas, Israel's God achieves unimpaired success: "He turns rivers into a desert and springs of water into thirsty ground; he turns fruitful land into salt waste." With the very same power, "he turns a desert into pools of water and parched land into springs of water. There he lets the hungry dwell" (Ps 107:33–35). He can return his people to the dried-up waste and from there give them again their vineyards and turn the valley of desolation into the gate of hope (Hos 2:17). Viewed thus the Hosea passage echoes the covert refutation of the Canaanite fertility-god myth.[81] This same refutation seems to underlie the pentateuchal trek account and also the desert visions of Deutero-Isaiah.[82]

79.   G. R. Driver translates, "land of decease" (*Ugaritic Myth* [Edinburgh: Clark, 1956] 107). This is hardly acceptable, since further on (67:6:5, 29–30) the "goodness of *ars dbr*" is referred to.

80.   The historization of Canaanite myth in the literature of the Hebrew Bible is a well-known phenomenon. A typical example may be found in Isa 51:9–11, where the mythical dismemberment of Rahab is welded with the historical tradition of the crossing of the Red Sea and is then projected into the vision of the return from the exile. See I. L. Seeligmann, *Voraussetzungen der Midraschexegese* ([VTSup 1, Congress Volume, Copenhagen 1953; Leiden: E. J. Brill, 1953] 169).

81.   E. Jacob identifies in the book of Hosea many more instances of refutation and rejection of Canaanite mythical traditions that had found popular acceptance among the prophet's contemporaries ("L'héritage cananéen dans le livre du prophète Osée," *RHPR* 3 [1963] 250–59).

82.   This technique of covert refutation of Canaanite mythology can be observed in the biblical creation story and certainly was applied also in other biblical traditions. See U. Cassuto, *A Commentary on the Book of Genesis* ([trans. L. Abrahams; Jerusalem: Magnes, 1961] 7ff.).

It should be clear that whatever its origin and subsequent development may be, the love-in-the-desert motif of Hosea does not give expression to a prophetic desert ideal, as has been and is still asserted by some scholars. At best it constitutes a fairly isolated and subsidiary theme in the prophet's thought. It is the result of a literary process of motif-fusion rather than an explicit expression of a theological or existential concept.

At this juncture the question must be raised whether or not such a concept can be discerned in the way in which Jeremiah developed this theme. Let us recall that in Hosea's version the motif depicts God's steadfast love for Israel in spite of the nation's iniquities. This love originally had been revealed in the setting of the Desert Trek, where it was coupled with the *expurgatory-transition* motif. In the book of Jeremiah the love theme takes a new turn. It now portrays Israel's affection for God in that remote historical period. At the same time the transition aspect of the trek motif is replaced by the "desolation aspect" of the wilderness motif: "Thus says YHWH, I remember the devotion of your youth, the love of your bridal days when you followed me in the wilderness, through a land that was unsown" (Jer 2:2). It must be admitted that Jeremiah's employment of the desert motif appears to reflect an appreciation of the desert period that deviates considerably from the disapprobation that surfaces in the pentateuchal traditions. If this distinct difference were to be explained as a deliberate deviation from pentateuchal historiography, a question would arise concerning the prophet's awareness of that tradition and his attitude toward it. But in fact no such reinterpretation has to be assumed. Like Hosea, Jeremiah never develops the historical desert reminiscence into a goal toward which he wants to guide the nation. Also in his view God's love for Israel, evoked by the memory of the nation's fidelity at the time of her youth, ultimately will express itself in a return from the מדבר into the restituted Land of Israel: "Thus says YHWH, 'The people that survived the sword [again] found favor in the wilderness.'" And he turns to his people saying: "I have loved you from of old; with loving-kindness I have drawn you [after me]. . . . Again you shall plant vineyards upon the mountains of Samaria; the planters shall plant and enjoy the fruit thereof" (Jer 31:2–5).

Jeremiah's apparent divergence from the pentateuchal presentation of the desert period therefore should be explained as a literary variation rather than as a case of a deliberate reassessment of history. The apparent contradiction may be resolved by our attempt to explain the love-in-the-desert motif as a fusion of two themes that were derived from different aspects of מדבר. I would describe the process as a combination of the love-in-the-drift theme with the Desert-Trek motif. Thus Jeremiah's presentation of the desert period does not evidence an unawareness of the pentateuchal traditions on the part of the prophet, nor does it imply a conscious reworking of these traditions. The variation, which indeed is present, cannot be construed to show that Jeremiah conceived of the desert period as Israel's Golden Age for whose return he nostalgically longed.

It is reasonable to conclude, then, that in both the books of Hosea and Jeremiah the modification of the appreciation of the trek period results from an unpremeditated process of literary variation and was brought about by the infusion into the desert motif of initially unrelated themes. The underlying factors are less of a conscious historiosophical character than of a literary nature.[83]

The last prophet and in fact the latest biblical source that makes extensive use of the desert motif is Deutero-Isaiah. Under the impression of the striking similarity between Israel's historical situation in Egyptian Bondage and in the Babylonian Exile, the prophet expresses his hopeful expectation of a new exodus and a new settlement in Canaan in terms and images that are clearly patterned upon the pentateuchal trek traditions. "The conception of the new exodus is the most profound and most prominent of the motifs in the tradition which Second Isaiah employs to portray the eschatological finale."[84] But Deutero-Isaiah does not merely borrow a theme from pentateuchal sources or from the prophets Hosea and Jeremiah who precede him. His utilization of the ancient material is selective and is subject to formative adaptation. He fully retains the established notion of the Desert Trek as a mere transition stage. However the original aspect of *rite de passage* for the sake of purification is completely overshadowed by the *divine-benevolence* theme. The shift of stress is easily explained. It arises out of the fundamentally different theological situation of postexilic Israel, compared

83. M. Fox concurs with my refutation of the desert ideal ascribed to Jeremiah but does not accept my explanation that the prophet's apparent approbation of the Desert Period results from a mixing of motifs ("Jeremiah 2:2 and the Desert Ideal," *CBQ* 35 [1973] 441–50). Following a suggestion by A. W. Streane (*Jeremiah* [CBC; Cambridge: Cambridge University Press, 1913] ad loc.) and by N. H. Tur-Sinai (פשוטו של מקרא [Jerusalem: Kiryat-Sefer, 1967] 3a.156), he takes חסד נעוריך to be an objective genitive which signifies God's love for Israel in her youth (cp. Jer 31:2–3), not Israel's love for God.

84. J. Muilenburg, "Isaiah," *IB* (Philadelphia: Abingdon, 1956) 602.

with that of the Exodus generation. While for the Exodus generation the desert became the locale of purification that perforce must precede the attainment of the Promised Land, the returning exiles had already successfully passed through the stage of catharsis, which they experienced in the destruction of the Temple and in the Babylonian Exile. The purging of the Exodus generation from the dross of sin and sinners was effected in the desert, so that only their sons, so far guiltless, reached the gates of Canaan (Num 14:20–37; Deut 1:35–36). The Israel of Deutero-Isaiah's time had been decimated by war, destruction, and dispersion. The returning exiles were the עשיריה, the "holy seed" which Isaiah of Jerusalem had envisaged (Isa 6:13; cp. Ezra 9:2). The new exodus fell to the lot of the faithful remnant, and the new trek through the desert could be freed from its purgatory qualities and concomitantly be invested with new images of promise and hope. Now the desert motif was wedded with the theme of the Davidic Covenant and with the vision of the restituted Jerusalem.[85] It is this fusion of the desert motif with the *remnant* idea and with the expectation of a restored Davidic dynasty which, as will be shown, constitutes the basis of the desert theme in Qumran ideology.

In sum, we may say that it is altogether futile to speculate on an imaginary prophetic desert ideal and to present it as the expression of a typical bedouin zest for freedom that was opposed to the monarchical regime.[86] The prophets did not reject the monarchy but rather accepted it as the form of government that had been divinely decreed for Israel at a specific juncture in its history. The king was conceived of as the pivot of the political order, just as God was in charge of the cosmic order. Disorder and anarchy result in a kingless situation, when the country is thrown back into desert-like chaos (Isa 3:1–12; cp. Hos 3:4–5). Kings did indeed fail in history and were rebuked and punished for their faults. But nowhere in prophetic literature did the experience of the historical failure of kings result in a request for the abolishment of kingship or for a return to "free" desert life.[87]

85. Cp. B. W. Anderson, "Exodus Typology in Second Isaiah," *Israel's Prophetic Heritage: Essays in Honor of J. Muilenburg* (ed. B. W. Anderson and W. Harrelson; New York: Harper, 1962) 181.

86. "L'atavisme bédouin, l'aversion innée du nomade pour les moeurs et la culture modernes, pour toute organisation politique centralisée, sont des tendances encore profondément enracinées chez Osée" (Humbert, *RHPR* 1 [1921] 115 [see above, n. 1]).

87. See S. Talmon, "Kingship and the Ideology of the State," *KCC*, 9–38.

In postdestruction literature the desert motif occupies an insignificant place. The focal point in history is transferred from preconquest times to the days of the monarchy. The House of David is now center stage and becomes a fertile source of literary imagery. Biblical eschatology, the vision of the messianic Golden Age, is conceived in terms of a revitalized and purified monarchical regime based on a "new covenant" between YHWH and the House of David. This concept is already present in the books of Amos (9:11–12) and Hosea (3:3–5) and gains momentum as the approaching end of Israelite sovereignty is perceived more clearly.

Ezekiel does not portray the future Davidic king in full detail. In essence his political message and vision of the future is not different from that of his precursors: in the ideal age to come, a reunited Israel, governed by one king and purified from idol worship, will again occupy the Land of Canaan (Ezek 37:21–27). When all had been said, Ezekiel and his contemporaries, like the prophets of preceding generations, would fully accept the strikingly realistic picture of the Golden Age that was painted by Jeremiah: "If you obey . . . indeed (and execute justice and righteousness), then there shall enter by the gates of this house kings sitting upon the throne of David, riding in chariots and on horses" (Jer 22:4; cp. 17:24–25, *contra* Deut 17:16).

VII

We turn now to the analysis of the desert theme in Qumran literature and theology. In view of the fact that the Qumran Covenanters had established their communal center in the reality of the Judean Desert, the comparative scarcity of references to the term מדבר and its cognates in their literature is rather surprising. Only twelve occurrences of מדבר are listed in the concordances[88] that cover the Qumran material published before 1960. Subsequent publications have not materially affected the picture. Some of these references occur in tiny fragments that remain unintelligible and therefore will not be considered here.[89] A classification of the occurrences of מדבר

---

88. A. M. Habermann, *The Scrolls from the Judean Desert* ([Tel Aviv: Machbaroth Lesifruth, 1959] 38 [Heb.]); K. G. Kuhn, *Konkordanz zu den Qumrantexten* (Göttingen: Vandenhoeck & Ruprecht, 1960) 115.
89. D. Barthélemy, O. P. and J. T. Milik, *Discoveries in the Judean Desert: Qumran Cave I* (Oxford: Clarendon, 1955) 1.130, frg. 29:5–6 and p. 144, frg. 42:6.

shows that the term is used once topographically and pertains there to the "Great Desert," which is located to the south of Palestine.[90] In one other case the cosmic creation aspect of the מדבר theme is involved.[91] Neither of these bears on the issue at hand.

Only one reference to מדבר is a direct reminiscence of the Desert Trek. It pertains, most significantly, to the extermination of the unbelieving desert generation (Deut 9:23): "And their males were cut off in the desert, and he [God] spoke to them at Kadesh: 'Go ye up and possess [the Land,' but they chose the desire of] their own spirit and hearkened not to the voice of their Maker—the commandments He taught them—and they murmured in their tents [cp. Ps 106:25]. And the anger of God was kindled against their congregation."[92] In selecting this pentateuchal passage in referring to the desert period, the author of the Zadokite Documents aligns himself with the overwhelming majority of the biblical writers in their depreciative attitude towards this historical period. He further clarifies his view by introducing into his exposition of the Deuteronomy passage the quotation from Psalm 106, which elaborates on the desert generation's recurring acts of rebelliousness against God. The historiographical review presented in Ps 106:13–33 is but a condensed catalogue of the nation's iniquities in the desert period, to the exclusion even of the signs of temporary remorse which the pentateuchal account has preserved. The Qumran author takes as gloomy a view of the Desert Trek as does the psalmist, if not a gloomier one. It is important to stress that like Psalm 106, which is of the "cultic-confession" type, the Zadokite Fragments express the very quintessence of the Qumranites' historiosophy. The arrangement of the book, the combination of historical reports with codices of legal injunctions and exhortatory orations, suggests that it was viewed by the Covenanters as the "New Law" conceived in the image of the Pentateuch, especially of Deuteronomy. The Covenanters' intense preoccupation with the materials assembled in the documents is illustrated by the fact that in the library at Qumran this composition survived in seven manuscripts and also was found in private collections.[93] "The number of

90. 1QM ii 12
91. 1QM x 12–13.
92. CD iii 6–9; Rabin, *Zadokite Documents*, 10–11.
93. M. Baillet, "Fragments du documents de Damas, grotte 6," *RB* 63 (1956) 513–23.

copies is higher than that of Pentateuchal MSS (except Deuteronomy) or of Jeremiah and Ezekiel, for example."[94] Therefore we may safely conclude that the passage from the Zadokite Documents quoted above succinctly expresses the Qumranites' criticism of the historical desert generation. Viewed in this light, their new trek into the desert cannot be judged an attempt to identify with values and to realize ideals which supposedly were inherent in the historical desert period. It can only be a reexperience of the *transition-and-preparation* motif that crystallized in the trek traditions.

That this is indeed the signification of the desert in Qumran theology becomes apparent when the desert motif is evaluated against the background of the Covenanters' vision of future salvation. In complete concurrence with the biblical Exodus-Trek-Conquest sequence, the retreat into the desert constitutes for them the hiatus between the historical exodus from Jewish society of their own days and their future conquest of Jerusalem and of the Land of Israel, which still lies ahead of them.

"It was perhaps felt that the present age of Israel's history should fittingly end, as it had begun, with a probationary period."[95] The interim period of the desert is but an extension of the obnoxious historical past and does not reach into the brilliant expanse of future salvation. The retreat into the desert is the last link with Israel's *Unheilsgeschichte,* which began with the generation of the Flood, continued into the days of Jacob's sons, to the exception of the patriarchal era, included the bondage in Egypt and the Desert Trek, and lasted throughout the times of the kingdom into the Second Temple Period[96] (cp. Ezekiel 20). This phase will end with the onset of the approaching ultimate redemption, of which the historical Conquest of Canaan was a mere deficient foreshadow that came to naught. "At the end [of this new interim period] of the forty years they [the wicked] shall cease to exist [יתמו] and no wicked man shall be found on earth. But the meek [עניים] shall inherit

94. F. M. Cross, *The Ancient Library of Qumran and Modern Biblical Studies* (New York: Doubleday, 1958) 60, n. 46.
95. F. F. Bruce, *Biblical Exegesis in the Qumran Texts* (Grand Rapids: Eerdmans, 1957) 26. See also N. Wieder, "The 'Law-Interpreter' of the Sect of the Dead Sea Scrolls: The Second Moses," *JJS* 4 (1953) 172; Yadin, מגילת בני אור בבני חושך ממגילות מדבר יהודה (Jerusalem: Bialik, 1955) 31ff. = *The Scroll of the Sons of Light against the Sons of Darkness* (trans. B. and C. Rabin; Oxford: Oxford University Press, 1962); H. Kosmala, *Hebräer-Essener-Christen* (Leiden: E. J. Brill, 1959) 66, 72–73, 171, n. 19.
96. CD ii 5–iv 4. Cp. J. M. Allegro, "A Recently Discovered Fragment of a Commentary on Hosea from Qumran's Fourth Cave," *JBL* 78 (1959) 142–47.

the earth and delight in peace abounding" (Ps 37:11).[97] This is an interest-ing piece of Qumran hermeneutics. With the aid of the transferred trek-terminology, the general motif of *the fall of the wicked* depicted in Psalm 37 is invested with specific Covenanter eschatology. The identification of their adversaries with the evil desert generation is made explicit by the reference to "forty years"[98]—a central trek motif—and is further fortified by the em-ployment in the pesher of typical trek-transgression terminology: הממרים,[99] יתמו,[100] the rebellious will come to an end, whereas on the other hand the Covenanters will inherit, יירשו,[101] the land in the same manner as the Con-quest generation had taken possession of Canaan.

There are in the Qumran writings, however, references to events that are set in the framework of the desert period and in which the Covenanters dis-cern prototypes of their own historical experiences. The images of the Teacher of Righteousness and certainly that of the Law Interpreter undoubt-edly were patterned upon the image of Moses.[102] Their personalities mirror a positive aspect of the מדבר motif in Qumran literature, just as the life-history of Moses reflects the biblical evaluation of the desert period.

The Teacher's struggle with the Wicked Priest is a reenactment of the strife of Moses and Aaron against the powers of evil that opposed them in their time: "For in ancient times Moses and Aaron arose by the hand of the Prince of Lights, and Belial raised Jannes and his brother by his evil device, when Israel was delivered for the first time. And in the epoch of the desola-tion of the land there arose the 'removers of the boundary' 'and they led Is-rael astray.'"[103] Moses had been appointed to bring Israel out of the Egyp-tian bondage; the Teacher was appointed to lead the Covenanters out of their bewilderment and distress. When they had become conscious of their shortcomings and their sins and for twenty years had craved in vain to be il-luminated, then "God 'considered their works,' for 'with a perfect heart' did they seek Him; and He raised for them 'a teacher of righteousness' to lead

---

97. J. M. Allegro, "A Newly-Discovered Fragment of a Commentary on Psalm XXXVII from Qumrân (4QpPs 37)," *PEQ* 86 (1954) 71; T. H. Gaster, trans., *The Dead Sea Scriptures in English Translation*, with introduction and notes (New York: Doubleday, 1956) 259.

98. Cp. also CD xx 14ff.

99. Cp. Num 20:10, 24; 27:14; Deut 1:26, 43; 9:7, 23–24; 31:27; Ps 78:17, 56; 106:7, 33, 43; 107:11; et al.

100. Num 14:34–35; Deut 2:14–16.

101. Cp. Num 14:24.

102. See Wieder, *JJS* 4 (1953) 158–74 (above, n. 94).

103. CD v 17–20.

them in 'the way of His heart.'"[104] Moses had been entrusted further with bringing "the Law" to the Children of Israel in the desert, and again the Teacher follows the same pattern. Remembering his covenant with the patriarchs, God "raised from Aaron 'men of understanding' and from Israel 'men of wisdom,' 'and he caused them to hear'; and they digged the well: 'the well which princes digged, which the nobles of the people delved with the staff' [cp. Num 21:18]. The Well is the Law. And those that digged it are 'they that turned [from impiety] of Israel.'"[105] In the characteristic Qumran pesher technique, the author identifies the "well" with "the Law," that is, with the Covenanters' law. But the specific wilderness setting in which the "well" episode is embedded in the Pentateuch is not commented upon, nor is it hermeneutically utilized in CD. The new significance of the "well" is in no way rooted in wilderness reality. It is again the historical event *in* the desert, not the existential experience *of* the desert which forms the basis of the Covenanters' reemployment of trek traditions.

There is a combination in the account of the historical desert period of a positive stratum on the one hand with a dominant negative stratum on the other hand. This results in an ambivalence of attitudes that makes impossible a full identification of the Covenanters with the Exodus generation. It also may explain the surprisingly weak echo of the pentateuchal desert in their literature. We further have to keep in mind the characteristics of the pesher technique, which plays an overwhelming role in the Covenanters' reactualization of biblical traditions. The pesher is employed preponderantly as a means to prove that the events which befell the "last generation," that is to say the יחד members, were actually foreshadowed in biblical prophetic literature, including "prophecies" in the Pentateuch, and to a lesser degree in other biblical compositions of an essentially nonhistoriographical character. The pesher technique is rarely, if ever, applied to traditions of a definable one-time historical nature. Thus the patriarchal narratives, or for that matter the historical records incorporated in the former prophets, are seldom utilized in the pesher literature. It is for these reasons that Deutero-Isaiah's desert imagery completely eclipses the actual trek period as a source from which Qumran authors derive the desert motif.

---

104. CD i 10–11.
105. Or "the repentants of Israel" (CD vi 2–5); see also Kosmala, *Hebräer*, 73, n. 32 (above, n. 94).

As said, in Deutero-Isaiah's desert vision, Israel is altogether free from the transgressions of which the trek generation so often is accused. The sin-and-punishment theme being absent, Isaiah's desert motif has become a pure and concentrated expression of the transition-and-preparation idea, which the post-trek generations perceived as the essential signification of the trek tradition. The reactualization of Deutero-Isaiah's desert in the Covenanters' conceptions could therefore be performed without the transformation of contents which would have been a *sine qua non* for such a reemployment of the pentateuchal traditions.

Thus the famous passage in Isa 40:3, "A voice cries, 'In the wilderness prepare the way of the Lord; make straight in the desert a highway for our God,'" was established as a central theme in the Covenanters' ideology.

Two references of great ideological import arise directly out of this Isaiah passage.[106] The day of the Qumranites' secession from Israel "is the time when the way is being prepared in the wilderness."[107] Again, even more explicitly it is stated that the Covenanters "are to be kept apart from any consort with forward men, to the end that they may indeed 'go into the wilderness to prepare the way [i.e., do what scripture enjoins]; Prepare in the wilderness the way . . . make straight in the desert a highway for our God.'"[108]

The Covenanters literally accept the prophet's call to go into the desert (Isa 40:3), expounding it as a summons to dissociate themselves from their sinful contemporaries (1QS viii 12–16) and to live in the desert as שבים לתורה, "returners to the Torah" (4QpPs 37 i 1–2),[109] according to the laws that had been revealed to them (1QS ix 19–20). This exodus from society turns them into שבי המדבר, "penitents of the desert" (4QpPs 37 ii 1), with the stress on *penitents,* who are assured of future salvation. But no desert ideal is involved. "Their retreat . . . is to be understood, not in a framework of nature-spirit dualism of Greek type, but in the ethical or "spirit-spirit" dualism of apocalypticism. They go into the desert for a season, to be born again as the New Israel, to enter into the Covenant of the last days."[110] One might even go one step further. The intellectualizing in-

---

106. Also 1QH viii 4–5 reflects Isaian language. Cp. Isa 41:19.
107. 1QS ix 19–20. Gaster, *The Dead Sea Scriptures,* 59 (see above, n. 96).
108. 1QS viii 13–14. Trans. Gaster, ibid., 56.
109. Allegro, *PEQ* 86 (1954) 71 (see above, n. 97).
110. Cross, *The Ancient Library of Qumran,* 56 (see above, n. 93).

terpretation of "going into the desert," as an effort to regain from there God's law, clearly indicates how far removed the Covenanters were from a *nature ideology* expressed in wilderness terms. The wilderness symbolizes the state of chaotic lawlessness that is the existential setting of the "man of scoffing who . . . [preached] to Israel 'waters of falsehood' and caused them to go astray in a wilderness, תוהו, without way."[111] The chaos has to be overcome from within so that a way may be paved for the new order, the New Covenant.[112] This new order, like Israel's settlement in Canaan, will not spring from an even-flowing progress of history but will be born out of turmoil and upheaval. The establishment of the New Jerusalem will be preceded by fierce battles against the powers of darkness. These are the ancient Wars of YHWH (Num 21:14) all over again, for which the Covenanters discipline themselves by the rules laid down in the War Scroll. In the description of the Last War, we encounter references to the מדבר that appear to be of decisive importance for the evaluation of the desert motif at Qumran. In this future context the Covenanters significantly present themselves as the Exiles of the Desert, גולת המדבר, who return from the Desert of the Nations, מדבר העמים,[113] in order to encamp in the outskirts of Jerusalem, מדבר ירושלים, on the eve of their onslaught on the holy city.[114]

The last-mentioned reference to מדבר ירושלים belongs to the ecological-connotation aspect of מדבר and can be disregarded in our discussion. The other two call for some comment. By designating their preeschatological—that is, historical—status as an "exile in the wilderness" the Covenanters emphatically present their desert period as a necessary evil and certainly not as a "mystic ideal."[115] The theological appellation Desert of the Nations given to their actual abode in the preredemption era again proves that they regarded the מדבר stage as an alien and unwelcome phase in their history. The term is appropriated from Ezekiel, who employs it in an oracle in which he likens God's future judgment of Israel to the judgment he meted out to the Exodus generation in the wilderness, "I will bring you into the wilderness

111. CD i 14–15.
112. Cp. also 1QH viii 4–5 and Isa 41:18.
113. The term recurs, partly in a lacuna, in 4QpIsaᵃ, a fragmentary pesher on Isa 10:28–11:4 (see J. M. Allegro, "Further Messianic References in Qumran," *JBL* 75 [1956] 174–87) and probably also in a fragmentary Hosea manuscript. See Allegro, *JBL* 78 ([1959] 145 [above, n. 95]).
114. 1QM i 2–3.
115. A. Dupont-Sommer, *The Essene Writings from Qumran* (Cleveland/New York: World Publishing Company, 1962) 169, n. 2.

of the nations; there will I confront you face to face. Even as I entered into judgment with your forefathers in the wilderness of the land of Egypt . . ." (Ezek 20:35–36). In all these three manifestations—in the Pentateuch, the book of Ezekiel, and the War Scroll—the מדבר is a typological crystallization of a predestined "mark time" on Israel's march towards redemption.

The foregoing analysis has shown that pentateuchal trek imagery is not altogether absent from the Qumran writings. Cross is right when he defines the Covenanters as "an apocalyptic community, a *Heilsgemeinschaft*, imitating the ancient desert sojourn of Mosaic times in anticipation of the dawning Kingdom of God."[116] However, it is of crucial importance to discern that the Covenanters reexperienced the desert of Mosaic time in reflections mediated by the visions of Ezekiel and Deutero-Isaiah.[117] They adopted the camp structure, not because it was best suited to desert conditions, but as a typological reflection of the historical pre-Conquest tribal organization. Both *camp* and *tribe* can be divorced from their historical setting and can be transferred as imagery into an altogether different ecological and sociological framework. As was already done by the author of the apocalypse that closes the book of Ezekiel (chapters 40–48), so also in Qumran literature this nomadic imagery was fused with motifs which are rooted in a sedentary state of life: a static sanctuary and the renascent Davidic monarchy. Thus the מחוקק of the pentateuchal "well" episode (Num 21:17–18), in whom the author of the Zadokite Documents recognizes the Law Interpreter, דורש התורה, is in the vision of the future joined by a scion of the House of David who is the realization of the מחוקק projected in Jacob's Blessing (Gen 49:10):[118] "For the מחוקק refers to the royal mandate; the families of Israel are the [military] units.[119] *Until* the rightful Messiah *shall come*, the shoot of David, for to him and to his seed has been given the royal mandate over his people for everlasting generations. . . ." Again, in a pesher on Nathan's prophecy (2 Sam 7:11–14): "He is the shoot of David who will arise with the Law Interpreter [דורש התורה] who . . . in Zi[on in the l]ast days; as it is writ-

116. Cross, *The Ancient Library of Qumran,* 56 (see above, n. 93).

117. Isa 35:8–10 may have been another biblical proof text on which the Qumran version of the Desert-Trek idea hinged.

118. Our translation differs somewhat from the one proposed by the editor of the fragment. Cp. Allegro, *JBL* 75 [1956] 174–75 [above, n. 112]).

119. Here we follow Y. Yadin's reading: *dglym.* See "Some Notes on Commentaries on Genesis XLIX and Isaiah from Qumran Cave Four" (*IEJ* 7 [1957] 66). Allegro reads *rglym* and translates "feet" (*JBL* 75 [1956] 174–75).

ten: And I will raise up the house [אוהל] of David that is fallen"
(4QpSam).[120]

In conclusion we may say that, true to biblical tradition, the desert initially was for the Qumran Covenanters a place of refuge from persecution to
which they betook themselves in spite of their innate fear of the wilderness.[121] Their secession from their sinful contemporaries was culminated in
the flight into the desert. Thus the wilderness developed the conceptual dimension of "retreat." Ultimately the desert became the locale of a period of
purification and preparation for the achievement of a new goal. This goal is
the conquest of the Holy Land, culminating in the seizure of Jerusalem and
the reestablishment of the supreme sanctuary of Israel, in which the Sons of
Zadok, YHWH's truly appointed priests, will officiate *in aeternum*. The
desert is a passage to this goal, not the goal itself.

In another context I endeavor to show that in their basic conceptual
framework the Judean Covenanters are true heirs to biblical Judaism.[122] This
dictum holds also for their utilization of the desert motif. Notwithstanding
adaptational variations, an unbroken line of interpretation of the desert tradition appears to lead from the Bible to postbiblical Jewish literature, of which
the Covenanters' writings are one manifestation. However, these dissenters
from the mainstream of Judaism in the Period of the Second Temple are not
the sole preservers of this chain of tradition. It can provisionally be stated
that the desert motif retains the same characteristics and in essence represents the same ideas in normative rabbinic literature as in biblical imagery.

The new breakthrough occurs in Christian literature that exhibits a
monastic orientation, when retreat from the world is raised from the status of
a temporary disengagement to that of a theological ideal. At the same time,
self-imposed poverty, frugality, and simplicity become invested with the
glory of self-abnegation, which is expected to clear the way for an un-
impeded access to individual salvation set in metahistory. It is in this context that the desert is freed from the biblical conception of a cursed waste-
land that must be traversed, serving as a bridge to communal redemption in
history. The primitivity of desert life that the Hebrews viewed as a frighten-
ing and unwelcome phenomenon, is now reinterpreted and joyfully accepted

---

120. Allegro, ibid.
121. See, e.g., 1QH viii 24. That passage is patterned on the equally fear-inspiring description of
     the wilderness in Jer 17:5–6; 48:6.
122. S. Talmon, "Between the Bible and the Mishnah," *WQW*, 21–52.

as a prerequisite for the longed-for experience of spiritual bliss. Terrestrial Jerusalem had been envisaged by the Israelites as lying beyond the fringes of the desert. The Christian vision of the celestial Jerusalem sprouts from within the confines of the wilderness.

It would be an intriguing exercise to trace the influence of this early Christian configuration of the biblical *desert motif* on modern Old Testament scholars' perception of a reputed *desert-ideal* in prophetic literature. However, the investigation of this issue requires an in-depth analysis which cannot be attempted in the present context.

"WISDOM" IN THE BOOK OF ESTHER

I

Tradition intended the book of Esther to be accepted as an accurate and reliable account of events which befell the Jewish exiles in the Persian Empire under the reign of King Ahasuerus, who was identified with Xerxes I (486–465).[1] The purported historiographical nature of the book is underlined by its concluding passage, Esth 10:1–3. Here the author deliberately employs technical terminology which is widely used in biblical historiography, especially in the books of Kings and Chronicles.

However, modern biblical scholarship has severely doubted the accuracy of the account given in the Esther story and "most scholars nowadays agree that the book in its present form does not relate real historical events."[2] It is a widely, though not universally, held opinion, first propagated by T. D. Michaelis in 1783, that the "chronistic" finale (Esth 10:1–3), which refers the reader to the "Chronicles of the Kings of Media and Persia" for further information on Ahasuerus and Mordecai, is to be judged a late apposition to the original compilation. Although there is no marked difference in style between the core of the book and the concluding passage,[3] certain discrepancies of contents are often deemed sufficient to warrant their separation.[4] The same has been said of the section immediately preceding the

---

1. This identification has been upheld on philological and archeological grounds by R. Stiehl ("Das Buch Esther," *WZKM* 53 [1956] 4–22).

2. H. Ringgren, "Esther and Purim," *SEÅ* 20 (1955) 5.

3. See H. Striedl, "Untersuchungen zur Syntax und Stilistik des hebräischen Estherbuches," *ZAW* 55 (1937) 73–108.

4. However, D. Daube ("The Last Chapter of Esther," *JQR* 37 [1946–47] 139–47) considers chap. 10 the crowning piece of the story. In it the author of Esther advocates the preference of orderly and regular royal taxation (Esth 10:1) over financial blood-letting and persecution, as were proposed by Haman in 3:9; 4:7; 7:4. Cp. further H. Gunkel, *Esther, Religionsgeschichtliche Volksbücher* ([ed. F. M. Schiele; Tübingen: Mohr, 1916] 46, n. 276).

"finale," which deals with the establishment of Purim as a national festival (Esth 9:20–32).[5]

In the Esther story itself, prominent details were pointed out that are inconsistent with what is known of Persian customs. The rather numerous legendary, even fanciful embellishments of the incidents reported further detract from the historical reliability of the account. However, there also have been scholarly attempts to uphold the historicity of the book of Esther. This was done by means of a reidentification of its central figures and by a resetting of the occurrences described, in historical periods and situations with which the details of the Esther story could supposedly better be squared than with the times of Xerxes I. Such an attempt was already made by Josephus (*Ant.* 11.6.11ff.), who retrojected the whole account into the reign of Cyrus the Great (559–530 BCE). Under this king, Mordecai, who had been exiled in 597, according to our book (Esth 2:6), could have been active without stretching his lifespan to an incredible length, as would be necessary if he was a contemporary of Xerxes I.

Some modern scholars have moved down the chronology of the story into the later Persian period. Gunkel decided on the times of Darius II (423–404) as the most likely date of its composition.[6] J. Hoschander suggests that Ahasuerus should be identified with Artaxerxes II (Mnemon, 403–358), whose name initially was mentioned in the story but later was suppressed for political reasons. Hoschander then proceeds to discover in the book of Esther allusions to historical events that occurred in the reign of that king.[7]

Others defined the book of Esther as a clever literary fabrication that is but a disguised report on historical facts that came to pass in Hellenistic or in Roman times and were retrojected into the Persian period for reasons of political expediency. Thus H. Willrich identified Ahasuerus with Ptolemy VIII (Physicon, 170 BCE).[8]

The book was sometimes described as a political satire that reflects the victory of Judah the Maccabee (= Mordecai) over the Syrian general

---

5. The scholarly discussion of the problems pertaining to the book of Esther is usefully summarized in the introductions to the Old Testament by O. Eissfeldt, *Einleitung in das Alte Testament* ([2d ed.; Tübingen: Mohr, 1956] 628–29) and A. Bentzen, *Introduction to the Old Testament* ([3d ed.; Copenhagen: Gad, 1957] 2.192–95).

6. Gunkel, *Esther,* 87.

7. J. Hoschander, *The Book of Esther* (Philadelphia: Dropsie, 1923). Most MSS of the LXX give the name of the Persian king as Αρταζέρζης (Esth 10:3).

8. H. Willrich, *Judaica: Forschungen zur hellenistisch-jüdischen Geschichte und Literatur* (Göttingen: Vandenhoeck, 1900) 1–28.

Nicanor (= Haman) on the 13th of Adar 161 BCE. The events would then fall into the reign of Antiochus IV (Epiphanes).[9]

A. E. Morris discovers in the book reflections of happenings that occurred earlier in the reign of Antiochus IV, in 175–172 BCE, "before Antiochus had proved himself to be an unjust tyrant." The story was supposedly composed by a hellenizing Jew, with possible "Sadducean" inclinations, who advocated an agreement with the foreign king. This attitude, says Morris, may explain the religious laxity apparent in Esther that is comparable to the spirit of Ecclesiastes.[10]

R. Stiehl, on the other hand, places the events somewhat later in Antiochus IV's reign. In her opinion the Mordecai-Haman struggle mirrors a Jewish insurrection against the Seleucid overlordship, represented by Haman ὁ μακεδών (Esth 9:24, LXX). In this fight the Jews were joined by the Persians and Elamites. The incident occurred after the Elamite revolt under Kamnashires I and before the emergence of the Parthians, which caused decisive changes in the political setup of the Ancient Near East. Therefore Stiehl presumes that the Esther story portrays a situation that prevailed between 160–140 BCE.[11]

P. Haupt suggested the Syrian Alexander Balas (153–140 BCE) as the most probable candidate for the Haman of our story.[12] R. Pfeiffer finds mirrored in it the sentiments of militant Jews in the days of John Hyrcanus (135–104 BCE), while Isidore Lévy and S. Perowne preferred to identify Ahasuerus with Herod the Great, who executed his wife Mariamne (= Vashti).[13]

All these theories have found little general support.[14] The proposed identification of persons and events is usually rather strained and sometimes farfetched. On the other hand there is a fairly universal agreement among scholars that the author of the Esther story generally shows an intimate

9. This theory is weakened by the statement found in 2 Macc 15:36 that the victory over Nicanor was celebrated "on the day preceding the day of Mordecai," which by that time must have been a well-known institution.
10. A. E. Morris, "The Purpose of the Book of Esther," *ExpTim* 42 (1930–31) 124–28.
11. Stiehl, *WZKM* 53 (1956) 4–22 (see above, n. 1).
12. P. Haupt, *Purim* (ed. F. Delitzsch and P. Haupt; BASS 6/2; Leipzig: Hinrichs, 1906).
13. R. H. Pfeiffer, *Introduction to the Old Testament* (2d ed.; New York/London: Harper, 1948) 745; Isidore Lévy, "La répudiation de Vasti," *Actes de XXI Congrès Internat. Oriental.* (1948–49) 114ff.; S. Perowne, *The Life and Times of Herod the Great* (London: Hodder and Stoughton, 1956).
14. Cp. Eissfeldt, *Einleitung* (see above, n. 5); A. Shalit, "אחשורוש," *EncMiq* 1.234–36; and H. Bardtke, "Estherbuch," *RGG* 3 (1958) 703–8.

knowledge of Persian court etiquette and public administration. He either must have had some personal experience of these matters or else was an extremely well-informed and gifted writer. If his tale does not mirror historical reality, it is indeed well-imagined. *Si non e vero e ben trovato*. His presentation of the relationship between the exiled Jews in the Persian Empire and their non-Jewish neighbors seems to reflect a true situation and cannot be shrugged off as a mere literary fantasy, even if in detail it has to be qualified.[15] Accordingly, many scholars prefer to content themselves with the guarded statement that, although we are not in a position to check on details, the book of Esther reflects conditions that prevailed in the eastern parts of the Persian Empire in the fifth century BCE. In essence it is most probably a true description of an actual sociohistorical situation, garnished with chronistic details of suspect accuracy. This analysis led to the definition of the book as a "historical novel," a definition that found favor with many scholars.[16]

II

The differentiation between a "historical" nucleus and a "novelistic" elaboration still does not do justice to the composite literary nature of the book of Esther in which further elements can be discerned. First of all we have to consider the relationship between the Esther-Mordecai story and the Purim chronicle. In the canonical book the story and the account of the establishment of Purim are inseparably bound up with each other. The incidents recorded in the story are actually represented as the very *raison d'être* of the festival, which was instituted as their annual commemoration. But scholars take a rather different view with regard to their relationship. True, it is widely agreed that from its inception the story was intimately connected with the Purim festival. It was, as Eissfeldt put it, "die Festlegende von Purim."[17] But this does not preclude, as the biblical account obviously im-

---

15. Y. Kaufmann, תולדות האמונה הישראלית (Tel Aviv: Dvir, 1959) 4.439–49; A. Shalit, *EncMiq* 1.234–36; N. Snaith, "The Historical Books," *The Old Testament and Modern Study* (ed. H. H. Rowley; London: Oxford University Press, 1951) 105–7; Bentzen, *Introduction,* 192 (see above, n. 5); Ringgren, *SEÅ* 20 (1955) 23–24.

16. See., e.g., Gunkel, *Esther,* 75–76; Eissfeldt, *Einleitung* (see above, n. 5); Bentzen, *Introduction,* 2.192–95; Kaufmann, תולדות.

17. Eissfeldt, *Einleitung,* 628.

plies, the possible preexistence of a Purim-like festival that was independent of the Esther story. In fact many scholars have endeavored to explain Purim as the Jewish variant of an originally heathen feast. P. Jensen and H. Zimmern[18] perceived mythological elements in the biblical book, which then led them to postulate the Babylonian New Year festival as the matrix of the Jewish Purim.[19] J. Lewy elaborated a theory previously proposed by P. de Lagarde that the very name *Purim* points to the derivation of the festival from the Persian New Year, Farvardīgān.[20]

Although some parallels between Purim and its supposed mythico-cultic precursors can be established, they are not concrete enough to postulate a direct derivation of the former from one of the latter. This conclusion is proved correct by Ringgren's detailed analysis and painstaking comparisons, which nonetheless have not materially affected the issue. It is for this reason that the reactions of scholars to these theories oscillate between O. Eissfeldt's cautious appreciation of possible New Year contents for Purim to Y. Kaufmann's wholesale rejection of them.[21]

But even Kaufmann would not discard altogether the assumption of an initial independence of Purim from the Esther story. Without committing himself to a detailed theory with regard to the genesis of the festival he concurs with the scholars who hold that it "was conceived sometime somewhere in the Persian Empire. From there it spread in the countries of the Diaspora and ultimately was introduced also in Palestine." Kaufmann concedes that "the festival preceded the book. Most likely its subject matter initially was narrated orally. In the course of time the splendid story of the festive event was composed, and then this wondrous tale on its part, without doubt, furthered the emanation of the festival."[22]

---

18. P. Jensen, "Elamitische Eigennamen: Ein Beitrag zur Erklärung der elamitischen Inschriften," *WZKM* 4 (1892) 47ff., 209ff.; H. Zimmern, "Zur Frage nach dem Ursprung des Purimfestes," *ZAW* 11 (1891) 157–69; and with modifications, E. Schrader, *Die Keilinschriften und das Alte Testament* (3d ed.; Berlin: Reuther and Reichard, 1902–03) 514–20. Also H. Cazelles, "Note sur la composition du rouleau d'Esther," *Lex tua veritas,* Festschrift für Hubert Junker (ed. H. Gross and F. Mussner; Trier: Paulinus, 1961) 17–29.

19. This hypothesis was restated by V. Christian ("Zur Herkunft des Purimfestes," *Alttestamentliche Studien F. Nötscher zum 60. Geburtstag dargeboten* [ed. H. Junker and J. G. Botterweck; Bonn: Hanstein, 1950] 33–37).

20. J. Lewy, "The Feast of the 14th Day of Adar," *HUCA* 14 (1939) 127–51; P. de Lagarde, *Purim: Ein Beitrag zur Geschichte der Religion* (AGWG 34; Göttingen: Dietrich, 1887).

21. Eissfeldt, *Einleitung* (see above, n. 5); Kaufmann, תולדות (see above, n. 15).

22. Kaufmann, תולדות, 448.

We do not intend to enter here into a discussion of the respective merits of the various theories presented in explanation of the genesis of Purim. The new material that has come to light since the publication of Kaufmann's, Eissfeldt's, and Bentzen's works, which surveyed the matter, has not decisively clarified the issue.[23] However we wish to point out the practically unanimous acceptance of the assumption that at some time, the non-Israelite forerunner of the Purim festival was celebrated in complete separation from the events recorded in the Esther story.

III

This opens the door for an investigation into the literary character and composition of the Esther narrative itself. The first question that now arises is whether the canonical version of the story is to be considered its original and its only form. Various scholars, setting out from different premises, have postulated that the narrative was extant also in other formulations. Some would pronounce the short summary near the end of the canonical book (9:20–28) to be the original account of the events which led to the establishment of the festival. The preceding chapters, i.e., the bulk of the narrative, present but enlargements and embellishments of a theme. In fact, as already stated, this passage (9:20–28) is often considered a separate composition which attached itself to the narrative. But there is nothing in it to recommend the suggestion that the Esther story grew out of it.

In contrast, Torrey assumed that originally the narrative was even more detailed than it is in the Hebrew version. He presupposes a "twofold Semitic tradition of the Esther narrative: the brief version which lies before us in the canonical book and a considerably longer Aramaic narrative, now existing in Greek in two distinct forms," the standard version and the Lucianic tradition. Torrey accords preference to the longer (Greek)[24] over the shorter (Hebrew) version, which he considers to be "an abbreviated translation from an Ara-

---

23. Cp. Cazelles, where additional literature is quoted ("Note," 17–29 [see above, n. 18]). See also R. Mayer, "Iranischer Beitrag zu Problemen des Daniel- und Esther-Buches" (*Lex tua veritas*, Festschrift für Hubert Junker [see above, n. 18], 127–36).

24. Out of a total of 270 verses in the LXX, Swete counts 107 that are not represented in the MT (*Introduction to the Old Testament in Greek* [Cambridge: Cambridge University Press, 1900] 257).

maic original."[25] The original Esther story had a distinctly literary motive and was most skillfully structured. The historiographically motivated Purim account was subsequently joined to it. In Torrey's words, "a fine bit of pure fiction has been fitted into a historical scheme."[26] The reputed "literary motive" is not further analyzed. Torrey contents himself with praising the competence of the author whose aim was "merely to tell a great story for its own sake; a story of universal appeal, to be enjoyed not only by the Jews but also by the members of every other nation."[27]

T. Gaster went one step further. He perceives in the biblical book a combination of two tales, one centering around Esther, the other around Vashti, both going back to a Persian original. These folktales dwelt on the wiles of women and their shrewdness *vis-à-vis* men, in a literary fashion comparable to that of Boccaccios' Decameron. Again, it is held that the stories were "retold with a Jewish coloration" and were adapted "to explain in terms acceptable to the Jews, the origin of a Persian festival which they had come to adopt. It is this naturalization that is alone responsible for the historical anomalies and the incongruities."[28]

The most recent attempt to explain the incongruities and anomalies found in the book is that of H. Cazelles. They are supposed to have arisen out of the fusion of two originally independent texts "l'un historique et l'autre liturgique." This combination resulted in the transfiguration of the initially heathen liturgy which now became a typical piece of biblical "histoire de salut."[29]

These propositions, hypothetical as they may be, have one feature in common. They arise out of the observance of the diversity of materials incorporated in the canonical book of Esther. Subscribing to the isolation of the narrative from the historiographical recast and from the cult-oriented

---

25. C. C. Torrey, "The Older Book of Esther" (*HTR* 37 [1944] 1–40, esp. p. 9). Torrey stated his views previously in a review (published in *JBL* 61 [1942] 130–36) of "*The Old Testament in Greek*, vol. III, 1. Cambridge 1940." G. Jahn had maintained that the Hebrew Esther is but a modified translation of the Greek version as presented in Codex B (*Das Buch Esther* [Leiden: E. J. Brill, 1901]).

26. Torrey, *HTR* 37 (1944) 21. Gunkel postulates a *Volkserzählung* that was utilized in the canonical book (*Esther*, 28).

27. Torrey, *HTR* 37 (1944) 14. The literary skill of the author of Esther has been praised by many other scholars. A fine analysis of his accomplishments is presented by S. D. Goitein (מגילת אסתר," עיונים במקרא") [Tel Aviv: Dvir, 1957] 59–72).

28. T. Gaster, *Purim and Hanukkah* (New York: Schuman, 1950) 35.

29. Cazelles, "Note," 23, 29 (see above, n. 18).

Purim account, we still feel that some further characterization of its literary type seems to be in order. This characterization shall now be attempted.

IV

We propose to define the Esther narrative as a *historicized wisdom-tale*. It may be described as an *enactment* of standard *wisdom motifs*, which are present also in other biblical narratives of a similar nature and which biblical literature has in common with Ancient Near Eastern wisdom literature, as defined by the literary-type analysis.

Even the cursory reader of the Esther story will discern in it typical wisdom themes and precepts which bring to mind associations with biblical and extrabiblical wisdom teaching.[30] To be sure, these constitute what may be styled "Wisdom of Scribes," as exemplified in Egyptian and Mesopotamian sources and as also represented in the early strata of biblical wisdom. Suffice it here to draw attention to the numerous examples of Egyptian wisdom teaching that are concerned with the education of court scribes and crown princes (cp. also Prov 30:1–9).[31] These teachings often take the form of a fable culminating in a moral or that of a wisdom-tale into which proverbial sayings are inserted or to which they are attached.[32] Such compositions are also well known from Mesopotamian literature.[33] A good example is the Aḥiqar novel that is preserved in its original Aramaic language in fragments of a manuscript dating from the fifth century BCE, discovered at Elephantine. The story itself was probably composed one hundred to one hundred fifty

---

30. Morris hinted at the similarity of the religious attitudes reflected in Ecclesiastes and Esther but did not follow up this lead (*ExpTim* 42 [1930–31] 124–28 [see above, n. 10]). Y. M. Grintz suggests that Judith's irony in dealing with Holofernes (Jdt 11:8, 16) might well constitute the first case of "such wisdom language in Hebrew prose (ספר יהודית [Jerusalem: Bialik, 1957] 54). We shall have occasion to show that in this as well as in other respects the book of Judith is probably influenced by the canonical book of Esther.

31. J. Fichtner, *Die altorientalische Weisheit in ihrer israelitisch-jüdischen Ausprägung* (BZAW 62; Giessen: Töpelmann, 1933) 13–14.

32. A representative selection of this type of literature may be found in A. Erman, *Die Literatur der Ägypter* (Leipzig: Hinrichs, 1923). See further J. B. Pritchard, ed., *ANET* (2d ed.; Princeton: Princeton University Press, 1955).

33. Cp. J. J. A. van Dijk, *La sagesse Suméro-Accadienne* (Leiden: E. J. Brill, 1953); S. N. Kramer, *History Begins at Sumer* (Garden City, N.Y.: Doubleday, 1956), chaps. 15–17; and also Pritchard, *ANET*.

years earlier.[34] Thus possibly not more than a century divides the writing of the Aḥiqar novel and the Esther narrative, which may well have originated in the fifth century. We shall have occasion to show that there are common motifs in these two literary creations that lend special meaning to their comparison. However, let it be stated from the outset that we do not assume any direct interdependence between these stories, but would explain the similarities as having arisen out of their affiliation with a common literary type, in which both are rooted.

In attempting to analyze the *wisdom* features of the Esther narrative, we are concerned predominantly with similarities in situations and with general trends and ideas that seem to be reflected in this narrative and in wisdom compositions, rather than with formal literary parallels. In the book of Esther proverbial language is not at all common. There are, however, some possible instances. The recurring phrase עד חצי המלכות וינתן לך (Esth 5:3), or ותעש (5:6; 7:2; 9:12), could well be of a proverbial nature.[35] Similarly Zeresh's words in recognition of Haman's impending downfall, אשר החלות לנפל לפניו לא תוכל לו כי נפול תפול לפניו (6:13), have a proverbial ring to them.

But these are exceptions, and on no account could it be suggested to define the book as a collection of wisdom sayings. What the Esther narrative in fact does is to portray *applied* wisdom. The outline of the plot and the presentation of the central characters show the wise man in action, with the covert, but nevertheless obvious, implication that his ultimate success derives from the proper execution of wisdom maxims, as set forth, e.g., in Proverbs, and to a certain degree, in Ecclesiastes.

The proposed recognition of a wisdom-nucleus in the Esther narrative may lead to a better understanding of some salient features of the canonical book that scholars often view with perplexity, even with consternation.

Thus it may help in explaining the disturbing lack of any specifically Jewish religiosity in the book, on which many a scholar has commented. In contrast to the author of Daniel, the author of the book of Esther is not at all troubled about the ritual difficulties which perforce must arise from Esther's residing at Ahasuerus's palace.[36] The problem of the observation of the dietary laws never becomes apparent in our book, while in the books of Daniel

---

34. These fragments will be quoted from H. L. Ginsberg's translation in *ANET*.
35. Gunkel considers this to be "Märchenstil" (*Esther*, 28).
36. See S. Talmon, "Daniel," *The Literary Guide to the Bible* (ed. R. Alter and F. Kermode; Cambridge, MA: Belknap, 1987) 353–55.

(1:8–16) and Judith (10:5; 12:1–4, 18–19) it figures rather prominently.[37] Altogether the book of Esther has what Torrey styles a "notoriously unreligious appearance,"[38] which sometimes has caused it to be blacklisted by theologians[39] and Bible scholars.[40]

Many a schoolboy has learned from his teacher's question, which has become commonplace, that Esther is the only book in the Bible in which the divine name is not mentioned even once. There is not a shred of evidence for the assumption voiced by some scholars that the names of God were excised by pious Jews from this "profane" book to keep them, so to speak, from defilement.[41] True we do know of the substitution in certain periods of epithets for the tetragrammaton and progressively also for other divine appellations. This was done for reasons of extreme piety and awe, or in order to combat their misuse for purposes of magic and sorcery. But at no time in history was Judaism given to an estheticism that could have caused the complete excision of all divine names from a biblical book, repulsive as its contents may be to the nineteenth-century theologian. As a matter of fact, religious sentiment and practices are not altogether absent from the scene in the book of Esther. Mordecai is confident that his people's salvation will come from some other, unidentified source, should Esther refrain from appealing to Ahasuerus on behalf of her kin, out of fear for her own well-being.[42] Again

---

37. The midrash sensed the problem and goes out of its way to assure us that Esther ate only her own food and did not partake of the dainties sent to her by the king, just as Daniel and his friends abstained from eating ritually proscribed food (2 *Midr. Panim Aḥerim*, p. 87, ed. S. Buber, 1886, p. 64; *Tg. Esth II* 2:9; *b. Meg.* 13a).

38. Torrey, *HTR* 37 (1944) 9 (see above, n. 25).

39. Most poignant is the often-quoted remark of Martin Luther: "Ich bin dem Buch und Esther so feind, dass ich wollte sie wären garnicht vorhanden, denn sie judenzen zu sehr und haben viel heidnische Unart" (*Tischreden* [Weimarer Ausgabe] 22.2080).

40. Luther's harsh dictum had a detrimental effect in this respect. Very typical is the judgment of G. Jahn: "Ich scheide gern von diesen einzigen mir widerlichen Buche des Alten Testaments aus welchem die Juden wegen seines gottlosen Inhalts den Gottesnamen entfernt haben [sic] welcher ursprünglich in ihm wie in jedem biblischem Buche enthalten war . . . Aus dem Kanon hätte dieses zur Travestierung geeignete Buch längst entfernt werden sollen" (*Esther*, xv [see above, n. 25]). Cp. further Eissfeldt, *Einleitung* (see above, n. 5); Bentzen, *Introduction*, 2. 192–95 (see above, n. 5).

41. See previous note. M. Steinthal thought that the absence of divine names from the book is best explained by its author's scepticism (*Zur Bibel und Religionsphilosophie* [Berlin: Reimer, 1890] 53ff.).

42. It is often presumed that the term put into Mordecai's mouth, אחר מקום (Esth 4:14), actually is a substitute for the divine name. Josephus interprets it this way: ἔσεσται μὲν αὐτῷ βοήτειαν παρὰ τοῦ Θεοῦ πάντας (*Ant.* 11.227; see further 11.279–82). See also *Midr. Leqaḥ Tob.* 4:14, ed. Buber, 1886, p. 103 (repr. Jerusalem: n.p., 1960).

Mordecai and the Jews throughout the Persian Empire moan and mourn when the king's approval of Haman's murderous intentions are made public in the form of a royal decree (4:1–3). They fast communally for three days when Esther prepares to set out on her fateful mission (4:16–17). But neither in the hour of their despair, nor later when they rejoice over the downfall of their enemies, do they offer prayers of supplication or thanksgiving, or invoke the name of God. All this is in striking contrast to the ways of other biblical and postbiblical figures, among them Nehemiah (Neh 1:4–11; 2:4; etc.), Daniel, and Judith, who like Mordecai and Esther experienced life in exile under Persian rule. Daniel and his companions implore God whenever they are in need of help (Dan 2:17–23; 3:16–18; 9:3–21), and so do the people of Bethuliah (Jdt 4:9–15; 6:18–21; 7:19–29). Daniel is reported to have offered prayers three times a day facing Jerusalem (Dan 6:11), while Judith makes her prayer coincide with the daily sacrifice in the Temple of Jerusalem (Jdt 9:1ff.; cp. further 12:7–8; 13:4–5, 17), and she concludes her mission with a thanksgiving psalm (Judith 16).

It would have been as easy to interpolate prayers into the book of Esther as supposedly to excise them from it, together with the divine names. The Greek translation, as is well known, does introduce the divine name into the text, as, e.g., in Esth 6:1: MT, בלילה ההוא נָדְדָה שנת המלך; LXX, ὁδὲ κύριος ἀπέστησεν τὸν ὕπνον ἀπὸ τοῦ βασιλέως τὴν νύκτα ἐκείνην (= נַדֵּד ה'). It credits Mordecai and Esther equally with prayers, and records these added prayer texts in full after Esth 4:15.[43] It is generally agreed that such interpolations were not uncommon in biblical books. Thus the psalm of Jonah (Jonah 2:3–10) is considered a late addition to the book, which in the view of most scholars was written in the postexilic period.[44] Similarly, Hannah's psalm and the psalm in Isaiah 12 are judged appositions to the books of Samuel and Isaiah, respectively. Why then should redactors and copyists have refrained from applying the same technique to the book of Esther?

43. So does Josephus (*Ant.* 11.229). The midrash puts a prayer of thanksgiving into the mouth of Mordecai when he mounts the king's horse, the symbol of his victory over Haman (*Midr. Abba Gurion*, p. 40a; *2 Midr. Panim Aḥerim*, p. 76). See also commentaries, e.g., C. A. Moore, *Esther* ([AB 7B; Garden City, NY: Doubleday, 1971] xxxii–xxxiv, lxiii–lxiv, 105–7) and D. J. A. Clines, *The Esther Scroll: The Story of the Story* ([JSOTSup 30; Sheffield: JSOT, 1984]).

44. A notable exception is Kaufmann, who assigns the composition of the book to a period prior to the rise of the Assyrian Empire (תולדות, 2.279–87, 605).

One is led to assume that the absence of prayer from the book is original, as is the absence of the divine names, and that these absences are due to the ideological setting of the book,[45] a setting that may be discerned also in other literary compositions of the Hebrew Bible.

The concept of an unspecified and remote deity devoid of any individual character as is prevalent in the Esther narrative, is also present in some specimens of biblical wisdom literature. In Ecclesiastes and especially in the Job dialogues, the nonspecific divine appellations, אל שדי, אלה, אלהים, etc., outnumber the tetragrammaton. This idea of an impersonal supernatural power can be traced to Ancient Near Eastern wisdom teaching. It is a salient feature of the essentially cosmopolitan nature of wisdom thought which aims at applicability to human situation generally, irrespective of politico-national or religio-national allegiances.

It is this characteristic that helps to explain the complete absence in the book of Esther of any reference to Jewish history. The one mention of Jeconiah's exile (Esth 2:6) is of mere chronistic interest and is of no consequence to events narrated. This detachment from historical consciousness stands in striking contrast to the pronounced history-awareness of most biblical writers and their apocryphal epigones.

Throughout the Bible occasions occur when in times of distress the nation or the individual appeal to God for help, confessing their sins in past times and present, and recounting God's deeds in days of old, to remind themselves, as it were, of the mercy and grace he had shown their forefathers. By and by these retrospective surveys of the *Heilsgeschichte* became fairly standardized and attained a fixed place in the cultic life of Israel.[46] From both these aspects, the literary and the cultic, the historical recitation was especially enjoyed in late biblical writings—Ezra, Nehemiah, and Chronicles—as well as in postbiblical books—*Jubilees,* Tobit, Mac-

---

45. This was recognized by Gunkel, who, however, did not pursue the matter further (*Esther,* 27, 80–81 [see above, n. 4]). Cazelles maintains that from the outset the author did not use the divine names, since he was aware of the heathen origin of the festival ("Note," 29 [see above, n. 18]).

46. I would suggest, with some hesitation, that in the cultic use of the *Heilsgeschichte* recitation, one may still discern undertones of sympathetic magic of which the biblical writers were no longer conscious. The recitation, just as the mytho-cultic act, aims at inducing the divine to perform again such wondrous deeds as are described in it. One might well compare some magical residues in prophetic literature, especially in the Oracles against the Nations.

cabees, and Judith, et al. In Jdt 5:5–22 even the Ammonite Aḥior tries his hand at such a recitation.[47]

Recitals of historic landmarks abound in all types of biblical writings except for one, wisdom literature, which "scarcely mentions the election of Israel or its history."[48] The covenant with the forefathers, the Exodus, God's love for the house of David, etc., which take so prominent a place in biblical historiography, prophetic writings, and psalmodic compositions,[49] are conspicuously absent from Proverbs, Job, and Ecclesiastes. Once more, the Esther story displays the same lack of historical depth and the ad-hoc mentality that characterizes the wisdom books.

The disinterest in Jewish history is matched by the absence from the book of Esther of any sign of affiliation with, or even a reference to, contemporaneous Jewry outside Persia, actually outside Susa. The Jewish community in this city is depicted as a self-contained unit that observes its own fast (Esth 4:16–17), although the king's decree constituted a threat to all Jews in the Persian Empire (Esth 3:8–15). The Susan Jews do not appeal for help or sympathy to their brothers in other parts of the Persian realm, including the land of Israel. How different is their attitude from that which manifests itself in the postexilic books of Ezra and Nehemiah, in Second Isaiah, or in some of the psalms (cp., e.g., Psalms 126, 137). The Elephantine papyri prove that approximately at the same time in which the Esther episode is set, Jews living in Egypt call upon the Palestinian community to intervene on their behalf with the Persian authorities.[50] The leaders in Jerusalem for their part strive to maintain contact with Egyptian Jewry. They endeavor to exercise their authority over them, at least in cultic matters, as may be learned from the "Passover edict" of Darius II,[51] or for a later period, from the report on the Greek translation of the Pentateuch, embedded in the Aristeas letter.[52]

---

47. Cp. also Jdt 8:11–27.
48. W. Baumgartner, "The Wisdom Literature," *The Old Testament and Modern Study* (ed. H. H. Rowley; Oxford: Clarendon, 1951) 211.
49. Especially in what may be termed "historiographical psalms." See "Did There Exist a Biblical National Epic?" in this vol., pp. 91–111.
50. A. Cowley, *Aramaic Papyri of the Fifth Century B. C.* (Oxford: Clarendon, 1923), nos. 30–32, pp. 108–26.
51. Ibid., no. 21, "The Passover Edict," lines 60–65.
52. Swete, *Introduction*, Appendix: "The Letter of Pseudo-Aristeas"; M. Hadas, *Aristeas to Philocrates* (New York: Ktav, 1951).

Nothing of the kind applies to the Esther narrative. The exiled Mordecai institutes new cultic laws binding on all Jews in the Persian realm (Esth 9:20–23, 30–31) without consulting with Jewish legal authorities in Jerusalem. In fact he acts like a later-age exilarch.[53] Thus the book of Esther stands out among the biblical narratives for its lack of even a vestige of common bonds with the land of Israel and its sacral institutions. In this respect it also has no equal in apocryphal literature. The book of Judith stresses that the people of Bethuliah, e.g., dare not desecrate time-honored commandments, even when life is in danger, without explicit permission of the High Priest and the elders of Jerusalem (Jdt 11:14).

We have no reason whatsoever to assume that in this matter the book truthfully puts on record actual historical facts. Whichever period in the Persian Era—or for that matter the Hellenistic era—one supposes to be reflected in the Esther narrative, none would allow, as far as historical evidence goes, for such a representation of the relationship of a diaspora center with the mother-community in Palestine. On the other hand, such misrepresentation of internal Jewish issues can hardly be due to the sheer inadequacy of an author whose detailed knowledge of Persian affairs is so highly praised by practically all students of the book of Esther.[54] Rather than ascribe this feature to the incompetence of the otherwise well-informed writer, one feels compelled to derive its explanation from his basic concepts and from the literary premises of the book, i.e., from his dependence upon nonhistorical and nonnational wisdom ideology.

V

It is wisdom atmosphere that gives to the Esther-Mordecai-Haman narrative its individualistic slant. In essence it depicts the timeless theme of in-

---

53. The rabbis were aware of this difficulty and therefore strove to present Mordecai as a scholar and teacher (*Midr. Leqaḥ Tob* 2:5, p. 94; *2 Midr. Panim Aḥerim*, p. 70; *Midr. Abba Gurion*, p. 36a). They further complemented the biblical story by interpolating messages that reputedly were sent by Mordecai to the prophets and elders in Jerusalem.
54. Ed. Meyer, *Geschichte des Altertums* (Stuttgart: Gotha, 1884–1902) vol. 3, part 2, pp. 5, 218; Gunkel, *Esther*, 54ff. (see above, n. 4); Ringgren, *SEÅ* 20 (1955) 23–24. (see above, n. 2). See also R. Mayer, "Iranischer Beitrag zu Problemen des Daniel- und Esther-Buches" (see above, n. 23).

triguing courtiers, whose battle is viewed against the background of the Persian court at the beginning of Ahasuerus's rule.

The author is so much absorbed in the portrayal of the central figures, their feats, and failures, that he completely neglects to supply the social setting that is amply provided in other biblical and postbiblical narratives of a historical or quasi-historical nature. Nothing is said about the organization of the Susa Jewish community and the occupations of its members. Altogether the town (עיר) of Susa appears like a mere annex to the acropolis (בירה). Neither Haman nor Mordecai seems to represent a group. Though the outcome of their struggle is expected to affect, and does affect, their families, followers, and coreligionists, in essence they fight their own duel. True, the canonical book wishes to present them as protagonists of two factions in the Persian Empire. But this presentation is only skin-deep and does not grow out of the core of the narrative. What is ultimately at stake is the position of one of the two at court. The contest will be decided upon, not by moral superiority or by divine grace, but rather by the ruthless application of all ruses found in the book of the "wise" courtier: "For by wise guidance you can wage your war, and in abundance of counselors there is victory" (Prov 24:6). The more seasoned and better skilled will prevail. Success assures the goodwill of the king, who judges by tangible results and not by motives: "A servant who deals wisely has the king's favor, but his wrath falls on one who acts shamefully" (Prov 14:35). The court is a slippery arena in which to fight. The rules are set by the king: "For the word of the king is supreme, and who may say to him, 'What are you doing?'" (Qoh 8:4); and the fate of vanquished and victor are decided upon by his whims: "A king's wrath is like the growling of a lion, but his favor is like dew upon the grass" (Prov 19:12; cp. 16:15).[55]

In this setting one cannot expect any attempt to relate the life of the individual or the group to a divine source that judges and decrees their fate by standards of moral behavior. The narrator of Esther's philosophy is anthropocentric. He never tries to probe into the underlying causes of woe or weal. They are the direct outcome of the immediate success of a formidable hu-

55. Cp. Aḥiqar 95–110.

man antagonist, or alternatively of the superior performance of the protagonist of his story.

It would appear that the author of the Esther narrative was himself
committed to the ideas and practices with which he imbues his *dramatis
personae*. It is the courtier-counselor's psychology, not that of the *misera
contribuens plebs*, as Gunkel would have it, that lies at the bottom of his interest in the intricacies of life at Ahasuerus's palace.[56] He describes in
detail the royal chambers, the monarch's festivities and revelries; praises the
excellence of the wines, the exquisiteness of dishes and furnishings. He
enjoys parading his intimate knowledge of harem affairs and court intrigues.
His tale brings to mind biblical descriptions of other courts, presented, e.g.,
in the Joseph story and in the book of Daniel. Solomon's palace as pictured
in 1 Kgs 5:1–8 and 7:1–12 falls into the same category. It is this court life
that is weighed and found lacking by another "wise man," the experienced
author of Ecclesiastes. He despaired of the conspicuous splendor (Qoh 2:1–
11), but the wisdom-groomed courtier expected it to fall to his share once he
attained the aspired goal, a position of confidence with a mighty ruler.

The typical product of wisdom education is the court scribe, the adviser
of kings, whose metier may take him to foreign countries and may bring him
into contact with foreign cultures. His loyalty is to his master, whoever he
may be. The counselor is a professional expert unfettered by national allegiances. His main concern is with the proper execution of his functions at
court, which may be as manifold as courtlife is multi-colored. In preparation
for his tasks he must have acquired a thorough knowledge of court etiquette.
He needs to possess administrative abilities to cope with sundry problems
that do not differ essentially from realm to realm.

Now both Mordecai and Haman admirably fit this pattern. In the course
of the story Mordecai rises to the rank of chief adviser to Ahasuerus, king of
Persia. This may well be an exaggeration on the part of our author, since a
foreigner would not have been allowed to attain such an elevated position in
the Persian realm. However, the exaggeration does not arise out of suspect
wishful Jewish thinking,[57] but rather out of a literary convention rooted in
the sociohistorical experience of the Ancient Near East. This is borne out by

---

56. Gunkel, *Esther*, 65 (see above n.4).
57. "Diese Erzählung bietet uns den vorbildlichen Fall dafür, wie aus einem Wunsche, eine
    Geschichte werden kann" (Ibid., 75). Cp. further L. B. Paton, *Esther* ([ICC; Edinburgh:
    Clark, 1908] 72).

the fact that Haman, Mordecai's predecessor, is also portrayed as a foreigner, reportedly of Amalekite extraction,[58] a detail which is especially stressed by Josephus: ἀλλότριος ὢν τοῦ περσῶν αἵματος (*Ant.* 11.12.277). And Haman can hardly symbolize the "successful Jewish exile," as does the figure of Mordecai in some views. But both can be easily squared with the image of the "foreign adviser," represented in the Bible by Daniel, Joseph, and possibly also Nehemiah, and in extrabiblical literature of a comparable date, by Aḥiqar and his nephew Nadin, all of whom "sit in the king's gate."[59]

Further support for this proposition may be derived from the attribution of royal descent to both Mordecai and Haman.[60] The story intends to establish a relation between Mordecai and the Benjaminite King Saul (Esth 2:5), while Haman reportedly descended from Saul's royal adversary (1 Sam 15:1–33), the Amalekite King Agag (Esth 3:1).[61] In rabbinic literature Haman is further connected, and even identified, with Amalek, who in his turn in a Yemenite Midrash is portrayed as one of Pharaoh's advisers at the Egyptian court.[62]

Mordecai and Haman do in fact resemble Joseph, Nehemiah, and Daniel, expatriated Jews who held office at foreign courts. However, at the

---

58. The assumed or factual reluctance of Persian rulers to employ foreigners as high officials may have been known to the translators and copyists of the LXX. One wonders whether this knowledge could not account for the (intentional?) rendering of Hebrew האגגי as βουγαιος in Esth 3:1, if Hoschander's (*Esther*, 21–27 [see above, n. 7]) and Lewy's (*HUCA* 14 [1939] 134–35 [see above, n. 20]) assumption is correct that the word is derived from Iranian *baga* ("god") and that it is a title that would identify Haman as a Mithras worshipper. Once the disturbing האגגי is removed, Haman might as well be conceived of as a Persian.

59. This technical term, which is often employed in the book of Esther (2:21; 3:2–3; 4:2; 5:9, 13; 6:10), pertains to the counselor's position as well, e.g., in Dan 2:49 and Aḥiqar 3:32–48. In Esth 2:19 the LXX render the Hebrew ישב בשער המלך very aptly: ἐθεράπευεν ἐν τῇ αὐλῇ.

60. This detail is accepted without question in rabbinic tradition and apparently also by Josephus (*Ant.* 11.212).

61. The far-flung account of the two protagonists' descent, if original, is motivated by more than a mere interest in genealogy. "Solche gelehrten Erinnerungen aus der heiligen Geschichte erwartete man nicht in diesem Zusammenhange" (Gunkel, *Esther*, 16 [see above, n. 4]). There seems to be a covert moral implied. Saul followed the wisdom precept which admonishes man to show clemency to his enemies (Prov 24:10–12, 17–18; 25:21–22). He spared Agag when this king was at his mercy and even suffered punishment for his deed (1 Sam 25:7–31). When the tables were turned and Agag's offspring Haman gains the upper hand over Mordecai, Saul's progeny, he displays no sign of compunction or mercy.

62. A. S. Yahuda, "A Contribution to Qurʾān and Ḥadīth Interpretation," *I. Goldziher Memorial Volume* (ed. S. Löwinger and I. Somogy; Budapest: Globus, 1948) 1.280–308.

same time, they have much in common with courtiers of presumably non-Israelite extraction who served as ministers at the court of Jerusalem[63] under David and Solomon: Seraiah (2 Sam 8:17) = Sheya (2 Sam 20:25) = Shisha (1 Kgs 4:3) = Shavsha (1 Chr 18:16), his two sons Elihoreph and Ahijah (1 Kgs 4:3), and Ado(ni)ram the son of Abda (1 Kgs 4:6; 12:18).

The attainment of a confidential position at court required much training. In order to be presentable to royalty and of use to monarchs, a man had to be well mannered, conversant with languages and public speech (Prov 22:11). He needed to be able to understand not only the language spoken at court, but also those of allies, vassals, and foes with whom the king conducted business.

Proficiency in languages and a skilled tongue coupled with an agile mind and readiness to act made a man proverbially fit to serve kings: חזית איש מהיר במלאכתו לפני מלכים יתיצב (Prov 22:29).[64] A comparison with Ps 45:2 (לשוני עט סופר מהיר), with Ezra 7:6 (והוא ספר מהיר בתורת משה), and especially with Aḥiqar 1 (אחיקר שמה ספר חכים ומהיר), makes it probable that in Prov 22:29 (quoted above) מהיר refers to the scribe. The accomplishments a מהיר is required to display are aptly described in an Egyptian document, a mock letter that reads like an examination paper for a graduating scribe, composed during the reign of Ramses I, by the royal official Hori, and presumably addressed to a younger colleague.[65]

Joseph quite obviously mastered the Egyptian language as well as Hebrew (Gen 43:23). Rabshakeh spoke Judean, Aramaic (Isa 36:1–21, especially vv. 11–13, and parallels), and doubtless also Assyrian. Nehemiah knew at least Persian in addition to Hebrew, and Daniel must have been fluent in Babylonian besides his native tongue.

Presumably Ahasuerus's advisers also possessed the required faculties. They were quick at hand with counsel when asked for it (Esth 1:13–21; 2:2–4) and knew when to speak up of their own initiative (7:9). Haman must

63. On this problem consult R. de Vaux, "Titres et fonctionnaires égyptiens à la cour de David et de Salomon," *RB* 48 (1939) 394–405; B. Maisler, "The Scribe of King David and the Problem of High Officials in the Early Israelite Kingdom," *BJPES* 13 (1946–1947) 105–14 (Heb.).

64. Cp. Sir 8:8 (ed. Segal 8:10).

65. A. Gardiner, ed., Papyrus Anastasi I, in *Egyptian Hieratic Texts* (Leipzig: Hinrichs, 1911) vol. 1. The Egyptian author of that document employs in transcription the Canaanite technical term *mahir*.

have excelled in these respects and thus won the confidence of the king (3:1–2), who was easily taken in by appearances.

The diversity of languages spoken in the Persian Empire is repeatedly stressed in the book of Esther. Royal decrees are always issued in the tongues of all the peoples who lived in the realm (Esth 1:22; 3:12; 8:9; cp. Dan 3:4, 7). It goes without saying that senior officials such as Haman and his successor Mordecai are expected to have had a fair knowledge of at least some of these languages. Though the canonical book does not indicate it, midrashic tradition hit the mark when it accredited Mordecai with the mastery of seventy tongues.[66] It is this accomplishment which, according to the Midrash, enabled Mordecai to understand the clandestine conversation of the two Persian courtiers who plotted against Ahasuerus (Esth 2:21–23).

True, Mordecai is not presented as a skilful speaker. He altogether avoids the limelight (Esth 2:22), keeps in the shadow, and prefers to pull strings, using Esther as his front. But Esther on her part quite decidedly masters courtiers' speech. She easily surpasses Haman in this field, as well as in adroit planning. In her dealings with Ahasuerus and Haman, she follows the directives of proverbial wisdom: "With patience a ruler may be persuaded, and soft speech will break the [strong] bone (Prov 25:15). Compared with her subtlety, Haman's actions appear piteously clumsy.

VI

The assumed existence of a wisdom-nucleus in the Esther narrative can be buttressed further by observing the basically typological approach of its author. Some details of the tale that are presented as historic facts actually appear to be elaborations of traditional themes. To an even higher degree, the typological concepts are apparent in the portrayal of the central figures in the drama enacted.

A quite definite wisdom motif is reflected in the relationship between Esther and Mordecai, the counselor who "sits in the king's gate" (Esth 2:19, 21). The wise Mordecai obviously was childless. For this reason he adopted a kinsman's daughter, an orphan without father or mother (Esth 2:7). He

---

66. One arrives at this conclusion by interpreting the name "Bilshan" adjacent to "Mordecai" in Ezra 2:2 and Neh 7:7 as an adjective derived from a contraction of בעל לשון, "master of tongues" (b. Menaḥ. 65a; 2 Panim Aḥerim, p. 62; Tg. Qoh 7:3).

educated the girl, in fact groomed her to take over from him at some future junction when his power should fail. The spectacular rise of a destitute orphan exiled in foreign lands to the exalted position of the spouse of the king of Persia clearly contains elements of a motif that is present in the Joseph and Daniel stories and *mutatis mutandis* is also found in late fairy tales, such as Snow White, Aschenbrödel, or The Ugly Duckling. However, in its combination with the theme of "adoption by a wise man," this motif can be traced directly to Ancient Near Eastern wisdom literature. It seems to be the traditional lot of the wise and the just to have the birth of sons delayed, as is the case with Abraham (Gen 15:1–3; 17:18) and King Danel of the Ugaritic legend; or to lose their progeny due to misfortune, like Job (1:18–21) and King Keret; or to be childless altogether. Sometimes the deficiency is ultimately remedied by the interference of the gods who are instrumental either in making the hero's wife fertile (Abraham, Danel) or in restoring the lost offspring (Job, Keret). In still other cases an adopted child takes the place of the longed-for son. It appears that in wisdom circles one tended to consider the adoption of a child a virtue rather than a last resort for the procurement of an heir. The wise person wished to be remembered by his spiritual attainments. These might better be implanted in an adopted son, chosen for his virtues, than in a legitimate child who may become a disappointment to his father. Such a "philosophy" is found in a piece of Egyptian wisdom literature preserved on a papyrus from approximately 1300 BCE, which assumedly stems from Thebes. Says the sage: "They [the wise] were not able to leave heirs in children . . . pronouncing their names, but they made heirs for themselves in the writings and in the [books of] wisdom which they composed." However, the reconciliation in childlessness does not stop short at the comfort of leaving "children of the spirit." The sage goes on to tell us that "the children of other people [probably orphans] are given to them [the wise] to be heirs, as though [they were] their own children."[67]

In semitic family society the wise person would not adopt just any orphan but would look for a suitable child among his kin. A kinsman can be trusted better than a stranger. Moreover, his adoption would also constitute a fulfillment of the sacred duty to stand by a needy relative. Thus the sage Aḥiqar adopts his sister's son Nadin and raises him in true wisdom tradition

---

67. Papyrus Chester Beatty IV (trans. J. A. Wilson; British Museum 10684), *ANET*, 431–32.

in order that he may inherit his own position at court. Now if we remember that the Aḥiqar story is a wisdom tale, that there is a "general resemblance between the ethics of Aḥiqar and Proverbs, Ecclesiastes, and Sirach,"[68] and that like the book of Esther the Aḥiqar tale has "no direct bearing on religion," a typological equation of the counselor Mordecai with the royal adviser Aḥiqar and the adoption of Esther with that of Nadin is obviously permissible.

Unfortunately, adopted children do not always turn out paragons of virtue, even if educated by a sage. And Nadin surely is an example to that effect. Once established at the king's court, he not only disregards his uncle's teachings, but also squanders his wealth. When reproached he brings his misdemeanor to a head by writing faked letters to the king of Egypt and the king of Persia and Elam, the archenemies of Esarhaddon. These letters contain proposals of conspiracy against the king of Assyria. Nadin signs them with Aḥiqar's name and then brings their contents to the knowledge of Esarhaddon, who without further inquiries commands Aḥiqar to be executed.

The Esther narrative takes a completely different turn. Mordecai's adoptee proves herself worthy of her foster father. She adheres to the precepts that he had taught her (Esth 2:20) and carries out his injunctions to the letter (2:10, 20; 4:15–16). In short, she is the exact opposite of Nadin and displays proverbial filial piety. So here, obviously, the parallelism with the Aḥiqar novel breaks down.

But might it not be that in spite of the differences, the basic common motif still underlies the Esther narrative, though in a form that gives witness to a process of its naturalization and adaptation to classical Israelite concepts? In Esther the figure of "the wise man's adopted son" has been split, so to speak. All the hoped-for expectations are realized in the glorious Esther, while the hatred, betrayal, and slander are transferred to a third figure, the malefactor Haman. Just as Nadin tries to destroy the king's faithful servant Aḥiqar by inciting Esarhaddon against him, Haman endeavors to do away with Ahasuerus's savior Mordecai with the aid of the unsuspecting king. Neither of the two potentates troubles himself to investigate the

---

68. E. J. Dillon, *Contemporary Review* (March 1888), as quoted in F. C. Conybeare, J. Rendel Harris, and A. Smith Lewis, *The Story of Aḥiqar* ([Cambridge: Cambridge University Press, 1913] xx; cp. also pp. xxxviii–xl). For a possibly direct transfer of motifs and expressions from Aḥiqar to the Hebrew biblical literature, see B. Klar, "From Aḥiqar to Jeremiah" (*Tarbiẓ* 20 [1940] 33–34 [Heb.]).

accusations brought forward by the informers but decrees the destruction of the innocent victims without much ado. This detail obviously is required for the proper development of the dramatic action. But at the same time, it is indicative of the concept of the proverbial "erratic king" found in wisdom literature.

With the dichotomy of the adoptive-child figure into a just and truly wise queen on the one hand, and a contriving, cunning counselor on the other hand, the stage is set for the specific dramatic arrangement of the Esther narrative. In order to make up for the resulting double representation of goodness by Mordecai and Esther, also "villainy," represented by Haman, is provided with a helpmate, his wife Zeresh. And just as Nadin and Aḥiqar contend for the good will of Esarhaddon, the fight in the Esther narrative is over Ahasuerus's benevolence. Accordingly it would appear that the dim figure of Vashti, the king's consort, is introduced for the sole purpose of establishing an equilibrium of the couple-arrangement that is peculiar to our narrative.

We can now turn to an analysis of the central characters in our story. The couple-arrangement, as outlined above, by itself indicates the "type" approach of the author.[69] One observes a marked homogeneity between the components of each pair. In all three cases the couple provides for a double representation of their inherent characteristics. True, there are some differences in the weight apportioned to the individual components. Vashti and Zeresh merely bring into more prominent relief the distinct features portrayed in their respective partners. In the Mordechai-Esther combination the relationship is reversed. Esther plays the major role. But this is the way the equilibrium of the triangle is maintained. The typological factor is further underlined by the lack of depth in the portrayal of the heroes, which becomes even more obvious in the bare delineation of the minor figures, e.g., Ahasuerus's courtiers, Esther's maids, or Haman's sons. In contrast to the biblical historical narrative, as best seen in the David stories, the heroes of the Esther narrative do not undergo any meaningful development. The situations change; the *dramatis personae* remain static in character.

Rather than ascribe this one-dimensional depiction of the main figures to the inadequate literary skill of the writer, as Gunkel asserts with regard to the introductory part of the narrative,[70] we tend to derive it from the moralizing tenor of the story. The author is not interested in the *dramatis personae* on their own account, but in the values, virtues, and vices which they repre-

69. Cp. Gunkel, *Esther*, 77–78, 88 (see above, n. 4).
70. Ibid., 8.

sent. In fact the glossing over of strictly individual traits enhances the general applicability of the moral illustrated and is perfectly in tune with wisdom narration.

In essence the three couples exemplify the traditional wisdom triangle: the powerful but witless dupe, the righteous wise, the conniving schemer. The "witless dupe" obviously is represented by Ahasuerus. One has often remarked on the unbelievable stupidity displayed by the king throughout our story. It is generally agreed that the portrayal of Ahasuerus, whom rabbinic tradition aptly styled הטפש[71] cannot reflect historical reality. In a masterful recounting, Gunkel brings to the foreground the prevailing features in the description of Ahasuerus and concludes that it was the author's intention to paint "das Bild eines persischen Herrschers, wie ihn sich die Untertanen vorstellen."[72] This statement is somewhat misleading. In the last analysis the Persian setting is of secondary importance. Ahasuerus is the personification of the traditional "witless king" out of the book of the wise. His figure has no intrinsic relations to Persian royalty but instead is an "ideal" type, which was conceived by an eclectic process of abstraction and simplification within a circumscribed literary tradition. This is the immature and gullible king of the pitiable land with which Qoheleth commiserates (Qoh 10:16; cp. Isa 3:4).

Wisdom teaching considers lack of wit not a regrettable inborn deficiency, but a punishable defect. The power of perception can be improved by proper training. Whoever neglected to be educated adequately must pay for his negligence. One can learn to size up a situation and to make the best of it. Therefore defeat is anathema, even if incurred in the pursuit of lofty principles. There is no room for the idealistic dreamer in the world of wisdom. Voluntary suffering, when it can be averted, becries the fool. For these reasons the author of Esther has not a word of pity, not to mention admiration, for Vashti, who forfeited a kingdom for mere sentiments of propriety. Such behavior can be attributed only to sheer foolhardiness, which makes Vashti a suitable companion for Ahasuerus.[73]

Ahasuerus is so easily deceived that his weakness becomes the source of his courtiers' corruption: "When a ruler pays attention to falsehood, all his

---

71. *Midr. Esth. Rab.* on Esth 1:4 applies to Ahasuerus the saying in Prov 29:11, which deals with the כסיל. See further *b. Meg.* 12b; *Midr. Esth. Rab.* on Esth 1:11; *Midr. Abba Gurion*, p. 14b; 2 *Midr. Panim Aḥerim*, p. 60.
72. Gunkel, *Esther*, 64 (see above, n. 4).
73. Midrashic exegesis sensed the noncommittal attitude of the biblical writer towards Vashti's courageous action and set out to discover the "true" reason for her refusal to comply with Ahasuerus's command in bodily blemishes with which she was temporarily afflicted (*b. Meg.* 12b).

servants [become] wicked" (Prov 29:12). Unaware of his folly, he becomes conceited, irritable, and unpredictable. Sitting at table with him is a precarious affair, since nobody can foresee his actions. The sage had in mind rulers like him when he advised: "When you sit to eat with a ruler, consider well what is before you" (23:1). And things *will* happen. The king's anger easily flares up, and woe to the man who caused it (20:2). His reactions are swift, uncontemplated, and therefore soon regretted. The sequence of emotions that recurrently is attributed to Ahasuerus is a stereotype in wisdom literature: his anger is kindled (Esth 1:12; cp. 7:7), he acts with inane haste (Esth 1:19–22), e.g., condemning a villain for a crime he had not committed (Esth 7:9), and regrets his deeds once he returns to his senses (Esth 2:1).

In the same fashion the Assyrian King Esarhaddon, enraged by the accusations of Nadin, orders the execution of the faithful Aḥiqar without even stopping to contemplate the matter, just as his father Sennacherib had acted in his time on a different occasion. That this is considered to be the proverbial "manner of kings" is aptly brought out in the continuation of the Aḥiqar novel. Pleading with his would-be executioner, Aḥiqar reminds him of that previous occasion when roles had been reversed. In a bout of sudden anger, Sennacherib had commanded Aḥiqar to kill the very man into whose hands he has now been delivered. Aḥiqar had spared the courtier, had hidden him, and then, he recalls, "after many days I brought you before King Sennacherib and cleared you of offenses before him, and he did you no evi[l]. Moreover, Sennacherib was well pleased with me for having kept you alive and not having killed you. Now do you do to me even as I did to you. Don't kill me. Take me to your house until other times. King Esarhaddon is merciful as any man [?]. In the end he will remember me and wish for my advice. Th[e]n you will [prese]nt me to him and he will spare me alive" (lines 49–54).

Sennacherib, Esarhaddon, and Ahasuerus did not intentionally do evil. Their behavior is immature. They can be led to acknowledge their mistakes, or at least to reconsider their hasty decisions. Thus Aḥiqar and Esther are able to prevent harm by speaking the right words at the appropriate time. This goes to prove that though "a king's rage is like the angel of death, a wise man will pacify him" (Prov 16:14).

VII

Before proceeding with our analysis, a short digression becomes necessary. "Wisdom" appears in the Hebrew Bible in two fairly clearly differenti ated forms. There is the eudamonistic, success-oriented wisdom that deals exclusively with the techniques of human behavior that ensure well-being and is not concerned with the spiritual contents of human life. This concept of wisdom may be regarded as just a variation of חכמה, as it manifests itself in the professional skill of artisans and craftsmen (Exod 36:1–8; 36:1–4). Such wisdom can be applied towards the achievement of evidently evil and immoral purposes. Thus Jonadab, Amnon's cousin and companion, is introduced in 2 Sam 13:3 as a "very wise man." But we learn immediately that in fact he is a cunning individual who without hesitation or pangs of conscience falls in with Amnon's carnal desires and shrewdly plans the rape of Tamar. It is this type of unscrupulous wisdom that leads to transgression and is condemned by the prophet: "They are wise to do evil, but to do good they do not know" (Jer 4:22). It plays havoc with accepted standards of right and wrong (Isa 5:20–21) and fosters reliance of man upon his own strength. Such wisdom results in being overbearing (ὕβρις), which is considered to be typical of the nations' wise men (Ezek 28:2–10; Obadiah 6–8), and which ultimately must come to ruin. It is personified in the character of the "wicked wise," and biblical teaching endeavors to overcome it by propagating the figure of the "righteous sage."

Pragmatic wisdom in its biblical garb progressively absorbs religio-moral ideas of a distinctive Israelite brand. The "wicked" is now conceived as the very opposite of the "wise" (Prov 20:26), who is tacitly equated with the "righteous" (Prov 25:5). The process culminates in the equation of חכמה with Torah in the late offshoot of this school of thought, the postbiblical Ben Sira. Now Mordecai is hardly equipped with the necessary traits to qualify for the "righteous wise" in Ben Sira's views. However, in contrast to Haman, who is personified "evil wisdom," Mordecai can pass muster as the representative of desirable "virtuous wisdom."

The true nature of the "wise" Haman escapes Ahasuerus. The author of the narrative, so to speak, identifies with the king and does not reveal the real motivations of his counselor until the story reaches its climax. Meanwhile he prepares his readers to expect Haman's ultimate downfall by demolishing step by step the myth of his wisdom. The man is shown to violate all the basic rules of wise behavior. His actions are guided by personal hatred and inane rage, which blind the wise man's eyes. Perceiving Mordecai's refusal to bow to him, Haman is filled with fury (Esth 3:5; 5:9). He contains himself for a while (5:10), but his anger overpowers him (an unpardonable sin in a sage; Prov 29:22). Says Aḥiqar, "I have lifted sand, and I have carried salt; but there is naught which is heavier than [grief]" (line 111). Haman becomes so obsessed with his hatred that it spoils even his joy over the distinction of being invited to the queen's table (*tend trois*), with only the king to share the honor (Esth 5:12–13). One surmises that he considers this invitation a great victory over "the Jew Mordecai," who being the queen's uncle and a courtier might have been expected to have precedence over Haman, or at least to be invited as well.

In his joy Haman also proves to be imprudent. The queen's invitation makes him exceedingly happy, just as the sight of Mordecai causes him unlimited pain. In fact he behaves like the uncontrolled, impetuous simpleton, lacking altogether the balance of mind required of the sage. Moreover he is loquacious. He discloses his sentiments and thoughts before others (Esth 5:10–13) like any proverbial fool (Prov 12:23), disregarding Aḥiqar's advice: "More than all watchfulness watch thy mouth, and [over] what [thou] h[earest] harden thy heart" (line 98). Worse than this, Haman acts when he is given to rage and thus incapable of proceeding with prudence. His impatience per force must lead to folly (Prov 14:17a; cp. 5:2). He overshoots his aim. Dissatisfied with punishing Mordecai for his impertinence, he plots genocide (Esth 3:6). Haman's intention to make all Jews suffer for the fault of one shows the incongruency of his actions. The discrepancy between the experience of personal slight and the wished-for mass retribution, subtly criticized in the book of Jonah, is viewed with surprising detachment on the part of the author of Esther. There is not a word of righteous indignation or of moral censure. This silence can be explained only by the complete certitude that such foolhardiness must come to ruin.

The first indication of Haman's imminent failure is given when in his conceitedness he can only think of himself as being the unnamed worthy subject whom Ahasuerus wishes to honor. This episode masterfully portrays the apparent wise person making a fool of himself (Esth 6:6–12). Haman does not perceive the sign of his impending doom when others already are certain of it (6:13).

So far Haman's punishment lies in his becoming the laughingstock of his contemporaries and of the reader, as befits the self-styled sage. He sneaks into his chambers "mourning and with his head hanging" (Esth 6:12). Again wisdom is proved right: "[At fi]rst a throne [is set up] for the liar, but in the e[nd they fi]nd out his lies and spit in his face" (Aḥiqar, line 133).

However, Haman the fool is also a fiend. He truly is the לץ of proverbial wisdom, the haughty man who does ill in his fury (Prov 21:24). His denouement comes at the very apex of the story from the hands of the wise Esther. It is Esther who introduces into our tale a new element. She designates Haman "evil," presents him as a foe and a scheming malefactor, and thus opens the king's eyes to Haman's true character. Now the story shifts to a new plane. The "evil" Haman is contrasted with Mordecai who had only "good" intentions for the king (Esth 7:6–9). The adjective *good* never had been used previously to characterize Mordecai, nor was *evil* employed to describe Haman. While in his capacity as apparent wise and actual fool, Haman was punished with ridicule; Haman the fiend is in for harsher treatment.

There are certain similarities in the character of the "witless king" and the "wicked wise." Both are possessed of power which, although derived from different sources, leads to overbearing hubris, with its accompanying impetuosity. The difference in the treatment of these two antitheses of the "truly wise" derives from the fact that the misdemeanor of the one is rooted in personal incapability, while in the other it arises from intentional malice and evil determination. For this they incur different punishments. Ahasuerus and Vashti, like Esarhaddon, are indeed chastised. Hardship affects them personally or afflicts their realm. However, being "fools," they should be given another chance. Therefore, they are not bodily killed. In eventually accepting the advice of their righteous counselors, Ahasuerus and Esarhaddon testify to the ultimate success of the "wise" and exemplify the hope which wisdom teaching holds out to the witless.

The punishment meted out to the "wicked wise" is of a different nature altogether. They have to bear the full brunt of the disaster that they had plotted to bring upon the "just sage": "The righteous is delivered out of trouble, but the wicked takes his place" (Prov 11:8). Both Nadin and Haman schemed to have their victims murdered; therefore, both meet with an untimely death (Ps 7:16; cp. Prov 26:27; Qoh 10:8). This basic proverbial maxim is reflected in the triumphant summary of the Mordecai-Haman strife in Esth 7:10: "So they hanged Haman on the gallows that he had prepared for Mordecai." Midrashic tradition elaborated on the theme and tried to read into this verse the notion of an exact "measure-for-measure" retribution:

"[Only] yesterday Mordecai had been marked for hanging; now he hangs his [would-be] henchman."[74]

In most versions of the Aḥiqar novel, Nadin's death is described as due to his swelling up and bursting asunder.[75] But in the most probably secondary Aesop variant of the story, "he is smitten by remorse and hangs himself."[76] This nuance enhances the similarity with Haman's fate and may well reflect another wisdom *topos*. Remember that the "wicked counselor" Ahitophel also strangles himself (MT: ויחנק = *Tg. Neb.:* ואתחניק), i.e., "hangs himself" (Gr: ἐτάφη), when Absalom disregards his evil advice (2 Sam 17:23).

The death of the "wicked" reestablishes the balance that had been precariously upset by his temporary ascendancy. It restores belief in the validity of basic wisdom concepts: the immediate and tangible retribution of one's deeds and the value of properly applied wisdom precepts.

The notion of retribution is obviously not a wisdom prerogative. It permeates the thinking of the biblical writers. However, while in biblical historical narration, prophetic teaching, cultic psalmody, and legal literature, retribution emanates from God, in the book of Esther it has no explicit divine source. Again, the Esther concept aligns itself with that of the proverbs quoted above, which also lack any religious motivation. In this respect the biblical material discussed here presents a more popular or more primitive stage of wisdom thought than the proverbs inserted into the Aḥiqar novel. The idea of mischievous harm boomeranging onto its perpetrator is expressed in the Aramaic Aḥiqar fragments as follows: "[Bend not] thy [b]ow and shoot not thine arrow at a righteous man lest God come to his help and turn it back upon thee. . . . From thee is the arrow, but from God is the guidance."

VIII

The introduction of the two contrasting terms "good" and "evil" with regard to Mordecai and Haman respectively at the very same juncture, under-

---

74. *Yalqut Shimʿoni*, section 1053. See further *Esth. Rab* on Esth 7:10 and *Midr. Abba Gurion*, p. 42.
75. Conybeare, Harris, and Lewis, *The Story of Aḥiqar*, xi (see above, n. 68).
76. Ibid., lxv.

lines the conception of these men as antithetical characters. Mordecai, complemented by Esther, displays all the basic accomplishments of the true sage that Haman and Zeresh so evidently lack.

The first person who expressly paid Mordecai the compliment of possessing wisdom was, to the best of my knowledge, Josephus. In *Ant.* 11.5.210 he attributes Mordecai's refusal to bow before Haman to his wisdom and his traditional customs: Μαρδοχαίου δὲ διὰ σοφίαν καὶ τὸν οἴκοθεν αὐτοῦ νόμου οὐ προσκυνοῦντος ἄνθρωπον. While Israelite/biblical νόμοι understandably could be taken to lie at the base of Mordecai's stubbornness (cp. Dan 3:12–18), Greek σοφία cannot serve as its explanation. The term testifies, rather, to Josephus' overall impression of the man as presented in the Esther narrative. Mordecai is indeed farsighted and tight-lipped. Not once does he discuss his thoughts or his actions with others. Except for Esther, whose help he requires, he confides in nobody, knowing that secretiveness goes with the wise courtier's *métier* (Prov 12:23) and that talkativeness spells disaster (Prov 13:2). He refuses to bow to Haman.[77] But he never troubles to explain his action, as do Daniel's friends in similar circumstances (Dan 3:17–18), probably in order not to incite further Haman's fury. Not once does he disclose his pardonable hatred, acting in accord with the rule: "More than all watchfulness watch your heart, for out of it are the issues of life" (Prov 4:23). Mordecai does not lose his temper and remains levelheaded, even in times of utter distress. He plans carefully and never rushes into action but bides his time, since "a man of patience is better than the mighty, and he that masters his spirit than he that conquers a city" (Prov 16:32). His foresight is proved when he sets up Esther in the palace, thus providing for a rainy day (Qoh 11:1). He ultimately prevails by showing genuine wisdom, which gives more strength to the wise than give ten (or "the wealth of," reading מֵעֹשֶׁר)[78] rulers to a city (Qoh 7:19; cp. 9:16).

---

77. In fact, wisdom teaching would advise him to do so: "Bow thy back to thy superior, thy overseer from the palace. [Then] thy household will be established in its property, and thy recompense will be as it should be" (Instruction of the Vizier Ptah-Hotep, line 440 [trans. J. A. Wilson; *ANET*, 414]). Cp. Aḥiqar, lines 142–44: "With him who is more exalted than thou, quarrel not. With him who is . . . and stronger than thou [contend not; for he will take] of thy portion and [add it to] his." See also Prov 8:1–2; Sir 8:1–2. Midrashic exegesis has it that Mordecai refused to bow to Haman because the latter carried heathen idols in his pockets (2 *Midr. Panim Aḥerim*, p. 81). *Midr. Esth. Rab.* and the LXX on Esth 3:7 tell us that Mordecai would bow only before God.

78. H. L. Ginsberg, *Studies in Koheleth* (New York: JTSA, 1950), following a suggestion by K. Galling.

In all his doings Mordecai is ably seconded by Esther, in whose very name the midrash discovers an indication of her secretiveness, ולמה נקרא שמה אסתר שמסתרת את דבריה.[79] She is like the wisest woman who builds up her house (Prov 14:1), and were it not for her designs, her people would have come to ruin (11:14).

Esther and Mordecai contrast Haman, not only in their roles as true sages, but also in their capacities as representatives of "goodness." Theirs is not the goodness of absolute morality. Such a concept would not square with the type of wisdom exemplified in the story. Their virtues become apparent in the subjection of their private interests to the requirements of the communal well-being, whereas Haman was prepared to sacrifice a nation in order to satisfy his personal hatred of one man. The "evil Haman" (Esth 7:6), whose intentions are vile (7:4; 9:24), is opposed by Mordecai, whom all his community welcome, and who "seeks good for his people" (10:3). The victory of Mordecai and Esther over Haman is a double score: the sage vanquishes the apparent wise, and the goodly/just, the evildoer. It therefore constitutes a valid reason for the jubilation of the Jews in Susa and throughout the empire (Esth 8:15–17; 9:18–19): "When the righteous prosper a city rejoices, and when the wicked perish there is cheer" (Prov 11:10). It befits wisdom teaching that the wicked Haman becomes the spoil of the righteous Mordecai (Aḥiqar 159–72). In keeping with the proverb that "the wealth of the sinner is safeguarded for the righteous" (Prov 13:22), Haman's possessions, after his execution, are transferred to Mordecai by royal decree (Esth 8:1–2). The story ends on the optimistic note, typical of popular wisdom, that a man's fate is meted out to him according to his deeds. Therefore, the righteous always may expect ultimately to have joy, while the wicked's hopes shall perish (Prov 10:28).

IX

In the canonical book of Esther, especially in the chronistic summary, Mordecai occupies the center of the stage. But in the last count it is the

---

79. *b. Meg.* 13a.

wise Esther who dominates the scene. In the course of events she ascends from the role of Mordecai's protegée to become her mentor's guardian. In fact she completely overshadows her uncle and outclasses his adversary Haman in the art of crafty planning and successful execution. In the end it is Esther's superior cleverness that saves the day.

In addition to her wits, Esther boasts physical attractions (Esth 2:7). Thanks to this combination she is much better equipped to deal with emergencies than was her beautiful but seemingly simple predecessor Vashti. It comes as no surprise that Esther's charm and good sense captivate chamberlain and king alike (2:9, 17). She finds favor with whoever beholds her (2:15). In short she achieves proverbial success (Prov 3:4).

Scholars are somewhat astonished at the fact that the Purim story actually centers around a heroine. It is clearly Esther who plays the decisive role in the development of events. One tends to consider this feature as stemming from the influence of the Hellenistic novel, which assuredly makes itself felt also in the apocryphal book of Judith.[80] This latter comparison is then adduced to strengthen the case for a second-century BCE dating of both Esther and Judith.

This argument appears to be inconclusive. The supposed impact of the Greek romance on these two novels remains to be proved. As it is, Cazelles, who bases his arguments on E. Rohde's studies,[81] prefers to date Esther earlier than the Greek romance, at least before this attained its full development.[82] Furthermore, Grintz has made a very strong case for dating Judith during the reign of Artaxerxes II (404–359/358), i.e., well into the Persian period.[83] This would necessitate an even earlier date for Esther, since Judith is tangibly patterned after Esther, as Grintz would also agree. The similarity in the general setup of the plot, in the characterization of the two heroines and in some features of their life history make an interdependence plausible. The elaboration of common themes (cp. Jdt 10:3; 16:8 with Esth 4:3, 16) and especially the somewhat verbose reiterative insistence of the author of Judith on the role played by a female in the drama (Jdt 9:10; 10:19; 13:15; 16:6), whereas in Esther the facts are allowed to speak for themselves, defi-

---

80. See, e.g., Bardtke's remarks (*RGG* 3 [1958] 703–8 [above, n. 14]).
81. E. Rohde, *Der griechische Roman und seine Vorläufer* (Hildesheim: Breitkopf und Härtel, 1960), reprint of 1st edition, 1876.
82. Cazelles, "Note," 20–21 (see above, n. 18).
83. Grintz, *Sefer Yehudith*, 19 (n. 16), 53, and 55 (see above, n. 30).

nitely indicate the dependency of Judith on Esther.[84] This, however, cannot gloss over the differences in attitudes and ideas that serve as bases for these two novels and on which we shall still have occasion to comment.

It is entirely feasible that the stories of both Esther and Judith are woven around a motif that occurs once more in Herodotus's account of the "slaying of the Magi" (3.68–70). This story is set in the time of Darius I (522–486), i.e., a generation before Esther and Mordecai. Herodotus relates that after the death of Cambyses (522), a certain Gaumata seized the reign, pretending to be Smerdis, Cambyses' brother, who in fact had been secretly executed by him. Instrumental in the discovery of the fraud is one of Gaumata's wives, whom her father had instructed to ascertain whether her husband's ears had been cut off, a defect by which the real identity of the fake Smerdis could be established. Defying danger, the daughter carries out the investigation while with Gaumata at night and forthwith reports to her father. The impostor is killed by the Persians together with his helpers, the Magi. In commemoration of this event, a festival is instituted, the Magophonia.

Now the theme common to the three tales, all set in the Persian era—a courageous woman rids, or helps to rid, her people of a tyrant—could well be rooted in a specific Persian motif.[85] However, as far as Esther and Judith are concerned, suitable prototypes are already found in the earlier books of the Hebrew Bible. Biblical writers were fully aware of the ageless truth that strong and powerful men are most easily overcome by female cunning. Delilah brings about the destruction of the invincible Samson (Judges 16). Siserah and Abimelech are slain bodily by women who are quick to grasp their chances (Judg 4:17–21; 5:24–27; 9:50–54). Kings whose perception is dimmed by rage or old age are especially prone to fall prey to female cleverness. Michal, Saul's daughter, makes a fool of her father in order to save her husband David from Saul's murderous intentions (1 Sam 19:11). She easily might have taken her cue from Rachel, who foiled her father Laban's plans, having recourse to a rather unfair ruse (Gen 31:34–35). Again, it is Bathsheba's hold over the aging David that is cleverly exploited by

---

84. We cannot enlarge here on this problem, which calls for a separate treatment.
85. We expect soon to have at our disposal at least one more extrabiblical narrative of a (pseudo-) historical nature set in the Persian Period. In "Le travail d'édition des fragments manuscrits de Qumran," J. Starcky announced the discovery of some fragments of which he remarks: "Les restes d'un texte pseudo-historique se situant a l'époque perse rappellent Esther ou Daniel" (RB 63 [1956] 66).

Nathan to set up his protegé Solomon on the throne of Israel (1 Kgs 1:11–31).

Apparently courageous and determined women were often found in wisdom circles. Thanks to the persuasive performance of the wise woman of Tekoa, David ended Absalom's exile and granted him permission to return to his house (2 Sam 14:1–24). It was the "wise woman of Abel of Bethmaacah" who saved her town from destruction (20:16–22), showing her superiority over men, again proving that wisdom is better than physical strength.[86]

Similarly, Esther's victory over the mighty Haman and the easily persuaded king is won, not by force, but by superior planning. It reads like a satire on the pitiful and self-deceptive attempts of Ahasuerus's boasting courtiers to preserve by sheer force the male's right to have the last word in his house (Esth 1:20–22).

Also Esther's exploitation of Ahasuerus's sexual desire for the achievement of her praiseworthy aims is not without precedent in the Bible. Tamar thus tricks her father-in-law into admitting that he had failed to do right by her (Gen 38:13–26). In spite of the different setting there is some dramatic similarity in Naomi's playing on Boaz's predictable appreciation of Ruth's beauty, displayed in suitable apparel (Ruth 3:1–4) to make him take action on her behalf, and in Mordecai's using Esther's charms to bring Ahasuerus around. Esther's character and matter-of-fact attitude are much more in line with the bearing and deeds of some biblical women than with the amorous pretenses coupled with physical courage that the inspired and patriotic apocryphal Judith displayed.

Biblical literature is not at all devoid of the eroticism that scholars single out in the Esther story. Many a passage in prophetic writings is highly charged with overt or covert eroticism. The unfaithful, sex-minded wife is a central figure in the Joseph narrative, with which the book of Esther has many features in common.[87] And after all, the book of Esther is much less outspoken in the description of female lures than is, e.g., the Song of Songs, or for that matter, the book of Proverbs (chaps. 5, 7). In short, there is no need to look further than biblical literature for prototypes of the wise and beautiful Esther, a woman who is the main character of a story.

---

86. Cp. further Qoh 9:14–15.
87. See below.

The foregoing remarks may have some bearing on the dating of the Esther story, since they circumscribe its affinities with and dissimilarities from comparable literature. By the introduction of female figures into the contest of courtiers, the Esther narrative parts company with Ancient Near Eastern wisdom literature. A comparison with the all-male outfit of the Aramaic Aḥiqar novel, set in Assyria, which in this respect displays what appears to be a basic principle with Mesopotamian and Egyptian wisdom literature, goes to show that the Esther narrative could not be derived solely or directly from these literary traditions. In Ancient Near Eastern wisdom, "woman" is discussed only in her relationship to "man," predominantly with regard to her connubial or familial duties, or adversely in the role she plays in the sex life of the male, especially the adolescent, whether in conjunction with fertility rites or in plain seduction.[88] It is only in biblical literature that women are deemed fit not merely to serve as objects in wisdom teaching but are also credited with subject-activities in this domain. True, in all instances (and the Queen of Sheba could be added to the roster above), wise women are exclusively occupied with what has been styled "popular pragmatic wisdom." They are prolific in the practical employment of wisdom maxims but are never reported to contemplate on profounder issues, such as the problem of divine retribution in which biblical wisdom thought culminates.[89] This analysis further substantiates the opinion voiced previously that the book of Esther is truly steeped in biblical wisdom thought and literary traditions.

On the other hand, the portrayal of Esther as a resolute and active queen may well be influenced by Persian motifs perceivable in addition to figures already mentioned, or by the שֵׁגַל of Artaxerxes, to whom Neh 2:6 alludes. Accordingly, we may discern in the Esther narrative three converging elements: an Ancient Near Eastern wisdom nucleus in a specific biblical variation, imbued with Persian literary motifs. This conflux constitutes a strong argument in favor of dating the composition of the Esther story in the begin-

---

88. Fichtner, *Altorientalische Weisheit,* 19–20 (see above, n. 31).

89. The possible Ancient Near Eastern roots of the female hypostization of "wisdom," which is found in biblical writings (Proverbs 8, 9; Job 28), does not disqualify this statement. O. S. Rankin concludes that the only traceable influence on the Hebrew Bible in this matter is Iranian (*Israel's Wisdom Literature* [Edinburgh: Clark, 1936] 222–64).

ning of the Persian era. The traditional setting of the book in the days of Xerxes I cannot be wide of the mark.

X

In the foregoing analysis we attempted to make explicit the presence of wisdom elements in the canonical book of Esther. We purported to show that the acknowledged diversity of literary elements in the book can be explained in part as arising out of the author's endeavor to present a generalizing wisdom tale and traditional wisdom motifs in a specific historical setting. We wish to stress, however, that the presentation in traditional imagery does not necessarily impair the possible authenticity of the historical situation that is described in the book.

It remains to be shown that both the literary type of the wisdom tale and the literary process of historicizing wisdom motifs present in the book of Esther can also be found in other biblical writings. We have remarked in passing on certain similarities between the Esther-Mordecai narrative and other biblical stories, which like it, center around historical or quasi-historical heroes who display characteristics akin to those exemplified by the central figures of that narrative. In all these stories we find a tendency to propagate abstract maxims of thought and behavior by means of their practical application in "real" historical situations. The combination of traditional motifs, presented in a (purportedly) unique historical garb, results in an ambiguity that determines the modern reader's attitude of apprehensiveness towards the "veracity" of these stories.

In some cases, as in the book of Jonah, a precarious balance between underlying traditional motifs and a possible historical actuality is maintained. In others the scales are tipped in favor of the literary component, due to the discovery of extrabiblical material which throws light on preceding developmental stages of the biblical narrative. The emergence of several Ancient Near Eastern versions of *le juste souffrant* has finally established the always-assumed type-character of the biblical Job story.[90] The existence of a just and wise Danel in Ugaritic literature,[91] together with the new

---

90. Van Dijk, *La Sagesse Suméro-Accadienne,* 118–33 (see above, n. 33).
91. C. Virolleaud, *La légende phénicienne de Danel* (Paris: Geuther, 1936); C. H. Gordon, *Ugaritic Manual* (Rome: Pontificium Institutum Biblicum, 1955) 179–84.

knowledge derived from the recently discovered Prayer of Nabonidus,[92] make it exceedingly probable that at least parts of the biblical book of Daniel are but a recast of traditional material.

However, it appears that the wisdom affiliations of the Esther narrative are best brought into relief by its comparison with the Joseph story. Some striking similarities between the plot underlying both these tales were assembled in a paper by Rosenthal, published in 1895.[93] Moreover, Rosenthal showed that in an astonishingly large number of instances the two literary compositions, one set in Egypt, the other in Persia, with at least a millennium between them, employ the same language, word for word. This cannot be considered a case of mere literary similarity but must rather be due to direct interdependence. Under existing conditions it was obvious that the author of Esther had consciously borrowed from the writer of the Joseph story.

This assumption can hardly be denied. The occasional verbatim identity of these literary units proves it to be correct. Also it is easily understood that similarities in situations and in the fate of the central characters were conducive to an influence of the Joseph story on the Esther-Mordecai narrative. They have in common, *inter alia,* the royal court setting and the rise of a destitute young Israelite to political prominence in his land of exile. But what is more important, they can be shown to belong basically to one literary type. In a most instructive paper, G. von Rad has brought to light the exceedingly strong wisdom elements in the Joseph story.[94] He has proved for this composition, what we have set out to do for the Esther narrative, namely that in essence the Joseph story illustrates the realization of wisdom precepts in practical life. Thus both the Joseph story and the Esther narrative represent a type of the historicized wisdom tale. Their similarities, therefore, are to be accounted for, not only by the probable interdependence, but also by their dependence upon one common literary tradition.

---

92. J. T. Milik, "Prière de Nabonide et autres écrits d'un cycle de Daniel," *RB* 63 (1956) 407–15; D. N. Freedman, "The Prayer of Nabonidus," *BASOR* 145 (1957) 31–32.
93. L. A. Rosenthal, "Die Josephgeschichte mit den Büchern Ester und Daniel verglichen," *ZAW* 15 (1895) 278–84; further: "Nochmals der Vergleich Ester-Joseph, Daniel," *ZAW* 17 (1897) 126–28; P. Riessler, "Zu Rosenthal's Aufsatz, Bd. 15. S. 278ff.," *ZAW* 16 (1896) 182. A paper by M. Gan goes over the same ground, taking its departure from the Esther narrative instead of from the Joseph story ("The Book of Esther in the Light of Joseph's Fate in Egypt," *Tarbiz* 31 [1962] 144–49 [Heb.]).
94. G. von Rad, "Josephsgeschichte und ältere Chokma," (VTSup 1; Leiden: E. J. Brill, 1953) 120–27 (reprinted in GSAT 8; München: Kaiser, 1958) 272–80.

INDICES

SOURCES

HEBREW BIBLE

Genesis					
1–11	97 98	14:5	79 79n 82	32:23–33	97
1:5	115n	15	212	32:25–33	212
1:26–30	181	15:1–3	274	32:29	96 97
2:5	98	15:10	115n	32:31	97 210
2:9	202	15:18	182	33	167
2:17	202	15:20	82	33:2	167
2:23	98	15:20–21	78	34	221
2:24	98	16:6–14	229	34:23	66n
3:9ff.	211	16:7	204	34:25–29	221n
3:19	189	16:12	222	34:30–31	221
4:1	202	16:13	204 206	35:1–15	148
4:3–5	115	17:1	200	35:7	201
4:11–12	223	17:1–14	182	35:9	200
4:13–16	221	17:15–19	182	35:9–15	182
4:17	202	17:18	274	35:29	188
4:23–24	221	18	212	36	140n
4:25	202	18:1–8	221	36:24	227 230
4:26	206	18:21	202	36:26	79n
6:1–4	80	19:1–8	221	36:31ff.	114
6:9–10	121n	19:5	202	36:31–39	113
6:13–22	190	19:8	202	37:36	122 123 124
7:1ff.	211	21:14	228	38	123
8:21	181	21:20	222 229	38:13–26	287
8:21–22	183	21:33	206	38:16	202
9:1ff.	211	24:29–33	221	38:26	202
9:5–6	223	25:8	188	39:1	122 123 124
9:8–10	131	25:17	188	42:9	73 201
9:8–16	183	25:18	222	42:12	72 201
9:8–17	190	25:27	222	43:23	272
9:9–15	181	26:1–5	182	45:2–20	126
9:12ff.	98	26:34–35	33	46:1ff.	123
9:12–17	181	27	167	46:6–7	176
9:15	189	27:3–4	222	46:7	120
9:16	181	27:30	114	46:7–27	119
9:20–21	167	27:37	116	46:8	119 120
9:21–23	201	27:46	33	46:8–27	119
9:23	167	28:10–22	148 212	46:28–50:26	119
9:32	118n	28:12	71	47:30	188
10:10	118n	28:13–15	182	48:3–4	182
11:9	73n	28:16	201	48:14	115n
12:6ff.	148	31:13	31	49	252n
13:1–4	148	31:34–35	286	49:1–27	175
		32:23–31	182	49:5–7	221

APOCRYPHA AND PSEUDEPIGRAPHA

QUMRAN MANUSCRIPTS

RABBINIC LITERATURE

TALMUD

MIDRASH

AUTHORS

Cowley, A. 152n 267n
Cross, F. M. 92 92n 106n 111n 152n 210n
  247n 250n 252 252n
Culley, R. C. 31n

D
Dahood, M. 37n 74n 84n 110n
Daiches, S. 27
Damrosch, D. 107n
Daube, D. 255n
Davies, W. D. 43n 74n
Delcor, M. 222n
Delitzsch, F. 157n 257n
Dhorme, E. 73n
Dietrich, M. 76n 77n
Dijk, J. J. A. van 262n 289n
Dillon, E. J. 275n
Donner, H. 76n 147n 204n
Douglas, Mary 13 13n
Driver, G. R. 68n 143n 220n 241n
Dubow, F. L. 99n
Dupont-Sommer, A. 251n
Durkheim, Emile 16

E
Edsman, C. M. 192n 213 213n
Edzard, D. O. 228n
Ehrlich, Z. 70 70n 71n
Eichrodt, W. 223n
Eisenstadt, S. N. 21n
Eissfeldt, O. 98 206n 256n 257n 258n 259
  259n 260 264n
Eliade, M. 53n 105n 161n 231n
Emerton, J. A. 31n
Engnell, I. 11n 23 23n 42n
Epstein, Y. N. 231n
Erman, A. 262n
Eshel, C. 70 70n 71n
Etzioni, A. 99n
Evans, D. G. 29 29n
Ewald 11

F
Fenton, T. L. 38n
Fichtner, J. 262n 288n
Finet, A. 228n
Fishbane, M. 60n 118n 120n

Fisher, L. R. 36n
Flight, J. W. 217 217n 218n
Fohrer, G. 206n
Fokkelman, J. P. 39n 125n 130n
Fox, M. 243n
Frankfort, H. 20 34 34n
Frazer, J. G. 14 14n 19 100 100n
Freedman, D. N. 152n 290n
Frick, F. S. 223n
Friedrich, W. P. 35n

G
Gaisser, J. 133n
Galling, K. 192n 283n
Gan, M. 290n
Gardiner, A. 272n
Gaster, T. H. 74n 230n 248n 250n 261
  261n
Geller, M. I. 22n 164n 220n
Gemser, B. 169n
Gerth, C. 208n
Gerth, H. H. 162n 222n
Gesenius, W. 52n
Ginsberg, H. L. 36 36n 37 38 39 85n 100
  101n 263n 283n
Ginzberg, L. 240n
Glatzer, N. N. 178n 192n
Goedicke, H. 138n 159n
Goetze, A. 72n
Goitein, S. D. 261n
Goldschmidt, Walter 48 49n
Goldziher, I. 271n
Gordis, R. 27 80n 162n
Gordon, Cyrus H. 23 220 220n 240n 289n
Goshen-Gottstein, M. H. 35n
Graetz, H. 110n
Graf 11
Gray, G. B. 94 94n
Gray, J. 77n 140 140n 141 141n 153n
Green, D. E. 206n
Greenberg, M. 211n 221n
Greenfield, J. 37n 152n
Greenstone, J. H. 26n
Gressmann, H. 94 94n 95 95n 96 96n
Grintz, Y. M. 262n 285 285n
Gross, H. 259n
Gruenbaum, M. 57n

ANCIENT AUTHORS

LIST OF ABBREVIATIONS

AB	Anchor Bible
AcOr	*Acta orientalia*
AGWG	Abhandlungen der Gesellschaft der Wissenschaften zu Göttingen
AION	*Annali (dell') Istituto Universitario Orientale di Napoli*
AJSL	*American Journal of Semitic Languages and Literature*
AnBib	Analecta biblica
ANET	J. B. Pritchard (ed.), *Ancient Near Eastern Texts Relating to the Old Testament*
AnOr	Analecta orientalia
AOAT	Alter Orient und Altes Testament
APOT	*The Apocrypha and Pseudepigrapha of the Old Testament*
ASGW	Abhandlungen der Philologisch: Historischen Klasse der Königlichen Sächsischen Gesellschaft der Wissenschaften
ASR	*American Sociological Review*
ASTI	*Annual of the Swedish Theological Institute*
ATD	Das Alte Testament Deutsch
AUSS	*Andrews University Seminary Studies*
BA	*Biblical Archaeologist*
BASOR	*Bulletin of the American Schools of Oriental Research*
BASS	*Beiträge zur Assyriologie und semitischen Sprachwissenschaft*
BDB	F. Brown, S. R. Driver, and C. A. Briggs, *Hebrew and English Lexicon of the Old Testament*
BHS	*Biblia hebraica stuttgartensia*
BibOr	Biblica et orientalia
BIES	*Bulletin of the Israel Exploration Society*
BJPES	*Bulletin of the Jewish Palestine Exploration Society*
BKAT	Biblischer Kommentar: Altes Testament
BZ	*Biblische Zeitschrift*
BZAW	Beihefte zur *Zeitschrift für die alttestamentliche Wissenschaft*
CAD	*The Assyrian Dictionary of the Oriental Institute of the University of Chicago*
CBC	Cambridge Bible Commentary
CTA	*Corpus des tablettes en cunéiformes alphabétiques*
EI	*Eretz Israel*
EncMiq	*Encyclopedia Miqraʾit (Encyclopaedia Biblica)*
ETR	*Études théologiques et religieuses*

EÜ	Einheitsübersetzung
EvT	*Evangelische Theologie*
ExpTim	*Expository Times*
GB	W. Gesenius-F. Buhl, *Hebräisches und Aramäisches Handwörterbuch über das Alte Testament*
GSAT	*Gesammelte Studien zum Alten Testament*
HAT	Handbuch zum Alten Testament
HB	Herder Bibel
HKAT	Handkommentar zum Alten Testament
HSLA	*Hebrew University Studies in Literature and the Arts*
HSM	Harvard Semitic Monographs
HSS	Harvard Semitic Studies
HTR	*Harvard Theological Review*
HUCA	*Hebrew Union College Annual*
IB	*Interpreter's Bible*
ICC	International Critical Commentary
IDB	G. A. Buttrick (ed.), *Interpreter's Dictionary of the Bible*
IDBSup	Supplementary Volume to *Interpreter's Dictionary of the Bible*
IEJ	*Israel Exploration Journal*
IES	Israel Exploration Society
IPS	Israel Publications Society
JANES	*Journal of the Ancient Near Eastern Society of Columbia University*
JAOS	*Journal of the American Oriental Society*
JB	Jerusalem Bible
JBL	*Journal of Biblical Literature*
JBR	*Journal of Bible and Religion*
JJS	*Journal of Jewish Studies*
JNES	*Journal of Near Eastern Studies*
JPS	Jewish Publication Society
JSOT	*Journal for the Study of the Old Testament*
JSOTSup	Journal for the Study of the Old Testament—Supplement Series
JSS	*Journal of Semitic Studies*
JTS	*Journal of Theological Studies*
JTSA	Jewish Theological Seminary of America
KAI	H. Donner and W. Röllig (eds.), *Kanaanäische und aramäische Inschriften*
KAT	Kommentar zum Alten Testament
KB	L. Köhler and W. Baumgartner, *Lexicon in Veteris Testamenti libros*

KCC	S. Talmon, *King, Cult and Calendar in Ancient Israel*
KHK	Kurzer Hand-Kommentar zum Alten Testament
KTU	*Kleine Texte aus Ugarit*
LCL	The Loeb Classical Library
NCB	New Century Bible
NEB	New English Bible
OrAnt	*Oriens antiquus*
OTL	Old Testament Library
PEQ	*Palestine Exploration Quarterly*
QHBT	F. M. Cross and S. Talmon, *Qumran and the History of the Biblical Text*
RB	*Revue biblique*
RES	*Revue des études sémitiques*
RevQ	*Revue de Qumran*
RGG	*Religion in Geschichte und Gegenwart*
RHPR	*Revue d'histoire et de philosophie religieuses*
RS	Ras Shamra
RSPI	L. R. Fisher (ed.), *Ras Shamra Parallels*, vol. I
RSV	Revised Standard Version
SB	Sainte Bible
SBS	Stuttgarter Bibelstudien
SBT	Studies in Biblical Theology
ScrHier	Scripta hierosolymitana
SEÅ	*Svensk exegetisk årsbok*
SOAS	School of Oriental Studies, University of London
SROT	S. Talmon, "Synonymous Readings in the Textual Tradition of the Old Testament," (ScrHier 8; Jerusalem: Magnes, 1961) 335-83
SSAW	Sitzungsberichte der sächsischen Akademie der Wissenschaften zu Leipzig
StThL	Studia theologica lundensia
TDOT	*Theological Dictionary of the Old Testament*
ThEx	*Theologische Existenz Heute*
TLZ	*Theologische Literaturzeitung*
TWAT	*Theologisches Wörterbuch zum Alten Testament*
TWNT	*Theologisches Wörterbuch zum Neuen Testament*
TZ	*Theologische Zeitschrift*
UF	*Ugarit-Forschungen*
UUÅ	Uppsala universitetsårsskrift

List of Abbreviations

VT	*Vetus Testamentum*
VTSup	Vetus Testamentum, Supplements
WC	Westminster Commentaries
WMANT	Wissenschaftliche Monographien zum Alten und Neuen Testament
WO	*Die Welt des Orients*
WQW	S. Talmon, *The World of Qumran from Within*
WZKM	*Wiener Zeitschrift für die Kunde des Morgenlandes*
ZAW	*Zeitschrift für die alttestamentliche Wissenschaft*
ZBK	Zürcher Bibelkommentar
ZDMG	*Zeitschrift der deutschen morgenländischen Gesellschaft*
ZDPV	*Zeitschrift des deutschen Palästina-Vereins*
ZS	*Zeitschrift für Semitistik*
ZWT	*Zeitschrift für wissenschaftliche Theologie*

ACKNOWLEDGEMENTS

I wish to thank the original editors and publishers for their kind permission to publish the following studies in this volume:

The "Comparative Method" in Biblical Interpretation: Principles and Problems, *Congress Volume: Göttingen 1977* (ed. J. A. Emerton; Vetus Testamentum Supplements 29; Leiden: Brill, 1978) 320–56.

The "Navel of the Earth" and the Comparative Method, *Scripture in History and Theology: Essays in Honor of J. Coert Rylaarsdam*. (ed. Arthur L. Merrill and Thomas W. Overholt; Pittsburgh Theological Monograph Series 17; Pittsburgh: Pickwick, 1977) 243–68. Translated from the Hebrew original: טבור הארץ והשיטה המשווה, *Tarbiẓ* 45 (1976) 163–77.

Biblical *repāˀîm* and Ugaritic *rpu/i(m)*, *Hebrew Annual Review: Biblical and Other Studies in Honor of Robert Gordis* 7 (1983) 235–49.

Did There Exist a Biblical National Epic? *Proceedings of the Seventh World Congress of Jewish Studies: Studies in the Bible and the Ancient Near East* (Jerusalem: Magnes, 1981) 2. 41–61.

The Presentation of Synchroneity and Simultaneity in Biblical Narrative, *Studies in Hebrew Narrative Art throughout the Ages* (ed. Joseph Heinemann and Shmuel Werses; Scripta Hierosolymitana 27; Jerusalem: Magnes, 1978) 9–26.

Polemics and Apology in Biblical Historiography: 2 Kings 17:24–41, *The Creation of Sacred Literature: Composition and Redaction of the Biblical Text* (ed. Richard E. Friedman; University of California Publications: Near Eastern Studies 22; Berkeley/Los Angeles: University of California, 1981) 57–68.

History and Eschatology in Biblical Thought, published as: *Eschatology and History in Biblical Judaism* (The Ecumenical Institute for Advanced Theological Study, Tantur, Occasional Papers 2; Jerusalem: Ecumenical Institute, 1986). Translated from the German original: Eschatologie und Geschichte im biblischen Judentum, *Zukunft: Zur Eschatologie bei Juden und Christen* (ed. Rudolf Schnackenburg; Schriften der Katholischen Akademie in Bayern 98; Düsseldorf: Patmos, 1980) 13–50.

The Concept of Revelation in Biblical Times, translated from the German original: Grundzüge des Offenbarungsverständnisses in biblischer Zeit, *Offenbarung im jüdischen und christlichen Glaubensverständnis* (ed. Jakob J. Petuchowski and Walter Strolz; Freiburg: Herder, 1981) 12–36.

The "Desert Motif" in the Bible and in Qumran Literature, *Biblical Motifs: Origins and Transformations* (ed. Alexander Altmann; Philip W. Lown Institute of Advanced Judaic Studies, Brandeis University: Studies and Texts 3; Cambridge: Harvard University, 1966) 31–63.

"Wisdom" in the Book of Esther, *Vetus Testamentum* 13 (1963) 419–55.